The Illusion of Full Inclusion

The Illusion of Full Inclusion

❖ ❖ ❖

A Comprehensive Critique of a Current Special Education Bandwagon

Edited by

James M. Kauffman

and

Daniel P. Hallahan

8700 Shoal Creek Boulevard
Austin, Texas 78757-6897

pro·ed

© 1995 by PRO-ED, Inc.
8700 Shoal Creek Boulevard
Austin, Texas 78757-6897

Library of Congress Cataloging-in-Publication Data

The illusion of full inclusion : a comprehensive critique of a current
    special education bandwagon / edited by James M. Kauffman and
    Daniel P. Hallahan.
       p.   cm.
    Includes bibliographical references and indexes.
    ISBN 0-89079-612-2
    1. Mainstreaming in education—United States. 2. Handicapped—
Education—United States. 3. Special education—United States.
I. Kauffman, James M. II. Hallahan, Daniel P., 1944–
LC4031.I45 1994   94-22139
371.9'046'0973—dc20   CIP

This book is designed in New Century Schoolbook and Helvetica.

Printed in the United States of America

1 2 3 4 5 6 7 8 9 10   99 98 97 96 95

Contents

◆ ◆ ◆

Preface

◆ ◆ ◆

IN ONE OF HIS MOST MEMORABLE ESSAYS, "Bandwagons Also Go to Funerals," the late Burton Blatt (1979) cautioned special educators about advocacy unrestrained by careful analysis and reliable data. A decade and a half later, Blatt's cautions need forceful reiteration, for in 1994 special education is in danger of riding the bandwagon called "full inclusion" to its own funeral.

What may be special education's largest bandwagon ever, one having gathered such great mass and momentum that it seems to many unstoppable, began its roll almost imperceptibly in the mid-1980s. Astute observers immediately warned that this bandwagon, although just forming, had all the potential for mischief of a loose cannon (Lieberman, 1985; Mesinger, 1985). Within 10 years, its size, velocity, and direction have become potentially fatal not only to those on board but to the entire special education community through which it is traveling.

The full inclusion bandwagon offers an attractive platform—the merger of special and general education into a seamless and supple system that will support all students adequately in general schools and general education classrooms, regardless of any student's characteristics. Those offering cautions warn that this platform, although having an appealing sheen, is not sufficiently substantial for students who make particularly heavy demands on any system of education. A single structure, critics argue, can be made sufficiently strong to support *some* students with disabilities in regular schools and classes, but it cannot offer equally effective support in the same place at the same time for all students; a special, supplementary structure is required to keep many students with special needs from dropping through the floor of public education.

This book is intended to show why full inclusion can provide only an illusion of support for all students, an illusion that may trick many into jumping on the bandwagon but is sure to produce disappointment, if not outrage, in its riders when the juggernaut crushes the students it was supposed to defend. The growth and increasing momentum of the full inclusion bandwagon have been due in part to the ready availability of books providing a rationale for scrapping the present special education structure altogether. Many of us who take a cautious deliberative approach to special education reform saw a need for a book warning of the dangers of embracing the illusory rhetoric of full inclusion.

We have organized the essays into three major sections. Part I provides context and historical perspective. Part II is a series of critiques of the full inclusion movement, with particular attention paid to conceptual and policy issues. Part III takes up various issues from the perspective of concern for groups with specific disabilities, including emotional or behavioral disorders (known by many different labels, but most commonly by *serious emotional disturbance*), learning disabilities, blindness, deafness, autism, and mental retardation.

Although many more cautionary writings are available than those we have been able to include in this volume, we believe these selections provide a good beginning for helping individuals interested in the full inclusion controversy in weighing alternatives to what has become increasingly popular but misguided rhetoric in school reform. In an appendix, we have included the statements of a variety of professional and advocacy organizations on this issue. Together, these essays and organizational statements will, we hope, be an effective tool for informing educators, advocates for students with disabilities, and policymakers of the disaster that we can still avoid—if we quickly, forcefully, and effectively unite to steer the full inclusion bandwagon away from its collision with the realities of childhood, schooling, disabilities, teaching, and parenting.

We thank the authors and publishers of the works that are reprinted in this volume for their permission to use their material. We are grateful also to Don Hammill and Lee Wiederholt for suggesting that we collect these essays and to PRO-ED for publishing them in a timely fashion.

Finally, we note that all royalty earnings from the sale of this book are assigned to the Eli M. Bower Endowed Fellowship Fund at the University of Virginia. The Eli M. Bower Fund provides an annual stipend to a graduate student in the Curry School of Education who is preparing to work with children with emotional or behavioral disorders.

J. M. K.
D. P. H.
Charlottesville, VA

REFERENCES

Blatt, B. (1979). Bandwagons also go to funerals: Unmailed letters 1 and 2. *Journal of Learning Disabilities, 12*(4), 17–19.

Lieberman, L. M. (1985). Special education and regular education: A merger made in heaven? *Exceptional Children, 51,* 513–516.

Mesinger, J. F. (1985). Commentary on "A rationale for the merger of special and regular education" or, Is it now time for the lamb to lie down with the lion? *Exceptional Children, 51,* 510–512.

Part I

Full Inclusion in Historical Context

For over 4 decades, many special educators have called for the inclusion of students with disabilities in general education schools and classrooms to the extent that such inclusion is appropriate for individual children. In the mid-1970s, the consensus of advocates for children and youth with disabilities was that these students should be a part of mainstream classes, when their special educational needs could be met there, and the mandate for education in the "least restrictive environment" (LRE) was thus incorporated into the Education for All Handicapped Children Act of 1975 (better known as Public Law 94-142, and later known as IDEA, the Individuals with Disabilities Education Act of 1990). IDEA also mandates that a continuum of alternative placements (CAP) be available to students with disabilities, under the assumption that an array of options ranging from full-time placement in general classrooms to placement in special residential schools or hospitals is necessary to meet the needs of individual students. Furthermore, IDEA mandates that appropriate education and related services and the least restrictive placement be determined on an individual basis; it proscribes decisions based on categorization of students.

Beginning in the early 1980s, some individuals and advocacy groups began challenging the concepts of LRE and CAP, arguing that the LRE—for all students—is the general school and general classroom and that a CAP is unworkable and unnecessary for providing appropriate education and related services. In essence, the argument of these advocates of full inclusion was that students with disabilities no longer be included in a general classroom when and to the extent appropriate, based on case-by-case evaluation; rather, they argued that students with disabilities should be treated, for purposes of placement, as a single category or class. All individual consideration was to be constrained by universal placement of students with disabilities in general schools and classes.

IDEA prescribes, first, the determination of appropriate education and related services and, only subsequently, that the least restrictive environment for delivery of those services be determined—in all instances, on a case-by-case basis. Contrary to IDEA, advocates of full inclusion call for a uniform placement decision *first,* followed by consideration of what might constitute an appropriate education and related services that could be delivered in that placement. Full inclusion makes placement the prepotent issue in special education; it defines as appropriate only that which can be delivered in the general school or general classroom.

The current full inclusion thrust has roots in the civil rights and educational reform movements of the late 1960s and early 1970s. Around that time, two articles that were particularly influential in shaping advocacy for mainstreaming in that era and setting the course toward full inclusion in the 1990s appeared in the journal *Exceptional Children.* They were Lloyd Dunn's 1968 piece ("Special Education for the Mildly Retarded—Is Much of It Justifiable?") and Evelyn Deno's 1970 article ("Special Education as Developmental Capital"). These articles provided impetus for the mainstreaming movement of the 1970s, which saw the rise of the resource room model as a means to the end of including students in more general classroom activities. In the 1990s, however, the resource model was decried as "segregationist" by advocates of full inclusion, who urged its abandonment in favor of a model of collaborative consultation between general and special educators.

In the first essay in Part I, we discuss the emergence of collaborative consultation, the favored service delivery model of the advocates of full inclusion, as a substitute for the resource room and mainstreaming. The next three essays in Part I (MacMillan, Semmel, & Gerber; Semmel, Gerber, & MacMillan; and Hallahan & Kauffman) are from a series of 25-year retrospectives on the articles by Dun and Deno, including evaluations of their historical significance and continuing legacy. Part I ends with three commentaries (by Bateman, Gallagher, and Morse) on the retrospectives and other issues related to the Dunn and Deno articles in the context of the full-inclusion movement.

Chapter 1

From Mainstreaming to Collaborative Consultation

Daniel P. Hallahan and James M. Kauffman

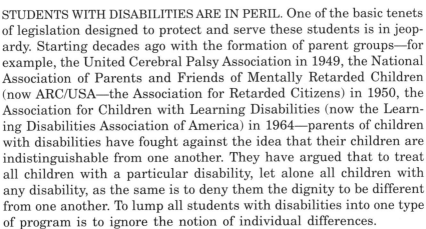

STUDENTS WITH DISABILITIES ARE IN PERIL. One of the basic tenets of legislation designed to protect and serve these students is in jeopardy. Starting decades ago with the formation of parent groups—for example, the United Cerebral Palsy Association in 1949, the National Association of Parents and Friends of Mentally Retarded Children (now ARC/USA—the Association for Retarded Citizens) in 1950, the Association for Children with Learning Disabilities (now the Learning Disabilities Association of America) in 1964—parents of children with disabilities have fought against the idea that their children are indistinguishable from one another. They have argued that to treat all children with a particular disability, let alone all children with any disability, as the same is to deny them the dignity to be different from one another. To lump all students with disabilities into one type of program is to ignore the notion of individual differences.

It was not until the passage of P.L. 94-142 in 1975 (reauthorized in 1990 as the Individuals with Disabilities Act or IDEA), however, that parents' dreams of the recognition of the individuality of their children began to gain widespread acceptance. As Bateman (1992) has noted, the heart of IDEA is the *individualized* [italics added] education program (IEP). School personnel are to treat each student

The case study "Yours, Mine, or Ours?": Steve Franklin that appears on pp. 10–15 is reprinted by permission of Daniel P. Hallahan and James M. Kauffman. Copyright 1994 by Daniel P. Hallahan and James M. Kauffman.

as having individual needs requiring individual programming. In keeping with this idea of the singularity of the IEP, the law further stipulates that the school district must make available a full continuum of alternative placements, including general education classroom placement on a full- or part-time basis, resource rooms, special classes, and special schools. In other words, there is an assumption that any single placement is not appropriate for meeting the diverse needs of all students with disabilities.

Little did the architects of this legislation know that within 2 decades entire school districts would be moving toward the virtual elimination of the continuum in favor of placing all students with disabilities in general education classrooms. Although schools may still officially declare that they offer a full continuum in order to comply with the law, we strongly suspect that in practice this is not the case. In effect, what many schools are doing is making the general classroom the placement of choice. We have been informed by some parents that unless they (the parents) mention other types of placements, these are never alluded to by school personnel. If parents want a more intensive setting, such as a resource room or self-contained classroom, they often must press the school system for such accommodations.

Until the early 1970s, the special self-contained classroom was the primary service delivery mode for providing special education. In this service delivery model, students attended the special class for most or all of the school day and had relatively little interaction with their nondisabled peers. In the 1970s, growing concern about the lack of research evidence demonstrating the effectiveness of special classes and about providing more "normalized" school environments for children with disabilities led to widespread adoption of resource services. To obtain these services, students went to a special resource room for only part (usually a relatively small part) of the school day. The rest of their time in school they were included in general classes with their nondisabled peers. The resource room was designed to allow more inclusion of students with disabilities in general classes and typical school activities. It was also thought to provide better articulation of special and general education, to encourage special education teachers to consult with their general education colleagues, and to attach less stigma to the students receiving special education.

Ten years later, in the 1980s, proponents of the regular education initiative (REI) and full inclusion condemned the resource room as well as the special self-contained classroom as ineffective, stigmatizing, and segregationist (cf. Blackman, 1992; Wang, Reynolds, & Walberg, 1988; Wang & Walberg, 1988). The proposal of the promoters of full inclusion, therefore, was to abandon the resource model along with any other models that involved removal of the student from the general classroom. The assumption of proponents of full inclusion is that what special educators are doing with students is good; *where* they are doing it is wrong. Blackman (1992) clearly articulated this position:

> *There is nothing pervasively wrong with special education.* What is being questioned is not the interventions and knowledge that has been acquired through special education training and research. Rather, what is being challenged is the location where these supports are being provided to students with disabilities.
> Special education needs to be reconceptualized as a support to the regular education classroom, rather than as "another place to go." Recent research suggests that what is so wrong about special education is the stigma and isolation that result from being removed from the regular education class for so long. We now have the effective strategies to bring help to the student rather than removing the student from the enriching setting of the regular education class. (p. 29)

The service delivery model proposed for full inclusion therefore is one in which students are not removed from general education at all; instead, all students are placed in general education classes, and all services are brought to them in that setting. Reports from the federal government document the movement toward placing a greater percentage of students with disabilities in general classrooms. As Table 1.1 depicts, from the 1987–1988 school year to the 1990–1991 school year, the percentage of students identified for special education services whose primary placement was in the general classroom increased by nearly 14%. Furthermore, most of this increase can be attributed to students with learning disabilities, whose primary placement in the general classroom increased by 28%.

Surprisingly, this table also suggests that for students with disabilities in general, and for those with learning disabilities in particular, the bulk of this movement to general education classrooms has come at the expense of resource room placements. Schools have apparently elected to begin the demise of the continuum of services by concentrating on filling general classrooms with as many students with disabilities as possible rather than closing down special classes. In fact, there has been a slight *increase* in the percentage of students served in special classes. Students with the milder disabilities (i.e., those in resource rooms rather than self-contained classes) would be the most logical to try to place in general education classrooms. In

TABLE 1.1. Students Ages 6 to 21 Years Served Under IDEA, Part B and Chapter 1, by Educational Environment

	All students with disabilities		Students with learning disabilities	
	1987–1988[a]	1990–1991[b]	1987–1988[a]	1990–1991[b]
Regular class	28.88	32.83	17.59	22.53
Resource room	39.98	36.46	59.14	53.67
Separate class	24.71	25.09	21.71	22.38
Separate facility	4.91	4.22	1.35	1.06
Residential facility	.80	.85	.09	.13
Other	.72	.56	.12	.23

Note. All numbers are given as percentages. [a]Source of data: U.S. Department of Education, 1990. [b]Source of data: U.S. Department of Education, 1993.

addition, perhaps resource rooms have proven to be the most vulnerable to closure because they do not have as long a tradition as the self-contained class, and what constitutes the ideal resource room arrangement has never been widely agreed upon. With such diversity of opinion concerning how resource rooms should operate, there has not been a unified voice defending them.

It may only be a matter of time before the individuals advocating for the general education classroom as the primary placement choice for all students with disabilities begin to make inroads on closing down special classes. Certainly, enough rhetoric has been generated to make one think that the collapse of the idea of a full continuum of placements is imminent. One possible scenario, however, is that the full inclusionists will have their way in abolishing resource rooms but will get stalled in their efforts to shut down special classes. It will be interesting to see if placements in special classes continue to increase. We do not know from the available federal data whether the increase in special class placements is coming at the expense of placements in separate facilities, in residential facilities, or in resource rooms. It would be ironic indeed if the full inclusion movement ends up resulting in students who would have been placed in resource rooms being placed in special classes. Such a phenomenon is not all that difficult to imagine, however. It may be that general education teachers will be able to accommodate the inclusion of some students with disabilities, but that they will also find some too difficult to handle. As resource rooms are eradicated to make way for inclusion in general classes, these more demanding students may find their way into special classes.

Whichever scenario ensues—the two-tiered general education class versus special class arrangement or the inclusion of all students in general education classes—the results will be devastating for students with disabilities. Both models are sink-or-swim configurations. The consequences of being in the mainstream may be the opposite of what is intended. In fact, case studies suggest that eliminating less restrictive pull-out options may result in some students being placed in more restrictive settings rather than less restrictive ones (Hallenbeck, Kauffman, & Lloyd, 1993).

Yes, some students now being served primarily in resource rooms or special classes could be spending more of their time in general education classes. But to propose that all students with disabilities can be educated all of the time in general education classrooms defies logic. The rest of the chapters in this book address the plethora of problems presented by the full inclusion model, but let us address just one enigma related to this paradigm—how will the field meet the teacher supply-and-demand problem intrinsic to well-conceived full inclusion models?

Most full inclusion enthusiasts are quick to point out that under their plans for restructuring services for students with disabilities there will still be a role for special educators. One of the ways that advocates of inclusion frequently propose special educators be used is in some type of collaborative consultation role. In contrast to the more traditional model of consultation whereby an "expert" provides advice or assistance to the classroom teacher, collaborative consultation is based on the premise of shared responsibility and authority between the special and general educators (West & Idol, 1990). A variation of collaborative consultation is cooperative teaching, in which both the special educator and the general educator teach together in the general education classroom.

There has been virtually no research on the effects of collaborative consultation and cooperative teaching on student learning, leading some writers to characterize these models as a "feel good approach" (Fuchs & Fuchs, 1992). Moreover, what research has been done suggests that it is an extraordinarily complex process and is largely dependent on the ability of the teachers involved to get along with one another (Nowacek, 1992; Reeve & Hallahan, 1994; Trent, 1992; West & Cannon, 1988). It is logical to assume that part of what makes for compatibility in collaborative consultation and cooperative teaching is mutual respect. The following case, based on an actual cooperative teaching situation (names and minor details have been changed) illustrates how fragile the notion of mutual respect can be.

"YOURS, MINE, OR OURS?": STEVE FRANKLIN

As a resource teacher for eighth-grade students with learning disabilities and/or behavioral disorders, Steve believed his first priority was to ensure that his students be successful in their mainstream classes. Thus, when he heard about the inclusion model, in the form of the resource teacher working in the general education class with his or her students and others, he was excited by the potential for actual team teaching. He was a first-year teacher at Wilson Junior High, however, and he did not want to "step on any toes."

He had heard that the English teacher with whom his students would be placed was excellent with special needs students—demanding and expecting the best, but not unrealistic in her expectations. These qualities, Steve thought, would help ease him, as well as his students, into this new inclusion model. Here, perhaps, would be a place where not only the children would feel part of the mainstream, but Steve as well could feel the satisfaction of working in the general classroom with students who demonstrated a wide range of strengths, abilities, and weaknesses.

As there were only 2 weeks left in the summer, Steve chose to waste no time in starting to build rapport with this teacher. He called her one evening to set up a meeting:

> "Hello, Pam, this is Steve Franklin. I've just been hired as the resource teacher next year, and I understand you will be teaching most of my students English. Would it be possible for us to get together sometime soon to discuss possibilities for how we envision our working roles and get to know each other's styles?"

> "Sure, let's meet at my house next Thursday. Right after noon is good for me; my kids are napping!"

> "Great, I'll see you then. I'm really looking forward to this; I've heard great things about your work with special needs students in your classroom."

On the appointed day, Steve and Pam had a very productive discussion about the inclusion model. Pam was highly receptive to the proposal, saying that in her 20 years of teaching, there had been several special educators who had worked with her in this capacity, and that, most often, it was very successful. She stressed that personal styles and philosophies played a key role in these interactions. She found that if the teachers kept open communication, the students invariably benefitted from this combination of professionals working toward similar goals.

The first day of school, seventh-period English in Room 317 had two teachers standing in front of the room. They introduced themselves to the students as Mr. Franklin and Ms. Jarinski, not differentiating their roles as special educator or general educator. Even for some of the resource students, this was their first contact with Mr. Franklin.

Steve and Pam stayed after school that day to do further planning for the first semester's goals and assignments, now that they had had the advantage of meeting the students with whom they'd be dealing. Steve was fascinated by Pam's creativity. He was also pleased to hear that Pam's expectations were no lower for his students than for the others, although she was amenable to suggestions he was making for certain accommodations. For example, Pam wanted students to read *The Outsiders* and write a summary and reactions to each chapter. Knowing that reading this book—let alone writing detailed analyses—would be difficult for some of his students, Steve created audiotapes for each chapter for those students with particularly low reading abilities. Also, for those who could read fairly well (i.e., at grade level) but who shied away from written language assignments, he believed that taking dictations of their summaries and reactions would be a more effective first-novel-of-the-year measure of their comprehension. Pam, it appeared, was pleased with these accommodations, and Steve thus felt reassured that she would be amenable to others he might make as the year progressed.

Each day Steve looked forward to seventh period. This was a time when he could work with a range of student ability levels that he hoped would be a "reality check"—a measure against which he could gauge the performance of the students in his caseload. In addition, in the general classroom he could see what behavior and learning patterns differentiated his students from the others. For example, Chris took an extra 3 to 5 minutes to get his materials out; Sherika seemed to be talking constantly to her neighbor (whomever it might be that day); Shawn and Joe couldn't keep their hands to themselves; April just gazed out of the window when directions were given; and Charles, being teased a lot for his weight and "strange" behaviors (picking his nose, talking to himself), always seemed dejected.

Because of all these individual differences and occasional need for crisis intervention, Steve's role in the classroom began to change from what he had originally planned. It suddenly seemed that Pam was the teacher in the front of the blackboard while Steve was "floating" through the classroom arena, helping to clarify directions, organizing students, editing students' writing, administering positive reinforcement to students who were behaving appropriately and on task, and defusing fights before they could occur (or dealing with the post-altercation discipline).

Frustrated and unsure of the situation, he discussed his concerns with Pam.

> "Am I doing a good job? I don't intend to sound unrealistic, but is this the way it's worked with the resource teachers involved in inclusion in the past?"

> "Steve, you're doing a fabulous job. I don't think I could reach this group if I didn't have your help. The things you do in class are so valuable, for all of the kids, not just the identified students."

> "Yeah, but I often think that if you didn't have to deal with the tough emotional and learning needs of my kids, your day would go much smoother. I wish I could do more for you than I do."

> "Hey, Steve, they're not just your kids, they're ours."

This woman was like a special educator's dream: her concepts of inclusion and her philosophy about the special needs children were so great, they were almost a cliché! Always in the back of Steve's mind, however, was the knowledge that this team of teachers led by Pam Jarinski did not have to take his caseload each year. They did not make any more money than the rest of the teachers in the school, and yet they dealt with some very tough issues concerning the students with specific disabilities. Steve wanted to know that he, and his students, would be invited back to this classroom next year and for years to come.

The difficulties in the seventh-period class continued, however. As the year went on, Steve and Pam became less and less anxious to teach this class. By the second 9-week grading period, Steve noticed that it was more than just "his students" who were difficult to instruct in this setting. Of course, part of the problem was that this was the last period of the day, and interactions had built to the boiling point with some of the eighth graders by the time they got to the class. Also, energy levels were low for those students who weren't out of their seat or talking with others; some seemed as if they could use that afternoon nap afforded to the lucky kindergartners! Looking at the "tired" ones made Pam and Steve feel even less successful. But the ultimate frustration for them was the disappointed, rolling-of-eyes look on the faces of the students who were there each day, ready to learn, but who had to wait out the disruptions of the students around them.

Steve continued to do much of the "behind the scenes" work, planning and organizing different activities for the class, but he was less and less at work in front of the class. It became evident, although Pam and Steve never spoke of it, that this was the way they would work: Pam in front, giving instruction, with Steve still "floating." He thought back to their original meeting, and the emphasis Pam had put on communication. They were both so busy keeping up with the kids, however, that they barely had time to talk anymore, until they saw each other in seventh period. And once there, they were two people in the same room doing entirely different jobs. When Pam had her planning period, Steve was pulling kids from their Enriching Arts classes, so he had a full resource class of six students. He could occasionally go next door to set plans for the day, but they rarely had the opportunity to sit down and discuss the numerous and varied interactions, responses, and difficulties that occurred in seventh period. Steve was really beginning to have difficulty with the concept of teacher collaboration as it was manifesting itself in Room 317. Although he maintained the utmost professional and personal respect for Pam, he could not help believing that this situation was not in the best interests of his students or from feeling dissatisfied with a lack of the team-teaching responsibilities he had hoped for.

Steve's internal pressure to do better got worse 1 day when a critique came from a new, unexpected source: a student. Shawn, one of the students with behavioral disorders, had continued to have trouble keeping his hands to himself, despite the contracts and self-monitoring strategies Steve had worked on with him. One day Steve had approached Shawn's desk, knelt down, and whispered to him to give Lucy's pencil back to her. Shawn turned away from him, saying, "You're not the teacher here, anyway. You're the resource teacher. You should be in your room helping kids and stuff."

Steve's first thought was, "Who is this little guy to tell me how I should do my job?" His second thought was the realization that not only he, but also the children, were confused about his role. Their experiences with their resource teachers would most likely have been in a pull-out model. They did not know all of the behind-the-scenes planning Steve did with Pam; what they saw each day in the class did not look much like a teacher partnership anymore.

On 1 day, the behavior of the class was particularly horrendous— bad enough that both Pam and Steve decided to spend some heart-felt, dedicated time after the long day to discuss their next move. The idea they came up with for behavior management centered on grouping the students into teams and giving each team token rein-forcement for appropriate behaviors (attention to task, helping team-mates, having materials out, etc.) and removing it for inappropriate behaviors (talking out, not having materials, not attending to task, etc.). They were very clear about the parameters for this system when they presented it to the students, yet they felt that it was not too complicated to work. The physical change to the classroom was fairly radical: They moved all of the desks to an empty room at the end of the hall and exchanged them for tables. They arranged the students into groups of four, mixing ability levels, but minimizing interaction and behavior difficulties. The tokens they gave were "fake" money bills that each group could amass and cash in at the end of the grading period. Each group's name was on the board, and money was taken away or given in the appropriate column, as deserved, in order that the students could immediately see their accumulation or loss of rewards.

This plan was fairly successful for a few weeks. Certain students motivated the others in their group to work hard, stay on task, and behave appropriately. When someone "messed up" (as they called it), it was not always Pam or Steve calling them on it; now the students had a major part in the behavior management.

Steve, however, still had a minimal part in the plan as far as classroom time was concerned. Pam was the one in front of the room with the chalk, so by mere fact of physical proximity to the "rewards" board, she was the one to award and withdraw the tokens. Steve had hoped this system would have afforded him a higher profile in the class.

After the novelty had worn off the token system, classroom prob-lems reappeared. Pam and Steve realized that keeping up with the system was more demanding of their time and patience than they had originally thought. Steve was disappointed that this was not working, but it was helpful for him to see that strategies that might work in the smaller group or in self-contained special education set-tings, were far more difficult to implement with the large group. As always, his admiration for what Pam's job was like did not change.

Steve was late to seventh period that next Monday, as he'd gotten his finger caught in his file cabinet rushing to tie up loose ends from sixth period and had gone to the clinic to put ice on it. It's amazing what can happen when you're gone for 10 minutes . . . .

He came to Room 317, opened the door, and saw many somber faces in front of him. They all looked at him and then at Ms. Jarinski. Steve sat down next to her at the table and furrowed his brow, waiting for some explanation about what was going on. Pam handed him a list of four students, all resource room ones, and said, loud enough for all the students to hear, "I think we have to self-contain these kids for the rest of the year. It goes against my philosophy, but they just can't seem to control themselves."

There were only 3 weeks left in school, and Steve was shocked. Without changing their IEPs, this would not be legal, and he did not feel that this should be the final solution, nor that it was a message he wanted to send these kids—that they were incapable of controlling their behavior and, thus, could not be accepted in the mainstream English class. What could he do without damaging his relationship with Pam?

Here we have an energetic, recent graduate of one of the finest special education training programs in the country, an individual who achieved a 3.65 grade-point average on his way to a master of education degree, an individual who, all of his professors and clinical instructors agreed, would make a fine special educator. To expect that this unseasoned special education teacher could immediately garner the respect of an experienced, competent general educator, however, is unrealistic. Given that there is already a shortage of nearly 27,000 special education teachers in the United States (U.S. Department of Education, 1993), how can the demand for experienced special educators who can function as credible collaborative consultants possibly be met?

Collaborative consultation may be one excellent service delivery model, but research and experience suggest that its success depends on two individuals having a chemistry and good transactions—a chemistry that is difficult to define and that occurs relatively rarely and transactions with uncertain effects on students. Through more research, we may be able to know better how to train collaborative special and general educators, but this will undoubtedly take years to achieve and may never be sufficient to supplant other service delivery models. Thus, the nagging $64,000 question is whether effective "support" from special educators could be harnessed for all students with disabilities under a full inclusion model. Neither the history of placement and service delivery models (cf. Kauffman & Pullen, 1989; Kauffman & Smucker, in press) nor an analysis of placement issues in contemporary special education (cf. Kauffman & Lloyd, in press) suggest an affirmative answer.

REFERENCES

Bateman, B. D. (1992). *Better IEPs*. Creswell, OR: Otter Ink.

Blackman, H. P. (1992). Surmounting the disability of isolation. *The School Administrator, 49(2)*, 28–29.

Fuchs, D., & Fuchs, L. S. (1992). Limitations of a feel-good approach to consultation. *Journal of Educational and Psychological Consultation, 3(2)*, 93–97.

Hallenbeck, B. A., Kauffman, J. M., & Lloyd, J. W. (1993). When, how, and why educational placement decisions are made: Two case studies. *Journal of Emotional and Behavioral Disorders, 1,* 109–117.

Kauffman, J. M., & Lloyd, J. W. (in press). A sense of place: The importance of placement issues in contemporary special education. In J. M. Kauffman, J. W. Lloyd, T. A. Astuto, & D. P. Hallahan (Eds.), *Issues in the educational placement of pupils with emotional or behavioral disorders*. Hillsdale, NJ: Erlbaum.

Kauffman, J. M., & Pullen, P. L. (1989). An historical perspective: A personal perspective on our history of service to mildly handicapped and at-risk students. *Remedial and Special Education, 10(6)*, 12–14.

Kauffman, J. M., & Smucker, K. (in press). The legacies of placement: A brief history of placement options and issues with commentary on their evolution. In J. M. Kauffman, J. W. Lloyd, D. P. Hallahan, & T. A. Astuto (Eds.), *Issues in the educational placement of pupils with emotional or behavioral disorders*. Hillsdale, NJ: Erlbaum.

Nowacek, J. E. (1992). Professionals talk about teaching together: Interviews with five collaborating teachers. *Intervention in School and Clinic, 27,* 262–276.

Reeve, P. T., & Hallahan, D. P. (1994). Practical questions about collaboration between general and special educators. *Focus on Exceptional Children, 26(7)*, 1–10, 12.

Trent, S. C. (1992). *Collaboration between special education and regular education teachers: A cross-case analysis*. Unpublished doctoral dissertation, University of Virginia, Charlottesville.

U.S. Department of Education. (1990). *Twelfth annual report to Congress on the implementation of the Education of the Handicapped Act*. Washington, DC: Author.

U.S. Department of Education. (1993). *Fifteenth annual report to Congress on the implementation of the Individuals with Disabilities Education Act*. Washington, DC: Author.

Wang, M. C., Reynolds, M. C., & Walberg, H. J. (1988). Integrating the children of the second system. *Phi Delta Kappan, 70,* 248–251.

Wang, M. C., & Walberg, H. J. (1988). Four fallacies of segregationism. *Exceptional Children, 55,* 128–137.

West, J. F., & Cannon, G. S. (1988). Essential collaborative consultation competencies for regular and special educators. *Journal of Learning Disabilities, 21,* 56–63.

West, J. F., & Idol, L. (1990). Collaborative consultation in the education of mildly handicapped and at-risk students. *Remedial and Special Education, 11*(1), 22–31.

———————————— **Chapter 2** ————————————

The Social Context:
Then and Now

Donald L. MacMillan, Melvyn I. Semmel, Michael M. Gerber

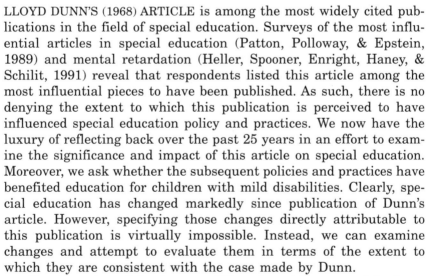

LLOYD DUNN'S (1968) ARTICLE is among the most widely cited publications in the field of special education. Surveys of the most influential articles in special education (Patton, Polloway, & Epstein, 1989) and mental retardation (Heller, Spooner, Enright, Haney, & Schilit, 1991) reveal that respondents listed this article among the most influential pieces to have been published. As such, there is no denying the extent to which this publication is perceived to have influenced special education policy and practices. We now have the luxury of reflecting back over the past 25 years in an effort to examine the significance and impact of this article on special education. Moreover, we ask whether the subsequent policies and practices have benefited education for children with mild disabilities. Clearly, special education has changed markedly since publication of Dunn's article. However, specifying those changes directly attributable to this publication is virtually impossible. Instead, we can examine changes and attempt to evaluate them in terms of the extent to which they are consistent with the case made by Dunn.

Consideration of the impact of Dunn's article on special education requires that one distinguish between Dunn's literal position and what some interpreted as "his message." That is, translators

Reprinted from "The social context of Dunn: Then and now," by Donald L. MacMillan, Melvyn I. Semmel, & Michael M. Gerber, *The Journal of Special Education,* Vol. 27, 1994, 466–480. Copyright © 1994 by PRO-ED, Inc.

extrapolated liberally from Dunn's words to suggest that no children with mild mental retardation required special day class placement, that no minority group children scoring in the 55 to 80 IQ range were "really retarded," and some even extended the arguments to apply to children with severe and profound disabilities—a population Dunn did not consider. Dunn certainly raised some issues that most, if not all, would contend needed addressing, such as the assumption that children with mild mental retardation constituted a homogeneous population and that self-contained special classes and the curriculum offered therein were appropriate for the students then served as mildly mentally retarded or educably mentally retarded.

SOCIAL CONTEXT IN 1968

In 1975, Lee Cronbach published a paper analyzing the five decades of controversy surrounding mental testing, and a number of his observations bear directly on the analysis of Dunn's article. Cronbach noted the importance of the social context in considering the receptiveness of society to positions advanced by individuals. For example, when in 1923 Brigham characterized certain immigrant groups as lacking intelligence, there was virtually no public outcry. Forty-five years later, however, when Jensen (1969) commented on black–white differences in IQ, he was vilified. Sentiment in the late 1960s was antagonistic to Jensen's views, leading many scholars and the public to react negatively, aggressively, and in considerable numbers. Similarly, understanding the reaction to Dunn's article also requires consideration of the social context in the late 1960s—the field was *ready* for his message. Consider the probable reaction to the same points had they been raised at the height of the eugenics scare. In fact, only a few years before Dunn's article, G. Orville Johnson (1962) published an article entitled "Special Education for the Mentally Handicapped: A Paradox," which appeared in the same journal, *Exceptional Children,* and in which many points similar to those raised by Dunn were presented. The reason for the meager reaction to Johnson's article and the warm reception to Dunn's is best understood in terms of the different social contexts at these two points in time.

In order to understand the reaction to Dunn's article one must appreciate the differences that existed then in special education child categories and the delivery system as contrasted with the present. Moreover, one must understand the social context that prevailed in the late 1960s, because this context explains, in part, the receptiveness of the field to Dunn's message.

Special Education in the 1960s

Romaine Mackie (1969) reported that between 1948 and 1966 there was a 400% increase in the number of students served as mentally retarded in public schools. Moreover, when President Ford signed P.L. 94-142 into law in 1975, mild mental retardation constituted the highest incidence of the exceptional child diagnoses (Reschly, 1988a). Programs for students with educable mental retardation were the most numerous of all special education programs, and they served the largest number of children receiving special education services. In the middle and late 1960s, the categories of mild handicaps and educable mental retardation were almost synonymous. The field of learning disabilities, as we know it today, was essentially nonexistent. While efforts on behalf of children with "minimal brain dysfunction" had emerged and Title I of the Elementary and Secondary Education Act permitted services for children with "specific learning disabilities," categories of exceptional children at the state level and in the U.S. Bureau for the Education of the Handicapped were hazy on mild handicaps other than mental retardation. This left public educators in a somewhat awkward position. That is, a youngster encountering persistent academic and/or social failure was eligible for special education services only if he or she could be found eligible for, and served in, the educable mental retardation (EMR) program. At the time, the Heber (1961) definition served as the guide for most state codes defining mental retardation, and that definition permitted identifying children as mentally retarded with IQs as high as 85, including children who in the American Association on Mental Deficiency classification scheme were categorized as mildly mentally retarded (IQ 55 to 70) and borderline mentally retarded (IQ 70 to 85). As such, EMR programs in the 1960s served a majority of children who would not qualify as mentally retarded today, and who also were, in many ways, much more capable students academically and socially, considering that approximately 3% of the general population score IQ 70 or below, while 16% score IQ 85 or below (see MacMillan, 1989, for a discussion).

Overrepresentation

Because IQ was one of the defining features of mental retardation, the differing distribution for African-American and white children (Kaufman & Doppelt, 1976) was to prove detrimental to EMR programs. One consequence of the use of IQ to establish eligibility, when coupled with the differing distributions for IQ by race and the disproportionate number of African-American children reared in poverty, was the overrepresentation of minority children in EMR programs (see Reschly, 1988b). Although recognized for years, this issue would precipitate a series of court cases challenging the fairness of identification procedures for minority children (see Elliott, 1987; Reschly, 1988b, for discussion).

Social Context

The thinking about mental abilities and factors influencing them was also changing in the 1960s. Two publications in the early part of the decade would profoundly change our thinking on the relative impact of genetics and the environment. J. McV. Hunt (1961) published *Intelligence and Experience* and Benjamin Bloom (1964) authored *Stability and Change in Human Characteristics*. Both were highly regarded scholars, and their message was clear: We had been underestimating the influence of environmental factors on intellectual development. In describing this period, Zigler and Muenchow (1992) wrote: "It seemed that the whole country was captured by an environmental mystique: It was as if the biological law of human variability had been repealed, and all that was known about genetics was being denied" (p. 10). A wave of early intervention projects followed and were interpreted by some as efforts to intervene in the lives of children coming from impoverished homes in the belief that the quality of the environment, particularly in the early years, was a central determinant of subsequent intellectual development. The early 1960s was a watershed in terms of a change in thinking on the part of psychologists and educators from a belief in the dominant role of genetics to an optimism regarding the power of the environment to alter the developmental trajectory of intelligence.

This "naive environmentalism" was not lost on some working in the area of mental retardation. A thorough treatment of the research and the interpretations of its results is provided by Spitz (1986). In describing this period, and in particular the role of Hunt's analyses, Spitz wrote: "Many influential workers considered that cultural deprivation was a major source of mild mental retardation, and consequently they prescribed early intervention as a preventive measure" (p. 86). In mental retardation circles, it was as if IQ were stable except in the range of 60 to 85 IQ, where the influence of the environment was operative in suppressing "true" scores in the normal range. Terms such as "pseudoretardation" and "The 6-hour retardate" were invoked to suggest that there were some cases who appeared on superficial measures (i.e., IQ, school achievement, etc.) to be mentally retarded but who were "not really retarded." Such thinking is even apparent in some of the classification schemes on the American Association on Mental Deficiency (AAMD), where "retardation due to psychosocial disadvantage" suggested that we knew what the etiology of mild retardation was—the effect of cultural deprivation.

Coupled with this belief in the power of the environment was the influence of sociologists on the thinking of special educators. Although Mercer's book, *Labeling the Mentally Retarded,* was not published until 1973, the data reported in that book were collected during the early 1960s. Sociologists examined the influence of institutions on individuals, and Mercer's earlier presentations, which predated Dunn's article, emphasized the "Anglocentric" nature of the public schools, the influence of the medical model on the classification procedures used in the schools, and how these served to erroneously identify minority children as EMR. In addition, the famous *Brown v. Board of Education* (1954) case, although decided over a decade previously, precipitated study of, and debate over, the effect of resources in schools on achievement differences, particularly as these pertained to black students. The post-Brown era included a serious examination of segregation/desegregation and the likely impact on school achievement. In essence, Dunn extended this examination to EMR classes, which were characterized at the time as suffering from de facto segregation. All of this made one of Dunn's major assertions very reasonable; namely, that if the public schools have denied equal educational opportunity to African-American children in the form of racial segregation, then is it not reasonable to assume that the special educational component of the public schools is implicated by identifying many African-American children as educably mentally retarded who are not, in fact, mentally retarded? Mercer's data seemed to support such an assertion, and those data were instrumental in the case presented by the plaintiffs in *Larry P. v. Riles* (1971, 1979, 1984).

UNIVERSAL PLACEMENTS, CURRICULUM, AND OUTCOMES

As noted in an earlier article (MacMillan, 1971), a major point made by Dunn was extremely helpful to the field. Namely, Dunn objected to the *universal* placement of students with educable mental retardation into self-contained special classes. At the time, special day class (SDC) placement was the service delivery model of choice, and it was universally applied to students with EMR. That is, if a student was certified as educably mentally retarded, he or she was placed and served in an SDC. Dunn appropriately noted the variability among students labeled EMR and questioned the appropriateness of the SDC and the nonacademic curriculum for *all* students so classified. Just as the predominant policy of assigning individuals with moderate, severe, and profound mental retardation in large residential institutions in the early decades of this century was found to be indefensible, so placement in special day classes for students labeled educably mentally retarded in the middle decades of this century was similarly misguided. Dunn challenged the utility of the special day class model for all students labeled educably mentally retarded, and outlined another service delivery model, the resource specialist teacher model, as potentially beneficial for a segment of the educably mentally retarded population. Some, unfortunately, interpreted Dunn's alternative model as a suggested replacement for the special day class model. Deno (1970) later explicated the need for a continuum of services, or cascade system, to accommodate the individual differences existing among students with disabilities.

In the years since Dunn's article appeared, we have witnessed the emergence of the resource specialist program (RSP) as the "almost universal" placement for students with mild handicaps. Mainstreaming, although difficult to define operationally (MacMillan & Semmel, 1977), entailed integration of students with mild handicaps with their nonhandicapped peers for some portion of the school day. In subsequent years we would experience pressure for the Regular Education Initiative (REI) (Will, 1984) and full inclusion—proposals that would shift responsibility for students with disabilities to regular education and would extend the range of children for whom integration was recommended. Throughout the period from 1970 to the present, the issue of *where* services are delivered remained the major topic of debate. Zigler, Hodapp, and Edison (1990), for example, invoked Bronfenbrenner's "social address" model of the environment, in which the only variable of importance is where the services are delivered. These authors noted that the field of mental retardation has been prone to conceptualize institutions "only as places, not as places *within which interactions occur*" (Zigler et al., 1990, p. 7). The preoccupation with settings and the apparent search for the universally best setting for delivering educational services to students with mild retardation deny the variability among children *and* the variability in social–psychological characteristics of settings within any given model (e.g., SDC, RSP). Project PRIME was the only comprehensive investigation of classroom observation variables among placement models that was conducted during the decade following Dunn's influential article (Kauffman, Agard, & Semmel, 1986). Results empirically demonstrated the wide variance within similarly classified classroom environments.

The civil rights movement, with its challenge to school arrangements on the basis of race, was not lost on special education. While special day classes had become the norm, the existence of a disproportionate number of minority children in these classes opened them to critical scrutiny as pockets of segregation within schools. This scrutiny, in turn, altered the fundamental way in which *schooling* was conceptualized and rekindled an awareness of individual differences. Special education was not a fixed set of clinical practices linked to a diagnosis or classification. Increased attention over the following decades was to be paid to individual differences within disability categories—an awareness that would lead logically to concepts of a "cascade" or continuum of services and the need for Individualized Education Programs (IEPs).

The shift from SDC to RSP as the preferred service delivery model had profound curricular implications as well. The curriculum orientation of the "EMR program" in place prior to Dunn's article, in fact, differed from the regular school curriculum in terms of goals, activities, and instructional units (see, e.g., DeProspo, 1955; Hungerford, DeProspo, & Rosenzweig, 1958; Kirk & Johnson, 1951). Although one might take issue with the appropriateness of this curriculum orientation for *all* students categorized as educably mentally retarded, the shift to RSP as the preferred service delivery model carried with it the adoption of the regular school curriculum, with its goals as appropriate for students with educable retardation, with the RSP services being designed to assist the student with the academic curriculum.

The primacy of the normal school curriculum had a long-standing tradition in the classification practices in mental retardation. The beliefs and practices dictated that there be a continuum of involvement in "normal" academic learning that should parallel students' relative severity of disability (e.g., educable mental retardation, trainable mental retardation, severe and profound mental retardation). Inability to learn in the normal curriculum was the original impetus for constructing an alternative curriculum for students with mental retardation, and it was the first step in the referral process for students being referred for psychological evaluation. The reasoning behind an alternative curriculum was that because the students could not learn in the curriculum designed to prepare them for normal occupations and life, they should be prepared for the inevitably limited social role that their level of ability dictated. Recommendation of the RSP model reiterated the belief that higher functioning students in the EMR category should learn the core curriculum to whatever extent possible. The validity of that position for the "higher functioning" students with educable retardation of the 1960s would prove difficult to test, because a change in the definition of mental retardation (Grossman, 1973) would eliminate children with IQs between 70 and 85 from eligibility.

CHANGES IN THE EDUCABLY MENTALLY RETARDED POPULATION

A central focus of Dunn's article was to question the utility of special education for many children then classified as mentally retarded who came from ethnic minority backgrounds. A disproportionate number of students with educable retardation were African-American (Reschly, 1988b), a fact that would precipitate litigation for the next 20 years (*Larry P. v. Riles,* 1971, 1979, 1984; *Marshall v. Georgia,* 1984; *P.A.S.E. v. Hannon,* 1980; *S-l v. Turlington,* 1979). It is important to realize that the educably mentally retarded population being addressed by Dunn resulted from the AAMD definition by Heber (1959, 1961). That definition permitted identification of individuals with IQs as high as 85 (actually 1 *SD* below the population mean). In 1973, AAMD published a new version of the definition (Grossman, 1973), which was responsive to the concerns raised regarding overrepresentation of minority group members, and shifted the upper cutoff from 1 *SD* to 2 *SD* below the mean (approximately IQ 70). The results of this change in definition include (a) a dramatic reduction in the number of children who are psychometrically eligible for classification as mentally retarded, and (b) a more patently disabled population with pervasive and serious learning problems (see MacMillan, 1989, for an extended discussion of these changes). Consider that Dunn's observations and recommendations for change were predicated on the previous definition of mental retardation and an educably retarded population that included youngsters who were far more capable than would be identified under the Grossman definition. Whether Dunn's concerns over achievement, stigmatization, negative effects of labels and segregation, self-fulfilling prophecies, and the like, extend to that segment of the mentally retarded population remaining after the change in definition, is open to conjecture. Nevertheless, his arguments concerning the negative aspects of the protective SDC for children with mild and borderline mental retardation can be found currently in much of the literature advancing full inclusion of children with severe handicaps—a literature with an even less substantive empirical basis than could be advanced by Dunn concerning children with mild mental retardation.

HOW BORDERLINE STUDENTS HAVE FARED: SOCIAL CONTEXT

Dunn hypothesized that the students in the EMR programs would fare at least as well in regular programs, although he was not specific in terms of which particular students (e.g., only those above IQ 70; minority students in the EMR category) were disserved by special education. In fact, Dunn listed a number of changes that had emerged in regular education that he believed would enable some/many students with EMR of the late 1960s to succeed in regular education. Debate centered on whether some children with EMR in the 1960s were "really retarded" or merely "6-hour retardates," but what was often overlooked was the fact that virtually all students placed in EMR programs at the time had been referred by their regular class teachers on the basis that these students were not keeping pace with their classmates. That is, referral was based on the teacher's perception that a child deviated markedly from classmates in achievement and social/personal adjustment and on the premise that the teacher had tried but failed to minimize the observed deficit. It was one thing to argue whether such children were truly mentally retarded; however, it was another to suggest that such children would be successful in regular education with no ancillary support, when they had not experienced success in earlier trials (Gerber & Semmel, 1984, 1985; MacMillan, Meyers, & Morrison, 1980).

Dunn also failed in his prognostications to anticipate changes that would occur in regular education that would reduce the likelihood for success by that segment of children targeted in his article. He apparently anticipated that the borderline students would be afforded more equal educational opportunity by being served in regular programs unlabeled. A number of features of special day classes, however, were sacrificed. For example, SDCs were characteristically associated with (a) low pupil–teacher ratios, (b) teachers with specialized training, (c) programs with vocational and social goals and sequences—and experiences for achieving these goals, (d) expenditures on the order of 1.75 to 2.5 times greater than costs per student in regular education ($2,000 to $4,000 more per student), and (e) greater individualization of instruction and periodic reviews of student progress (Reschly, 1988b). In exchange, these students were enrolled in regular programs with little or no ancillary services. Moreover, in the 1980s there was pressure to "return to basics" and to reinstitute "standards" viewed by many critics of public education as sorely lacking. These sentiments are captured in the report entitled *A Nation at Risk* (National Commission on Excellence in Education, 1983), in which consternation was expressed over the lack of standards indicated by diploma recipients who were barely literate. One response to this press for excellence came in the form of proficiency assessments, known as minimum competency examinations. Legislation was passed in some 40 states requiring minimum competency tests, frequently required in order for students to graduate from high school.

Dunn and his supporters who urged the return of children with EMR to regular grades did not anticipate these changes in regular education—changes that would dramatically compromise the chances of the borderline students to receive a high school diploma. In his provocative article, Dunn offered achievement data from efficacy studies to suggest that students in the IQ range of 70 to 85 achieved "significantly better" in regular grades. Overlooked was the fact that "significantly better" did not translate into achievement at grade level. In their review of the efficacy and mainstreaming literature, Semmel, Gottlieb, and Robinson (1979) reported that the highest mean reading achievement test score for students identified as educably retarded was 3.8, regardless of their age or the setting in which they were taught. It is instructive to note that the Balow, MacMillan, and Hendrick (1986) report on grade equivalence required to pass minimum competency tests indicated that not one district adopted a reading level anywhere near as low as 4.0 to pass the competency examination. As a result, those students who Dunn argued would be better accommodated in regular grades are very unlikely to achieve in reading at a level that would permit them to pass the minimum competency test (MCT) required for receipt of a high school diploma.

In a recently completed project (MacMillan, Balow, Widaman, & Hemsley, 1993), the educational circumstances of borderline students (i.e., IQ < 85 and achievement in the lowest quartile) were contrasted with those of learners with mild handicaps served by special education and regular class contrasts. The "back to basics" curriculum provides borderline students with a traditional academic curriculum, courses required for high school graduation, and proficiency tests. Failure of a proficiency test, or subtest, in ninth grade frequently results in the student being programmed into a remedial class until the student passes the proficiency test. For each remedial class taken, one less elective course can be taken by the student. MacMillan et al. (1993) found several interesting features of these remedial classes. First, they had disproportionately high ethnic minority enrollments, and the degree of the disproportion became greater as grade level increased. The "overrepresentation" noted by Dunn for EMR classes is currently present in remedial classes for students failing MCT subtests. The educational site of overrepresentation has shifted from EMR classes to remedial classes; however, the two types are comparable in that they *both* enroll a homogeneously grouped population with low academic achievement including a disproportionate number of ethnic minority students. A second finding was that the more remedial classes in which a student was enrolled, the less "relevant" they viewed the curriculum in terms of preparing them for their future.

Semmel, Gerber, and MacMillan (see Chapter 3) collected longitudinal data demonstrating the effect of the academic orientation at the school level provoked by the recent "effective schools" and "school improvement" policy movements in general education on children with mild handicaps. Two-year academic gain on the California Assessment of Proficiency (CAP) Tests for schools as a whole was negatively correlated with 2-year academic gain of special education elementary school students with mild handicaps. This empirical finding supported the earlier contention of Zigmond and Semmel (1988), who contended that the economic need to compete with Pacific Rim nations has been the impetus for growing pressure on the schools for increasing the competency of pupils in mathematics and science. This general education policy initiative has provoked a significant increase in academic press for achievement in the schools. This trend is associated with greater frustrations, failures, and increased dropout rates among the most "nonacademic" children with mild handicaps in the schools.

The bright future for borderline students seen by Dunn in 1968 has proven to be an illusion. In 1968, students with generalized achievement deficits and IQs in the 70 to 85 range were portrayed by Dunn as candidates for success in regular education classrooms because of innovations and changes in practices in regular education. Although his argument that they were "not really retarded" was later reinforced by the AAMD (Grossman, 1973), even the most ardent critic of EMR programs would not have denied that these students presented persistent and serious academic difficulties. What awaited these students in regular education was a curriculum that was highly academic, a paucity of ancillary support services to meet their needs, large classes, and course requirements and MCTs that were serious barriers for them in light of their academic problems. Moreover, Gottlieb's (1981) analysis of the extent to which mainstreaming resulted in anticipated benefits to children with mild retardation provides further evidence that Dunn's anticipated consequences concerning achievement, social acceptance, and avoidance of de facto segregation have not been realized.

SHIFT FROM EMPIRICISM TO ADVOCACY

In an earlier critical analysis of Dunn's position, MacMillan (1971) noted that the 1968 article lacked scholarly rigor. In many ways, Dunn utilized empirical data like the proverbial tippler who uses a lamppost—for support rather than illumination. Dunn argued for the relatively positive effects of regular classes based on the lack of empirical results of the "efficacy studies" of special classes (see Semmel et al., 1979; Semmel, Peck, & Lieber, 1985). Hence, the empirical support generated to buttress his views placed him in the weak scientific position of arguing in favor of a condition based on the lack of support for the efficacy of a contrasting condition (i.e., SDC). Furthermore, his review of empirical evidence on a given point (e.g., impact of labeling, existence of a self-fulfilling prophecy) was neither comprehensive nor penetrating. Instead, Dunn tended to selectively cite a study or two that supported a point he was making, and in the process, ignored other evidence that failed to support or even contradicted the evidence he cited. For example, Dunn argued that the label "mentally retarded" was not worn as a badge of distinction. He then extrapolated from Goffman's (1963) work on mortifications of self and stigma and Rosenthal and Jacobson's (1968) study on self-fulfilling prophecy in an attempt to empirically validate the assertion he was making, namely, that labeling children "mentally retarded" does irreparable harm to them. The Rosenthal and Jacobson study had been roundly criticized (see Elashoff & Snow, 1971; Thorndike, 1968). Goffman's research involved members of religious orders, the military, and incarcerated individuals who experienced removal of personal clothing and possessions, extreme regimentation of their daily lives, 24-hour close supervision, and the like. These are hardly analogous to the experiences of a child placed in a special day class. Moreover, Dunn ignored empirical evidence presented regarding the extension of Goffman's hypotheses to a mentally retarded population, albeit in a different environment, by Edgerton and Sabagh (1962). These investigators reported that higher functioning clients with mental retardation actually benefited from aggrandizements of the self by virtue of comparing themselves to less capable residents of the institution into which they were placed. On the broader topic of labeling children mentally retarded, MacMillan, Jones, and Aloia (1974) failed to confirm the negative effects hypothesized by Dunn. For a more detailed critique of the empirical evidence cited by Dunn (1968), see MacMillan (1971).

MARGINAL ROLE OF EMPIRICISM IN POLICY: AN UNFORTUNATE LEGACY

Special educational practices for children with EMR had been subjected to extensive, if not always sophisticated, empirical validation for years prior to publication of Dunn's article. Leaders in the field, such as Samuel Kirk (1964), Herbert Goldstein (1963, 1964, 1967), and Samuel Guskin and Howard Spicker (1968) had published extensive reviews of research summarizing critically the empirical evidence on various educational practices concerned with children with EMR. Most, if not all, of the research summarized in these reviews focused on the effects of educational practices (placement, methods of instruction, curriculum, etc.) on the child/adolescent/adult with EMR. Of importance to the present discussion is that researchers in special education sought *evidence* on which to try certain things, change practices, and recommend policy. It should also be noted that the focus of these efforts was on *outcomes*.

Coinciding with the publication of, and reactions to, Dunn's article is a shift away from focusing on outcomes and a new emphasis on *inputs*—that is, gaining *access* to regular classes for students with mild handicaps and to special education for those heretofore denied a public education because they were perceived as being too handicapped to benefit. The period of the early 1970s serves as a sort of watershed; since that time policies and treatments have been recommended, in many cases devoid of empirical support that they will in fact have a positive impact on children with mental retardation. Zigler et al. (1990) capture this shift:

On the one hand, it is our duty to gather and evaluate information, to participate in our work as responsible scientists. Yet all too often, each side of the normalization debate has lapsed into an advocacy or apologist role vis-à-vis group homes or large institutions or mainstreamed versus special education classrooms.

This sort of dogmatism intrudes as well into professional advice concerning the best placements for each specific retarded person. Nowadays, professionals often insist they know best, instructing families about what to do with their children or what to do with their retarded adult offspring. Again, a look at history provides us with instructive examples. Some years ago professionals advised institutionalizing most retarded individuals; today families who institutionalize their family members are made to feel inadequate or guilty, and these are problems that can be as long-lasting and hurtful as the actual difficulties of dealing with a mentally retarded loved one. (p. 9)

While policy reform relative to special education was under way prior to 1968, the change in the basis on which academics urged change appeared to be informed by Dunn's strategy. Ride the tide of sentiment! Increasingly we see those in the academic community eschewing the need for evidence, and instead relying on ideology and slogans as the basis for the changes sought. "Label jars, not people" was the simplistic solution to some for the complex issue of classification. To the question of what evidence suggested a certain change in services being advocated, a frequent response was, "It didn't require Lincoln to have a research study to know that slavery was wrong." No longer were "best practices" determined by evaluation designs; rather, they were determined by those with the loudest voices, catchiest slogans, and most ability to simplify.

The current state of affairs in special education represents the most unfortunate legacy from Lloyd Dunn. He failed to review the evidence in a scholarly manner, he made broad, sweeping generalizations, and he recommended a blueprint for change that lacked any empirical support. Moreover, some of his disciples compounded these problems by misrepresenting what Dunn had stated or by blatantly extrapolating from his article to populations of children with disabilities not considered by Dunn. To his credit, he read the climate in the field and anticipated properly the reception his criticism and recommendations for change would receive. Within a short time, the professional publications in special education would abound with self-flagellation concerning all the ills of special education, usually ignoring the variation within categories of children, variations in specifics of any single administrative model or instructional strategy, and clearly taking on a sociological flavor in regard to the issue of how institutions harm people. Interestingly, special educators contributing such pieces typically saw no problems in general education and frequently none inherent in the individual child. School psychologists were portrayed as individuals ferreting out students with disabilities where no disabilities actually existed, and the tools they used were assailed in the courts and in the literature as causal factors in the academic problems encountered by children. In the 25 years since the Dunn article appeared, there has been a stream of topics in print and delivered at conferences suggesting that the "problem" would be solved if we abolished residential institutions, intelligence tests, special education settings, and disability categories and refrained from the use of categorical labels. Unfortunately, the simplistic casting of special education issues fails to capture the multivariate nature of the problems and thereby misleads those who would study the "problem" in the simplistic fashion suggested. A quote from H.L. Mencken summarizes this problem: "For every complex issue there is a simple answer, and it is wrong" (cited in Zigler & Hodapp, 1986, p. 223).

In the ensuing years, "advocacy" has become the umbrella term to subsume any number of activities designed to bring about change in the field of disability. Certainly, advocacy on behalf of children is desirable; however, the brand of advocacy we have seen has increasingly been "program advocacy" rather than "child advocacy." Advocacy on behalf of deinstitutionalization, mainstreaming, behaviorism, abolishment of aversives, facilitated communication, the Regular Education Initiative, and full inclusion, to mention only some, has been characterized by the uncritical advancement of a point of view in the absence of, or a disregard for, the evidence on the effects of that "program" on children. The noted psychologist Lee Cronbach (1975) distinguished between advocacy and scholarship:

> There is a fundamental difference between the style of the advocate, in law and in journalism, and the style of the scholar. An advocate tries to score every point, including those he knows he deserves to lose. The advocate who bridles his partisanship places his side at an "unfair" disadvantage. Our scholars chose to play advocate when they went before the public, and they abandoned scholarly consistency. (p. 12)

In this passage, Cronbach has captured the essence of what all too often has passed as scholarship in the special education literature. Ideology backed by testimonial has led to advocacy for certain practices as being the panacea, with a blatant disregard for the individual differences inherent in the population classified as disabled or within any one of the disability categories. Kauffman and Hallahan (1993) have vividly described the use of the term "all" in much of the reform literature describing entry level skills *all* children will bring to school, levels of achievement in math and science which *all* children will surpass; statements that fail to consider the severe disabilities present in *some* children. Advancing a treatment for *all* children in effect argues for the abandonment of *some* for the betterment of *others*. There is danger inherent in assuming that one treatment is appropriate for all children, or that a given treatment is never appropriate for any child.

Program advocacy, such as that mentioned above, gives the distinct impression to legislators and others concerned with special education that we know what works and how to best serve children with disabilities. However, after a decade of effort to implement some of Dunn's proposals, Gottlieb wrote that an "appropriate education for mentally retarded children has not yet been developed" (1981, p. 118). Similar conclusions have been reached by most empiricists taking a child perspective and examining the consequences of various educational placements and instructional procedures on child outcomes (e.g., achievement, social status, self-concept).

In closing, we reiterate our agreement with those who advocate for the rights of children with disabilities to free *access* to all of the real and potential advantages of education. However, we maintain a strong commitment to maximizing personal, social, and academic *outcomes* for these citizens throughout their lives. Advocacy demands compelling moral and ethical argument to achieve policy objectives. Effective educational interventions, however, demand empirical validation and demonstrable generalization. Advocacy defines opposing positions and perceptions as impediments to desired goals. Science, on the other hand, thrives on variation and controversy. Advances in new knowledge grow from testing competing views. Part of the tragedy of the contemporary atmosphere is that would-be reformers frequently denigrate the mores of science in the name of advocacy. They often promote and rationalize their subjective views as if these were buttressed by scientific rigor. There also appears to be a growing trend among some advocates to stifle debate about how children with disabilities are to be educated. Clearly, at a time when children with disabilities and special education are in danger of losing the protected resources and commitment won after long struggle, Dunn's views must not be uncritically embraced as an historical "affair complete." Rather, we advocate for continued professional debate and research on the salient issues that Lloyd Dunn so dramatically brought to public attention 25 years ago.

AUTHORS' NOTE

This chapter was supported, in part, by grants HC023C20002, H023C80072, and H023C30103 from the U.S. Department of Education to the first author, and grant H023C90038 to the Special Education Research Laboratory, University of California, Santa Barbara.

REFERENCES

Balow, I. H., MacMillan, D. L., & Hendrick, I. G. (1986). Local option competency testing: Psychometric issues with mildly handicapped and educationally marginal students. *Learning Disabilities Research, 2*(1), 32–37.

Bloom, B. S. (1964). *Stability and change in human characteristics.* New York: Wiley.

Brigham, C. C. (1923). *A study of American intelligence.* Princeton NJ: Princeton, University Press.

Brown v. Board of Education of Topeka, 347 U.S. 483, 493 (1954).

Cronbach, L. J. (1975). Five decades of public controversy of mental testing. *American Psychologist, 30,* 1–14.

Deno, E. (1970). Cascade system of special education services. *Exceptional Children, 37,* 229–237.

DeProspo, C. (1955). A suggested curriculum for the mentally retarded. In M. Frampton & E. Gall (Eds.), *Special education for the exceptional* (Vol. 3, pp. 472–478). Boston: Porter Sargent.

Dunn, L. M. (1968). Special education for the mildly retarded—Is much of it justifiable? *Exceptional Children, 35,* 5–22.

Edgerton, R. B., & Sabagh, G. (1962). From mortification to aggrandizement: Changing self-conceptions in the careers of the mentally retarded. *Psychiatry, 25,* 263–272.

Elashoff, J. D., & Snow, R. E. (1971). *Pygmalion reconsidered.* Worthington, OH: C.A. Jones.

Elliott, R. (1987). *Litigating intelligence.* Dover, MA: Auburn House.

Gerber, M., & Semmel, M. I. (1984). Teacher as imperfect test: Reconceptualizing the referral process. *Educational Psychologist, 19,* 137–148.

Gerber, M., & Semmel M. I. (1985). Microeconomics of referral and reintegration: A paradigm for evaluation of special education. *Studies in Educational Evaluation, 11,* 13–29.

Goffman, E. (1963). *Stigma.* Englewood Cliffs, NJ: Prentice-Hall.

Goldstein, H. (1963). Issues in the education of the educable mentally retarded. *Mental Retardation, 1,* 10–12.

Goldstein, H. (1964). Social and occupational adjustment. In H. A. Stevens & R. Heber (Eds.), *Mental retardation: A review of research* (pp. 214–258). Chicago: University of Chicago Press.

Goldstein, H. (1967). The efficacy of special classes and regular classes in the education of educable mentally retarded children. In J. Zubin & G. A. Jervis (Eds.), *Psychopathology of mental development* (pp. 580–602). New York: Grune & Stratton.

Gottlieb, J. (1981). Mainstreaming: Fulfilling the promise? *American Journal of Mental Deficiency, 86,* 115–126.

Grossman, H. J. (Ed.). (1973). *Manual on terminology and classification in mental retardation.* Washington, DC: American Association on Mental Deficiency.

Guskin, A. L., & Spicker, H. H. (1968). Educational research in mental retardation. In N. R. Ellis (Ed.), *International review of research in mental retardation* (Vol. 3, pp. 217–278). New York: Academic Press.

Heber, R. (1959). A manual on terminology and classification in mental retardation. *American Journal of Mental Deficiency, 56,* Monograph Supplement (Rev.).

Heber, R. (1961). Modifications in the manual on terminology and classification in mental retardation. *American Journal of Mental Deficiency, 65,* 499–500.

Heller, H. W., Spooner, F., Enright, B. E., Haney, K., & Schilit, J. (1991). Classic articles: A reflection into the field of mental retardation. *Education and Training in Mental Retardation, 26,* 202–206.

Hungerford, R., DeProspo, C., & Rosenzweig, L. (1958). Education of the mentally handicapped in childhood and adolescence. In S. C. DiMichael (Ed.), *Vocational rehabilitation of the mentally retarded* (pp. 47–63). Washington, DC: U.S. Department of Health, Education, and Welfare, Office of Vocational Rehabilitation.

Hunt, J. M. (1961). *Intelligence and experience.* New York: Ronald Press.

Jensen, A. R. (1969). How much can we boost IQ and scholastic achievement? *Harvard Educational Review, 39,* 1–123.

Johnson, G. O. (1962). Special education for the mentally handicapped: A paradox. *Exceptional Children, 19,* 62–69.

Kauffman, J. M., Agard, J., & Semmel, M. I. (1986). *Mainstreaming: Learners and their environments.* Cambridge, MA: Brookline Books.

Kauffman, J. M., & Hallahan, D. P. (1993). Toward a comprehensive delivery system for special education. In J.I. Goodlad & T.C. Lovitt (Eds.), *Integrating general and special education* (pp. 73–102). New York: Macmillan.

Kaufman, A. S., & Doppelt, J. E. (1976). Analysis of WISC-R standardization data in terms of the stratification variables. *Child Development, 47,* 165–171.

Kirk, S. A. (1964). Research in education. In H. A. Stevens & R. Heber (Eds.), *Mental retardation: A review of research* (pp. 57–99). Chicago: University of Chicago Press.

Kirk, S. A., & Johnson, G. O. (1951). *Educating the retarded child.* Boston: Houghton Mifflin.

Larry P. v. Riles. (1971). Civil Action No. 71-2270 (N.D. Cal. 1971).

Larry P. v. Riles. (1979). 495 F. Supp. 926 (N.D. Cal. 1979) (decision on merits).

Larry P. v. Riles. (1984). United States Court of Appeals. Ninth Circuit. No. 80-427. January 23, 1984. Trial Court Decision Affirmed.

Larry P. v. Riles. Civil Action No. 71-2270 (N.D. Cal. 1971). 495 F. Supp. 926 (N.D. Cal. 1979) (decision on merits). United States Court of Appeals, Ninth Circuit, No. 80-427. January 23, 1984, trial court decision affirmed.

Mackie, R. (1969). *Special education in the United States: Statistics 1948–1966.* New York: Teachers College Press.

MacMillan, D. L. (1971). Special education for the mildly retarded: Servant or savant? *Focus on Exceptional Children, 2,* 1–11.

MacMillan, D. L. (1989). Equality, excellence, and the EMR populations: 1970–1989. *Psychology in Mental Retardation and Developmental Disabilities, 15*(2), 1, 3–10.

MacMillan, D. L., Balow, I. H., Widaman, K. F., & Hemsley, R. E. (1993). *Minimum competency tests and their consequences* (Final Report). Riverside: School of Education, University of California at Riverside.

MacMillan, D. L., Jones, R. L., & Aloia, G. F. (1974). The mentally retarded label: A theoretical analysis and review of research. *American Journal of Mental Deficiency, 79,* 241–261.

MacMillan, D. L., Meyers, C. E., & Morrison, G.M. (1980). System identification of mildly mentally retarded children: Implications for interpreting and conducting research. *American Journal of Mental Deficiency, 85,* 108–115.

MacMillan, D. L., & Semmel, M. I. (1977). Evaluation of mainstreaming programs. *Focus on Exceptional Children, 9*(4), 1–14.

Marshall et al. v. Georgia, U.S. District Court for the Southern District of Georgia, CV482-233, June 28, 1984; Affirmed (11th cir. no. 84-8771, Oct. 29, 1985); Order, February 13, 1987.

Mercer, J. R. (1973). *Labeling the mentally retarded.* Berkeley: University of California Press.

National Commission on Excellence in Education. (1983). *A nation at risk: The imperative for educational reform.* Washington, DC: Author.

PASE (Parents in Action on Special Education) v. Joseph P. Hannon, U.S. District Court, Northern District of Illinois, Eastern Division, No. 74 (3586)(1980).

Patton, J. R., Polloway, E. A., & Epstein, M. H. (1989). Are there seminal works in special education? *Remedial and Special Education, 10*(3), 54–59.

Reschly, D. J. (1988a). Introduction. In M. C. Wang, M. C. Reynolds, & H. J. Walberg (Eds.), *Handbook of special education: Research and practice.* (Vol. 2, pp. 3–5). Oxford, England: Pergamon Press.

Reschly, D. J. (1988b). Minority mild mental retardation: Legal issues, research findings, and reform trends. In M.C. Wang, M. C. Reynolds, & H. J. Walberg (Eds.), *Handbook of special education: Research and practice* (Vol. 2, pp. 23–41). Oxford, England: Pergamon Press.

Rosenthal, R., & Jacobson, L. (1968). *Pygmalion in the classroom: Teacher expectation and pupils' intellectual development.* New York: Holt, Rinehart & Winston.

S-1 v. Turlington, Preliminary Injunction, U.S. District Court, Southern District of Florida, Case No. 79-8020-Civ-CA WPB (1979).

Semmel, M. I., Gottlieb, J., & Robinson, N. M. (1979). Mainstreaming: Perspectives on educating handicapped children in the public schools. In D. Berliner (Ed.), *Review of research in education VI.* Washington, DC: American Educational Research Association, Peacock Publishers.

Semmel, M. I., Peck, C., & Lieber, J. (1985). Effects of special education environments: Beyond mainstreaming. In J. Meisels (Ed.), *Mainstreaming the mildly handicapped child* (pp. 165–192). Hillsdale, NJ: Erlbaum.

Spitz, H. H. (1986). *The raising of intelligence: A selected history of attempts to raise retarded intelligence.* Hillsdale, NJ: Erlbaum.

Thorndike, R. L. (1968). Review of R. Rosenthal and L. Jacobson, *Pygmalion in the classroom. American Educational Research Journal, 5,* 708–711

Will, M. (1984). Educating children with learning problems: A shared responsibility. *Exceptional Children, 52,* 411–415.

Zigler, E., & Hodapp, R. M. (1986). *Understanding mental retardation.* New York: Cambridge University Press.

Zigler, E., Hodapp, R. M., & Edison, M. R. (1990). From theory to practice in the care and education of mentally retarded individuals. *American Journal on Mental Retardation, 95,* 1–12.

Zigler, E., & Muenchow, S. (1992). *Head Start: The inside story of America's most successful educational experiment.* New York: Basic Books.

Zigmond, N., & Semmel, M. I. (1988). Educating the nation's handicapped children. In K. Lloyd (Ed.), *Risking American education competitiveness in a global economy: Federal education and training policies, 1980–90.* Arlington, VA: Center for Educational Competitiveness.

Chapter 3

A Legacy of Policy Analysis Research in Special Education

Melvyn I. Semmel, Michael M. Gerber, Donald L. MacMillan

◆ ◆ ◆

ONE CONCEIT IN CELEBRATING 25th anniversaries is the belief that the number of years passed are a valid indication of our relative maturity as a field of scholarship and educational practice. Surviving long enough to have a history, much less to reminisce and commemorate, is an accomplishment of sorts. Ideas, like other living things, do tend to evolve, but in intellectual competition as in natural history, there are no guarantees.

Almost 100 years ago, urban public schools embraced special day classes as part of a solution to the enormous effort that universal education demanded of regular classroom teachers, especially when students with mental retardation were present (Sarason & Doris, 1979). Sixty years later, Lloyd Dunn rhetorically mused in his now well-known article (Dunn, 1968) about whether separate classes for students with mental retardation were justifiable.

Another quarter century passes, and in 1993 we now find zealous reformers wondering aloud if much of special education itself is justified. Echoing some of the same arguments made by Dunn (unproved efficacy, possible harm), contemporary reformers call for new, comprehensive, effective school programs; updated, more demanding curricula; and full inclusion of "all" students.

Reprinted from "Twenty-five years after Dunn's article: A legacy of policy analysis research in special education," by Melvyn I. Semmel, Michael M. Gerber, & Donald L. MacMillan, *The Journal of Special Education,* Vol. 27, 1994, 481–495. Copyright © 1994 by PRO-ED, Inc.

In another chapter in this book (MacMillan, Semmel, & Gerber), we point out that Dunn's article became well known more for its contribution to a particular advocacy than for its contribution to special education scholarship. We suggest that the subsequent quarter century has been marked by much confusion between advocacy, on one hand, and scholarship, on the other. This Janus-like condition amplifies the level of contention among special educators without necessarily altering the material reality of schools. Many authors, in fact, have pointed out repeatedly that modern initiatives aimed at reintegrating students with disabilities into general education most often originate with special educators! It appears that special educators may actually take such initiatives more seriously and embrace their reformist intent more readily than do their general education colleagues (Kauffman, Gerber, & Semmel, 1988; Semmel, Abernathy, Butera, & Lesar, 1991). Indeed, reformist zeal and vision constitute a substantial part of the historical traditions of special education as a field of practice (Sarason & Doris, 1979; Hendrick & MacMillan, 1989).

The question remains: What does our history teach? How is our scholarship, if not our advocacy, better informed because of the history we, as a field, have experienced?

LEARNING FROM OUR HISTORY

The 19th-century German philosophy professor, Hegel, held a generally negative view about society's ability to learn from its history: "What experience and history teach is this—that people and governments never have learned anything from history, or acted on principles deduced from it" (Hegel, 1857, see Introduction).

One of Hegel's better known devotees, himself a passionate activist more interested in changing the world than understanding it, added his own twist to Hegel's idea of historical dialectic: "Hegel says somewhere that all great events and personalities in world history reappear in one fashion or another. He forgot to add: the first time as tragedy, the second as farce" (Marx, 1967, p. 5).

The "tragedy" of Dunn's 1968 article was that, in riding the rising tide of antisegregation sentiment spurred by the civil rights movement, he helped drive a powerful ideological wedge between advocates for special education and advocates for ethnic and racial minorities—advocates who should have found common cause in the public school system's chronic lack of tolerance for human differences

(Gerber, 1989). Instead, with Dunn's unwitting assistance, special education in the late 1960s and early 1970s was successfully cast as one of the villains in the civil rights melodrama. The "smoking gun" was "overrepresentation" of minority students in classes for students with mental retardation, a strange concept that simultaneously embraces a normative concept of social equality (i.e., the "over" part) while depending heavily on a belief in biogenetic difference (i.e., the "representation" part). No one, presumably, was arguing that there was not some real incidence of mental retardation within minority groups, only the degree to which bias skewed the identification rates between groups (Gottlieb, Semmel, & Veldman, 1976).

The debate about identification and racial bias in special education created notoriety rather than insight. It created an image of special educators, made bold by some self-serving, pseudo-scientific argument, acting in the interest of racists and bigots. Somehow, it seemed, special education had hypnotized the entire general education establishment—teachers, administrators, and policymakers—into believing in the construct of mental retardation, particularly among ethnic and racial minorities, and in "special" education as its solution.

This was, and continues to be, denial on a massive scale. The public schools, via politicians and administrators, operate special education to satisfy a variety of purposes, some undoubtedly more defensible than others. Any variance between special education's unchanged goals—to minimize the handicapping consequences of significant differences while supporting the effectiveness of regular classroom teaching—and observable practices is not a product of some massive deception or misuse of science by a splinter group of reactionary professionals. Rather, these discrepancies arise from the multipurpose complexity of public schooling in our society including, in some circumstances, motives and methods that are not above reproach.

History does, in fact, record that the earliest "ungraded" classes freely mingled immigrants, non-English speakers, and racial minorities, who may or may not have been "truly" retarded, with children who most certainly were. However, history also records that special education as a "policy," not as the collection of its specific habilitative or teaching practices, was a creature of the public school system, not of an unusually powerful special education lobby. The carefully drawn, empirically minded, clearly articulated ungraded class movement begun in New York in the first years of the century was led by bold, visionary reformers. The rapid diffusion and adoption of the "ungraded class" concept around the country, though, was not because every local administrator or school board agreed with New York progressivist ideas. Separate classes were a good practical tool of management whether one separated children for "good" or "bad" reasons.

The distinction between special education policy and practice is important to understanding the field after Dunn's article. Special education is the whole of its structures and functions as encouraged or permitted by the public school system, on one hand, and what particular special education teachers do or intend to do for each identified student, on the other. What describes the "system" is not necessarily what describes actual practice or results. This distinction is easily lost even by those deeply involved in special education. The truth is, and always has been, that the school system created the segregationist tendencies of special education for very practical, economic reasons. Historically, when the political climate dictates that these tendencies should be viewed as repugnant to a democratic society, those who lead the public school system follow the band. However, when they do, they exhibit a cynical form of historical and institutional amnesia. They certainly seem to have no moral compunction about denying their paternity and abandoning their offspring (e.g., see National Association of State Boards of Education, 1992).

California's experience, we think, has been illustrative. The state was among those that led the post–civil rights special education reform movement in the early 1970s. It was the locus of two, still-controversial antidiscrimination law suits (*Larry P. v Riles,* 1972; *Diana v. State Board of Education,* 1970) brought by minority rights advocates. General decertification of thousands of minority children previously classified as mentally retarded actually began some years earlier. In 1972, though, a state "master plan" instigated two reforms of the type that Dunn's 1968 article seemed to envision. In its new special education policy, California created generic service categories (i.e., learning handicapped, severely handicapped), purportedly to defeat the stigma thought to be associated with conventional disability labels like "mental retardation," and in an attempt to balance ethnic proportions among the educably mentally retarded (EMR) population. It also established resource specialists to consult with and assist regular classroom teachers in teaching learning (i.e., mildly) handicapped students. The resource specialist program (RSP) was supposed to provide an alternative to segregated settings, including self-contained special education classrooms. However, the intent of this earlier reform movement and its actual functioning in practice diverged almost immediately. Nothing in the practice of identifying students for "learning handicapped" programs, rather than programs for students classified as educably mentally retarded, learning disabled, or emotionally disturbed, prevents stigmatization. Stigmatization is a social process related to rejection. It stems from people's attitudes and behavior, not from terminology. If teachers and administrators, both in word and deed, avoid or deny responsibility for children with disabilities, no reworking of terminology will prevent stigmatizing processes from developing. The intended neutrality of the classification "learning handicapped" deceived no one. In short order, "LH" became as omnipresent in professional vocabulary as "LD" or "EMR" were elsewhere, with much the same effect on parents, teachers, peers, and the identified children themselves.

In light of current proposals to deliver special education in regular classrooms through consultation and collaborative teaching models, it is also revealing, we think, that California teachers who were named to play the new role of "resource specialists" were never provided a suitable means for penetrating and influencing general education classroom practices nor the administrative and real dollar investment necessary to make them credible as a "resource" to their general education colleagues (Semmel & Ballard-Campbell, 1983). Looking simultaneously at the past and at the future, we fear that contemporary reform rhetoric about "full inclusion," as well as about consultative and collaborative models of service delivery, will not only fail to benefit from the tragic past experience, but also will command such little real commitment of resources as to be a farce.

School Resources and Social Integration

About the same time that Dunn began drafting his 1968 article, James Coleman's study of differences between segregated schools was beginning a chain reaction that would instigate a decade of explosive debate, research, and political reaction (Coleman et al., 1966). The fury of the debate was a measure of how deeply Coleman's findings had contradicted popular beliefs and uncritical assumptions about how and what schools produce by the activity that occurs behind the doors of classrooms. Coleman's analysis of a massive amount of data had failed to provide unequivocal proof that segregated, more poorly resourced African-American schools produced lower achievement than better resourced, segregated white schools (Coleman et al., 1966). Worse for those who advocated for federally funded compensatory education programs, these data provided only meager evidence that differences in amounts of directly purchasable resources in schools, including general characteristics of teachers, accounted for differences in achievement outcomes. The grossly simplified message that most captured the attention of the media was that schools made little difference beyond differences that were innate or the result of socialization and family. The deeper, more troubling implication, however, was that differential spending as part of a planned intervention strategy to boost achievement of low-achieving students, particularly minority students, was futile.

By the end of the 1960s, accumulating data from preschool model demonstrations and early data from compensatory education programs began to be interpreted to suggest that differential federal spending did not alter fundamental differences in ability or achievement. In 1968, Jensen fomented an already inflammatory situation with publication of his interpretation that average IQ differences between white and African-American students represented relatively permanent innate differences between these groups, differences not subject to modification through education.

Even before the decade ended, though, the policy arguments for desegregation had shifted away from a differential school resource argument (i.e., separate, but not equal) to a social integration argument. In this latter formulation, it was not necessarily true that "white" schools had more or better teaching resources, it was rather that "white" schools had "better" students whose achievement-oriented, achievement-ready backgrounds created a powerful environmental press for academic attainment. Therefore, social integration would provide social modeling of higher aspirations, skills, and motivation to minority students whose segregated school environments produced a defeating climate of failure and hopelessness.

Although there may have been merit to the conclusion that decades of social discrimination, segregation, and economic impoverishment had produced a "deprived" population less ready or able to learn than their advantaged peers, it was foolish to believe that mere juxtaposition of white and African-American students would cancel the bill that white America had accumulated. Therefore, much of the passion expended on forcing or resisting busing was wasted; it yielded little real effort to meet the educational needs of low-achieving students. Although racial segregation in schooling was a destructive practice, it was unlikely that it caused underachievement in any simple, mechanical way. Confusing the social *goal* of equal opportunity with *place* of opportunity distracted social scientists as well as the lay public from attention to what were appropriate educational means to reach desired ends.

DUNN IN THE CONTEXT OF THE NATIONAL CIVIL RIGHTS MOVEMENT

Seen against the backdrop of the movement to reduce racial segregation, Dunn is probably not deserving of either as much criticism as he has received for betraying special education nor as much praise as he has received for being a visionary. Many of the students who participated in Dunn's studies of curriculum and testing materials in the early 1960s were African-American students classified as mentally retarded in Tennessee schools. As civil rights advocates successfully characterized school special education placement practices as inherently or overly biased, with the unspoken goal of segregating African-American students within schools, Dunn surely realized, as did many others, that identification of minority students as mentally retarded and the placement of these students in self-contained special classes were no longer politically or socially viable options. The force of this social movement would not be stopped by empirical evidence that such placements were educationally appropriate, even if such evidence were available. Dunn, as a senior leader in the field of special education, experienced no epiphany, but only a sober assessment that times had changed and so must special education practice.

Two pieces of evidence support this interpretation. The first comes from a close reading of the 1968 article. Dunn goes to great lengths to focus his critique continually on issues related to minority students. The second piece of evidence is that, although Dunn was instructionally involved with the dissemination of special education research literature to his doctoral students, his article revealed an utter lack of a critical review of empirical evidence supporting his arguments.

True, Dunn probably intended his article as a polemic, not a scholarly review. But just as true, if credible evidence had been available, it would have been foolish of him *not* to marshal it in support of his position. The fact of the matter, we now know, is that the "efficacy studies" of special versus regular classes provided ambiguous and contradictory evidence, at best (Semmel, Gottlieb, & Robinson, 1979; Semmel, Peck, & Lieber, 1985).

Most importantly, though, Dunn, like many other researchers concerned with special class "efficacy," didn't or couldn't grasp the significance of nonrandom selection of students for special versus regular class placement. To appreciate this fact fully requires more than a statistical argument. Rather, it requires a different theory about identification and referral processes as they relate to school environments. For the most part, scholarship on mental deficiency was deeply committed to the belief that mental retardation, as expressed behaviorally in schools, was a direct reflection of an innate condition. Therefore, concern was focused on accurate detection and identification of a visible, obvious difference. Institutional racism, Dunn and others reasoned, created biased identification practices, thus thwarting objective "scientific" measurement and analysis. This undesirable intrusion into what was thought to be an ever clearer, ever more precise diagnostic process was rationalized as a kind of "error," which once removed would reveal those who were "truly" retarded.

In thinking this way, Dunn's error was not to believe in innate differences, but only to believe that the context of identification was largely irrelevant to how these differences manifested themselves in everyday life. This is a view to which we also must plead guilty (Gerber & Semmel, 1984a; MacMillan, Meyers, & Morrison, 1980). That is, Dunn could see only that a valid, scientifically grounded process could be undermined, not that the process itself, whatever its output, was as integral to the phenomenon of disability and as real as individual differences were real.

The Dual Character of Special Education

As justifiable attacks on racism and social systems of exclusion intensified in the late 1960s, special education—that is, the *idea* of "special" education itself, not just some of the practices associated with it, became an unintended victim. The reason is that special education's historical origins in the public schools was a marriage of mixed motives and economic necessity from the very start. It was a creature of public schooling as much or more than it was a creation of clinical and empirical science in medicine or psychology. It has always reflected some of its traditional progressivism, dating from Elizabeth Farrell's association with Lillian Wald's settlement house on Henry Street near P.S. 1 in New York, and the zealous social movements of which public schooling was a significant part in the first decades of this century (e.g., see Hendrick & MacMillan, 1989; Sarason & Doris, 1979). However, it also has always represented some of the extreme pragmatism that contributed to the rapid proliferation of a few dozen experimental "ungraded" classrooms into thousands of special classes by the late 1920s. In its progressive, proactive personality, special education was the work of visionaries, individuals who truly meant "all" when they envisioned public schooling (e.g., Hungerford, DeProspo, & Rosenzweig, 1958). In its pragmatic, reactive form, special education was the work of administrators who, with scarce resources, sought to manage a complex set of operations toward multiple goals, only one of which may have been the education of low-achieving students.

The civil rights movement of the 1960s simply heightened recognition of this dual character of special education. The passage of the Education for all Handicapped Children Act of 1975 (EHA, or P.L. 94-142), the first *national* policy on special education mandating how schools and school people should behave, brought special education's pragmatic character to the foreground. However, in doing so, national special education policy also exposed public schooling to new scrutiny and criticism, as well as schools that attempted to fulfill the federal mandate.

Whereas before Dunn's article, special educators tended to focus strongly on issues, such as identification and curriculum, with a view to *long-term* outcomes (e.g., employability), after Dunn's article, the focus shifted to the fairness and appropriateness of identification, assessment, planning, and programming *procedures* themselves. A scholarly field used to thinking that appropriate schools could be built up around knowledge of individual differences now faced a world in which the behavior of schools in compliance to policy determined what would be considered individual differences. A different type of scholarship was needed, one that could embrace the compensatory, reciprocal relationship between real individual differences, on one hand, and schools and school policy, on the other (Ballard-Campbell & Semmel, 1981; Gerber & Levine-Donnerstein, 1989; Gerber & Semmel, 1984a; Gerber & Semmel, 1984b).

The simple message of EHA had two parts. First, find and provide *appropriate* public education for individual students with disabilities based upon their *unique* needs, not the characteristics associated with some broad class of disabilities. The second was, don't discriminate; children and their families have a right not to be mistreated. Dunn's vision was too restricted to see the way in which EHA would build logically and simultaneously on both special education's historical goals and the civil rights movement stimulated by disenfranchised minorities (Semmel, 1986). In the end, Dunn only expressed as future hope what had already been decided by state and local educational authorities: Minority students classified as educably mentally retarded had to be decertified. In fact, California began this effort in the same year that Dunn's article was published, and the federal government authorized expenditure of compensatory education money for a little-known handicapping condition called "specific learning disabilities."

Couching special education in civil rights constitutional terms resulted in a gradual substitution of procedural compliance foci for instructional innovation. Ultimately, mindless regard for procedure over substance, compliance over purpose, led to a reaction in the 1980s. Part of this reaction was pragmatic. Special education as mandated was costly and frequently challenged the values and modes of decision making from which schools derived their essential character. But part of the reaction came from special educators themselves—the old "visionary" character reasserting itself. Once again, when special education visionaries speak of "all" students and "full" participation, they mean it quite literally. When they focus on outcome-based education, they do so with a commitment to development of powerful instructional tools and curricular approaches. Once again, though, the language of improvement is employed as well by school pragmatists who use it rhetorically to press and defend their concern, not for differential outcomes and curriculum, nor even for equality-seeking processes or procedural fairness, but rather for the structural arrangements and placements—the inputs—that promise greater managerial control of limited resources.

REFORMING THE REFORM: BEYOND DUNN'S LEGACY

Thus far, we have argued that Dunn's article was primarily a reaction to civil rights concerns already permeating school reform of the late 1960s. The modern incarnation of Dunn's ideas—the Regular Education Initiative (Kauffman et al., 1988; Semmel et al., 1991; Will, 1986)—centers on structures and placements rather than compelling individual differences, on *inputs* rather than *outcomes*. Its favored form of argument, like Dunn's, is moral and polemical rather than empirical. In fact, the empirical literature was, and remains, difficult to interpret.

Some years after Dunn published his 1968 article, and after the civil rights movement yielded EHA, Madden and Slavin (1983) revisited the research on special education effectiveness to compare outcomes related to different placements. The available evidence was still surprisingly scant. Most work suffered from the same selection bias that characterized earlier studies (see Semmel et al., 1979; Semmel et al., 1985). Whatever the reasons were for placing apparently equivalent students in different settings, it was still unlikely that such decisions were random. The best research supporting regular versus special class placement—really, a single study by Calhoun and Eliot (1977)—was able not only to randomly assign students identified as educably mentally retarded, but also to rotate their teachers across the different settings to remove teacher effects.

It is important to note, however, that the degree to which these researchers were able to create a controlled experiment was equal to the degree to which their placement alternatives departed from reality. Ecological validity was sacrificed for internal validity. Leaving aside for the moment the questionable treatment of the educable mentally retarded sample as being homogenous based on IQ alone, there are several interesting facts about this study that illuminate the direction of special education after Dunn.

First, the researchers used only special education teachers in both settings. Second, the instruction was "individualized" for all students. Third, specific, or very limited, outcomes were inspected. Even then, significant differences were not general across all measures. For example, reading measures tended to differ, while math measures did not. Fourth, and most telling, even the best research reviewed by Madden and Slavin (1983) constructed but did not sample environments. It is one thing to construct an environment for experiment or model demonstration, and quite another to claim that its relative success supports widespread imitation and adoption as a matter of policy.

Dunn's article, driven as it was by concern for systematic schooling and desegregation, marked the beginning of the recognition that school environment not only was a constraint on special education, but also specifically shaped the processes of identification, referral, assessment, placement, and instruction of children with disabilities. If Dunn closed one door, the EHA opened the next. Special education in national policy attained the character of a defined system with researchable parameters, a characterization quite different from one that focuses on type of disability and instructional techniques or materials. The academic fields on which special education historically drew its tools—psychology, medicine—had few means for studying schools or school systems (Semmel et al., 1985).

Tolerance Theory: Juggling Means and Variances in Schools

In the late 1970s, Byron Brown and Daniel Saks tried to explain poor mean achievement gains in schools receiving Chapter 1 funds

(Brown & Saks, 1981). They used the concept of "joint production functions," which, unlike previous use of the "production functions" model, viewed schools as *jointly* (i.e., simultaneously) producing multiple outcomes with the same fixed amount of resources. In this view, each student is a unique "product," not merely a part of some aggregate amount of achievement produced by the school.

Specifically, Brown and Saks recognized that Chapter 1 funds were targeted for students who, by definition, were not modal in their poor responses to "traditional" instruction. Therefore, they reasoned, estimates of mean achievement for a school would seriously underestimate the effects of differential effort on behalf of slow learners if the net effect of that effort was to raise the achievement of these students toward the baseline average. That is, effective, schoolwide efforts to raise slow learner achievement would tend more to narrow variance than to increase the mean. A search for mean gains, therefore, could miss clear evidence that compensatory education resources had been used effectively.

Gerber and Semmel (Gerber & Semmel, 1984; Gerber & Semmel, 1985; Semmel, 1986) built a special education theory by adapting the microeconomic arguments used by Brown and Saks. "Tolerance" theory (Gerber, 1989; Gerber & Semmel, 1985) sought to describe school system principles that produced segregation (e.g., referral) and integration (e.g., inclusion) phenomena with regard to students perceived to be very difficult to teach but without regard to their entitlement classification. Students at risk for identification and special treatment, like those identified as "disadvantaged" in Chapter 1 schools, bid for or are targeted for additional effort to increase their level of achievement. Given that critical resources (e.g., instructional effort) are always relatively scarce, teachers in classrooms must either skew their efforts toward fairly unresponsive learners and relinquish opportunity to obtain large mean gains, or they can assign such learners to special status, thereby exempting themselves from making continued instructional efforts for these students. In the formal special education structure that accompanied EHA, assignment literally means assignment to another class or to another teacher. Inversely, meaningful reintegration of difficult-to-teach (e.g., disabled) students requires teachers' commitment to allocate sufficient instructional effort for the newly enfranchised student.

In tolerance theory, instructional "effort" is intentionally an abstraction of the complex ways individual teachers apply their motivation, knowledge, skills, and experience to devise learning activities suitable for different students. Madden and Slavin (1983), for example, realized that all instructional effort was not the same or a simple function of placement. Teachers vary in their ability to devise instructional arrangements that effectively minimize—maximize "tolerance" for—individual differences exhibited by learners:

> It is likely that a regular classroom using individualized instruction can accommodate a wide range of student abilities, so that the interaction between IQ level and setting seen (in some studies) may be specific to situations in which no special accommodations are made for very low achieving students in the regular classes. (Madden & Slavin, 1983, p. 560)

Obviously, capacity to exert effective effort, and thus capacity to be effective with a broader range of different learners, can be increased for the school as a whole by providing new resources (e.g., other teaching staff), either to the classroom or to some other location in the school (e.g., remedial labs, special day classes, resource rooms, etc.). Also, school officials may seek to directly increase particular teachers' motivation, knowledge, or skills so that instructional capacity within their classrooms increases. However, from a tolerance theory perspective, it is evident that the integration of children with disabilities in a general education class has the effect of increasing ability variance, with concomitant increases in instructional demands; this, in turn, results in a need for augmented allocation of resources from school sources. In a zero sum resource environment, such shifts in school assets will surely diminish the variance of extra-class interventions for children with disabilities. If the school's goal is success for all pupils in the general education class, and some children do not succeed, then alternative school interventions can be offered only through diminishing the resources available for general education. Hence, reinstituting needed interventions within schools can result in inefficient use of scarce resources and harmful disruptions in the general education classroom program. It is evident that there is a pressing need to determine a calculus for maximizing efficiency and instructional flexibility in meeting the needs of all children in the schools (see Semmel & Gerber, 1990, for a critique of the Success for All and other REI interventions).

Although tolerance theory views teachers as the most important allocators of their own instructional effort, it recognizes that classrooms are not freestanding enterprises. Rather, they are part of a complex organization of people and activity that manifests itself as a particular culture, climate, and environment. Many researchers have agreed that schools that produce higher mean achievement tend to be organized for and characterized by greater cohesion of values, knowledge, and goals. Thus, teachers' allocation decisions are influenced from sources outside the classroom, including formal local, state, and federal policies, as well as their schools' parents, colleagues, and administrators. Dunn's article reflected a preoccupation with the *classroom* placement as the unit of concern with virtually no consideration for variations among *schools* that may be associated with differential achievement and social effectiveness with children having disabilities. The school effectiveness and school reform movements of the 1980s following the earlier alarms of Coleman's (Coleman et al., 1966) report, alerted the field to the important potential contributions of school environments to school achievement (Murphy, 1990). Contemporary special education policy research has moved beyond classroom placement type comparisons in recognition of the importance of complex interactions between subordinate and superordinate environmental hierarchical levels of schooling (Semmel et al., 1985; Semmel, Gerber, & Abernathy, 1993). For example, proponents of REI frequently argue that schools that are effective with general education students are equally effective with special needs students. New instructional technologies are thought to be powerful enough to accommodate the instructional burdens introduced as a function of increasing ability variance in the general education classroom (e.g., cooperative learning, consulting teacher model, peer tutoring).

The School Environments Project (SEP)

A longitudinal research project being conducted at The University of California, Santa Barbara (Semmel & Gerber, co-directors) is seeking to empirically explain how and how well schools, as units of analysis, rather than classrooms, accommodate extreme individual differences. The SEP research team is explicitly investigating whether schools thought to be relatively effective based on extant criteria (e.g., see Purkey & Smith, 1985) are similarly effective with the students they have identified for special education services (see Semmel et al., 1993).

A subsample of 33 elementary and 25 junior high schools was selected for more intensive study from a large probability sample of Southern California schools. To determine relative effectiveness of schools within these samples, measures of general school achievement were compared to measures of achievement for students each school had identified for special education. Specific measures included 5 years of state standardized achievement testing, socioeconomic status, mobility, and minority status indicators, and results from on-site, individually collected measures of academic performance, self-esteem, and school adjustment from a 10% to 20% sampling of students identified as learning handicapped (California's "generic" label for students with various mild disabilities).

After several years of study, and contrary to claims made by many contemporary proponents of special education reform, SEP researchers have been unable to find evidence of any strong positive relationships between general school achievement and special education students' academic performance, self-esteem, or school adjustment. That is, schools that do relatively well with respect to general academic achievement are *not* the same schools that can be characterized as doing relatively well with their special education populations. In fact, a negative relationship was revealed by an analysis of 2-year gains by each school's special education student population as a function of gains in general achievement.

Figures 1 and 2, drawn from Semmel, Gerber, and Cook's (in preparation) SEP substudy, are graphical representations of this latter series of analyses. Figure 1 shows a statistically significant regression of special education reading performance on the Basic Academic Skills Sample (BASS) (Deno, 1989) on schoolwide reading achievement on the California Achievement Program (CAP) ($p < .003$, Adj. $R^2 = .25$). The relationship for junior high schools (see Figure 2) was not as strong and was not statistically significant

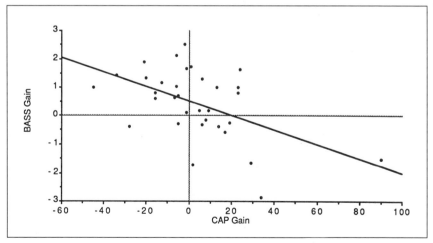

FIGURE 1. Two-year reading gains for 33 elementary schools' special education students (Basic Academic Skills Sample) as a function of general school reading improvement (California Achievement Program).

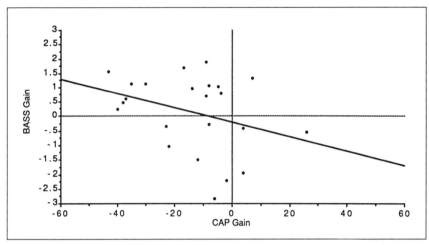

FIGURE 2. Two-year reading gains for 25 junior high schools' special education students (Basic Academic Skills Sample) as a function of general school reading improvement (California Achievement Program).

($p < .11$, $R^2 = .07$). We speculate that these results reflect the impact on pupils with disabilities of increased academic emphasis in "effective schools." As schools respond to pressures of the most recent school improvement reforms for increasing academic achievement, under conditions of diminishing resources, they may adaptively develop strategies for increasing school means—to the detriment of their nonmodal special education pupils.

SUMMARY AND CONCLUSIONS

Lloyd Dunn stunned the special education community in 1968 with a severely critical review of practices that were then common for students with mild disabilities, particularly those with mental retardation. He was particularly critical of what was perceived as unnecessary if not discriminatory tendencies to overidentify and place minority students in classes for students with mild mental retardation.

We have argued that the strong antisegregation sentiments of the 1960s contexualize the crisis that Dunn's rebuke and recommendations created for the field of special education. The historically and generally poor ability of public schools to accommodate individual differences, regardless of their character or source, was an easy and long overdue target of the civil rights movement. Special education, as a function of public schooling, may have reflected but did not originate this intolerance. Progressive visionaries and managerial pragmatists have always seen special education as a vehicle for accomplishing their separate purposes, even while employing the same rhetoric of reform and claiming the same goal—namely, to improve the educational outcomes for *all* children. Their sometimes conflicting impact on special education scholarship, as well as advocacy, continues to the present moment.

Dunn's legacy has been a tendency to hold special education unfairly accountable for many of the structural and ideological limitations of the larger public schooling system that produces and defines it. On the positive side, critiques by Dunn and others led researchers and practitioners to focus more deliberately on how that larger system works. National public policy in special education, while encouraging a drift into more procedural than instructional or curricular emphases, did stimulate development of research that attempts to integrate context and policy effects in the study of individual differences of learners.

The more negative result of Dunn's assault on pre-EHA special education, however, has been to reawaken tension between visionaries and pragmatists, a tension that historically fills the air with more rhetoric than scholarship. Contemporary reformers also evoke Dunn to support their proposals, and by so doing promote more defense of the *principle* of special school responses to difference than empirical inquiry into the nature and potential of those responses. Moreover, before the very thin literature supporting Dunn's views is used to suggest massive restructuring of schools along the lines of even successful experimental models, we should consider the rather poor record of transporting and replicating such demonstrations across the range of naturally occurring school environments. The sobering fact that we've seen reform before, and heard exhortations to adopt this or that panacea, indicates a prior need to understand how and why school environments vary so greatly with respect to their potential to accommodate individual differences.

AUTHORS' NOTE

This chapter was supported, in part, by Grant No. H023C90038 from the U. S. Department of Education, Special Education Programs, to the Special Education Research Laboratory, University of California, Santa Barbara, and Grant Nos. HC023C20002 and H023C80072 to the third author.

REFERENCES

Ballard-Campbell, M., & Semmel, M. I. (1981). Policy research and special education: Contemporary research issues affecting policy formation and implementation. *Exceptional Education Quarterly, 2*(2), 59–67.

Brown, B. W., & Saks, D. H. (1981). The microeconomics of schooling. In D. Berliner (Ed.), *Review of research in education* (Vol. 9, pp. 217–254). Washington, DC: American Educational Research Association.

Calhoun, G., & Eliot, R. (1977). Self-concept and academic achievement of educable retarded and emotionally disturbed pupils. *Exceptional Children, 44,* 379–380.

Coleman, J. S., Campbell, E. Q., Hobson, C. J., McPartland, J., Mood, A. M., Weinfeld, R. L., & York, R. L. (1966). *Equality of educational opportunity.* Washington, DC: U.S. Government Printing Office.

Deno, S. (1989). *Basic academic skills sample.* Duluth, MN: University of Minnesota.

Diana v. State Board of Education, C-70-37(RFP Dist. N. Calif.) (1970).

Dunn, L. M. (1968). Special education for the mildly retarded: Is much of it justifiable? *Exceptional Children, 35,* 5–22.

Gerber, M. M. (1989). The new "diversity" and special education: Are we going forward or starting again? *California Public Schools Forum, 3,* 19–31.

Gerber, M. M., & Levine-Donnerstein, D. (1989). Educating all children: Ten years later. *Exceptional Children, 56,* 17–27.

Gerber, M. M., & Semmel, M. I. (1984a). Teacher as imperfect test: Reconceptualizing the referral process. *Educational Psychologist, 19,* 137–148.

Gerber, M. M., & Semmel, M. I. (1984b) Policy analysis research training in special education. *Teacher Education and Special Education, 7*(2), 66–74.

Gerber, M. M., & Semmel, M. I. (1985). Microeconomics of referral and reintegration: A paradigm for evaluation of special education. *Studies in Educational Evaluation, 11,* 13–29.

Gottlieb, J., Semmel, M. I., & Veldman, D. (1976). Retarded children mainstreamed: Practices as they affect minority group children. In R. Jones (Ed.), *Mainstreaming and minority children* (p. 223–243). Reston, VA: Council for Exceptional Children.

Hegel, G. W. (1857). *Philosophy of history.* New York: Collier & Sons.

Hendrick, I., & MacMillan, D. L. (1989). Selecting children for special education in New York City: William Maxwell, Elizabeth Farrell, and the development of ungraded classes, 1900–1920. *The Journal of Special Education, 22,* 395–417.

Hungerford, R., DeProspo, C., & Rosenzweig, L. (1958). Education of the mentally handicapped in childhood and adolescence. In S.C. DiMichael (Ed.), *Vocational rehabilitation of the mentally retarded* (pp. 47–63). Washington, DC: U.S. Department of Health, Education, and Welfare, Office of Vocational Rehabilitation.

Jensen, A. R. (1968). Social class, race, and genetics: Implications for education. *American Educational Research Journal, 5,* 1–41.

Kauffman, J. M., Agard, J., & Semmel, M. I. (1986). *Mainstreaming: Learners and their environments.* Cambridge, MA: Brookline.

Kauffman, J. M., Gerber, M. M., & Semmel, M. I. (1988). Arguable assumptions underlying the Regular Education Initiative. *Journal of Learning Disabilities, 21*(1), 6–11.

Larry P. v. Riles, USLW2033 (US June 21) (1972).

MacMillan, D. L., Meyers, C. E., & Morrison, G. M. (1980). System identification of mildly mentally retarded children: Implications for interpreting and conducting research. *American Journal of Mental Deficiency, 85,* 108–115.

Madden, N. A., & Slavin, R. E. (1983). Mainstreaming students with mild handicaps: Academic and social outcomes. *Review of Educational Research, 53,* 519–569.

Marx, C. (1967). *The eighteenth brumaire of Louis Napolean.* New York: International Publishers.

Murphy, J. (Ed.). (1990). *The educational reform movement of the 1980s.* Berkeley, CA: McCutchan.

National Association of State Boards of Education. (1992). *The report of the NASBE study group on special education.* Alexandria, VA: Author.

Purkey, S. C., & Smith, M. S. (1985). Effective schools: A review. *The Elementary School Journal, 83,* 427–452.

Sarason, S., & Doris, J. (1979). *Educational handicap, public policy, and social history.* New York: Free Press.

Semmel, M. I. (1986). *Special education in the year 2000 and beyond: A proposed action agenda for addressing selected issues.* Proceedings of the CEC Invitational Symposium on the Future of Special Education, Council for Exceptional Children, Reston, VA.

Semmel, M. I., Abernathy, T., Butera, G., & Lesar S. (1991). Teacher perceptions of special education reform: An empirical study of the Regular Education Initiative. *Exceptional Children, 58,* 9–24.

Semmel, M. I., & Ballard-Campbell, M. (1983). *Role delineation of the program specialist and the resource specialist under the California Master Plan for Special Education* (Final Report). Santa Barbara: University of California, Special Education Research Institute.

Semmel, M. I., & Gerber, M. (1990). If at first you don't succeed, bye, bye again: A response to general educators' views on the REI. *Remedial and Special Education, 4*(4), 53–59.

Semmel, M. I., Gerber, M., & Abernathy, T. (1993). *The relationships between school environment variables and educational outcomes for students with mild disabilities* (SERL/SEP Research Report). Santa Barbara: University of California, Special Education Research Laboratory.

Semmel, M. I., Gerber, M., & Cook, B. (in preparation). *Regression of special education reading performance (BASS) on schoolwide reading achievement* (SERL/SEP Research Report). Santa Barbara: Univeristy of California, Education Research Laboratory.

Semmel, M. I., Gottlieb, J., & Robinson, N. M. (1979). Mainstreaming: Perspectives on educating handicapped children in the public schools. In D. Berliner (Ed)., *Review of research in education* (Vol. 7, pp. 223–279). Chicago: Peacock Publishers.

Semmel, M. I., Peck, C., & Lieber, J. (1985). Effects of special education environments: Beyond mainstreaming. In J. Meisels (Ed.), *Mainstreaming the mildly handicapped child* (pp. 165–192). Englewood Cliffs, NJ: Erlbaum.

Will, M. (1986). Educating children with learning problems: A shared responsibility. *Exceptional Children, 52,* 411–415.

Chapter 4

Toward a Culture of Disability

Daniel P. Hallahan and James M. Kauffman

◆ ◆ ◆

WHEN EVELYN DENO AND LLOYD DUNN wrote their now classic articles (Deno, 1970; Dunn, 1968), we (Hallahan and Kauffman) were doctoral students. If our memories serve, both of us sensed from the reactions of our professors, as well as our own reading, that these articles would be catalysts for much-needed change. That these two articles struck responsive chords is not surprising, given the state of special education and the social–political climate in academia and the country at the time. Institutionalization of persons with disabilities was still common, and the separate, self-contained special education class reigned supreme as the service delivery model of choice. Exposés of horrible conditions in all too many residential institutions had recently surfaced (e.g., Blatt & Kaplan, 1966; Wiseman, 1967), and efficacy studies purporting to show the inadequacy of special classes were proliferating. The moral imperative for change spelled out by Deno, and even more forcefully by Dunn, found a receptive audience in the special education professorate and the graduate student body, both of which had been actively involved in the mounting social unrest on college and university campuses that had begun several years earlier. It was easy to draw parallels between the injustices heaped upon African Americans and the perceived discrimi-

Reprinted from "Toward a culture of disability in the aftermath of Deno and Dunn," by Daniel P. Hallahan & James M. Kauffman, *The Journal of Special Education,* Vol. 27, 1994, 496–508. Copyright © 1994 by PRO-ED, Inc.

nation against people with disabilities. Both articles capitalized on their era's commitment to political activism and social justice.

Although published over 2 decades ago, we still find much wisdom in the Deno and Dunn articles. For example, Dunn warned of special educators "living at the mercy of general educators who have referred their problem children to us" (Dunn, 1968, p. 5). Special education is still largely in the position of looking to general education to define its own identity. Deno's cascade was a simple but logical graphic describing an inverse relationship between severity of disability and intensity of needed services. The cascade served as a rationale for the "least restrictive environment" clause that, in 1975, became a hallmark of Public Law 94-142 (now IDEA), a clause that still serves us well as a guiding principle for placement decisions.

Given the seminal role of these two articles in legislation and the professional literature of special education, it is ironic that both articles contained the seeds of ideas now having the potential to destroy the field. It is doubly ironic that Deno's cascade itself is in danger of demolition and that some of the arguments for razing it were contained in Deno's own article. We contend that the articles by Deno and Dunn, especially the latter, contained arguments consistent with today's zeitgeist—the spirit of our time that identifies special education as more harmful and evil than helpful and good—and that these ideas have been exploited by those who would save children, their families, and the public the "pain" of special education.

The low esteem in which the conceptual bases of special education and its practices are now held by many advocates of reform (e.g., Lipsky & Gartner, 1991) may contribute to the fact that special education teachers leave the profession in droves every year (see Singer, 1992, for discussion of attrition of special education teachers). It is also not surprising that special educators continue to kowtow to school psychologists and their armamentarium of tests rather than rely on their own clinical judgment in decisions regarding identification (see Bateman, 1992, for discussion of the critical importance but neglect of professional judgment). Today's special educators are made to feel like pariahs when critics describe the profession as segregationist (Stainback & Stainback, 1991; Wang & Walberg, 1988), insinuate that special education treats children as if they were not fully human or worthy of respect (Lipsky & Gartner, 1987), and suggest that good teaching would obviate the need for special education (Algozzine, 1993). If we were to believe its most vitriolic critics, special education teachers are responsible for harming children irreparably by labeling them and segregating them from their friends, all in order to provide them with instruction that is less adequate than what they would receive in general education.

We are not blaming Deno and Dunn directly for what we perceive to be the beginnings of the collapse of special education that is currently taking place. It would be folly to try to make the case that their articles led directly to the erosion of special education. Nevertheless, many who currently call for the elimination of special education as an identifiable entity (e.g., Gartner, Lipsky, S. Stainback, & W. Stainback) cite notions similar to those of Deno, and especially Dunn, in making their case. Among other things, Deno questioned the existence of a separate system of special education, and Dunn cited the literature purporting to show the deleterious effects of special class placement and labeling of special education students.

DENO'S ARGUMENTS

Special Education as a Separate System

Deno asked:

> Does special education need to exist at all as a separate administrative system? Further, if it needs to exist now because of conditions that prevailed in education in the past and may still exist at this time, should special education assume it must always exist as a separate delivery system? . . . Might not special education be in a healthier state if it assumed that its ultimate objective is to work itself out of business as a social institution, to turn over to the regular education mainstream whatever helpful technology it develops so that the handicapped children can be a part of that mainstream? Wouldn't it be remarkable if special education could be a profession not afraid to change and not afraid that its role and livelihood were threatened as the ability of others to deal with individual differences expands? (Deno, 1970, p. 233)

It is one thing to hold up the notion of working oneself out of business as a lofty, idealized goal—one that we should be working toward, but one that we recognize as not reachable within our lifetime. It is another to take the goal literally. It is laudable for members of any helping profession to want to see their client base disappear. But physicians, psychologists, and social workers would not seriously entertain the idea that sickness, mental illness, and social deprivation will be totally eliminated any time soon. Why should it be any different for disabilities requiring educational treatment?

Deno suggested developing and turning over to the regular education mainstream educational technologies that would enable students with handicaps to be part of that mainstream. We agree with that objective but are skeptical about whether achieving that objective will contribute to special education's being able to go out of business. In fact, as Kauffman (1990) has suggested, achieving that objective might actually contribute perpetual new business to special education.

Deno's conception of education and variance is static; it does not take into consideration the inevitable variance in outcomes or the capacity of education to increase variance in students' performance. If special education develops truly effective technologies and regular education actually adopts them and applies them to new generations of students, then we might expect increasing variance in student outcomes. This phenomenon, coupled with the fact that other forces in our society are producing larger numbers of children with more complex and serious problems that make their accommodation in school more difficult, is likely to keep special educators busy well into the 21st century, perhaps even into the 22nd.

We cannot envision the eradication of disabilities or the elimination of the need for special instruction of students with disabilities. In fact, trends indicate the opposite. The prevalence of students with disabilities has increased fairly steadily since the mid-1970s, when the federal government began keeping such statistics. Some have argued that such increases, especially in the case of learning disabilities, wherein most of the increase has occurred, are due to misdiagnosis. Hallahan (1992), however, has argued that the increases are more than likely real. Increases in poverty, drug abuse, family instability, and so forth, have led to more children at risk for disabilities at all degrees of severity. These social factors may result in both physical (e.g., central nervous system dysfunction) and psychosocial (e.g., lack of family support) vulnerability. And learning disabilities may be a particularly sensitive barometer of the impact of these physical and social insults because "it takes lower levels of biomedical and psychological stress to result in a mild disability than a severe disability" (Hallahan, 1992, p. 524). And Hallahan has speculated that, even in socioeconomically advantaged environments, the increase in learning disabilities may be partially explained by an increase in academic expectations by the schools and a decrease in family succor due to a siphoning off of familial attention to other activities (e.g., television and video games within the home and after-school activities—sports, dance lessons, piano lessons—that require transportation outside the home).

We can from another perspective also make a strong case that there is an increasing rather than a decreasing need for special educators to work with these students with disabilities. General educators are even less able to deal with students identified as disabled than they were when Deno published her article. The demands placed on teachers today are overwhelming. Not only are they being asked to do more than ever with regard to curriculum content, but they are faced with more and more students who are not even identified for special education but who have a host of problems. U.S. Senator Daniel Patrick Moynihan (1993) noted the trend to "define deviancy down." As he said:

> I proffer the thesis that, over the past generation, . . . the amount of deviant behavior in American society has increased beyond the levels the community can "afford to recognize" and that, accordingly, we have been re-defining deviancy so as to exempt much conduct previously stigmatized, and also quietly raising the "normal" level in categories where behavior is now abnormal by any earlier standard. (p. 19)

Moynihan cited sociologist Emile Durkheim's (1938) theory stipulating that the level of deviancy a society recognizes will remain stable over time. In times when deviancy is on the increase, society normalizes that which was previously considered abnormal in order to keep deviancy at a tolerable level.

Need for an Ecological Perspective

Another point Deno, as well as Dunn, made is that the field of special education needed to take more of an ecological perspective toward disabilities: "The emphasis on 'defect' residing in the child tends to focus attention away from the external variables which educators might be in a position to do something about" (Deno, 1970, p. 232). At the time, this viewpoint no doubt needed more emphasis. Many practitioners and researchers assumed that any and all problems of students were located within the students themselves. When Deno's article appeared, however, the field was moving swiftly to adopt a focus on environmental factors. The ecological approach was all the rage. For example, the highly visible Head Start early intervention programs of the 1960s were founded on the philosophy that changing young children's environments would prevent later learning problems. In special education, William Rhodes's work was calling attention to the importance of an ecological approach to emotional disturbance (Rhodes, 1967; Rhodes & Head, 1974; Rhodes & Tracy, 1972a, 1972b).

Unfortunately, in the rush to adopt an ecological philosophy, many professionals tripped over themselves to point the finger at the environment as the culprit, ignoring a significant part of the equation—the child. Bell and Harper (1977), among the first to point out the lopsided nature of much of the research on early childhood, demonstrated the significant effects that infants and young children can have on their caregivers. Their research signaled a recognition among child developmentalists that a truly ecological perspective considers reciprocal effects of child and environment as well as the understanding that problems are not located solely in the child or the environment, but in both.

It is our observation that the lesson from Bell and Harper (1977) has been largely ignored by special educators. When today's theoretician in special education speaks of an ecological approach, he or she is usually talking about an almost exclusive emphasis on environmental variables. In the field, this translates into the notion that the onus of learning failures is solely the teacher's. Again, the teacher is the ogre.

This reluctance to identify any part of the problem as residing within the child has been fueled by, and/or given rise to, the current popularity of social constructivist interpretations of disability (Ferguson, Ferguson, & Taylor, 1992). Of course, disability is socially constructed. Learning disabilities, *as we know them,* would not exist in a society that did not value literacy. And, as Moynihan (1993) has pointed out, we can redefine behavioral deviance as we may wish, though not without social consequences. The fact is, however, that we live in a society that values literacy and one that has not yet become inured to every form of social deviance.

We are not denying the value of recognizing the socially constructed nature of disability and the contributions of those who have urged us to consider disabilities within this framework. We think it important, however, to point out the potential dangers in holding an exclusively constructivist position. We speculate, for example, that the facilitated communication bandwagon that so many have boarded without credible scientific evidence as to its effectiveness—and in the light of much evidence to the contrary (F/C Under Siege, 1993; Green, 1992; Thompson, 1993)—would not have left the station had not so many professionals been primed to view disability as residing anywhere but in the child. But what is more germane to our thesis is that overzealous constructivism leads to a devaluation of the special education teacher. Faced with the most difficult-to-teach students, it can only be disheartening to be told that you and your profession are part of the problem, not part of the solution.

DUNN'S ARGUMENTS

Efficacy of Special Classes

Dunn drew heavily on what have come to be known as the "efficacy studies"—the substantial body of research focused on comparisons of students with disabilities educated in regular versus special classes. His conclusions:

> These results are well known ... and suggest consistently that retarded pupils make as much progress in the regular grades as they do in special education.... Efficacy studies on special day classes for other mildly handicapped children, including the emotionally handicapped, reveal the same results. (Dunn, 1968, p. 8)

What Dunn failed to point out is that virtually all of these studies were flawed because they did not include random assignment of students to classes. And those efficacy studies conducted since Dunn's article have had the same problem. (It is difficult for researchers to get around the ethical and legal problems associated with randomly assigning students to conditions when placement is supposed to be based on their best interests.) Thus, those selected by the school system to go into special classes very likely had learning problems that were more severe and less tractable.

In those rare studies using random assignment, the results were, if anything, favorable toward the efficacy of special classes. In what many have considered the best controlled study of the effects of placement on academic achievement, researchers found that students with mental retardation with IQs between 75 and 85 benefited more from regular classes, whereas those who had IQs below 75 benefited more from special classes (Goldstein, Moss, & Jordan, 1965). It is interesting to note that, using today's definition of mental retardation, which uses an IQ cutoff of 70 or 75 and below, those students in the high IQ group would not have qualified for identification as mentally retarded. Regarding self-concept, in another study using random assignment, researchers obtained similar results (Budoff & Gottlieb, 1976). Those with high learning potential fared better in regular classes, and the opposite was true for those with low learning potential.

Given the fact that the results of the vast majority of the efficacy studies were suspect and that the few studies that were well done were supportive of special classes, we find it disconcerting that so many today continue to cite the efficacy studies directly as evidence that special classes are ineffective or refer to them indirectly by saying that research has failed to demonstrate the effectiveness of special classes. For example, Gartner and Lipsky (1989) maintained that efficacy studies show "little or no benefit for students of all levels of severity placed in special education settings" (p. 13; see also Lilly, 1988; Wang & Walberg, 1988). It is all the more aggravating because researchers have pointed out the flawed nature of the efficacy studies for some time (e.g., Gottlieb, Alter, & Gottlieb, 1983; Keogh & Levitt, 1976; MacMillan & Becker, 1977).

In many ways, the efficacy studies are irrelevant to today's context. The vast majority of them were conducted between 1950 and 1980. We can hope, if not assume, that both mainstreaming practices and special education instruction have improved since these studies were conducted. For example, today's proponents of special classes would not want their position judged on the basis of programs using Frostig worksheets, and today's proponents of regular classes would probably find it vexing to make comparisons in which students are placed in general education classes that are not using such strategies as cooperative learning.

Even if today's researchers were to conduct efficacy studies using random assignment and were to find significant differences in favor of placement in general education classes, this finding would perhaps justify the reduction in the number of special classes, but not their elimination. In educational research comparing groups of students, some subjects in each of the groups invariably end up performing or behaving more similarly to subjects in the other group than to subjects in their own group. In other words, there is almost always some overlap of the distributions of the two comparison groups. Because of the mandate to provide the most appropriate education to *each* student with a disability, it would be unethical to eliminate special classes unless research consistently demonstrated that general education classes were superior to special classes and there was virtually no overlap between the distributions on the dependent variables. An exception to this might be research showing that for a substantial number of students, special classes were harmful—for example, a finding that special classes made students regress in their behavior or in some way worsened their condition or damaged their well being.

Effects of Labeling

Some opponents of special classes, indeed, do make the claim that the well-being of students is jeopardized by special class placement. They claim that the mere labeling of the child as disabled damages his or her self-concept and motivation to learn. Furthermore, they assert that labels result in the public viewing the labeled persons negatively.

Dunn cited some of the literature purporting to show that labeling has deleterious consequences, and critics of special education today continue to make reference to this body of research. Some grudgingly admit the usefulness of labeling "as a tactical matter of the moment" but "in the longer run ... reject the entire labelling activity" (Lipsky & Gartner, 1991, p. 45). Numerous reviewers of research on the effects of labeling, however, have noted the contradictory findings (Gottlieb & Leyser, 1981; Keogh & Levitt, 1976; MacMillan & Becker, 1977; MacMillan, Jones, & Aloia, 1974). Some investigators have found poorer self-concepts for those in special classes compared with those in general education classes, and some have found the opposite. Furthermore, most of these studies also suffer from the flaw of lack of random assignment, although research has been clearer in showing that placing disability labels on persons leads others to view them differently (Foster, Ysseldyke, & Reese, 1975; Salvia, Clark, & Ysseldyke, 1973).

Antilabeling and Shame

The fact that labels alert others to the differences of persons with disabilities, however, does not necessarily mean that they will view the labeled individuals negatively. Yes, labels can lead others to view persons in a stereotypical way. One can make just as strong a case, however, that labels can help explain behavior that is out of the ordinary and lead to a better understanding and sensitivity toward the labeled person. For example, without the learning disability label, a student not doing well in school might be considered lazy. The label can help to make society understand that the aggravating or frustrating behavior of students with disabilities is not typically intentionally aggravating and frustrating. Labels may also help explain to the persons with disabilities, themselves, their own behavior. It may be that some persons with learning disabilities are relieved to know that they differ from others because they have an identifiable condition, such as learning disabilities or attention deficit disorder, that can be ameliorated.

Labels, in and of themselves, are not evil. How they are interpreted by others and by the labeled person determines whether they are harmful or ameliorative. The challenge is to educate society to use labels to arrive at a better understanding of persons with disabilities, to avoid overgeneralizing or stereotyping based on labels, and to see the individual behind the label. The challenge is also to help persons with a disability to use their label as a basis for self-understanding, not as an excuse for failure to learn what they are able, a justification for choosing unacceptable behavior, or a reason to feel unworthy.

Currently, those involved in the special education scene are spending an inordinate amount of time concerned about the use of labels. Journal editors are insisting on certain turns of phrase (e.g., "students with learning disabilities" rather than "learning disabled students"). Some professionals smugly consider the "proper" use of terminology as a litmus test for true professionalism and empathy. Perhaps the height of absurdity relative to the business of creating inoffensive labels was demonstrated by the National Cristina Foundation, which in 1991 offered a cash prize of $50,000 for the best way of referring to people ordinarily called disabled or handicapped (Shapiro, 1991). Out of the 66,000 entries, the winning entry was "people with differing abilities"!

Sensitive reference to people's disabilities is undoubtedly good. We are not suggesting a return to the terms "idiot" and "imbecile," nor are we suggesting the careless use of labels. And we admit our preference for the current "people with . . ." terminology. But the zeal and self-righteous way in which many have introduced these changes does smack of political correctness. Furthermore, Wolfensberger's (1991) claim that such practices reflect lysenkoism (emphasis on environmental and somatic influences on heredity) is consistent with our argument that people with disabilities do have something inherently different about them; social construction does not explain the whole story.

What is most unsettling about the current apprehension about using offensive labels is that it may have just the opposite of the intended effect. Inadvertently, it may be sending a message to persons with disabilities and their families that having a disability is something to be ashamed of. Extreme concern regarding labels may reflect an unwillingness to confront the realities to which the labels refer.

Labeling and Positive Identity

It is interesting that many deaf persons and many blind persons have eschewed the new terminology. The deaf community, for example, prefers to be called "the Deaf." They also have looked suspiciously on the current inclusion movement, with many of them preferring separate settings or even residential institutions (Lane, 1987).

The deaf view themselves more as a cultural group than a disabled group (Padden & Humphries, 1988). Although we might wish to debate, albeit not strongly, whether deafness is a disability, there is no doubt that there is a deaf culture. The fact that many deaf couples would prefer to have deaf rather than hearing children is convincing evidence of the strength of that culture. In many ways, the deaf are proud of their deafness.

Major segments of the blind community have also reacted negatively to politically correct labeling. At its 1993 annual convention, the National Federation of the Blind (NFB) adopted a resolution rejecting the use of terms such as *hard of seeing, visually challenged,* and *people with blindness.* The NFB passed a resolution that states that such labels are "totally unacceptable and deserving only ridicule because of their strained and ludicrous attempt to avoid such straightforward, respectable words as *blindness, blind, the blind, blind person,* or *blind persons*" (Jernigan, 1993, p. 867).

Vaughan (1993), writing in the NFB's *The Braille Monitor,* questioned the use of people-first language on two grounds:

> First, the awkwardness of the preferred language focuses on the disability in a new and potentially negative way. In common usage positive pronouns usually precede nouns. We do not say, "people who are beautiful," "people who are handsome," "people who are intelligent," etc. Under the guise of the preferred language crusade, we have focused on disability in an ungainly new way but have done nothing to educate anyone or change anyone's attitudes.
>
> Second, we are told that preferred usage will cause us to focus on the whole person. In the best of all possible worlds, where ignorance, stereotypes, and advantages over others do not exist, this might be the case. But until we reach that condition—and that will be a long time coming—might it not be preferable to use language that reflects the actual experience of most disabled people? (p. 869)

TOWARD A CULTURE OF DISABILITY

Perhaps those who work in other areas of special education should take a cue from the deaf and the blind communities regarding the value of culture. For example, it might be beneficial for persons with learning disabilities to consider themselves as part of a learning disability culture. Maybe they should learn to embrace having a learning disability as being part of their identity, part of who they are.

Some indirect evidence for the value of building a learning disability culture comes from data on successful adults who are learning disabled. Researchers have found that successful young adults with learning disabilities, although not defining themselves solely by their learning disability, were better able than unsuccessful young adults with learning disabilities to refer to themselves as learning disabled. Unsuccessful adults, on the other hand, tended to deny their learning disability, refused to associate with other persons with disabilities, and avoided disabled student service centers in college (Spekman, Goldberg, & Herman, 1992). In a similar vein, Gerber, Ginsberg, and Reiff (1992) have found in their qualitative interviews that highly successful adults with learning disabilities engage in "reframing." For example, one of their interviewees stated: "I need to be proud of myself. As long as I was ashamed of being LD, it was difficult to proceed" (p. 481).

A frequent argument against separate classes, self-contained as well as resource, is that they are bad for students with disabilities because students see only inappropriate role models and are unable to interact with and learn from students without disabilities. Perhaps association with others who have similar problems could be used to transmit the culture of what it is like to be learning disabled, mentally retarded, and so forth. This would require a shift, however, in how disability and disability labeling is viewed. In our view, we should weigh the possibility and probability of reducing stigma and increasing learning by banning labeling and grouping by disability against the feasibility and likelihood of reducing stigma and increasing learning by developing esprit de corps among congregations of people with disabilities. Among individuals with other identifying differences, regular congregation is seen as a vital part of identity and support (e.g., senior citizens, veterans of foreign wars, recovering alcoholics, parents of children with specific disabilities). We agree with Edgar and Siegel (in press):

> In a naive and overzealous rush to implement fully inclusive school
> environments, we risk overlooking and discarding the discovery of
> identity, common will, and support that comes from the opportunity
> to congregate with those engaged in struggles that share character-
> istics of ability, culture, status, or environment.

It may be inappropriate to suggest that all people with disabilities should be proud of their labels. For example, we would not want to see couples with emotional or behavioral disorders wanting to have children with these disorders. But we do think that the notion of promoting the cultural aspect of one's disability does have merit for some purposes. Young children with attention deficit disorder, for example, could learn much from adults and older children with the same condition. The passing on of insights and information gained through experience to younger generations is something that has proven invaluable to deaf children and to blind children, and this is why so many of the deaf and the blind have resisted the closing of residential institutions. Perhaps we need ways whereby students with other types of disabilities can learn from their elders and their age peers.

Much of what we are discussing relates to what Minow (1987) has called the "difference dilemma," the question of whether we should focus on the disability or ignore it. By labeling the student for special services, we are focusing on the disability and calling attention to the fact that the person is different, thereby risking stigma and discrimination based on that difference. On the other hand, by not labeling the student and so not providing special services, we run the risk of stigma and discrimination "based on majority practices, such as tests, norms, and judgments forged without regard for difference, or with regard solely for the perspective, needs, and interests of the dominant group" (p. 378).

We think there is another equally knotty problem, what we shall call the "values dilemma," that makes working in the area of special education so difficult. This is the tension between working toward eradicating or reducing disabilities while at the same time working toward helping the public to attach positive value to those who have a disability. To the extent that we place a negative value on disability and treat it as an undesirable characteristic that we would like to change or help the individual overcome, we risk fostering negative attitudes toward those who have it. On the other hand, to the extent that we place a positive value on disability and treat it as a desirable characteristic or as inconsequential, we risk exacerbating the individual's handicap in our society and the stigma and rejection that accompany it. We suspect that others have as difficult a time as we do balancing our response to this dilemma. We think it crucial, however, that the field continue to work toward two goals: reducing disability and its effects, on the one hand, and, on the other, fostering the positive valuing of individuals with disabilities.

Finally, we offer that place of instruction should have relatively little to do with the acceptance of people with disabilities by the public and by themselves. In some ways, the radical inclusionists have unwittingly adopted a cynical view of the public and of people with disabilities. They have sold short society's and disabled people's competence to conceptualize the problem of acceptance without regard to place of education. They have assumed that perceptions are so colored by where instruction takes place that they induce an inability to recognize a person's worth and individuality as separate from where they are educated. What we should be striving for is self-acceptance and societal acceptance of people with disabilities regardless of where they receive their instruction. Why can't our goal be to make people understand that, even though Johnny and Shenika receive their instruction in a different class for some or part of the day, they are every bit as worthy of respect as the rest of society? Why should we not celebrate differences in where students receive their instruction, not just the differences in their personal characteristics? Our hope is that before we reach the 21st century, we will have a kinder and gentler culture of disability and that "we will understand that special education has no holy place and no promised land" (Kauffman, 1992, p. 344).

AUTHORS' NOTE

Preparation of this chapter was supported in part by the University of Virginia's Commonwealth Center for the Education of Teachers. We are grateful to the center's director, Robert F. McNergney, for his helpful commentary on the manuscript.

REFERENCES

Algozzine, B. (1993). Letter to the editor: Splitting hairs and loose ends: Answering special education's wake-up call. *The Journal of Special Education, 26,* 462–467.

Bateman, B. D. (1992). *Better IEPs.* Creswell, OR: Otter Ink.

Bell, R. Q., & Harper, L. V. (1977). *Child effects on adults.* Hillsdale, NJ: Erlbaum.

Blatt, B., & Kaplan, F. (1966). *Christmas in purgatory: A photographic essay on mental retardation.* Boston: Allyn & Bacon.

Budoff, M., & Gottlieb, J. (1976). Special-class EMR children mainstreamed: A study of an aptitude (learning potential) X treatment interaction. *American Journal of Mental Deficiency, 81,* 1–11.

Deno, E. (1970). Special education as developmental capital. *Exceptional Children, 37,* 229–237.

Dunn, L. M. (1968). Special education for the mildly retarded—Is much of it justifiable? *Exceptional Children, 35,* 5–22.

Durkheim, E. (1938). *The rules of sociological method* (8th ed.). New York: Free Press.

Edgar, E., & Siegel, S. (in press). Post-secondary scenarios for troubled and troubling youth. In J. M. Kauffman, J. W. Lloyd, T. A. Astuto, & D. P. Hallahan, (Eds.), *Issues in the educational placement of pupils with emotional or behavioral disorders.* Hillsdale, NJ: Erlbaum.

F/C under siege. (1993). *Autism Research Review, 7*(1), 2, 7.

Ferguson, P. M., Ferguson, D. L., & Taylor, S. J. (Eds.). (1992). *Interpreting disability: A qualitative reader.* New York: Teachers College Press.

Foster, G. G., Ysseldyke, J. E., & Reese, J. H. (1975). "I wouldn't have seen it if I hadn't believed it." *Exceptional Children, 41,* 469–473.

Gartner, A., & Lipsky, D. K. (1989). *The yoke of special education: How to break it.* Rochester, NY: National Center on Education and the Economy.

Gerber, P. J., Ginsberg, R., & Reiff, H. B. (1992). Identifying alterable patterns in employment success for highly successful adults with learning disabilities. *Journal of Learning Disabilities, 25,* 475–487.

Goldstein, H., Moss, J., & Jordan, L. J. (1965). *The efficacy of special training on the development of mentally retarded children.* Urbana: University of Illinois Press.

Gottlieb, J., Alter, M., & Gottlieb, B. W. (1983). Mainstreaming mentally retarded children. In J. L. Matson & J. A. Mulich (Eds.), *Handbook of mental retardation* (pp. 67–77). New York: Pergamon Press.

Gottlieb, J., & Leyser, Y. (1981). Facilitating the social mainstreaming of retarded children. *Exceptional Education Quarterly, 1*(4), 57–69.

Green, G. (1992, October). *Facilitated communication: Scientific and ethical issues.* Paper presented at the E. K. Shriver Center University Affiliated Program, Waltham, MA.

Hallahan, D. P. (1992). Some thoughts on why the prevalence of learning disabilities has increased. *Journal of Learning Disabilities, 25,* 523–528.

Jernigan, K. (1993, August). The pitfalls of political correctness: Euphemisms excoriated. *The Braille Monitor,* 865–867.

Kauffman, J. M. (1990, April). *What happens when special education works? The sociopolitical context of special education research in the 1990s.* Invited address, Special Interest Group: Special Education Research, annual meeting of the American Educational Research Association, Boston.

Kauffman, J. M. (1992, October). Special education into the 21st century: An educational perspective. *Challenge for change: Reform in the 1990's. Conference proceedings, 16th national conference of the Australian Association of Special Education.* Perth, Western Australia: Author.

Keogh, B. K., & Levitt, M. L. (1976). Special education in the mainstream: A confrontation of limitations? *Focus on Exceptional Children, 8,* 1–11.

Lane, H. (1987, July 17). Listen to the needs of deaf children. *The New York Times,* p. A35.

Lilly, M. S. (1988). The Regular Education Initiative: A force for change in general and special education. *Education and Training in Mental Retardation, 23,* 253–260.

Lipsky, D. K., & Gartner, A. (1987). Capable of achievement and worthy of respect: Education for handicapped students as if they were full-fledged human beings. *Exceptional Children, 54,* 69–74.

Lipsky, D. K., & Gartner, A. (1991). Restructuring for quality. In J. W. Lloyd, N. N. Singh, & A. C. Repp (Eds.), *The Regular Education Initiative: Alternative perspectives on concepts, issues, and models* (pp. 43–57). Sycamore, IL: Sycamore.

MacMillan, D. L., & Becker, L. D. (1977). Mainstreaming the mildly handicapped learner. In R. D. Kneedler & S. G. Tarver (Eds.), *Changing perspectives in special education* (pp. 208–227). Columbus, OH: Merrill.

MacMillan, D. L., Jones, R. J., & Aloia, G. F. (1974). The mentally retarded label: A theoretical analysis and review of research. *American Journal of Mental Deficiency, 79,* 241–261.

Minow, M. (1987). Learning to live with the dilemma of difference: Bilingual and special education. In K. T. Bartlett & J. W. Wenger (Eds.), *Children with special needs* (pp. 375–429). New Brunswick, NJ: Transaction Books.

Moynihan, D. P. (1993). Defining deviancy down. *The American Scholar, 62*(1), 17–30.

Padden, C., & Humphries, T. (1988). *Deaf in America: Voices from a culture.* Cambridge, MA: Harvard University Press.

Rhodes, W. C. (1967). The disturbing child: A problem of ecological management. *Exceptional Children, 33,* 637–642.

Rhodes, W. C., & Head, S. (Eds.). (1974). *A study of child variance, Vol. 3: Service delivery systems.* Ann Arbor: University of Michigan Press.

Rhodes, W. C., & Tracy, M. L. (Eds.). (1972a). *A study of child variance, Vol. 1: Theories.* Ann Arbor: University of Michigan Press.

Rhodes, W. C., & Tracy, M. L. (Eds.). (1972b). *A study of child variance, Vol. 2: Interventions.* Ann Arbor: University of Michigan Press.

Salvia, J., Clark, G. M., & Ysseldyke, J. E. (1973). Teacher retention of stereotypes of disability. *Exceptional Children, 39,* 651–652.

Shapiro, J. P. (1991, August 25). In search of a word for (shhh!) disabled. *The Washington Post,* p. C4.

Singer, J. D. (1992). Are special educators' career paths special? Results from a 13-year longitudinal study. *Exceptional Children, 59,* 262–279.

Spekman, N. J., Goldberg, R. J., & Herman, K. L. (1992). Learning disabled children grow up: A search for factors related to success in the young adult years. *Learning Disabilities Research & Practice, 7*(3), 161–170.

Stainback, W., & Stainback, S. (1991). A rationale for integration and restructuring: A synopsis. In J. W. Lloyd, N. N. Singh, & A. C. Repp (Eds.), *The Regular Education Initiative: Alternative perspectives on concepts, issues, and models* (pp. 226–239). Sycamore, IL: Sycamore.

Thompson, T. (1993, January). A reign of error: Facilitated communication. *Kennedy Center News,* No. 22, Vanderbilt University.

Vaughan, C. E. (1993, August). People-first language: An unholy crusade. *The Braille Monitor,* 868–870.

Wang, M.C., & Walberg, H. J. (1988). Four fallacies of segregationism. *Exceptional Children, 55,* 128–137.

Wiseman, F. (Director). (1967). *Titicut folies* [Film]. Cambridge, MA: Zipporah Films.

Wolfensberger, W. (1991). Reflections on a lifetime in human services and mental retardation. *Mental Retardation, 29*(1), 1–15.

Chapter 5

Who, How, and Where: Special Education's Issues in Perpetuity

Barbara D. Bateman

MAJOR THEMES SEEN OFTEN in this retrospective include who we are as special educators and how we practice our profession, who should be served by special education, individualization of services, and special education placements. These same issues were central in special education before Dunn (1968) and Deno (1970) and appear destined to remain with us, even though they are potentially solved by the Individuals with Disabilities Education Act (IDEA). The IDEA addresses eligibility, individualization, and placement squarely and reasonably. It is an ironic tribute to the parents and special educators of the 1960s and 1970s who foresaw and addressed these issues that they are nevertheless still tearing at the fabric of special education in the 1990s.

Perhaps it is no surprise that the old-timers in special education know that many of the issues haven't changed in an even longer time, as illustrated by a personal example. As a woefully under-educated, naive, and not-yet-certified special education teacher in the mid-1950s, I went to a state residential school for the blind to teach a class of eight children who were blind, multiply handicapped, and, except for Jerry, functioning at a severely or profoundly retarded level. They ranged from 6 years to 12 years old. Two were not toilet

Reprinted, with changes, from "Who, how, and where: Special education's issues in perpetuity," by Barbara D. Bateman, *The Journal of Special Education*, Vol. 27, 1994, 509–520. Copyright © 1994 by PRO-ED, Inc.

trained, two were nonambulatory, and only Jerry had language beyond echolalia. Jerry was the youngest in the class, very verbal and very bright, and his only disability was congenital blindness. He was mobile, curious, and courageous. With little education, a bare classroom devoid of equipment or supplies, no budget, no aide, and one bathroom at the far end of the wing, this "teacher" could not begin to serve that class of children appropriately, and it was clear that Jerry was being served the least well of all. Without consultation or permission, I naively suggested to Jerry's mother that she place him immediately in a public school. Public schools were responding then to the wave of children blind due to retrolental fibroplasia, and many were already implementing itinerant and resource room programs for children with visual impairments. In fact, many of the older students who lived at that residential school for the blind attended the local public high school. We didn't call it mainstreaming, integration, or inclusion, but just attending school.

Immediately after Jerry's mother withdrew him in favor of public school, I was on the carpet and nearly under it for causing the school to lose the per capita state funding it received for every enrolled student. This aftermath was predictable and unpleasant, and it encompassed the major issues with which we still struggle—who we special educators are and how we practice our profession, who we are to serve, individualization of services, and placement concerns.

SPECIAL EDUCATION AS A PROFESSION

Hallahan and Kauffman (see Chapter 4) are concerned that the seeds of destruction of the special education profession inadvertently sown by Dunn (1968) and Deno (1970) may be sprouting. No doubt, the profession has grown a few big weeds in recent years, but the field of special education will survive. Special education, by whatever name or organizational structure, is inherent in the bell-shaped distribution of many human learning characteristics. Regular education, even reformed or renamed, is a system that by its very essence is group oriented. Even if it were to adopt an individualized approach to the group enterprise, that individualized approach would be less than maximally effective and appropriate for the students at the extremes, the outliers. As long as resources are finite, regular education will have fallout. The fallout may be shifting and relative, as it always has been, and special educators will be there struggling with how to designate the children and how and where to serve them. The forces that gave rise to special education are basic and strong and are not going to go away. They may be temporarily glossed over or stifled, and that is a concern. If the foundations of the profession are eroded away under the current assault, or the next, the rebuilding process will be difficult, expensive, and time-consuming. But it will happen.

Special educators are the progeny of both science and compassion, and like all of our species we bring diverse values to our chosen profession. It is no wonder, therefore, that we are not all of one mind or cut from the same cloth. Some of the divisions between camps are deep and wide. These divisions have been variously described.

Deno spoke of two opposing armies of special educators divided over the very nature of special education as a discipline. One camp would have had us focus only on individuals; the other would have preserved categorical labels as a means of preserving identity and funding. Hallahan and Kauffman note the same split today and observe that labeling can focus unduly on negative aspects of disability, yet not labeling may result in no services being provided. More on this problem later.

Semmel, Gerber, and MacMillan (see Chapter 3) focus on the dual aspects of progressivism and pragmatism. The pragmatists' interest they characterize as the "structural arrangements and placements—the inputs—that promise greater managerial control of limited resources." This reactive concern is in stark contrast, they say, to the progressive visionaries in special education who proactively and literally mean "full" participation by all students. When these progressive visionaries focus on outcome-based education, they envision powerful curricular and instructional interventions. Semmel et al. observe that prior to Dunn, special educators focused on long-term outcomes, and after Dunn, on the equity of procedures, at least until the mid-1980s, when the visionaries arose again. This outcome versus process distinction is a pervasive and fundamental one. Finn (1990) believes a fundamental paradigm shift is under way in all of education—away from education as process to education as outcome, that is, the result of process. Finn noted that during a paradigm shift, both "conflicting world views can exist side-by-side for many years, perhaps for generations" (p. 586). In special education, both views are alive and well.

That special education should be so divided is not surprising. Some people are drawn to special education just as to regular education by a set of values we could describe as holistic and child centered. They value children's engagement in the process of education, be it placement in a regular class, a cooperative learning group, or a developmentally appropriate practice engaged in with a chronologically age-appropriate peer. Inclusion is a process, not an outcome.

Others are drawn by the traditional scientific aspects of special education and place more emphasis on outcomes and their assessment. This division is not sharp, perfect, or unique to special education. But it is there. A closely related and fundamental distinction that seems to cut across many others can be drawn by the extent of a special educator's reliance on data. This is not to say that all data-based decision makers are always on the same side of every issue, but it is to say that they can and do communicate. The often unbridgeable communication chasm is between those educators—special or regular—who look primarily to hard evidence and those who do not.

MacMillan, Semmel, and Gerber (see Chapter 2) make this exact distinction between program advocacy and child advocacy. Program advocacy, for example, on behalf of deinstitutionalization and full inclusion, has disregarded evidence about the effects of the program with children. MacMillan et al. plead for empirical validation and demonstrable generalization of intervention effects. These pleas go largely unheard by those whose primary focus is on the process of intervention or on the structure of a placement rather than on the accomplishment of specified outcomes.

Semmel et al. (Chapter 3) suggest that Dunn's legacy included this renewed tension between visionaries who want to reform without adequate data and managerial pragmatists, and they say it was after Dunn that special education's focus shifted away from outcomes to process and to the fairness of procedures. To the extent that this shift has occurred, it is an aspect of education's never-ending effort to achieve both equity and excellence, although they often seem at least partially mutually exclusive.

Closely related to the fact that not all special educators are empiricists is the fact that our discipline seems not to learn from our own history. In Deno's (1994) words, we fail to recognize that today's "bright idea" may have already been tried and abandoned for good reason. Cuban (1990) pointed out that education "reforms do return again, again, and again. Not exactly the same as before or under the same conditions, but they persist" (p. 11). Special educators fail to learn from the past because we fail to teach the past or perhaps we sometimes, being taught, choose to ignore the lessons. A discipline that has no sense of its own past not only repeats its mistakes, but also spins in place, failing to advance on the solid foundation of research. We now have a generation of graduate students in special education who have never heard of Precision Teaching or Project Follow-Through and who have no idea that the concept of learning styles was thoroughly studied over 30 years ago and found wanting, to give just three examples. Sadly, hundreds more could be cited.

Gottlieb, Alter, Gottlieb, and Wishner (1994) noted that many of the problems and unresolved issues the field faced 25 years ago are still with us today. Artiles and Trent (1994) observed that 25 years after Dunn and Deno we are still grappling with the issues of overrepresentation of and appropriate services for minority and/or poor children, and they said that one reason for our failure to move on is our failure to look at the problems in historical perspective. However, special education graduate students who are told to use only references and research less than 10 years old do not know that such problems and issues have already been raised. We must stop throwing away our history and begin teaching it and using it. Wheels truly do not need reinvention.

Relationships Between Special Educators and Regular Educators

An ongoing, troublesome aspect of working as a professional special educator has been an often difficult relationship with some regular educators. Dunn (1968) reflected, "We have been living at the mercy of general educators who have referred their problem children to us" (p. 5). We frequently, if not always, believed we could serve those children better than regular education did. As a result, communication between special and regular educators sometimes encountered difficulties around this perception that special educators were, or considered themselves, better trained and qualified. However, Dunn believed that we were in fact ill prepared and ineffective, at least with the socioculturally deprived slow learners about whom he was concerned. And he believed that by 1968 regular teachers were "increasingly better trained to deal with individual differences" (p. 10), but that there was yet a way to go. Perhaps regular education has now gone that distance, and that is why many now believe a proper model for delivery of special education is one where special educators work with regular educators, on their own turf, to deal with the entire class, including the children who have disabilities. It may be, too, that the stresses on regular education have increased to the point that teachers welcome help from any source, even one perceived as elitist.

Perhaps the real plea to special educators from their regular education counterparts is to either enable them to comfortably serve students with special needs or remove them. If we do neither, communication deteriorates and pressures mount.

WHO IS TO BE SERVED?

Special education is now both a service to children with disabilities and a safety net to some of the regular education fallout, by whatever changing name, and regardless of whether it is the best system to do the catching. Must there be fallout from regular education? As Hallahan and Kauffman (see Chapter 4) point out, as regular education uses more effective methodologies, the variance in student outcomes will increase, not decrease. As I said before, regular education by its very essence deals with norms, averages, and groups, while special education focuses on outlier individuals, a difference that underlies much of the tension between special education and regular education. Better regular education results in more outliers, not fewer. Another reason for fallout is that regular education sometimes adopts unproven practices that result in increased fallout. For example, it is painfully ironic that as the evidence on the importance of phonological awareness and segmentation skills in learning to read becomes ever more conclusive, regular education rushes to adopt beginning reading approaches that minimize or omit altogether phonologically based instruction. Whenever instructional gaps or lapses appear or grow in regular education, the pressure of increased numbers needing better instruction is felt by special education.

Another factor in increased fallout is the inability of regular education to individualize. This hesitation is perfectly highlighted in the discipline of special education students. Only the rare regular education administrator understands either the educational or legal necessity for individualized disciplinary procedures and consequences for students whose disabilities cause their misconduct. Other issues related to individualization are treated later. Here the point is that there are and will always be students who require more individualization than regular education can provide.

In addition to failures in instruction and individualization, we are also seeing an actual increase in the proportion of children with categorical disabilities. Hallahan and Kauffman's (Chapter 4) discussion of this increase, especially in children with learning disabilities, is compelling and correct. Gottlieb et al. (1994) also discussed those increases and predicted that the children will be increasingly impaired. Let us just hope that 25 years further down the education road, no one has to write that we ignored these warnings or these children's needs.

Most districts seem now to serve and collect subsidies for both categorically defined IDEA students and many others who do not qualify but who are labeled learning disabled. We also frequently hear that some children who need services are not being served because they do not fit the eligibility criteria. When we place a child in special education who ought not be there, often Dunn's socioculturally deprived slow learner, it is the fault of none but special educators themselves. Every child to be served under IDEA must need special education in order to be eligible (34 CFR 300.7(a)(1)). Furthermore, professional judgment, not test score, must always be the final authority in eligibility decisions. If we choose to yield to pressure from regular educators, we are only delaying the day we all look unblinkingly at the needs of children now in the gap between regular and special education.

Given that we are legally and in every other way free to serve only and all the children who we professionally believe ought to be served, why are so many special educators upset about the population actually served? A few outright erroneous decisions are made, often because they are made by people who don't know the child well and/or because of improper reliance on tests. Better training can provide the correction for those cases. However, professional judgment, observation procedures, portfolios, or curriculum-based assessment, standardized tests, or any combination thereof will never be perfect 100% of the time. There will always be room for legitimate discussion about the effects of the diagnostic processes used on the numbers of children deemed in need of services.

Another not-so-legitimate source of variation in numbers served is the reliance upon those discrepancy formulas that allow identification of only a preset percentage of students as learning disabled. Few practices speak any more clearly to our loss of the vision of a child-centered discipline providing individualized services to children in need.

Another source of dispute is the extent to which a particular regular education program is able to serve children. Some districts, schools, and teachers can adequately serve a wider range of children than can others. Therefore, some children need special education in one district and not another and therefore are eligible in one and not the other. We could develop eligibility criteria that would ignore this match between the child and the educational system, but to do so would favor foolish consistency, which is hardly a virtue. Arguably, then, we have two somewhat different populations in those who have actual mental or physical disabilities and those who, for the reason discussed or others, such as cultural difference, fail to thrive in regular education. An issue that preceded Dunn and Deno, was addressed by them, and remains with us today is whether special education ought to serve all those children who are not successfully served in regular education—for whatever reason—or only those students who have actual disabilities and therefore need special services. One reason this is an issue is that somehow we have allowed the monetary subsidization of some special education students to become our sole focus.

The field has acted as if the IDEA subsidy for providing a free, appropriate public education to defined groups had somehow prevented states or local districts from appropriately serving additional children who do not meet the IDEA criteria. Nothing could be further from the truth. Those who wish to identify and serve additional children simply on the basis of need, failure, percentile, or achievement measures are totally free to do so. They may not, however, charge taxpayers in other states for that decision. In short, a state or district may continue to provide special education to categorically defined IDEA students and receive a small federal subsidy for so doing. It may also provide special education, without the federal subsidy, to any other students it wishes. The choice of who to serve may and should be made on professional grounds, not on funding.

When we receive a subsidy for doing what's right, that may be helpful. However, it is not good to fail to serve children because we aren't paid a bonus to do it, nor is it good to claim falsely that a child fits the subsidy definition, even if the primary motivation is service.

Another aspect of who ought to be served by special education involves gender disproportion, a glaring but largely ignored phenomenon. Studies often report gender differences or nondifferences on some dependent variable, but much less is said about the fact that special education serves two boys for every one girl. The easy rejoinder is a combination of "boys have more disabilities" and "girls conform better to schools' behavioral expectations." Both are somewhat more easily said than established. For example, recent evidence suggests that reading disabilities may actually occur equally in males and females, contrary to most U.S. data on referrals and groups served. Amidst all the far worse sex discrimination in this country in 1993, underrepresentation of girls in special education may not be a large issue. It is, however, deserving of more attention than it receives. The underrepresentation of girls is obviously disproportional, but disproportion in itself is not desirable or undesirable. Legally, disproportion is discriminatory only when it is detrimental and lacking sufficient justification. Certainly, Dunn and his current followers believe that overrepresentation of some minority groups in special education is detrimental, unjustified, and therefore discriminatory. If this is so, is it not also the case that underrepresentation of girls would be beneficial for them? Both arguments are true only if special education services are deemed detrimental. A far more defensible position is that special education services may be either detrimental or beneficial, depending on the facts of a given case.

Disproportion may or may not be discriminatory, but ignoring it probably is. However, serious sex discrimination does still go on in special education. Referrals, evaluation processes, instructional programs, vocational opportunities, and more still reflect the sexism of the broader society. In addition, sexual victimization of students with disabilities, especially girls, is appalling and increasing. One might have predicted that special educators would be in the forefront of combatting sex discrimination. Perhaps in the future we will be.

Another recurring question surrounds the shift from a melting pot model to a salad model of how society addresses diversity. Schools still largely reflect one major cultural and socioeconomic strand. We now see substantial mismatches between some schools and some cultural strands. It takes time for better matches to evolve, and the pace of change may never again be slow enough to eliminate all mismatches. Special education has tried to deal with some of these mismatches. It has not been perfect; it has been available. Gottlieb et al. (1994) argued that special education has not been an effective intervention for inner city children. One might ask whether educators are of one mind about what *has been* effective for low-achieving and/or low-ability students falsely or mistakenly labeled learning disabled. Inadequate regular education is not the answer, nor is inappropriate special education. As Gottlieb et al. said, neither cures poverty. Later I will look at one possible approach to the cultural–socioeconomic mismatch problem.

In sum, it seems that we have some students who do well in regular education and some who do not. The latter seem to be divisible into students with disabilities and some who fail for other reasons. It is this latter group that has caused so much concern.

INDIVIDUALIZATION

In the early 1960s and into the 1970s, the basic special education delivery model was categorical, not individualized. This was true for both placements and programs. Sarah was diagnosed as brain injured, so she was placed in a class of brain-injured children and taught by a method said to be for brain-injured and hyperactive children. In its extreme form, this could result in overlooking or downplaying much about Sarah's individual, unique needs.

This categorical service delivery model was so pervasive and ingrained that it was to us then as water is to fish. We didn't know it was there, it was just the omnipresent given. One aspect of the phenomenal appeal of the original Illinois Test of Psycholinguistic Abilities (ITPA) was that it provided a way to individualize instruction and to organize educational programs around skills rather than labels. Popular as the ITPA was, it had not totally revolutionalized practice by the time Deno (1994) urged individualization rather than categorization of program and services. She acknowledged her earlier fear of categorization and reemphasized her concern. She lamented the new categories of disability (presumably autism and traumatic brain injury) and preferred the safety net concept be used to define the population to be served by special education, rather than the categorical disability approach.

This debate might be resolved by recognizing that under IDEA, categorical information is required for eligibility only. All program and placement decisions are mandated to be totally individualized, and categorical decision making is prohibited. Special education has admittedly had a difficult time letting go of the categorical model, even though the law disallows it. The issue of labeling overlaps almost totally with that of categorization. One slight connotative difference, however, is that perhaps we fear a label has been affixed to the child without a connection to a subsequent action. Categorization seems to imply some more purposeful behavior with an intended action to follow. The term "label" also seems to connote a greater possibility or fear of stigma than does categorization.

Hallahan and Kauffman's (see Chapter 4) analysis of the effects of labeling should and will become required reading for the next generation of special educators. One small postscript example might be added to the concern that current apprehension about labels may actually send an unintended message of shame. The parents, advocates, and courts who urge that a child who has a disability must be placed with those who do not have a disability too often send the message that children who have disabilities are not peers and are not fit to be with. Something is terribly and not very subtly insulting about saying a bright student with learning disabilities ought not attend a special school with other students who have learning disabilities because he or she needs to be with nondisabled students.

Another facet of individualization is how a student is treated within the educational system. Who among us has not heard an educator say, "If I make an exception for one, I'll have to make an exception for all, and I can't and I won't"? To make an exception is to individualize. Regular education by its present nature imposes limits on the individualization that can be accomplished. Special education has a mandate, on the other hand, to provide an individualized education program for every child served under IDEA.

This divergence between the two systems may be increased by the drive for excellence that is part of current reform. Semmel et al. (Chapter 3) report that schools that have good regular education programs are not the same schools that have effective special education. Semmel et al. suggest that diminishing resources, combined with reform pressures, may result in increasing regular education use of practices that are not effective for special education students.

While the goal, as Deno suggested, is individualization for all children, disabled and nondisabled alike, it may be nearly impossible to implement individualization for all within economic constraints. Even if one had unlimited resources, it is possible that the means of individualization that are effective for special education students might not be the same means as those for regular education students.

Deno's interest in individualization went beyond instructional program concerns into the arena of placement. In commenting on the cascade of services as it was implemented in Minnesota 2 decades ago, she observed that no one had assumed that mainstreaming would be appropriate for all children (Deno, 1994). This leads to our next ever-present issue—placement.

PLACEMENT

Placement issues loom as large as any raised in this retrospective view of the last quarter century of special education. Over a decade before Dunn's 1968 article, a course on gifted children was taught by James Gallagher. In the context of acceleration versus enrichment versus homogeneous grouping, he said something I recall as, "It isn't how you pile up the children that matters, it's what you do in the piles." I am now very sure he said it much more elegantly, but this profound and simple concept has been affirmed repeatedly as special education struggles ceaselessly with questions of how to best pile (place) children in the education setting.

The current placement battle rages over full inclusion versus the individualization placement decision-making process required by law. The substance of the war is placement of children, while its style reflects a deep and wide chasm dividing special educators. Individualized placement decisions can be made only if there is a continuum or variety of placements from which to select. The shape of Deno's cascade of services was tapered to reflect the numbers of children who need each level of service. In a strange twist, that numerical taper is now believed by some to reflect not only the amount of "restrictiveness" but also amount of "goodness" in the placements depicted.

Snell and Drake (1994) were extremely critical of Deno's cascade, claiming that it has "unfortunately" dominated the organization of special education. They characterized the cascade and its legal identity—the continuum of alternative placements—as "label, separate, and educate." They asserted that the cascade model requires that students must qualify for placement with nondisabled peers and that disability labels are rigidly associated with placement location. Further, they claimed that the legally mandated continuum is obsolete and prevents interaction with age peers. To whatever extent, if at all, any of these assertions is true, both the law and Deno's concepts are being violated. The position taken by Snell and Drake and other full inclusionists appears to be that only chronological age need to be considered in placement decisions. No legal or factual basis for this position is made explicit. Nor has it been evident to most courts. In a fairly typical case, the United States Fourth Circuit Court of Appeals dealt with the placement of 16-year-old Michael. His IQ was 72, his academic level about fourth grade, and he worked successfully at a fast food restaurant and related well to other teenagers in several small continuing groups, although he also had some difficulties with communication and social skills. The court approvingly noted the lower court's conclusion that at Annandale High School, which served 2,300 students, few of whom were disabled, Michael had "no appropriate peer group academically, socially, or vocationally." The court therefore upheld his placement at a vocational center 13 miles from his home, rather than at the public high school. The court also spoke to the fact he would have been simply monitoring classes at the high school and said that the disparity between his cognitive level and that of the other students would mean that he would glean little from the classes and his work would be at a much lower level than his classmates (DeVries v. Fairfax County School Board, 1989). The emphasis on access to typical, chronological-age peers seen in much of the advocacy for full inclusion is confusing, especially in light of the equally adamant support for "developmentally appropriate practices" now heard in many education reform circles.

Snell and Drake (1994) saw "no-referral intervention" as central to all successful reform. All students would be automatically placed in neighborhood schools, and yet at the same time the law's procedural safeguards would be continued. However, intervention without referral, evaluation, and identification would be a clear violation of several important procedural rights. Automatic placement with no individual decision making and with consideration only for chronological age also violates some very important procedural rights protected by IDEA. If in fact one advocates repeal of rights and protections central to IDEA, that advocacy might better be done openly. The placement battle illustrates perfectly the division in the field between process and outcome focus, between program advocacy and child advocacy, and between scholarly research and social philosophy.

A FEW FINAL THOUGHTS

Too many special educators are burning out after only a few years. Teachers' workloads are so heavy that teachers cannot be as effective as they want to be and know how to be. Much of the load is unproductive and unnecessary paperwork that results from administrators' lack of understanding of the law and fear that dire consequences will follow a failure of the forms. Most of these fears are groundless, although some state departments have put excessive and burdensome requirements on districts that go far beyond federal law. The field must find ways to reduce the paperwork and shift it away from teachers. Too often, the team concept, which is mandatory in the evaluation, program, and placement functions of IDEA, becomes translated in practice into the teacher assuming all the logistical and paperwork duties.

In addition to undue burdens of grossly misconstrued legal requirements and impossible caseloads, teachers must also build bridges with regular educators, sometimes in the face of value differences, half-hearted cooperation, and communication difficulties. Special education has never been a soft job, and it won't be one soon. Nevertheless, or perhaps because of that, the profession continues to attract outstandingly capable, dedicated, and hard-working people who care and who help children succeed against the odds. The details will change over the next 25 years, but the basic story line will be similar.

The Children We Serve

As a step toward better formulation and solution, we asked an observer from Venus to check out the U.S. education scene. Venus found that we have three groups of children—REKS, SPEKS, and OEKS. The regular education kiddos' (REKS) and special education kiddos' (SPEKS) education programs are reasonably under control, according to Venus. However, near chaos reigns for the others (OEKS). They are fallout—Dunn's socioculturally deprived slow learners and today's urban students with learning disabilities (Gottlieb et al., 1994). Who is responsible for their education? asked Venus. Until that fundamental question is answered, and answered fully in terms of funding and delivery systems, we cannot begin to resolve the issues. Perhaps instead of a perverse tug-of-war over the "others" by two camps that seem not to want the victory, a third camp will emerge. Already there are many individual program tents in it—remedial reading, "chapter," at-risk, "just say no," and more.

Deno (1994) believes that it is not ethical for regular education to be required to serve those children special education finds not eligible, given that regular education has already failed with them. We special educators often deplore what Deno characterized as bits and pieces, narrow legislation, separate bureaucracies, and fragmented services. However, the federal control we and Deno believe is excessive does not in any way limit who may be served. It only defines the students who must be served and prescribes procedures and protections for them. Let us immediately and clearly recognize that special education may serve all the children we wish to. Only we can decide which, if any, students we will serve beyond those who are IDEA-eligible. Special education has the expertise, but have we the necessary determination?

Individualization

One vital key to true individualization is constant monitoring of program efficacy. Gottlieb et al. (1994) proposed the innovative notion of trying special education intensively for a defined, limited period of time, and if it doesn't work, moving on to something else. While there are not a lot of something elses, the concept of preset time limits is well worth exploring. Evaluating interventions within a specific time frame is precisely what Individualized Education

Program (IEP) objectives ought to be doing (Bateman, 1992). Too many IEP objectives are distinctly not serious, are barely measurable, and almost never measured. Once again, interestingly, we find that IDEA already provides the means, albeit neglected and abused, to the desired outcome.

Placement

Dunn advocated for socioculturally deprived, low socioeconomic students who were *labeled* mentally retarded, not who *were* mentally retarded. His thesis was that these children should not be labeled retarded and should not be placed as if they were retarded. In the best of the efficacy studies, Goldstein, Moss, and Jordan (1965) found that students in the 75 to 85 IQ range benefited more from regular classes, just as Dunn believed.

Under IDEA, every student whose education can be achieved satisfactorily in the regular classroom is entitled to be placed there. To insist that any one placement must be the only one for all children, regardless of unique needs or disabilities, is contrary to common sense and to law. Such decisions ought to be made on the basis of what is likely to be, and then shown to be, efficacious for each individual student.

One Last Thought

Special education today, just as 25 years ago, stands at a crossroads being challenged by divisions within. Differences within can keep us vibrant and growing as a discipline, or they can temporarily destroy us. These are chaotic and difficult times for all of education. Special education is vulnerable in the midst of reform. We must eschew slogans in favor of data, program advocacy in favor of child advocacy, and process focus in favor of outcome focus if we are to serve children effectively. Efficacy may be as much the issue as ethics in the tug-of-war between equity and excellence in the nation's schools.

REFERENCES

Artiles, A. J., & Trent, S. C. (1994). Overrepresentation of minority students in special education: A continuing debate. *The Journal of Special Education, 27,* 410–437.

Bateman, B. (1992). *Better IEPs*. Creswell, OR: Otter Ink.

Cuban, L. (1990). Reforming again, again, and again. *Educational Researcher, 19*(1), 3–13.

Deno, E. (1970). Special education as developmental capital. *Exceptional Children, 37*, 229–237.

Deno, E. (1994). Special education as developmental capital revisited: A quarter-century appraisal of means versus ends. *The Journal of Special Education, 27*, 375–392.

DeVries v. Fairfax County School Board, 882 F.2d 876, (4 CA, 1989).

Dunn, L. M. (1968). Special education for the mildly retarded—Is much of it justifiable? *Exceptional Children, 35*, 5–22.

Finn, C. E. (1990). The biggest reform of all. *Phi Delta Kappan, 71*, 585–592.

Goldstein, H., Moss, J., & Jordan, L. J. (1965). *The efficacy of special training on the development of mentally retarded children.* Urbana: University of Illinois.

Gottlieb, J., Alter, M., Gottlieb, B.W., & Wishner, J. (1994). Special education in urban America: It's not justifiable for many. *The Journal of Special Education, 27*, 453–465.

Snell, M. E., & Drake, G. P., Jr. (1994). Replacing cascades with supported education. *The Journal of Special Education, 27*, 393–409.

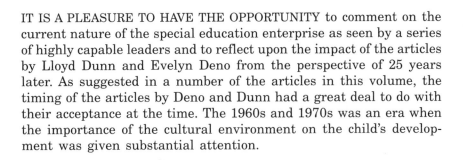

Chapter 6

The Pull of Societal Forces on Special Education

James J. Gallagher

IT IS A PLEASURE TO HAVE THE OPPORTUNITY to comment on the current nature of the special education enterprise as seen by a series of highly capable leaders and to reflect upon the impact of the articles by Lloyd Dunn and Evelyn Deno from the perspective of 25 years later. As suggested in a number of the articles in this volume, the timing of the articles by Deno and Dunn had a great deal to do with their acceptance at the time. The 1960s and 1970s was an era when the importance of the cultural environment on the child's development was given substantial attention.

CORRELATION VERSUS CAUSATION

It is always difficult to distinguish causation from correlation in a series of events, even with the advantage of retrospective insight. To cite a personal example, one time when I was first taking tentative steps toward learning to cook, I was preparing a meal and turned on the oven. Immediately all the lights in the house went out. Not only

Reprinted, with changes, from "The pull of societal forces on special education," by James J. Gallagher, *The Journal of Special Education,* Vol. 27, 1994, 521–530. Copyright © 1994 by PRO-ED, Inc.

did all the lights in the house go out, but all the lights in the neighborhood went out! The first agonizing thought to cross my mind was, "What have I done?" The answer of course was, "Nothing"; a failure in a power station had occurred as I turned the switch on the oven. But it is a typical human foible that we ascribe larger influences to our own actions than are justified.

There would seem to be a major parallel here about our arguments inside special education and the reality of its role in general education. To assume that the arguments that Deno and Dunn produced were the determining factor in the final decision to modify the patterns of American education is to be similarly ego involved. There is considerable evidence to suggest that such a conclusion is far from the truth. What was influencing policymakers, and what will influence the restructuring of education for the 21st century, will have more to do with larger societal issues and values than in-house arguments within our small subset of education.

The articles by Lloyd Dunn (1968) and Evelyn Deno (1970) *were* representative of these larger societal forces at work in the late 1960s, but it was these larger influences, in my opinion, that were the driving force to change special education. The drive toward desegregation and the heightened social consciousness of discrimination as a way of life surely had more to do with the reshaping of special education at that time than any of the arguments within the field (see Semmel, Gerber, & MacMillan, Chapter 3).

Certainly no credence can be given to the notion that our programmatic structures were changed as the result of comprehensive research results that have yielded evidence moving us in one direction or another. Instead, it seems that the forces and people driving public policy often tend to extract, often from the research community and literature, those elements that seem supportive of the idea that they wish to promulgate and to ignore those that do not seem to support the current fashion (Gallagher, 1989). Such neglected research can hibernate in scholarly anonymity for a decade or more, only to be rediscovered when a different social and policy fashion comes into being.

In order for us to adequately understand our situation and for us to correctly identify what is needed to change it, we need to take a step back and look at these larger forces that seem to be affecting our organizations and institutions as well as our teaching methods. It is these hidden or more distant forces that I will focus on. The other articles in this issue [Ed. note. *The Journal of Special Education,* Vol. 27, No. 4] have touched upon these forces at one time or another (see, e.g., Gottlieb, Alter, Gottlieb, & Wishner, 1994).

EXPECTATIONS, OVER AND UNDER

What should we expect from our programs for exceptional children, given strong and positive educational intervention? The answer depends on our perception of the cause of the exceptionality in the first place. There has been substantial discussion about the likelihood that a poor cultural environment is responsible for a child being identified as mildly mentally retarded or learning disabled. We should ask questions about this assumption that rarely were asked in the 1970s. We have the luxury of posing issues long after the time when fundamental assumptions should have been challenged.

For example, consider a child of 6 now testing in the mentally retarded range of development. What do we have a right to expect of such a youngster who would benefit from an outstanding educational intervention program? Do we believe that such a youngster might become a neurosurgeon or a lawyer? Or if not that, then perhaps the head of a dressmaking company or a director of a construction crew? Not any of those things? Despite an outstanding intervention program? When we ask such questions, and answer them, we begin to see our own limited expectations for our educational intervention program. We are not downgrading our programs to adjust this limited impact on the child. These limitations are biological or constitutional in nature; they are present and largely determine the result in adulthood no matter what the nature of the educational program might be.

The tale of the Japanese admiral is illustrative of our problem:

> During World War II a Japanese admiral was faced with a very difficult decision as to what path his fleet should take in the war in the Pacific. Having been excellently educated at UCLA, he knew games theory and decision theory and put his skills and knowledge to work. He carefully calculated the weights that should be applied to his two reasonable options and carefully selected which option held out the best opportunity for him.
>
> Sad to say for the Japanese admiral, his choice turned out most unhappily. His fleet was destroyed and he was disgraced. A natural question that could be posed is why, with his knowledge and skills, did he make such a mistake? Why did he choose the wrong path? The answer to this puzzle is even more interesting because, as it turns out, the admiral did not make a mistake. In fact, he *had* chosen the best of those paths available to him. The problem was that neither choice offered much hope for his fleet and his decision was only to maximize what turned out to be an unhappy set of choices under any circumstances.

When we apply this story to the situation faced by the 6-year-old youngster who has been identified as mentally retarded, we face a similar situation. We are faced with the same problem as the Japanese admiral: None of our potential options is extraordinarily favorable. We are faced with trying to maximize what is likely to be, in the end, a limited outcome no matter what choice we make.

We do not expect our 6-year-old youngster to become a neurosurgeon or a lawyer. We will be happy if he or she will become a skilled worker who is able to be self-sufficient and who is able to obtain consistent employment. When we try to assess the effectiveness of our educational intervention programs, we need to keep in mind the story of the Japanese admiral. We must understand that we have a limited set of options, and that, in all too many cases, few of the probabilities are in our favor.

If we are depressed by such facts, we shouldn't be. The fact that the youngster with cerebral palsy does not win the 100-yard dash does not make our habilitation program a failure, nor that our deaf child does not play Hamlet. We have to find a path between underestimating the potential of the child and being unrealistically optimistic about the outcome.

It is our expectations, our often unreasonable flights of fancy, that cause us to be depressed or to expect too much from ourselves and our colleagues, when we do, in fact, have the skills to help the child have a productive and happy life.

SPECIAL EDUCATION AS WE KNOW IT

There is little doubt that an era of special education ended in the late 1960s coincident with the publication of the two articles by Lloyd Dunn and Evelyn Deno. As many of the articles in this issue have pointed out, the reason for the impact of the two articles was only partially due to the arguments presented; it was also due to the times and the ecological circumstances. The articles were persuasive to many in the field of special education, who correctly perceived that they were telling the truth about our limitations (Edgar & Polloway, 1994).

Prior to the Dunn and Deno articles, there seemed to have been an unwritten treaty established between general education and special education. The essence of the treaty was that special education would agree to take from general education those students who were the most difficult to teach and most behaviorally difficult to manage in the classroom. In exchange, teachers and administrators in general education would support special education and its requirements for additional resources, with only the unspoken proviso that under no circumstances would special education bring these children back into the regular program. This treaty has now been broken by the new philosophy of *full inclusion,* and neither the special educators nor general educators are likely to be totally satisfied with the new situation.

The problem with the Dunn argument against special classes for children with mental retardation is that it assumed that if one type of environmental modification is a "failure," then "success" must lie in the opposite model. Instead, as Semmel et al. (Chapter 3) point out, success under any circumstances is a very difficult concept to identify or achieve, regardless of the type of environment or program that is provided to these students. In addition, there is very real evidence that the population of students now labeled as mentally retarded is quite different than it was merely a decade ago, when many youngsters of borderline mentality (based on IQ) were still being included in programs for students with mental retardation (Polloway, Patton, Smith, & Roderique, 1991).

As pointed out by Hallahan and Kauffman (Chapter 4), one of the limitations of special education has been to specify what "success" means in an educational program for children with mental retardation. Surely it does not mean that the students will perform at an average or superior level in academic coursework. It must mean, as Edgar and Polloway (1994) pointed out, that there should be an emphasis on outcomes of the program and the nature of the curriculum necessary to generate such outcomes. The outcomes that we are looking for are some kind of viable employment in adulthood and a reasonable life-style so that the student can enter the work force and have a productive and happy life. But to reach that goal, much work needs to be done at earlier stages of development.

SPECIAL EDUCATION AND DISCRIMINATION

We need to reassess at what developmental stage the decision should be made to separate those students who we expect will become skilled or semi-skilled workers from those students who are going on to more advanced and professional types of education. The reluctance to make this decision has stemmed in no small matter from educational administrators' fear of being called unfair. There is hardly a more devastating charge in the current social climate than to accuse someone of being unfair or discriminatory in their decision making toward various ethnic or social groups (Artiles & Trent, 1994).

The consequence of the fear of being accused of discrimination is that the decision to separate students for differential programming is delayed and delayed again by educational decision makers until relatively late in the secondary school program, by which time many students have been referred to special education or have been so discouraged and disheartened by their educational experience that they have dropped out, either physically or mentally, from the schools.

It is interesting to speculate the extent to which issues such as ability grouping would currently be before the public if the proportions of minority students in special education programs matched their proportions in the general population. In my opinion, it is the fear of courts and court action against special education for being discriminatory toward minorities that has been one of the prime driving forces toward restructuring of special education. Artiles and Trent (1994) spelled out the concern about overrepresentation. But what is overrepresentation? If children grow up in an environment unfavorable to education—or to the valuing of long-term goals, or of compliance to adult demands—then why should we be surprised that more youngsters from such families would be in educational difficulty than their proportions in the society?

In the end, it is the ability to master knowledge systems and to practice desirable skills that determines the success of students. Just as there is a disproportion of ethnic and racial membership in the National Basketball Association (no Asians, an "overrepresentation" of African-American players), which rather truly represents the degree to which these physical skills have been honed over hours of practice, so it is also true that there is disproportionality of ethnic and racial groups in areas where reading and studying are concerned. This is not to deny that there is justification for the concern of minority advocates that *some* special education programs have become dumping grounds where students have been put aside as a bother to the general education program. Any overall structural solution to our problem must deal with the issue of discrimination.

SPECIAL EDUCATION AS AN ENTRY TO SERVICES

Deno's cascade of services, now being interpreted as a comprehensive set of services and programs to meet the needs of varying levels of child problems in the educational setting, appears to be a reaction to an earlier structural problem in education. In many school systems, the only way to provide extra services to young children in educational difficulty was to refer them to special education because that is where the school psychologists, the counselors, and the specially trained teachers were housed. It has been the inadequate special resources provided to the general education stream that has been the problem for educators interested in helping students.

Chalfant's (1987) teacher referral teams represented one constructive approach to this problem of too many referrals to special education, invoking the strategy of case staffing children in educational difficulties *before* they are referred to special education and recommending courses of action that can be taken by the classroom teacher. Under such programs, it is possible to defer or eliminate many referrals to special education by making meaningful changes in the general education program for these students having educational problems.

EDUCATIONAL REFORM, RESTRUCTURING, AND FULL INCLUSION

We seem to be in another critical transitional era similar in this respect to the general social climate in which the Dunn and Deno articles appeared a quarter century ago. The present seems to be a watershed in education, a time when major changes are expected and anticipated by political decision makers. Too little has been made of the significance of the National Governor's Conference of 1989, wherein 50 governors of all conceivable political persuasions signed off on the "National Goals for Education" (America 2000) and the president of the United States adopted these goals as his own. Such an event could only have been possible if there were widespread dissatisfaction with the educational status quo.

If we are correct in our earlier assumption that larger social forces are at work in the shaping of educational policy, then what are those forces this time? Clearly, there is concern for equity in education. Are children of poor families or families from culturally different backgrounds getting a fair chance at a quality education? Fairness and equity are the key concepts, and the educational reaction to such concerns has been to return to an educational setting where children of all levels of ability, achievement, motivation, and family backgrounds would be together, more or less, ensuring that no group has been siphoned off and placed in an inferior setting with less opportunity.

Somewhat paradoxically, there also is a societal concern about excellence, particularly with the various studies showing American students lagging behind badly in comparison with other national groups of students (Stevenson & Lee, 1990). How this is affecting education currently seems to be largely in the assessment area, where talk of world class standards and authentic assessments is widely heard.

Children with disabilities are brought along in this values scheme with the concept of *full inclusion,* meaning that children with disabilities will be educated with children without disabilities and that no separate educational channels should be supported except under the direst of circumstances (Biklin, Ferguson, & Ford, 1989; Brown & Snell, 1993; Stainback, Stainback, & Forest, 1990). In this way, fairness, rather than discrimination, can be demonstrated, and children with disabilities, who have much to learn from their social peers, can have a more defensible education.

The article by Gottlieb et al. (1994) stressed the community-based education idea. Their concern is that "educational inclusion" will merely replicate an earlier model that has proven to be a failure for those students identified and referred to special education. One of the major differences in our thinking patterns must be to stop thinking of education as a place (school) and think of education as a continuing community responsibility. This is particularly true for students with severe learning disabilities or mental retardation, who can often learn much more in a job than they can by sitting in a classroom.

If families in desperate economic and social conditions are sending their children to the schools, then the solution is only partly within the school and partly within the community itself to change the unfavorable environment in which these students exist. At the present time, there would seem to be a radical swing from the concept that the problem exists *entirely* within the child to the equally unjustified conclusion that the problem lies *entirely* within the environment. Many of the people in the educational restructuring movement (e.g., Oakes, 1985; Slavin, 1988) seem to want to create an educational environment in which there is not only equal opportunity, but also equal outcomes. The rather banal slogan, "All children can learn," deliberately ignores the significant proposition that all children will not learn at the same pace or from the same base of knowledge.

One essential difficulty of the full inclusion philosophy is that it presumes that the children with learning disabilities or with mental retardation would be studying the same curriculum as the average student—but perhaps at a slower pace (Will, 1984). In reality, at the middle school or junior high school level, many specialists in the field of mental retardation stress a *functional curriculum* with concrete tasks and usable skills, such as computing sales tax, reading job descriptions, or writing a menu for a balanced diet (see Kauffman, Chapter 8). Many specialists recommend a curriculum for such students that focuses on learning useful skills and understandings that do not require a heavy burden of generalization or transfer (Deshler & Schumaker, 1986; Robinson, Patton, Polloway, & Sargent, 1989). Such a functional curriculum is not the preferred intellectual meal, however, for above-average students on their way to college. Nor is the abstract generalization required by the curriculum in college preparatory classes the proper educational diet for children with mental retardation.

THE INTEGRATION OF SPECIAL AND GENERAL EDUCATION

The problem of the melding of special education and regular education really is one of organization and structure. How does one administer the special services needed for exceptional children within a given school system? Should there be a parallel organization within the school system in which the director of curriculum for the regular program is paralled to the director of special education, and there are various parallel levels of organization creating a special organizational unit of special education? Such an organizational structure has often been designed as a parallel system encouraging little communication between general education and special education. How does one integrate such programs at some point below the superintendent level (Goodlad & Field, 1993)?

We should be clear in our understanding that the issues here involve more than just educational efficiency (Cullen & Pratt, 1992). They are, instead, issues of power and influence. If special education becomes merely a minor part of the general education system, then special education loses its voice in the power circles of the educational system and loses much of its ability to influence policy in that system at the local, state, and federal levels. One major question is, who sits at the table, who is "in the room" when the major policy issues of the schools are being considered? If there is a director of special education visible in the hierarchy of the school program, then it is likely that that person will be sitting in the room where the policy decisions are made. If special educators are merely one of many assistants to the general education administration, they likely will not be participants in policy meetings. Apart from anything else, this absence removes an important voice for the child who is different from key decisions in the school system.

And what are we to make of the Peter Pan phenomenon that seems to be gripping both regular and special educators, that is, the temptation to consider that all children will remain forever within the 10- to 12-year range? Few children with disabilities will go to law school or medical school, or even to college, so somewhere in the developmental progression in education these children should be separated from their nondisabled peers. How and when should this be done?

Also, is there not a considerable literature in special education suggesting that a goal of vocational success for children with mental retardation has to be planned long before the student is 17 or 18 but rather, must begin in a functional curriculum at middle school or before? So, how can we achieve both goals—a differentiated curriculum for exceptional children, but within the same social setting with other students?

SPECIAL EDUCATION RESPONSIBILITIES

Well, if we are being driven by these larger social forces, what are we to do? Are we merely a cue ball on the pool table of life to be pushed here and there as outside forces dictate? Not at all! We as special educators would seem to have two major sets of responsibilities; first, within the special education community, second, outside that community.

Special educators have been blamed for so many things that are clearly not their fault or responsibility that it becomes an easy excuse for special educators to say they have been the victims of social policy. But there is one responsibility that special educators should not avoid, and that is the design of a developmental curriculum from age 4 or 5 to adulthood that delineates the necessary tasks and skills to be learned at each educational level for the exceptional child, and the progressive building on prior skills that will lead to the child's becoming an effective worker and citizen. We have too often focused on a narrow band of the developmental process. Full inclusion is something that would seem to be most applicable to 8- to 10-year-olds but certainly not 13- to 15-year-olds (Skrtic, 1991). Full inclusion may fit into a part of a total developmental process, but only a part, and the maintenance of such strategies across the entire age range of growing up is clearly inapplicable.

The responsibilities outside the special education profession require us to point out forcefully that there is something amiss in the full inclusion plan—that fairness does not consist of educating all children in the same place at the same time (and with the same curriculum?) but in ensuring that the student has basic needs met and is traveling a well-thought-out road to a career and a satisfying life style. Whether that means being in the same educational setting from middle school onward is highly dubious in my opinion. It is not that we oppose "fairness"; rather, we wish to define it in a more appropriate way.

CONTRIBUTIONS OF SPECIAL EDUCATION

In the past, special education has been a leader in fields such as educational technology and the use of psychological services. Special education, once again, has an opportunity to lead in multidisciplinary programming with an emphasis on the family in the early childhood field. Part H of IDEA has encouraged the states to provide a comprehensive, multidisciplinary, interagency program for infants and toddlers with disabilities and their families (Gallagher, Trohanis, & Clifford, 1989).

It is always easier to introduce substantial changes in the service delivery patterns when you are starting from scratch, as in the early childhood area, as opposed to trying to change well-established patterns, as would be necessary in the public schools. The long experience of special education in working with families and with working across agencies and disciplines can establish the pattern that will shape the early childhood field, as the general education early childhood effort is only now beginning to gather steam (Gallagher, 1989).

The future that we face may well require us to be sociologists and anthropologists as well as diagnosticians and planners of curriculum. We must be aware of those social forces that often are more important than the arguments within the academy in determining the shape of the future.

REFERENCES

Artiles, A. J., & Trent, S. C. (1994). Overrepresentation of minority students in special education: A continuing debate. *The Journal of Special Education, 27,* 410–437.

Biklin, D., Ferguson, D., & Ford, A. (1989). Schooling and disability. Part II. *Eighty-eighth yearbook of the National Society for the Study of Education.* Chicago: University of Chicago Press.

Brown, F., & Snell, M. E. (1993). Meaningful assessment. In M. Snell (Ed.), *Instruction of students with severe disabilities* (4th ed., pp. 61–98). New York: Merrill.

Chalfant, J. (1987). Providing services to all students with learning problems: Implications for policy and programs. In S. Vaughn & C. Bos (Eds.), *Research in learning disabilities: Issues and future directions.* Boston: Little, Brown.

Cullen, B., & Pratt, T. (1992). Measuring and reporting student progress. In *Curriculum considerations in inclusive classrooms: Facilitating learning for all students* (pp. 175–196). Baltimore: Brookes.

Deno, E. (1970). Special education as developmental capital. *Exceptional Children, 37,* 229–237.

Deshler, D. D., & Schumaker, J. B. (1986). Learning strategies: An instructional alternative for low-achieving adolescents. *Behavioral Disorders, 7,* 207–212.

Dunn, L. (1968). Special education for the mildly retarded—Is much of it justifiable? *Exceptional Children, 35,* 5–22.

Edgar, E., & Polloway, E. A. (1994). Education for adolescents with disabilities: Curriculum and placement issues. *The Journal of Special Education, 27,* 438–452.

Gallagher, J. (1989). The impact of policies for handicapped children in future early education policy. *Phi Delta Kappan, 71,* 121–124.

Gallagher, J., Trohanis, P., & Clifford, R. (1989). *Policy implementation and P.L. 99-457.* Baltimore: Brookes.

Goodlad, J. I., & Field, S. (1993). Teachers for renewing schools. In J. Goodlad & T. Lovitt (Eds.), *Integrating general and special education* (pp. 229–252). New York: Merrill.

Gottlieb, J., Alter, M., Gottlieb, B. W., & Wishner, J. (1994). Special education in urban America: It's not justifiable for many. *The Journal of Special Education, 27,* 453–465.

Oakes, J. (1985). *Keeping track: How schools structure inequality.* New Haven, CT: Yale University Press.

Polloway, E., Patton, J., Smith, J., & Roderique, T. (1991). Issues in program design for elementary students with mild retardation: Emphasis on curriculum development. *Education and Training in Mental Retardation, 26,* 142–150.

Robinson, G., Patton, J., Polloway, E., & Sargent, L. (1989). *Best practices in mild mental disabilities.* Reston, VA: Council for Exceptional Children.

Skrtic, T. (1991). *Behind special education.* Denver, CO: Love.

Slavin, R. (1988). Synthesis of research on grouping in elementary and secondary schools. *Education Leadership, 46,* 67–77.

Stainback, S., Stainback, W., & Forest, M. (Eds.). (1990). *Educating all students in the mainstream of regular education.* Baltimore: Brookes.

Stainback, S., Stainback, W., & Slavin, R. (1989). Classroom organization for diversity among students. In S. Stainback, W. Stainback, & M. Forest (Eds.), *Educating all students in the mainstream of regular education.* Baltimore: Brookes.

Stevenson, H. W., & Lee, S. (1990). Context of achievement. *Monographs of the Society for Research in Child Development, 55.*

Will, M. (1984). Educating children with learning problems: A shared responsibility. *Exceptional Children, 52,* 411–415.

Chapter 7

Comments From a Biased Viewpoint

William C. Morse

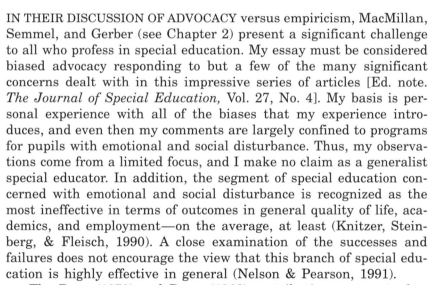

IN THEIR DISCUSSION OF ADVOCACY versus empiricism, MacMillan, Semmel, and Gerber (see Chapter 2) present a significant challenge to all who profess in special education. My essay must be considered biased advocacy responding to but a few of the many significant concerns dealt with in this impressive series of articles [Ed. note. *The Journal of Special Education,* Vol. 27, No. 4]. My basis is personal experience with all of the biases that my experience introduces, and even then my comments are largely confined to programs for pupils with emotional and social disturbance. Thus, my observations come from a limited focus, and I make no claim as a generalist special educator. In addition, the segment of special education concerned with emotional and social disturbance is recognized as the most ineffective in terms of outcomes in general quality of life, academics, and employment—on the average, at least (Knitzer, Steinberg, & Fleisch, 1990). A close examination of the successes and failures does not encourage the view that this branch of special education is highly effective in general (Nelson & Pearson, 1991).

The Deno (1970) and Dunn (1968) contributions came at what was, for me, an interesting professional time. We were working in two school districts to transfer some of the techniques developed at

Reprinted, with changes, from "Comments from a biased viewpoint," by William C. Morse, *The Journal of Special Education,* Vol. 27, 1994, 531–542. Copyright © 1994 by PRO-ED, Inc.

a group therapy camp for disturbed boys to public school settings where programs for disturbed pupils lagged behind other specializations. The standard assistance was referral to child guidance clinics when referral was possible. School liaison was rare and limited. School psychologists and school social workers were growing in numbers but still inadequate. The education–mental health liaison had a fundamental dissonance then that persists today; it makes one wince to hear present predictions that final solutions for programs for disturbed pupils will be achieved through the shotgun marriage of the two agencies (Morse, 1992). Until both disciplines change substantively, there will be limited gains for their students/clients.

At any rate, we were working in two school systems to develop programs for disturbed pupils. One development eventually became the crisis of helping teachers using Life Space Interviewing: This style of aid flourished in the two systems until the legal requirements of the federal legislation co-opted resources. In this approach, children did not have to be labeled or admitted by formal special education rituals, were not removed from the mainstream as home base, and service was based on actual behavior. Simultaneously, the two school systems were initiating another service of the "cascade," special segregated classes employing both intensive special education and mental health intervention. And along came Dunn and Deno.

My reaction to Dunn was very superficial. As the excitement grew, I ignored his arguments as too broad, really conclusions from too little evidence. None of this was on the sophisticated grounds brought forth in the current papers. Dunn said nothing about the quality of the classes: A rotten class is a rotten class, special or regular. I knew of efforts to help disturbed kids that were really deleterious. Anyway, he was speaking of students with mental retardation, and I held then and now that there are differences in what particular special children need and where they can best be served. As an individual psychologist, I find it uncalled for to consider all children with the same designation as equal, as is done for a class action decision. Also, it would have been interesting to know if certain children in either of Dunn's settings made progress while others might have regressed. My suspicions about unanalyzed average differences have grown with the years.

Then and now, I wondered at the big impact of Dunn's article. Several of the current authors bring out that Dunn found a cordial climate where many professionals were suspicious about the promises of special education classes as they existed. As to the disproportion of African-American students, failure to compare similar white socioeconomic groups prevents clarification of what part of overrepresentation is prejudice, as poverty is a devastating condition for all children, as Gottlieb, Alter, Gottlieb, and Wishner (1994) demonstrated so vividly. But added to poverty is the overt and covert racial prejudice, which most of us have seen firsthand, the causes and possible cures for which were analyzed in detail by Artiles and Trent (1994). This prejudice is reflected throughout education in discipline, exclusions, and career counseling, as well as special education.

As several of the authors state, Dunn should be neither damned nor praised for all that is attributed to his article. The total inclusion push became powerful not on the basis of Dunn, but as a product of a particular interpretation of a civil rights extension to those with disabilities, combined with severe budget problems in education. Such a combination of holiness and financial stress is difficult to resist, as is all too evident. Some professionals who helped to bring about the current rash of criticisms by overpromising results for special education classes are now overpromising again for inclusion. Who was in charge when we separated beyond functional need, ignored parents, neglected racial prejudice, and created a massive self-perpetuating infrastructure of rules and regulations? All of us were involved. If special education does collapse, there are many of us who participated. For those who are socioemotionally disturbed, it is professionals who are giving the sage advice to imitate mental health and deinstitutionalize. Will we put them on streets or in the school halls, or remove them to solitary home-bound teaching?

Inclusion for students who are socially and emotionally disturbed has usually been accompanied by diminished services: In one district where they closed their day school but did maintain the same level of inservice, it was necessary to hire many additional staff to serve the dispersed population. Often, total inclusion is in reality for all but the disturbed pupils. Regardless of Dunn, these two school systems went ahead with plans for segregated classes, with integration where possible. In retrospect, we erred in not maximizing integration through creative planning. Since there was a waiting list of pupils with severe disturbance, there was no worry about those with mild disturbance being included. We did not see Dunn's propositions as being prescriptive for all extruded special education students. It is interesting that, as the plans for the two systems evolved, one school allowed only 1 year of separate class while the other had no limit. And it soon became clear that some children needed more than the special class. Because there were no day schools then, this meant hospital treatment—even more exclusion. We were fortunate to have a high-quality service available. Parents, for the most part, had high hopes for the special class placement: For once, they were not bombarded with calls from school to come and get their unmanageable offspring. Parents were not required to accept counseling, only to come to the regular parent–teacher conference. At the time Dunn wrote, none of us saw that he boded ill for special education. We were deaf to the possibility and blind to our own shortcomings.

One of the biggest changes in special education has taken place in ideology. Now there are those special educators who see their field as corrupt and damaging to children, even though they continue to produce new crops of teachers every year through their classes. Yet, at least in the area of disturbance, there are those special teachers working on the front line who still feel they are doing the right thing to help youngsters through special classes. Given a modicum of support, they continue to work and even in some cases to turn pupils' lives around in spite of confounding pupil ecologies. Turning around one life makes the class cost-effective to the community, to say nothing of the child's life gains. But the work is very taxing, and the field continues to have the highest turnover rate. Lack of adequate support, stultifying rules, and outlandish expectations induce fatigue.

In contrast to my reaction to Dunn's article, my reaction to Deno's article was positive. I saw it as relevant and encouraging to what the school districts were planning. The cascade concept supported our plans. Decisions were made informally at the start, justice being subject to professional ethic. We were not aware then that we were party to a buildup of a legal bureaucracy, especially one that was part and parcel of the increasingly flawed general educational system (Skrtic, 1991). We did worry about how one could decide where on the continuum of service to best help a student. Trial and error was patently unfair. Unfortunately or not, depending upon one's viewpoint, the promise of a continuum was never fully realized in most programs countrywide. Even when complete, every level felt helpless, with some children too damaged to respond to the resources available to them. The point is that, if Deno's cascade is to function as intended, there must be an assurance of services and utilization of services for that small percentage of the most serious cases.

Studying these sophisticated papers reflecting on 25 years of Deno and Dunn, one is impressed by the erudition and insight displayed. The experience is like attending an advanced special education seminar. In fact, this issue could be a text for such an enterprise. Even those who try to keep abreast of the literature on these matters stand to be impressed by the scrutiny of the literature and the astute search for meaning as well as the additional original research reported. Of course, there is the advantage of hindsight. What would these authors have written at the time of the original publications?

Some of Dunn's references were suspect even then, and the violation of the scientific paradigm of randomness should have been evident. Ecological considerations have reduced blame of the victim to a considerable degree. The basic orientation has also changed from process to final outcome evaluation. In this respect, the outcomes for students who are disturbed are the poorest: The quality of their lives, school level, and employment all are discouraging. Follow-up studies suggest that, if you want the most favorable results, you should assess outcomes within a short time after intervening: The longer the delay, the more these pupils slip back *on the average,* even though some do successfully join the mainstream. This again illustrates that special education is not about categories, although such arguments are an academic pastime. It is about individual children, not labels. Disturbed children represent a polyglot group with even more polyglot environments. In what cases is special education the significant cause of success or failure in outcomes when the youngster usually goes back to the same school, family, and community ecology that was influential in creating the initial plight that made for eligibility? It is painful to acknowledge that special education was never meant to meet mental health needs of children and youth in the first place, but only to give some sort of emotional bandages, and then only for certain ones (not to exceed 2% of the population) whose school learning was fouled up by their emotional state. Surveys show that, at a minimum, twice that number are seriously disturbed and some 12% more are known to need some assistance. The valiant effort to reach parents (who have rights but not obligations and are often overwhelmed themselves) pays off when it can be managed. But the ecology is frequently impervious to change (Morse, 1993). Chaos theory certainly applies to the field of special education, as Guess and Sailor (1993) suggested. We are in an enterprise far too complex for simplistic answers.

UNDERLYING ISSUES

As one studies the two original articles and this current set, certain underlying issues emerge. Although these issues are not always explicit, each of us holds a position on these variables, and these positions bear on subsequent argument. Overt or covert, such positions become predispositions for advocacy decisions.

Does extruded special education have the potential for helping youngsters or is it inherently a flawed and negative intervention?

Another seldom-discussed matter in all the arguments about where the child sits is the real issue of the appropriateness and quality of what the child gets. Several of the authors point this out. There are individual differences in classes as well as differences in individuals, and by what criterion do we randomize classes? Dunn must have had some high-quality classes and some low, as well as pupils in each who flourished and others who regressed. The question for research should be this: For what pupils are what class elements appropriate? There are obviously indications and contraindications, as results in general are variable. It already looks as if, for children who are disturbed, ecological factors rather than class factors may be dominant in the long run. Generalizations in special education are as spurious and primitive as comparing those who had therapy with those who didn't, with no control of the essential variable: therapy. The match of templates between individual need and what is provided is at issue (Bem, 1979). Special education is supposed to be an individualized matter, and as yet we depend upon average differences (sometimes of minimal practical significance) for policy decisions, rather than examining subprofiles or templates.

Do the negative aspects of special education inevitably overbalance the positive? If special education means a lower teacher–pupil ratio, individualization, and highly trained teachers, how can it be a negative influence unless miserably executed? Once, when we were meeting to place a special pupil back in good old regular education, the receiving teacher could not see the value of haste. "You have the ideal education now, which I wished I had—small group, individualized curriculum. Every pupil should have it so good, especially some of my 28." There are still those who see special education as health producing rather than as a fatal disease. MacMillan, Semmel, and Gerber (see Chapter 2) raise this issue. Perhaps negative attitudes can be managed by special education subcultures, as Hallahan and Kauffman propose, or by direct counseling, as I have found. Of course, there will need to be overall antidiscrimination efforts as well, because we live in a scapegoating culture. Some of our pupils who are disturbed fought over being called "retards." They announced they were not "retards" but "disturbed." We cannot ignore the meaning of a label to the child who is given it, even though most have previously undergone self- and peer-labeling.

Rejecting the value of special education, as many pupils do, is a generic problem in education today, when many high school students hold negative attitudes about their education. They are joined by some high-powered critics. The services of education and the mode of delivery must be seen as relevant by the consumer. One self-referred adolescent refused the peer efforts at negative contagion because, as he told them, he saw the special class as a solution to his dilemma. The impact of being special turns out to be an individual person–ecology matter. Yet there are a number of special educators who "know" that special education is evil for all pupils. In the subtle process of any human helping, can we operate on pretense?

What should be the obligation of education in general to society, and in turn what should be the relationship of special education to general education? What purpose is assigned these two agencies? There is obvious disparity in the answers to this question. An economist once wrote that the function of the schools as a societal grant agency is to provide a massive child-sitting service and to keep adolescents off the streets and out of the employment market. The chain of relationships between society, education, and special education embodies profound philosophical arguments; we all have our opinions. Neither regular nor special education is a free-floating operation. We resist special education as handmaiden to regular education, thus "letting regular education continue in errant ways." Special educators seem to be embarrassed by being forced to play second violin. Because the community seldom speaks with one voice, there are many power plays and compromises concerning obligations. General education finds itself forced to add to the basics in response to societal problems, from driver education to AIDS education. Special education adds new categories.

So much depends upon societal attitudes toward special children, which have waxed and appear now to have plateaued if not waned in the financial crisis. Outcome data replace guilt as a driving force. The papers collected in this issue are attentive to the social changes in the last 25 years and the implications for special services. Social change, as Deno emphasized (1994), is a euphemism for the disintegration of the child-raising function. Neither regular education, with its push for excellence and higher graduation requirements, nor special education, with its spawning categories, has taken change seriously. At best, as Guess and Sailor (1993) have stated, the educational agencies look piecemeal at the situation, which calls for massive and coordinated alterations in society itself. Who really believes the changes proposed for Education 2000 will be accomplished? If the predictions turn out to be accurate, what will happen to special education?

Rather than Bushism dreams, we can best expect spots of progressive change in the configurations of education, not universal metamorphosis. When change happens, it will be the consequence of a coming together of a series of conditions welded in shape by astute and ethical local leadership. It is fascinating how, when there is a scarcity of resources to help students in dire need, such as Gottlieb et al. (1994) described, special educators distort their system to get help for children by making them special pupils. It is easier to do this than to get the proper changes in the system. We are reminded again of the late Eli Bower's comment that institutions that start out to serve children gradually convert to the cause of self-perpetuation.

Perhaps some of the differences of opinion about the original two articles go back to assumptions about the respective roles of regular and special education in society. Fred Weintraub (personal communication, 1992) once explained that there are three different basic assumptions about education. One is that equity means providing each student with the same opportunity and that those who can learn do, with an expected range in achievement. A second theory is that we give to each on the basis of individual need, thus eliminating individual differences in accomplishment. A third is that we give to each according to need but still expect significant individual differences. The variant paradigms are latent in the minds of administrators, teachers, and parents in every Individualized Education Program conference.

At a gross level of abstraction, we all agree that every child deserves a free appropriate, public education. The pinch comes in allotment of scarce resources. It is similar to the public debate on health care: Who is to get how much? When it comes to tax support, districts that are eliminating distinctly visible special education programs (saving money in a reduction of the hands-on time by assuming that consultation will suffice) are finding it more difficult to pass taxes—no visible program, no money. I have heard one national leader of inclusion mention (but only in passing) that our special funds are something we will have to protect as we move to full inclusion. Next fantasy? It would be helpful if writers during the great debates would post their position on the role of regular education vis-à-vis special education.

A related source of different opinions rests in beliefs concerning the mutability of individual differences. Our youngsters represent the extensions of the distribution in various dimensions. We hold different ideas about how and what children can learn. In truth, there may be no general answer to mutability, even though we hold our positions on the debate. The body politic led by the always changing scientific zeitgeist expects greater or less potential from environmental interventions. We are now seeing the ascendance of the neural–chemical explanation for variant behavior, even to the point of differential biological etiology for various modes of aggression!

Chemical treatment is rising in importance. Even though the resolution of the malleability debate can be achieved only in a specific individual situation, some apply a fixed view to a variety of conditions in planning meetings. If a practice helps one child, it should also work for any child, and the school should implement the practice. In some instances, the sponsors of cures refuse to allow any evaluative research. Special education becomes a matter of faith.

Perhaps the most important contribution of the federal legislation was the recognition of individual differences as the cornerstone for the new special education. While we are all equal before the law in certain regards, we are not all equal before the blackboard. There was even the faint hope that regular education might embrace the concept and do away with their 12 categories known as grades. Some schools have achieved the semblance of individual planning. The preschool legislation requires a family plan—every child should have a continually evolving, developmentally appropriate life plan. The legislation made explicit the most important premise: Each child goes to her or his own school. Teachers are often hard put to motivate attendance at the school where they teach. However, we all know teachers who do pass this miracle every day, at least until the pupils are adolescents. Incidentally, the article on adolescence by Edgar and Polloway (1994) addressed a neglected aspect of individual differences—developmental age differences. The world of the child changes with age, and so must special education. Specifically, the implication of inclusion–separation will differ with age as well as specific individual factors.

Unfortunately, the individual differences that dominate the narrow-gauge, regular educational assembly line have to do with cognitive intelligence. As Gardner's (1991) conceptualization indicates, this is but one of the seven multiple intelligences. Special education has yet to capitalize on his formulation. There are individual differences not only in child capacity, but also in how various pupils learn. Part of the time, the arguments we have reside in our concepts of each child's uniqueness and the individuality of learning.

The power and central place of caring in special education is often ignored. Special education is billed as a caring enterprise. Such an illusive quality as caring finds no home in our research, yet it may be a crucial variable. Perhaps because of my focus on pupils who are disturbed, I look for more attention to affective components in children's lives. Edgar and Polloway (1994) did indicate the need for caring. Several authors speak of self-concept and self-esteem, which are not always clearly distinguished. Hallahan and Kauffman (see Chapter 4) discuss the ambiguity of the research on self-esteem in special pupils. Because of the centrality of self-esteem and self-efficacy, perhaps each concept deserves more attention. As Markus and Nurius (1986) have demonstrated, children have more than a single self-concept tied to their hopes for the future: Some future selves are fearful and others encouraging as they relate to sense of self-efficacy in controlling their lives. In talking with special children, it is seldom that the special education experience has been deeply related to the present and future self-potentials. Special education is just another adult manipulation in the pupil's oft-manipulated life. Adolescents often say, in retrospect, "If it hadn't been for that class and teacher, I would have never made it." The point of beginning in special education is to seek relevance to the self in this non-choice "opportunity." It is psychological abuse to ignore the meaning to the individual. The most difficult challenge is education for the delinquents who have lost hope. Many of them also believe the future self is in the hands of fate; as one said, "fifty-fifty"—it's college or prison for the future self. Deno (1994) talked in general about the social malaise, and she might even have gone sharper. There are special pupils who live in constant fear for themselves and their protectors. There are classes and even schools where our pupils don't feel protected.

Special education is declared a caring profession, yet little is said about the rehabilitative function of teacher caring as an essential special education ingredient, even in the discussion of the increasing number of children stultified by not being cared for. How many of Dunn's classes were caring places? It is difficult to be a partial surrogate parent to 30 youngsters and no simple matter even with 10. Caring by consultation requires even more imaginative extension. Yet caring is what many special children most need. Caring requires hands-on relationships. We would like to remake families as the central source of essential caring. Sometimes we can: Too often such changes elude us. The school and other agencies will have to become caring if we expect to socialize our children and make them secure in this neglectful society. Noddings (1992) has delineated the challenge. Sarason (1985) for the first time added education to the mental health holy trinity in his book on caring and compassion. Of course, a special class does nothing more than increase the opportunity for caring; it does not give a guarantee.

While somewhat fleeting attention is given to the emotional life of pupils and teachers, there are glib expectations of great positive changes in public and teacher attitudes toward special children. This seems especially dubious in the present "skinhead" climate. But there is no argument that it is a task we must undertake. My caution: Go easy on the wishful thinking, and do not make our special children pay the price of exaggerated anticipations of acceptance.

There are a number of cogent observations about how society has changed in the years since the original articles, starting with Deno (1994). We have moved from a nation at risk to a nation of children at risk. In spite of well-intended Great Society programs, we now have an underclass in which poverty dooms the lives of many children, as Gottlieb et al. (1994) so well demonstrated. When these social changes are added up, it makes for a different world of childhood and thus a presumed different school life. The battle has been joined in the school change literature between excellence goals for world competition and the goals of compensatory support to meet the needs of those who are deprived. The matrix of forces from populist to professional is played out in local and state school boards, currently only superseded by budget dilemmas. While all levels of society are at risk for reactions to the vast social changes depicted, there is a concentration of multiple risk factors in large population centers. Studies in one state indicate that half the students are at risk for unproductive lives. While special education gets the fallout of the regular school, the regular school gets the fallout of society. It has been pointed out that the majority of the children in some schools are candidates for special services: Gottlieb et al. (1994) made this only too clear. The conditions are more than poverty, though they find poverty the major culprit. There is also the massive social disorganization in basic cultural institutions, particularly the family and the economy. Will the family structure restabilize or further diffuse? Will there ever be enough jobs above subsistence level to go around in the future? And are not special students the most in jeopardy?

The enormity of the task confronting us encourages retreats to the latest announced rapid cure-all for special children. Eli Bower characterized what happened to community psychology as a retreat to private office practice when confronted with the dismaying task of changing the community life. While pondering these papers, one can wonder if we are belaboring the most important issues. Certainly, the papers shed new light on special education with careful presentation of research. But is this where it's at?

Finally, are we paying enough attention to the impact of research findings and policy decisions on the role of the primary help given, the regular and special teacher? Several of the papers, particularly those of Semmel, Gerber, and MacMillan (see Chapter 3) and Hallahan and Kauffman (Chapter 4), took the refreshing stance of including the service deliverer in their analyses. Mandates come down from on high, but the nature of the child's experience is largely formulated by the regular or special teacher and the integrity of the support. If there are advantages to a special class, large credit goes to the teacher. If there are advantages to the mainstream class, again we must credit the teacher and the elements of the work setting. Special teachers often report their greatest frustration is not the problem children but the problem system, which stymies what they could be doing. In fact, many effective teachers are habitual rule breakers.

With the increased numbers of high-need, developmentally unfinished children in regular classes today, many teachers find themselves fatigued to the point of zombie-like responses. Daily survival becomes the main goal (Tompkins & Tompkins-McGill, 1993). If one asks an audience of teachers how many would quit and take another equal-pay position, it is not uncommon that half the professionals would leave. The turnover of teachers of students who are socially and emotionally disturbed is at the crisis level.

Whatever the argument concerning inclusion, what happens to the teacher role has to be a primary concern, second only to what happens to the child. There are examples of included children who are there but who are "out of it." They are sitting in a regular education seat but lost in the process because there is not enough square inch of teacher to individualize—which is the birthright of special education. This is not to say that there are no teachers who have the Midas touch, but there are many who do not. If inservice education (or preservice for that matter) were as successful as some seem to expect, we would not have many of the problems we now face. Many of the difficulties teachers face every day result from contagion and require group rather than individual solutions. Teachers are group workers, but most have little or no training in group dynamics.

ARE THERE HOPEFUL SIGNS EMERGING FROM OUR CHAOS?

Most of our authors give attention to what can be done about the problems their research raises, sometimes presenting solutions in explicit detail. Twenty-five years hence we will know how realistic the ideas were. Twenty-five years ago, and again today, much hope for a more justified special education rests on pending changes in regular education. Current crises and dissatisfaction with schools have produced federal, state, and local mandates for change, usually with little said about special education. Advocates of equity and excellence spar. Often the courts become the decisive arbiter. School reorganization ranges from waiting it out until the craze dies down, to cosmetic alterations and occasionally a significant revolution. Because reorganization emphasizes local empowerment and community participation, the tendency is to spend considerable effort on process and committees. Building principals, in whom local empowerment takes place, are confronted with power loss and role changes. Leadership by committee is a new turn for the educational bureaucracy. Local empowerment counters the imposition of any model or even effort to examine critically the available wisdom on problems. Each effort is an individual case study. We are a diverse society, so we expect diverse outcomes. But it would expedite matters to have some promising images as guidelines.

One of the few writers concerned with both how children learn and what they need to learn is Gardner (1991) and, to a lesser extent, Noddings (1992). It is interesting that both go back to Dewey, although with some critical additions. Gardner emphasizes relevancy, apprenticeship, and what he calls natural museum-type learning based on work being done in schools where he develops his ideas. Often special education is virtually ignored in school reorganization. For disturbed pupils, William Rhodes is about to publish a new curriculum/method aimed at empowering the students to control their own lives. This constitutes a specific example of restructuring in one area of special education. As important as cooperative learning and collaboration are, do we not have to go beyond this level for needed changes?

There is not much discussion about the role of prereferral to foster inclusion, though this is required in some special education programs. As an intervention, prereferral intends to reduce certifications by maximizing assistance in the mainstream setting. While the goal is to save money and prevent the negative effects of certification, if adequate service can be generated to alleviate the impasse of both the child and the teacher, what could be better as a first step in rational inclusion?

One of the resources not emphasized by Deno is crisis intervention support to the pupil, teacher, and classroom at the point of the pupil's failure to cope. If we are to include pupils who are disturbed, we need to have some immediate rescue service, such as the helping or crisis teacher mentioned above. This is direct hands-on service, not consultation. Intimate collaboration with the classroom teacher is essential. Such assistance need not require certification or separation beyond processing the precipitating episode, be it acting out or depressive withdrawal. But it also becomes the natural way to move in on persistent problems in a sustained way. Diagnosis is continual and driven by the particular problem rather than by the certification label. Because the curriculum aspects as well as behavior may be involved, the crisis person is trained both in teaching and mental health skills. It would seem that inclusion for pupils who are disturbed implies an available crisis resource.

But to some there is one movement pending that supersedes these changes. Thinking in broader terms of social restructuring to meet the needs of all children, there is the concept of the Full Service School (FSS). Perhaps I am enthusiastic about this new approach because it is the logical way to improve not only special education for children who are disturbed, but also the multiple service needs of many other children and their families. There are two major thrusts to agency collaboration. One is the generation of a community-based comprehensive spectrum of services (Epstein, Quinn, Nelson, Polsgrove, & Cumblad, 1993) called the Child and Adolescent Service System Program (CASSP) (Stroul, 1985). The obstacles to getting broad agency collaboration are formidable, as anyone who has tried to get even two agencies to cooperate will attest (Schlenger et al., 1992).

A more manageable effort is the full-service school (FSS), an alternative being developed in Florida and being monitored by Lynn Lavely and Neal Berger at the College of Education in the University of South Florida. In the FSS, community agencies serving children and their families have representatives on the school campus. The goal is one-stop service aimed at family preservation by connecting parents and children with relevant services through a case coordinator. The interagency working group proposes that a full-service school serve as a central point of delivery for whatever education, health, social/human, and/or employment services are locally needed. A possible advantage is that, rather than expending huge amounts of energy to get agency collaboration, the thrust is providing actual services to those in need. The essential point is that restructuring schools or special education, no matter how well done, will not necessarily serve the needs of children, especially special children. The school cannot and should not be expected alone to meet all needs of children. The idea of "ancillary" as applied to special education services is misleading. No needed service is ancillary. The FSS is service oriented to individualized planning. There is also evidence of the various disciplines participating with teachers in relevant curriculum as well.

Finally, it will not suffice just to articulate services if the services continue doing their business as usual. All services, not just the school, face the need to reinvent their practice and become more caring. If education needs to restructure practice to be responsive to the social realities of the day, should not the same hold for health, mental health, legal, and welfare services as well?

REFERENCES

Artiles, A. J., & Trent, S. C. (1994). Overrepresentation of minority students in special education: A continuing debate. *The Journal of Special Education, 27,* 410–437.

Bem, D. J. (1979). Assessing persons and situations with the template matching technique. In L. R. Kahle (Ed.), *Methods for studying person-situation interactions* (pp. 1–17). San Francisco: Jossey-Bass.

Deno, E. (1970). Special education as developmental capital. *Exceptional Children, 37,* 229–237.

Deno, E. (1994). Special education as developmental capital revisited: A quarter-century appraisal of means versus ends. *The Journal of Special Education, 27,* 375–392.

Dunn, L. (1968). Special education for the mildly retarded—Is much of it justifiable? *Exceptional Children, 35,* 5–22.

Edgar, E., & Polloway, E. A. (1994). Education for adolescents with disabilities: Curriculum and placement issues. *The Journal of Special Education, 27,* 438–452.

Epstein, M. H., Quinn, K., Nelson, C. M., Polsgrove, L., & Cumblad, C. (1993). Serving students with emotional and behavioral disorders through a comprehensive community-based approach. *OSERS, 5*(1), 19–23.

Gardner, H. (1991). *The unschooled mind: How children think and schools should teach.* New York: Basic Books.

Gottlieb, J., Alter, M., Gottlieb, B. W., & Wishner, J. (1994). Special education in urban America: It's not justifiable for many. *The Journal of Special Education, 27,* 453–465.

Guess, D., & Sailor, W. (1993). Chaos theory and the study of human behavior: Implications for special education and developmental disabilities. *Journal of Learning Disabilities, 27*(1), 16–34.

Knitzer, J., Steinberg, Z., & Fleisch, B. (1990). *At the school house door.* New York: Bank Street School.

Markus, H., & Nurius, P. (1986). Possible selves. *American Psychologist, 41,* 954–969.

Morse, W. C. (1992). Mental health professionals and teachers: How do the twain meet. *Beyond Behavior, 3*(2), 12–20.

Morse, W. C. (1993). Ecological approaches. In T. R. Kratochwill & R. J. Morris (Eds.), *Handbook of psychotherapy with children and adolescents* (pp. 320–356). Boston: Allyn & Bacon.

Nelson, C. M., & Pearson, C. A. (1991). *Integrating services for children and youth with emotional and behavioral disorders.* Reston, VA: Council for Exceptional Children.

Noddings, N. (1992). *The challenge to care in the schools: An alternative approach to education.* New York: Teachers College Press.

Sarason, S. B. (1985). *Caring and compassion in clinical practice.* San Francisco: Jossey-Bass.

Schlenger, W. E. et al. (1992). The evaluation of state efforts to improve systems of care for children and adolescents with severe emotional disturbances: The CASSP initial cohort study. *The Journal of Mental Health Administration, 19,* 131–143.

Skrtic, T. M. (1991). The special education paradox: Equity as the way to excellence. *Harvard Educational Review, 61,* 85–99.

Stroul, B. (1985). *The child and adolescent service system program (CASSP) system change strategies.* Washington DC: CASSP Technical Center at Georgetown University.

Tompkins, J. R., & Tompkins-McGill, P. L. (1993). *Surviving in schools in the 1990s.* Lanham, MD: University Press of America.

Part II

Policy Analyses
and Commentaries

The essays in Part II address the conceptual bases and policy implications of the inclusion movement. The Regular Education Initiative (REI) was an important precursor of the later inclusive schools movement. The first essay discusses the emergence of the REI, its connections to the conservative political agenda and rhetoric of the 1980s, and its implications for special education. The second explains why the movement to merge general and special education is misguided and offers an alternative set of assumptions regarding the relationship between general and special education. The third essay calls for reform of special education that could be considered radical in that it would be based on measured changes based on careful, logical analyses and reliable empirical data rather than on simplistic images and ideologies. Finally, in an essay explaining how special education has been radicalized by the full inclusion bandwagon, Fuchs and Fuchs expose the relationships among advocacy groups, and their agendas, that have put the field in increasingly dangerous straits.

Together, these commentaries and analyses raise questions about how and why the full inclusion movement has become the focal point of controversy in special education. They also raise questions about the conceptual bases of full inclusion and offer alternative views on what a prudent course for the field would be.

Chapter 8

The Regular Education Initiative as Reagan-Bush Education Policy: A Trickle-Down Theory of Education of the Hard-to-Teach

James M. Kauffman

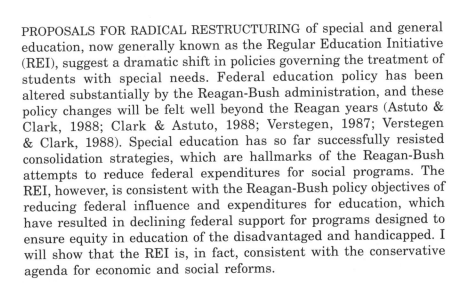

PROPOSALS FOR RADICAL RESTRUCTURING of special and general education, now generally known as the Regular Education Initiative (REI), suggest a dramatic shift in policies governing the treatment of students with special needs. Federal education policy has been altered substantially by the Reagan-Bush administration, and these policy changes will be felt well beyond the Reagan years (Astuto & Clark, 1988; Clark & Astuto, 1988; Verstegen, 1987; Verstegen & Clark, 1988). Special education has so far successfully resisted consolidation strategies, which are hallmarks of the Reagan-Bush attempts to reduce federal expenditures for social programs. The REI, however, is consistent with the Reagan-Bush policy objectives of reducing federal influence and expenditures for education, which have resulted in declining federal support for programs designed to ensure equity in education of the disadvantaged and handicapped. I will show that the REI is, in fact, consistent with the conservative agenda for economic and social reforms.

One of the primary hypotheses on which the REI is based is that students with disabilities would be best served by the improvement of education for *all* students, such that students of every description are fully integrated into regular classes, no student is given a special designation (label), costs are lowered by the elimination of special budget and administrative categories, the focus becomes excellence for all, and federal regulations are withdrawn in favor of local control. This hypothesis is parallel to Reagan-Bush economy theory, often known colloquially as a trickle-down theory, which is based on the presumption that the greatest benefits will be accrued indirectly by economically disadvantaged citizens under a policy designed to benefit more advantaged citizens directly. The implementation of economic policies based on trickle-down theory has produced a mighty river of prosperity for America's most advantaged citizens, but only dust for many who are homeless, poor, hungry, or otherwise markedly economically disadvantaged (see Minarik, 1988). Implementation of education policies based on a trickle-down hypothesis will very likely produce parallel results for those students who learn most easily and those who are most difficult to teach—high performers will make remarkable progress, but the benefits for students having the most difficulty in school will never arrive. Ironically, some of the most vocal advocates of the REI are special educators who appear to be apolitical or politically liberal and who seem unaware of the fact that the reforms they support are part of a conceptual revolution, a political strategy, and a policy initiative, all of which are inimical to the improvement of services to handicapped and at-risk students.

THE REI AS CONCEPTUAL REVOLUTION

Those advocating radical reform of special education suggest revolutionary changes in the way educators think about the problems of teaching and managing classes in which there is extreme diversity. They reject assumptions that have been the foundation of special education services in American public schools for over a century (cf. Hallahan & Kauffman, 1988). These foundational ideas include the following:

1. Some students are very different from most in ways that are specific regarding education, and special education—not the usual or typical education—is required to

meet their needs. In the context of public education, these students should be identified as *exceptional*. Excluding gifted and talented students, exceptional students are handicapped.

2. Not all teachers are equipped to teach all students. Special expertise is required by teachers of exceptional students because such students present particularly difficult instructional problems. Most teachers are neither equipped by training nor able in the context of their usual class size to ensure an equal educational opportunity for handicapped students.

3. Students who need special education, as well as the corresponding funds and personnel that are required, must be clearly identified to ensure that they receive appropriate services. Special services will be compromised or lost unless both funding and students are specifically targeted.

4. Education outside the regular classroom is sometimes required for some part of the school day to meet some students' needs. Removal of an exceptional student from the regular classroom may be required to (a) provide more intensive, individualized instruction, (b) provide instruction in skills already mastered or not needed by nonhandicapped students in the regular class, or (c) ensure the appropriate education of other students in the regular classroom.

5. The options of special education outside the regular classroom, and special provisions within the regular classroom, are required to ensure equal educational opportunity for exceptional students. The most important equity issue is the quality of instruction, not the place of instruction.

Advocates of the REI urge the adoption of very different assumptions (Biklen & Zollers, 1986; Gartner & Lipsky, 1987, 1989; Lilly, 1988; Lipsky & Gartner, 1987; Pugach, 1987, 1988; Reschly, 1988a, 1988b; Reynolds & Wang, 1983; Reynolds, Wang, & Walberg, 1987; Snell, 1988; S. Stainback & W. Stainback, 1987, 1988, 1989; W. Stainback & S. Stainback, 1984; Taylor, 1988; Wang, Reynolds, & Walberg, 1986, 1988; Wang & Walberg, 1988; Will, 1984, 1986a, 1986b, 1988, 1989). The most radical proposals—in effect suggestions to merge general and special education—include the following premises (see Gartner & Lipsky, 1987, 1989; Lipsky & Gartner, 1987; S. Stainback & W. Stainback, 1985, 1987, 1988, 1989; W. Stainback & S. Stainback, 1984):

1. Students are more alike than they are different, even in the most unusual cases. The same basic principles apply to the learning of all students. Consequently, no truly special instruction is needed by any student. It is therefore not the case that there are different kinds of students. The exceptional–nonexceptional and handicapped–nonhandicapped distinctions are not useful for education purposes.

2. Good teachers can teach all students; all good teachers use the same basic techniques and strategies. Teaching all students well requires that the teacher make relatively minor adjustments of strategy or accommodation for individual differences. Therefore, truly special training is not required for handicapped students or for their teachers. Special education has become a convenient way for general educators to avoid their responsibility to teach all students, leading to a decrement in the quality of instruction for all students.

3. All children can be provided a high-quality education without identifying some students as different or special and without maintaining separate budgets, training programs, teachers, or classes. Special targeting of funds for specific students is inefficient, confusing, and unnecessary. No student will be shortchanged in a system designed to provide a high-quality education for every student.

4. Education outside the regular classroom is not required for anyone. All students can be instructed and managed effectively in regular classrooms. Moreover, the separation of students from their ordinary chronological-age peers is an immoral, segregationist act that has no legitimate place in our free and egalitarian society.

5. Physically separate education is inherently discriminatory and unequal. The most important equity issue is the site, not the quality, of instruction, for if handicapped students are educated alongside their nonhandi-

capped peers, then and only then can they be receiving an equal educational opportunity.

Advocates of the REI reject the current so-called "segregationist" special education and propose a new, "integrated" model in which all students are special. The proposed new special education will be completely, or at least mostly, invisible because it will retain only the best of the outmoded and flawed dual system of special education and general education.

REI advocates suggest that current special education stigmatizes and segregates children needlessly and without benefiting them; it *should not* work, because it is separate and discriminatory. The new special education will not require labeling, will not result in stigmatizing children, and will be effective because it will be an integral part of education for *all* children.

Currently, according to REI advocates, general education is rigid, ineffective, and unable to tolerate any but the slightest differences among students; it *cannot* work, because teachers are not expected to deal with difficult students. The new general education will be supple, flexible, appropriate for all children; it will be successful for all children because teachers will know and take pride in the fact that they are expected to teach *every* child assigned to them—to provide excellence for all and failure for none.

Some advocates of the REI have compared current special education to South Africa's policy of apartheid (Lipsky & Gartner, 1987) and to slavery (Stainback & Stainback, 1988). The conclusion by these advocates of the most radical reform is that nothing short of *total* integration of general and special education *can* work to the ultimate benefit of children. Even more moderate proposals for the reform of the relationship between general and special education (e.g., Reynolds et al., 1987; Wang et al., 1986, 1988; Will, 1984, 1989) include the suggestions that (a) most students currently identified as handicapped have only minor problems, (b) general educators can be expected to manage these problems with little assistance, (c) no reliable differences can be found between difficult-to-teach at-risk students and difficult-to-teach students identified as handicapped, (d) effective strategies for teaching and managing most handicapped students in general education are readily available, and (e) the most effective way to serve most handicapped students is not to have separate special programs for them but to improve education in general. The suggestion that the general improvement of education is the best strategy for educating handicapped students—a trickle-down theory of educational benefit—is consistent with the Reagan-Bush administrations' education policy and political strategy.

THE REI AS POLITICAL STRATEGY

The REI bears all the markings of the Reagan-Bush agenda for education. Admittedly, many of the proponents of the REI may not have political motivations. In fact most of the proponents of the REI, were they to compare themselves to Ronald Reagan and George Bush, probably would see themselves as representing the opposite end of the political spectrum. A closer look at the proposals known as the REI would show, however, that they are aimed at decreasing federal support for education, including the education of vulnerable children and youth. These policies represent a shift away from the historical federal role of supporting compensatory programs for the most needy students (Verstegen, 1987).

One of the key players in the REI is former Assistant Secretary of Education and Director of the Office of Special Education and Rehabilitative Services, Madeleine Will, a Reagan political appointee (see Will, 1984, 1986a, 1986b, 1988, 1989). Supporters of proposals for radical reform frequently cite her statements that are critical of the current fragmented approach to the education of handicapped and at-risk students, her questioning of the necessity for a dual system of special and general education, her concern about the stigmatization of students identified as handicapped, her suggestion that parents of children who are failing in school may too often want their children to qualify for special programs, her opinion that separate education is inherently unequal (based on the 1954 Supreme Court decision, *Brown v. Board of Education of Topeka*), and her request for increased collaboration between special and general educators (e.g., Lilly, 1988; Lipsky & Gartner, 1987; Reschly, 1988a; Snell, 1988; S. Stainback & W. Stainback, 1987; Wang et al., 1986, 1988). The calls for reform by the primary political appointee of the Reagan-Bush administration in special education have been consistent with Reagan-Bush policies regarding the education of disadvantaged and at-risk students. These policies have had a negative effect on funding for students at risk, including handicapped children (Verstegen, 1984, 1985; Verstegen & Clark, 1988).

Reagan-Bush education policy consisted primarily of three strategies: (a) fostering an image of achieving excellence, regardless of substantive change, (b) federal disengagement from education policy, and (c) block funding of compensatory programs. All three strategies have had a negative effect on programs for students with special needs. The changes in education following the publication of *A Nation at Risk* (National Commission on Excellence in Education, 1983) consisted almost entirely of higher academic standards, an emphasis on competition, calls for stricter discipline, and exhortations to teachers to do better. These changes seem to have made little difference in the actual quality of education, involving primarily the management of image and public relations (Clark & Astuto, 1988). These changes, though perhaps salutary for more advantaged and capable students, have created a mainstream ever more difficult for and less accommodating of students with special needs (Braaten, Kauffman, Braaten, Polsgrove, & Nelson, 1988; Woodring, 1989).

Federal disengagement from educational policy involves scaling down the federal role and emphasizing local control (Astuto & Clark, 1988). As Verstegen (1987) noted, the Reagan-Bush move toward federal disengagement has broken with 200 years of federal concern for fostering equality and the common good, and it has endangered programs and services for the most needy of students. "The pendulum has swung, and we witness the turning back of the hands of time" (Verstegen, 1987, p. 548). The move toward block funding as opposed to separate categorical programs, supported by the argument that separate programs are duplicative and wasteful and that all students will profit from better integrated programs, has resulted in fewer dollars flowing to programs for handicapped and at-risk students. Verstegen and Clark (1988) reported that from 1981 to 1988 federal funding for elementary and secondary education dropped by 28% (in dollars adjusted for inflation); the biggest decrease (76%) was in special programs, "the heart of the block grant that was designed to support state and local efforts toward school improvement" (p. 138).

> Even the most favored programs . . . were losers. Supported by a very effective local and national lobby, education for the handicapped avoided being folded into the block grant, fought off the Administration's proposed budget cuts, but nevertheless lost 6% to inflation between 1980 and 1988. By contrast, compensatory education, which lacked an equally effective lobby, lost 25% during a period when the crisis in urban education led the Carnegie Foundation for the Advancement of Teaching to describe the students in big-city schools as "an imperiled generation." (Verstegen & Clark, 1988, p. 138)

Reagan-Bush policy initiatives were able to achieve many of their political goals, in spite of their nefarious effects on equity, primarily because they focused on a small number of very specific issues with high emotional appeal and offered simplistic answers to complex problems. Efficiency in an era of deficit spending, higher academic standards and tighter discipline in a time of perceived decline in student achievement and behavior, school prayer in the context of resurgent religious conservatism, and the pledge of allegiance in a time of renewed patriotism are prime examples of such issues. To the extent that emotional appeals and simplistic answers were made the focus of reform rhetoric, they obscured substantive analyses; the administration was successful in selling a package of empty promises.

Advocacy for the REI rests primarily on the emotional and public relations appeal of the proposed reforms, not on logical or empirical analyses of the probable consequences of those reforms. The REI as a political strategy, then, is rhetoric organized around four primary emotion-laden topics: (a) integration (with racial integration as a metaphor for integration of the handicapped), (b) nonlabeling (especially slogans such as "rights without labels"), (c) efficiency (i.e., deregulation and decentralization), and (d) excellence for all (the capstone of a trickle-down theory of educational benefit to handicapped students).

Integration

One of the most powerful emotional appeals of the REI is its comparison of special education to racial discrimination. Will (1984) and Gartner and Lipsky (1989) cited the U.S. Supreme Court decision in *Brown v. Board of Education of Topeka* and the discredited doctrine of "separate but equal" as justification for the integration of handicapped students into regular classrooms; advocates of the REI have compared special education to apartheid (Lipsky & Gartner, 1987) and to slavery (S. Stainback & W. Stainback, 1988). Questions about the similarities and differences between race and disability must be raised, as must questions regarding the conditions under which separate education of handicapped students entails discrimination. Are comparisons of special education to racial segregation and slavery appropriate, or are they unfitting? For several reasons, the race metaphor is an inappropriate way of thinking about disability.

First, equating ethnic origin with disability is demeaning to racial groups suffering discrimination on the basis of trivial differences, and it trivializes the needs of people with disabilities, whose differences require accommodations far more complex than disallowing skin color as a criterion for access or opportunity. Second, the physical, cognitive, and behavioral characteristics of handicapped children and youth are more complex and relevant to learning and to the function of schools in our society than is ethnic origin. Separate education may indeed be inherently unequal when separateness is determined by a factor irrelevant to teaching and learning (e.g., skin color), but separateness may be required for equality of opportunity when separation is based on criteria directly related to teaching and learning (e.g., the student's prior learning, the concepts being taught, the teacher's preparation). Were this not so, all manner of grouping for instruction would be struck down as inherently unequal. Third, skin color (the primary basis of racial discrimination) involves difference along a single dimension requiring simple adjustments of educational policy to accommodate an entire group of students; disabilities, on the other hand, are extremely diverse and require highly individualized and sometimes complex accommodations of educational programming. As Singer (1988) noted, Public Law 94-142 guarantees *procedural* rights, not rights to specific curricula or services, because only the procedures designed to effect appropriate education could be prescribed for so diverse a population as handicapped children. Fourth, the moral basis of the legal entitlement of handicapped students to special education (i.e., unusual or atypical, sometimes separate, education in contrast to the usual or typical education, even if the typical education is of high quality) is derived from the extraordinary educational requirements imposed by their characteristics. Finally, unlike characteristics of race or ethnic origin, disabilities often are malleable. Handicapped individuals may therefore pass from one classification to another during the course of their development and education, requiring a more carefully weighted approach to legal rights involving separation.

The civil rights issue for racial and ethnic minorities is one of access to the same services provided to others, regardless of their characteristics; the civil rights issue for handicapped students, however, is one of access to a differentiated education designed specifically to accommodate their special characteristics, even if accommodation requires separation. Thus the REI advocates who invoke *Brown v. Board of Education of Topeka* obfuscate the civil rights issues for handicapped students. Nevertheless, the call for total integration of all handicapped students and the comparison of special education to such unsavory practices as racial discrimination and slavery have enormous emotional appeal and create the image of moral superiority for advocates of radical change. As long as advocates of the REI can brand their critics "segregationist" and alternatives to total integration "segregationism" (Wang & Walberg, 1988), or compare special education to slavery (Biklen, 1985; S. Stainback & W. Stainback, 1988) or apartheid (Lipsky & Gartner, 1987), they maintain a significant public relations advantage, regardless of any deeper analysis of the issue of integration. This public image approach without regard for underlying substance is consistent with the Reagan-Bush approach to decision making on social issues and appears to have been supported by that administration's primary political appointee in special education, Madeleine Will.

Nonlabeling

Advocates of the REI argue that labels for handicapped students are unjustified because they require arbitrary decisions regarding relatively trivial and continuously distributed variables (e.g., W. Stainback & S. Stainback, 1984), that labeling unnecessarily stigmatizes students (e.g., Will, 1989), and that students' rights can be ensured without labels (e.g., Lipsky & Gartner, 1987). The images of capricious labeling and stigmatization of children are extremely distasteful, and the notion of rights without labels has enormous surface appeal. Yet, closer analysis of the antilabeling rhetoric of REI advocates reveals that it is a hollow promise.

Stainback and Stainback (S. Stainback & W. Stainback, 1989; W. Stainback & S. Stainback, 1984) argued that there are not two kinds of children, handicapped and nonhandicapped, because children so designated are similar in more respects that they are different and because the designations involve arbitrary decisions regarding children's levels of functioning. Their argument could be extended, of course, to apply to the classification of children along any continuous dimension—tall–short, fat–thin, healthy–sick, weak–strong, old–young, or hungry–well fed, for example. It is a truism that all children share many characteristics of humanity, yet no two are exactly alike. If we do not draw distinctions among children along important dimensions, however, we do not provide for their differences. Moreover, the arbitrary choice of a criterion for definition is unavoidable for any continuously distributed variable. Decisions to classify some babies as having low birthweight or recognize some children as obese are not condemned merely because such decisions require an arbitrary choice of criteria involving weight, or because the criterion established is less than perfectly predictive of important consequences for individuals.

Arbitrary decisions involving characteristics distributed along a continuum are frequently necessary to promote social justice, even though the arbitrary criterion is less than perfectly correlated with the performance of responsibility in question. A case in point is the voting age established for our political process. The decision to grant the right to vote to citizens 18 years and older rather than 21 was arbitrary; voting age could be changed at will. And, while some 18-year-olds exercise their right with a high degree of responsibility, others do not. Moreover, only a day of life may separate one young person who is granted the right to vote from one who is denied the right, and some 14-year-olds are better prepared to vote than are many 18-year-olds. Yet, to argue against the establishment of an arbitrary voting age would reduce the right to vote to an absurdity. We know that suffrage for 3-year-olds would make a mockery of the democratic process. But would suffrage for 17-year-olds? Perhaps not. Where do we draw the line? Clearly, if we care about social justice, we must establish an arbitrary criterion. And, just as clearly, we must establish arbitrary criteria for inclusion in specific educational programs if we want our education system not to mock our intelligence.

To return to the Stainbacks' argument, if there are not two kinds of children, how many kinds are there? One? Fourteen? As many kinds as there are children? If every child is considered either the same as all others or unique for instructional purposes, what are the implications for grouping children for instruction? Should students be randomly assigned to teachers? If students are not randomly assigned, then are we not admitting that we have some basis for categories of students? A basic premise of effective education is that instructionally relevant categories of students must be identified. Although the current categories of problem learners need to be redefined, available data do not support the contention that these categories are unrelated to instructional needs (Keogh, 1988). Clearly, the assumptions that different kinds of students cannot be reliably distinguished and that they must not be identified need rethinking.

The problem of the stigma associated with special education labels and services is persistent. The negative aspects of labeling, one of which is stigma, appear to have been overestimated, however, compared to the benefits (Hallahan & Kauffman, 1988; Singer, 1988). Advocates of the REI frequently opine that students experience problems because they are labeled (e.g., Biklen & Zollers, 1986). Singer observed that "the learning disabled did not create their problem; they were given a label because of their problem. By extension, taking away their label will not make their problem disappear" (1988, p. 412). Moreover, interviews with children suggest that many feel more stigmatized if they are given extra help in their regular classroom than if they are pulled out for assistance in a separate class

(Jenkins & Heinen, 1989). This finding lends support to Singer's (1988) observation that stigma is more a function of recognition of differences in the academic performance and social behavior of handicapped children than of the labels used for these differences. Thus, we must consider whether labels and the stigma associated with them are entirely avoidable.

Popular among advocates of the REI is the suggestion that students could be assured of appropriate educational services to meet their needs without categorical labels (Gartner & Lipsky, 1987; Lipsky & Gartner, 1987; Reschly, 1988a; S. Stainback & W. Stainback, 1985, 1987, 1989; W. Stainback & S. Stainback, 1984). Nevertheless, "rights without labels" appears to be a euphemism of the Reagan era, a slogan creating the image of concern for equal rights while rendering equity of a substantive level impossible. Candor compels the admission that we could not ensure the rights of disabled individuals who are not labeled—whose disabilities have become essentially invisible or unmentionable to us. One is forced logically to conclude that, if "rights without labels" is a viable concept, disabled people need only their rights to the same services as nondisabled people. But do handicapped students need only the ordinary, not special, allocations of funds, equipment, instruction, or access?

The nonsense of "rights without labels" is easily revealed by applying this slogan to a noneducation example involving labeling and the rights of people with disabilities—handicapped parking. Could people with disabilities be assured of preferential parking without labeling cars or spaces? Could unmarked spaces be effectively reserved? Could spaces be reserved for "handicapped only" without revealing which persons have a right to preferential parking? Obviously, "rights without labels" is a conundrum. Moreover, it captures the essence of the Reagan-Bush approach to equity: It is the appeal to become blind to differences, which has immediate emotional appeal but makes affirmative action, compensatory programs, and special educational accommodation impossible.

How can the rights of handicapped students be guaranteed without our talking about those students as having different needs or instructional requirements? If differences are talked about, then we label them and risk stigmatizing students; without labels, we must simply ignore students' differences. This is a terrible dilemma, as Minow (1987) recognized, but this point must not be missed: We ignore what we do not label. Some labels are known to be more accurate or more palatable or less damaging than others. Surely the most humane and least damaging labels must be sought, but to suggest that no child should be labeled handicapped or disabled, or to attempt studiously to avoid all labels, is clearly inane and opens the door to apathy and indifference.

Another argument of REI advocates is that too much energy and money are spent determining students' eligibility for special programs (e.g., Reschly, 1988a). Without labels, advocates argue, not only could the stigma of identification be avoided but enormous economies would be effected. Yet, the absence of publicly stated eligibility criteria and the evaluation and labeling they entail would mean the absence of special services or any requirement of parental participation in decision making.

> It remains unclear how students can be assured of receiving designated services if their eligibility is not determined. If eligibility decisions are not made, it might then be assumed that all students would be eligible for all services. That all students should receive all services is a proposal which can hardly be taken seriously. If all students are eligible for all services but only some students receive them, then both eligibility decisions and special services become covert. . . . (Council for Children with Behavioral Disorders, 1989, p. 204)

That covert eligibility decisions are intended by some proponents of educational reform is no longer in question. "The districts [with schools restructured for high performance] would not be required to publicly identify the students who would otherwise be segregated into special classes" (National Center on Education and the Economy, 1989, p. 23). This is quite clearly an appeal to revert to the very conditions that gave rise to the Education for All Handicapped Children Act—schools could determine students' eligibility for special services without parental notification or consent.

The effects of nonlabeling were recently examined by Feniak (1988) in England and Wales. In these countries, sentiment for integration and egalitarianism, in addition to concern over the stigma associated with labels, led to the legislative abolition of categories of handicap in 1981. But, as Feniak's analysis shows, the 1981 Education Act abolishing categorical labels had precisely the opposite effect of that intended by advocates of reform. Students are still labeled, but now only covertly. Moreover, the absence of labels obscures the extent to which children's special needs are being met. Monitoring of programs designed to meet students' special needs is made impossible because insufficient records are kept regarding children's characteristics.

> It is difficult to know how students are chosen to receive either a "developmental" curriculum, a "modified" curriculum or a "main-

stream plus support" curriculum since the new [reporting] format drastically reduces the amount of information which is supplied. . . . The net result is that the needs of these students are not being addressed. (Feniak, 1988, p. 122)

Like the issue of integration, the nonlabeling issue is exploitable for its public relations value. It is also consistent with the Reagan-Bush administration's approach to equity issues, which relies on the surface appeal of nondiscrimination without analysis of the deeper meanings for individuals with a history of disadvantage.

Efficiency

REI proponents appeal to the financial savings to be reaped by restructuring what they deem to be duplicative, inefficient, and fragmented programs for handicapped and at-risk students (e.g., National Center on Education and the Economy, 1989; Reynolds et al., 1987; Wang et al., 1988; Will, 1984, 1986a, 1986b, 1989). Their proposal is to combine the administration and funding of all special or compensatory programs into a single unit. In some cases, this noncategorical approach has been extended to encompass all education funding, special and general (e.g., Gartner & Lipsky, 1987; Lipsky & Gartner, 1987; W. Stainback & S. Stainback, 1984). With fewer administrative structures and regulations, these advocates argue, education will become more flexible, adaptive, efficient, and powerful. Such reasoning is immediately attractive to most administrators and other fiscal agents, many of whom have been persuaded of the advantages of deregulation and of combining programs into block grants for funding, as advocated by the Reagan-Bush administrations. As mentioned previously, however, analyses of Reagan-Bush policies have shown that the results have been decreases in funding for programs and services for children at risk (Clark & Astuto, 1988; Verstegen, 1987; Verstegen & Clark, 1988).

Combining general and special education budgets and services or combining all compensatory programs would almost certainly have the effect of decreasing the special services available to handicapped students. Specific budget lines are set aside for whatever purposes are deemed more important. Individuals who wish to achieve a specific financial goal must scrupulously set aside funds for that specific purpose. The same principle applies to the budgets of public institutions. In this era of deficit spending, the appeal to efficiency through block funding and deregulation is politically savvy. Ironically, politically liberal proponents of the REI are supporting an initiative that policy analyses indicate is virtually certain to retard or reverse progress in providing services to handicapped students (cf. Verstegen, 1985; Verstegen & Clark, 1988).

The appeal to efficiency raises equity issues for handicapped and at-risk students, and these issues encompass more than macro-analyses of funding formulas (Colvin, 1989). The issues also demand classroom-level microeconomic analyses of resource allocation. Such analyses suggest that teachers always face a dilemma in the allocation of their resources when teaching a group. Teachers must choose between (a) allocating more time to the production of expected mean outcomes for the group, which sacrifices gains of the least capable learners, or (b) allocating more time to the least capable learners to narrow the variance among students, which inevitably sacrifices achievement of the students who learn most easily. Teachers cannot avoid this dilemma, which would be made more painful by the inclusion of more difficult-to-teach students in regular classrooms (Gerber & Semmel, 1985; Kauffman, Gerber, & Semmel, 1988). Moreover, the problem could be eased only by a massive infusion of resources into general education. In the context of scarce resources and an emphasis on competitive excellence (typically defined as higher mean achievement gains) (see National Center on Education and the Economy, 1989), it is not difficult to predict how most classroom teachers would most often choose to allocate their time and effort.

Excellence

The Reagan-Bush position on education was that we must focus on excellence in our schools, and that excellence and equity are not competing issues. This doctrine suggests that to the extent that we foster excellence among our best students and schools, we will foster the same among our least capable students and our poorest schools. This trickle-down theory of education will work very well for the educationally advantaged, but not for educationally disadvantaged or handicapped students. Excellence and equity are always competing issues; what is gained in one is lost in the other. Excellence requires focusing support on the most capable learners; equity requires the opposite.

In an apparent variation on the themes of efficiency and excellence, some proponents of the REI suggest that education should be made special for all students because all students have special needs (Gartner, 1989). This would spare students the trauma of being labeled and save school districts the cost of identifying eligible students and administering special programs (see also Gartner & Lipsky,

1987, 1989; Lipsky & Gartner, 1987; W. Stainback & S. Stainback, 1984). Although every student is different from every other, and every student can (and should) be recognized as an individual, the sugges-tion that every student be given a special education is as vacuous as the notion that all students can be above average. Moreover, the feasibility of changing general education dramatically so that what has not worked for a century—providing an appropriate education for every student in general education, handicapped or not—will work now must be questioned (Kauffman, 1988b; Singer, 1988).

The history of education does not suggest that a single program of general education has ever been so supple or accommodating of extreme heterogeneity of learners as to serve *all* students well, nor does a logical analysis suggest that such a program is possible, par-ticularly when its focus is excellence defined as higher mean achieve-ment. Certainly, instruction could be (and should be) improved for all students. Nevertheless, "excellence for all" is a conundrum that appeals simultaneously and contemptuously to American pride and egalitarianism. The National Center on Education and the Economy, in its publication *To Secure Our Future* (1989), has sketched a plan for restructuring elementary and secondary education for high per-formance: "The challenge is to provide *an elite education for every-one*" (p. 9). As ludicrous as the notion of the ubiquitous elite may be, it is apparently proposed with no lack of seriousness and with full understanding of its public relations value.

Unless the call for excellence includes the protection of educa-tional resources for handicapped students at the expense of higher mean performance for the larger student body, however, it is an appeal to widen the gap between educational haves and have-nots. Unfortunately, *To Secure Our Future* does not propose the protection of funding for handicapped students. Indeed, it proposes a program design in which *high-performance schools* could combine funds for a variety of compensatory programs, including funds under the Educa-tion for All Handicapped Children Act (National Center on Education and the Economy, 1989, p. 23).

THE REI AS A FLAWED POLICY INITIATIVE

Besides the vacuousness of the political ideology driving the REI, there are at least four other reasons to question whether it can be successful in accomplishing the goals of its proponents: (a) a lack of support from key constituencies, (b) the illogic of its basic premises,

(c) a lack of specificity in the proposed restructuring, and (d) the proponents' cavalier attitude toward experimentation and research. Similar observations prompted Singer to describe the REI as "deeply flawed" (1988, p. 419).

Uninvolved Key Constituencies

Perhaps the most startling fact about the REI is that it is not, as its name implies, an initiative of general educators. Rather, it represents the self-criticism of some special educators and an apparent attempt by those special educators to suggest to general educators that they must take the initiative in solving the instructional problems of handicapped and other difficult-to-teach students (Braaten et al., 1988; Singer, 1988). But, as Singer asked, "What leads special educators to believe that regular educators are willing to take back responsibility for special needs children?" (1988, p. 416). If regular classroom teachers do not assume ownership of the REI as their agenda, can it succeed? Perhaps millions of teachers could be coerced into accepting the REI as a fait accompli. But if they were so compelled, could the proposed reforms succeed in an atmosphere of coercion?

Moreover, no evidence has been brought forward to suggest that most special education teachers see the REI as *their* agenda or believe that it will work. How could the REI succeed without the clear consensus of practitioners? Recent surveys of hundreds of general and special education practitioners in various regions of Virginia (Smith, 1988) and in 15 different states (Anderegg, 1989) found that most of the practitioners did not agree with many of the propositions on which the REI is based.

A few professional organizations (e.g., National Association of School Psychologists) and advocacy groups (e.g., National Council of Advocates for Students) have gone on record as supporting reforms associated with the REI (see Reschly, 1988a). It is important to note, however, that several professional organizations in special education, including the Council for Children with Behavioral Disorders (CCBD) and the Teacher Education Division of the Council for Exceptional Children (TED), have expressed grave reservations about these same reforms (CCBD, 1989; TED, 1986). Moreover, some advocacy groups (e.g., Joint Action Committee of Organizations Serving the Visually Handicapped, National Association of the Deaf) have offered testimony to Congress complaining that the "generic mainstreaming" suggested by advocates of the REI is inappropriate (Viadero, 1989, p. 26).

The parents of handicapped students are a very strong advocacy group in special education, without whose support major policy changes are almost certainly doomed. Yet it seems unlikely that most parents would support the REI. A major 5-year research project begun in 1982, the Collaborative Study of Children with Special Needs (Singer & Butler, 1987), involving five large school districts from various regions of the country, suggested that parents of handicapped children who were receiving special education in pull-out programs would have been reluctant to see their children returned to general education.

> Regardless of site or family background, parents of special education students were generally very satisfied. They were satisfied with their children's overall education program and related services, with their social interaction with other students, with the administration and teaching in the special education program, and with the facilities.
>
> These findings are in marked contrast to parental views prior to the implementation of PL 94-142. In fact, the researchers believe that parents of special education students are more satisfied with the public schools than parents of school children in general. (Robert Wood Johnson Foundation, 1988, p. 10)

In short, proponents of the REI appear to be gambling unwisely that their proposals will be successfully implemented, for they have not built the necessary base of support among critical constituencies (Davis, 1989). The only hope of conservative politicians who support the REI appears to be that the public relations value of integration, nonlabeling, efficiency, and excellence will carry the day, for any deeper analysis of the issues may make the REI a political time bomb.

Illogical Premises

The students the REI is concerned about are those whom general education has failed. As Keogh noted, "It is strange logic that calls for the regular system to take over responsibility for pupils it has already demonstrated it has failed" (1988, p. 20). Advocates of the REI conclude that special education also has failed these students, both procedurally and instructionally, and that radical reform is therefore necessary to provide effective instruction and procedural protection (e.g., Biklen & Zollers, 1986; Gartner & Lipsky, 1987; Lipsky & Gartner, 1987; Wang et al., 1988). Singer (1988) and others (e.g., Braaten et al., 1988; CCBD, 1989) have noted the illogic of the suggestions that (a) although special education has failed, it has insights to offer general education about how to keep students from failing, and (b) procedural protections that have not worked in special education will now work in general education. A more rational suggestion is that if special education has developed powerful interventions, they should first be implemented reliably in special education settings, then applied experimentally in general education. A more reasonable gamble with students' procedural rights would be first to find ways of effecting them more fully under current regulations for education of the handicapped, then to see whether they could be guaranteed in general education, and with fewer regulations. Note that if proponents of the REI admit that special education has indeed developed successful interventions and procedural protections, one of their major lines of argument for reform is vitiated.

Supporters of the REI argue implicitly and explicitly that general education today, compared to only a few years ago, is better equipped to learn how to deal with the problems of handicapped students. But "special education was the solution to the regular educator's thorny problem of how to provide supplemental resources to children in need while not shortchanging other students in the class. Nothing else has happened within regular education to solve this problem" (Singer, 1988, p. 416). Keogh (1988) noted that the REI is being proposed in the context of widespread criticism of regular education and its inadequacy for pupils who do not have particular educational problems. Moreover, the instructional reforms so far implemented in general education are those known to be most likely to fail with at-risk students (Carnine & Kameenui, 1989).

In brief, the illogic of the REI is readily apparent. Its implementation would be based on a crumbling conceptual foundation and would likely compound the difficulties now experienced by general education in meeting the needs of an extremely diverse student body.

A Lack of Specificity

The proposals advanced by proponents of the REI are remarkable in their lack of detail regarding critical aspects of how special and general education should be restructured. For all the talk of restructuring and redeployment of personnel, there have been few suggestions and no real specifics regarding who would be responsible for what problems, or how and where services would be made available to students (McKinney & Hocutt, 1988a). Although Wang et al. (1988) and Will (1984, 1986a, 1986b, 1989) decried the lost instructional time entailed by pull-out programs, they offered no specifics regarding the time saved by alternative assignment of personnel— except, of course, the implication that no instructional time is lost when no student is pulled out of one class for instruction in another place. If, however, *special* instruction and related services are still to be available as reform advocates suggest (i.e., special services are not to be abandoned), then it is not clear how such services would be provided without a loss in some category of regular instructional time.

Reschly's (1988a) suggestion that special education reform will be furthered by a revolution in the roles of school psychologists is an example of enthusiasm for the REI without the level of specificity needed to make the arguments for reform believable. Reschly calls for school psychologists to spend less time evaluating students for eligibility for special programs and more time consulting with teachers regarding the resolution of difficult instruction and behavior management problems. As Kauffman (1988b) pointed out, however, were the anticipated revolution in school psychology to occur, and were it to result in all school psychologists doing nothing other than consulting with teachers, the average classroom teacher could not expect more than 30 to 40 minutes of consultation per week. Whether this level of service would be sufficient to help most regular classroom teachers cope with particularly difficult-to-teach students— especially if the number of such students in regular classrooms was increased by the dissolution if most or all of special education—is not known but seems doubtful.

The suggestion of Reynolds et al. (1987) and Will (1984, 1989) that special education teachers' roles should be restructured to include more work with regular classroom teachers and Pugach's (1988) proposal that special education should be included in the training of all teachers also require considerable elaboration before they can be entertained seriously as alternatives to the current arrangement. If special education teachers were to assume more responsibility for assisting regular classroom teachers, what scheduling changes would be necessary? How much assistance (i.e., minutes of consultation per day or week) would be available to the average regular classroom teacher? If special education training were required of all teachers, how much training could be offered, and from whom? What range of students would regular classroom teachers then be able to work with successfully?

In brief, the REI appears in some respects to be a strategy without tactics, a top-down reform of education without full consideration of the implications of change for frontline educators or students. To the extent that the REI involves deregulation (or an alternative mode of regulation based on reward for high performance, as suggested by the National Center on Education and the Economy, 1989), it appears to be an expression of faith that local education agencies will find solutions to educating difficult-to-teach students within a unitary system structured for high performance—a faith not based on evidence of past success. Given the recent concern of general educators for competitive excellence, it behooves proponents of the REI to state explicitly and in considerable detail how restructuring special and general education will address the problems of students with histories of school failure.

A Cavalier Attitude Toward Experimentation and Research

Critics of the REI concede that special education has serious problems that must be addressed. They do not, however, agree with many of the REI proponents' interpretations of the research. Critics do not agree that research supports the following conclusions by REI advocates: (a) Special education pull-out programs are not effective, (b) referrals to and placements in special education programs are out of control, (c) the stigma of identification for special education outweighs the benefits, (d) students seldom or never exit special education, and (e) tested alternatives to the current system are available (see Anderegg & Vergason, 1988; Braaten et al., 1988; Bryan, Bay, & Donahue, 1988; Bryan & Bryan, 1988; Carnine & Kameenui, 1989; CCBD, 1989; Fuchs & Fuchs, 1988a, 1988b; Gerber, 1988; Hallahan, Keller, McKinney, Lloyd, & Bryan, 1988; Kauffman, 1987, 1988a, 1988b, 1989; Kauffman et al., 1988; Kauffman & Pullen, 1989a; Keogh, 1988; Lieberman, 1985; Lloyd, Crowley, Kohler, & Strain, 1988; McKinney & Hocutt, 1988a, 1988b; Mesinger, 1985; Schumaker & Deshler, 1988; Singer, 1988; Vergason & Anderegg, 1989). Indeed, these conclusions can be reached only by ignoring the research supporting conclusions to the contrary.

The conclusion that special education resource instruction is ineffective requires that one ignore evidence from meta-analysis (Carlberg & Kavale, 1980) as well as individual studies showing that such pull-out instruction has been effective for some students (e.g., Marston, 1987–88; O'Connor, Stuck, & Wyne, 1979). The conclusion that special education referrals are out of control is not confirmed by recent data from urban schools (Buttram & Kershner, 1989). Interviews with children have shown that they do not necessarily see being pulled out of regular classes for special instruction as more embarrassing or stigmatizing than receiving help from a specialist in their regular classes (Jenkins & Heinen, 1989). Singer (1988) reviewed evidence that the percentage of handicapped students returned to general classes is not as "embarrassingly low" (p. 367) as critics (e.g., Gartner & Lipsky, 1987) have charged. Alternatives to current pull-out programs are not clearly supported by research (Hallahan et al., 1988).

A careful examination of all available research reveals that the evidence regarding most aspects of special education is mixed. Research supports the plausibility of the conclusion that special education as currently structured (though not always as practiced) can be highly effective and cost efficient. "Proponents of the [REI] argue that the best solution is to abandon the current system, but in doing so, I fear that we would be throwing out the baby with the bath water" (Singer, 1988, p. 419). A prudent approach to research on the current problems of special education would be to seek ways to make the current system more effective, as well as to seek additional alternatives to the current system (Kauffman & Pullen, 1989b).

Another concern of critics of the REI is the response of some REI proponents to research evidence that is not entirely supportive of their proposals and claims. For example, a meta-analysis of the efficacy of special class placement (Carlberg & Kavale, 1980) is cited by proponents of the REI (e.g., Gartner & Lipsky, 1987; Lipsky & Gartner, 1987) as evidence of "little or no benefit for students of all levels of severity placed in special education settings" (Gartner & Lipsky, 1989, p. 13). Moreover, Gartner and Lipsky's interpretation of Carlberg and Kavale's (1980) findings is cited by other proponents of the REI in support of their contention that special classes per se have been ineffective (e.g., Lilly, 1988; Wang & Walberg, 1988). Carlberg and Kavale's analysis showed, however, that although regular classroom placement produced slightly better results than special class placement when all types of students were considered together and when students with a low IQ were considered alone, special class placement produced substantially better outcomes than regular class placement for students classified as learning disabled (LD) and behaviorally disordered/emotionally disturbed (BD/ED). Thus, citing Carlberg and Kavale (1980) to support the argument that special classes for all types of mildly handicapped students are ineffective is a distortion of fact.

> For LD and BD/ED children in special classes . . . an improvement of 11 percentile ranks resulted from their placement. Thus, the average BD/ED or LD student in special class placement was better off than 61% of his/her counterparts in regular class. . . . When

exceptional children were placed in special classes on the basis of low IQ, they did not respond as well as their regular class counterparts. The situation was reversed with respect to LD and BD/ED children, who were found to show greater improvement in the special class. A 99% confidence interval around the ES [effect size] for the LD and BD/ED categories ranged from 0.7 to .75; there is a high probability that these children demonstrate a better response in special classes than their counterparts in regular classes. (Carlberg & Kavale, 1980, pp. 301–302)

The centerpiece of the reform rhetoric of many REI advocates has been the Adaptive Learning Environments Model (ALEM), a program of individualization developed by Margaret C. Wang and her colleagues (e.g., Wang, 1980; Wang & Birch, 1984; Wang, Peverly, & Randolph, 1984). Reviews of the literature have concluded, however, that evaluations of the ALEM suffer from very serious methodological weaknesses (Bryan & Bryan, 1988; Fuchs & Fuchs, 1988a, 1988b; Hallahan et al., 1988). When calls are made for experimental trials regarding alternatives to the current system (e.g., Reynolds et al., 1987), *experiments* should be taken to mean well-controlled studies from which one could make generalizations according to the canons of scientific research. Yet the response to criticism of ALEM research has been to skirt the issue of methodological limitations and call the position of critics "segregationism" (Wang & Walberg, 1988).

Finally, some reform advocates (e.g., Biklen, 1985; Lipsky & Gartner, 1987; S. Stainback & W. Stainback, 1988) trivialize or disparage experimental trials and empirical data, arguing that restructuring the current pull-out system is a moral imperative. Critics of the REI, on the other hand, argue that advocacy and policy regarding the education of handicapped and other difficult-to-teach students must be informed by reliable empirical data, and that moral imperatives in special education and other compensatory programs cannot be fully determined in the absence of such data (e.g., Carnine & Kameenui, 1989; CCBD, 1989; Fuchs & Fuchs, 1988a, 1988b; Hallahan et al., 1988; Lloyd et al., 1988; Singer, 1988).

CONCLUSIONS

The REI should not be questioned merely because it may have emanated in part from the Reagan-Bush administration. Rather it should be questioned because of its insubstantial empirical and rational bases and because of where it may be moving public education. The fact that the REI is consistent with the policies of a popular previous administration and appears to be finding the favor of the Bush-Quayle administration (Miller, 1989), however, may explain why it continues to receive support from some quarters and poses a more serious challenge to education that if it had no political base. The REI, though deeply flawed, is not a dead issue.

The nature of policy options should be considered in analyzing the REI and its alternatives. Policy always represents a trade-off of benefits and relative advantages, never a final solution to the problems it is designed to address. The policy options for addressing a given problem are generated by one or more conditions that present dilemmas or points of choice—scarcity, preferences or beliefs, relative advantage, and accidental circumstances. In the case of the REI, fiscal constraints are a scarcity condition obviously motivating the attempts to combine programs into more efficient packages, regardless of the consequences for at-risk students. The belief systems represented by the REI are peculiar in that both conservative ideology (e.g., focus on excellence, federal disengagement) and liberal rhetoric (e.g., nonlabeling, integration) are combined to support the diminution or dissolution of a support system for handicapped students. The relative advantage given to handicapped students by the REI is primarily cosmetic; ironically, the substantive losers are those students whom the policy is ostensibly designed to benefit. Finally, the resurgence of political conservatism following a period of rapid expansion of social programs is an accidental social circumstance providing fertile ground for faulty belief systems that allow political justification for the loss of the relative advantage formerly granted to persons with disabilities. More careful attention to the nature of, and trade-offs entailed by, the options selected for support and implementation might help us achieve more meaningful reform of education.

Meaningful reform of education cannot be achieved without ownership of that reform by the teachers who will be called upon to implement it and by the parents who support it. Attempts to reform institutions without the support of primary constituencies almost always are disasters. If the REI, or any other set of proposals for reform, is to have any reasonable chance of success, much more groundwork will need to be laid at the classroom practitioner and parental levels.

The REI has as its primary goal changing the place of instruction from special to regular classrooms. Special education should be pursuing the goal of more effective and humane education for handicapped students—helping these students to learn more academically, feel better about themselves and about school, and relate more adaptively to others. The *primary* objective should be more effective education; the *secondary* objective should be to provide that treatment in the least restrictive or most normalized setting. In pursuing both objectives, the achievement and socialization consequences of educational options must take precedence over the immediate consequences of place or location. As noted recently by prominent behavior therapists,

> freedom of individual movement and access to preferred activities, rather than type or location of placement, are the defining characteristics of a least restrictive environment. . . . Consistent with the philosophy of least restrictive yet effective treatment, exposure of an individual to restrictive procedures is unacceptable unless it can be shown that such procedures are necessary to produce a safe and clinically significant behavior change. It is equally unacceptable to expose an individual to a nonrestrictive intervention (or a series of such interventions) if assessment results or available research indicate that other procedures would be more effective. . . . Thus, in some cases, a client's right to effective treatment may dictate the immediate use of quicker acting, but temporarily more restrictive, procedures. (Van Houten et al., 1988, pp. 382–383)

Given the research available today, the generalizations that education in separate classes is never effective and that effective education in regular classrooms is feasible for *all* handicapped students (even for all mildly and moderately handicapped students) are indefensible. A policy mandating placement of all handicapped children in general education under the assumption that pull-out programs have been shown to be ineffective for all students and integrated education of all handicapped children is known to be feasible would be based on a gross misinterpretation—and a grotesque misapplication—of research.

The assumption that students with mild disabilities are those most easily integrated into general education may not be warranted. Integration of students with severe disabilities into regular classrooms may in many cases be more feasible than integration of those with mild or moderate disabilities. Teachers and peers may more readily make allowances for the characteristic social behavior and academic performance of a student whose disability is obvious to the casual observer than for the characteristics of one whose difference is more subtle. In fact, mild or moderate, but nonlabeled and persistent, deviations from expected social behavior and academic performance may present the most difficult problems with regard to teacher tolerance and peer acceptance.

Efforts should be focused on incremental improvements in the current system through research, training, careful and logical analysis of strategies, and rigorous analysis of policy. Radical reforms or revolutions should be attempted only after clear empirical bases for such reforms have been established. Whenever possible, reliable data should be used in making decisions about the structure of special and general education. In the absence of reliable data, careful, logical analyses, not presumptive assertions of moral superiority, should guide decisions. Furthermore, in evaluating learning environments for handicapped students, professional judgment alone is insufficient for decision making—parental opinion and choice regarding effectiveness and restrictiveness must be considered as well.

The REI is a complicated set of issues that demands careful analysis and challenges us to seek more effective ways of integrating many handicapped students into the mainstream. The simplistic answer to the REI of maintaining the status quo must be rejected, as must the equally simplistic notion that all handicapped students must be fully integrated into general education, regardless of what the data or rational analyses suggest. The statements by Madeleine Will and other advocates of the REI notwithstanding, special education is an integral part of American public education, not a separate system. It is, indeed, an identifiable and special part of public education that can be legislated or regulated into or out of existence. But it can be erased from our consciousness and ledgers only at great peril to handicapped students. Thus, proposed reforms of public education should include revitalizing this invaluable part of the system to make it serve its special purposes more effectively, rather than dismantling it. This revitalization might best be accomplished by combining a commitment to higher professional standards of training and performance for special education teachers and administrators with strategies designed to improve the effectiveness of general educators.

AUTHOR'S NOTES

Preparation of this chapter was supported in part by the University of Virginia's Commonwealth Center for the Education of Teachers. Opinions expressed herein are my own and do not necessarily represent positions of the Commonwealth Center.

I am grateful to Terry A. Astuto, Daniel P. Hallahan, Robert F. McNergney, Donald L. Roe, and Deborah A. Verstegen for their helpful comments on earlier drafts of the manuscript.

REFERENCES

Anderegg, M. L. (1989). *Regular educators' responses to three key issues of the regular education initiative: An investigation of regular educators' experiences.* Unpublished doctoral dissertation, Georgia State University, Atlanta.

Anderegg, M. L., & Vergason, G. A. (1988). An analysis of one of the cornerstones of the regular education initiative. *Focus on Exceptional Children, 20*(8), 1–7.

Astuto, T. A., & Clark, D. L. (1988). State responses to the new federalism in education. *Educational Policy, 2,* 361–375.

Biklen, D. (Ed.). (1985). *Achieving the complete school.* New York: Columbia University Press.

Biklen, D., & Zollers, N. (1986). The focus of advocacy in the LD field. *Journal of Learning Disabilities, 19,* 579–586.

Braaten, S. R., Kauffman, J. M., Braaten, B., Polsgrove, L., & Nelson, C. M. (1988). The regular education initiative: Patent medicine for behavioral disorders. *Exceptional Children, 55,* 21–27.

Bryan, T., Bay, M., & Donahue, M. (1988). Implications of the learning disabilities definition for the regular education initiative. *Journal of Learning Disabilities, 21,* 21–28.

Bryan, J. H., & Bryan, T. H. (1988). Where's the beef? A review of published research on the Adaptive Learning Environment Model. *Learning Disabilities Focus, 4*(1), 9–14.

Buttram, J., & Kershner, K. (1989, March). *A second look at special education in urban districts.* Paper presented at the annual meeting of the American Research Association, San Francisco.

Carlberg, C., & Kavale, K. (1980). The efficacy of special versus regular class placement for exceptional children: A meta-analysis. *The Journal of Special Education, 14,* 295–309.

Carnine, D., & Kameenui, E. (1989). *The regular education initiative and children with special needs: A false dilemma in the face of true problems.* Unpublished manuscript, University of Oregon, Eugene.

Clark, D. L., & Astuto, T. A. (1988). *Education policy after Reagan—What next?* Occasional Paper No. 6, Policy Studies Center of the University Council for Educational Administration, University of Virginia, Charlottesville.

Colvin, R. L. (1989). School finance: Equity concerns in an age of reforms. *Educational Researcher, 18*(1), 11–15.

Council for Children with Behavioral Disorders. (1989). Position statement on the regular education initiative. *Behavioral Disorders, 14,* 201–208.

Davis, W. E., (1989). The regular education initiative debate: Its promises and problems. *Exceptional Children, 55,* 440–446.

Feniak, C. A. (1988). Labelling in special education: A problematic issue in England and Wales. *International Journal of Special Education, 3,* 117–124.

Fuchs, D., & Fuchs, L. S. (1988a). An evaluation of the Adaptive Learning Environments Model. *Exceptional Children, 55,* 115–127.

Fuchs, D., & Fuchs, L. S. (1988b). Response to Wang and Walberg. *Exceptional Children, 55,* 138–146.

Gartner, A. (1989, April). *Beyond mainstreaming: A critical look at integrating students with disabilities.* Conference presentation, Buffalo, NY.

Gartner, A., & Lipsky, D. K. (1987). Beyond special education: Toward a quality system for all students. *Harvard Educational Review, 57,* 367–395.

Gartner, A., & Lipsky, D. K. (1989). *The yoke of special education: How to break it.* Rochester, NY: National Center on Education and the Economy.

Gerber, M. M. (1988). Tolerance and technology of instruction: Implications for special education reform. *Exceptional Children, 54,* 309–314.

Gerber, M. M., & Semmel, M. I. (1985). The microeconomics of referral and reintegration: A paradigm for evaluation of special education. *Studies in Educational Evaluation, 11,* 13–29.

Hallahan D. P., & Kauffman, J. M. (1988). *Exceptional children: Introduction to special education* (4th ed.). Englewood Cliffs, NJ: Prentice-Hall.

Hallahan, D. P., Keller, C. E., McKinney, J. D., Lloyd, J. W., & Bryan, T. (1988). Examining the research base of the regular education initiative: Efficacy studies and the adaptive learning environments model. *Journal of Learning Disabilities, 21,* 29–35.

Jenkins, J. R., & Heinen, A. (1989). Students' preferences for service delivery: Pull-out, in-class, or integrated models. *Exceptional Children, 55,* 516–523.

Kauffman, J. M. (1987). Research in special education: A commentary. *Remedial and Special Education, 8*(6), 57–62.

Kauffman, J. M. (1988a). Lessons in the nonrecognition of social deviance. In R. B. Rutherford, C. M. Nelson, & S. R. Forness (Eds.), *Bases of severe behavioral disorders of children and youth* (pp. 3–19). Boston: Little, Brown.

Kauffman, J. M. (1988b). Revolution can also mean returning to the starting point: Will school psychology help special education make the circuit? *School Psychology Review, 17,* 490–494.

Kauffman, J. M. (1989). *Characteristics of behavior disorders of children and youth* (4th ed.). Columbus, OH: Merrill.

Kauffman, J. M., Gerber, M. M., & Semmel, M. I. (1988). Arguable assumptions underlying the regular education initiative. *Journal of Learning Disabilities, 21,* 6–11.

Kauffman, J. M., & Pullen, P. L. (1989a). REI movement throwing baby out with the bath? *Virginia Journal of Education, 82*(8), 16–19, 27.

Kauffman, J. M., & Pullen, P. L. (1989b). A personal perspective on our history of service to mildly handicapped and at-risk students. *Remedial and Special Education, 10*(6), 12–14.

Keogh, B. K. (1988). Improving services for problem learners: Rethinking and restructuring. *Journal of Learning Disabilities, 21,* 19–22.

Lieberman, L. M. (1985). Special education and regular education: A merger made in heaven? *Exceptional Children, 51,* 513–516.

Lilly, M. S. (1988). The regular education initiative: A force for change in general and special education. *Education and Training in Mental Retardation, 23,* 253–260.

Lipsky, D. K., & Gartner, A. (1987). Capable of achievement and worthy of respect: Education for handicapped students as if they were full-fledged human beings. *Exceptional Children, 54,* 69–74.

Lloyd, J. W., Crowley, E. P., Kohler, F. W., & Strain, P. S. (1988). Redefining the applied research agenda: Cooperative learning, prereferral, teacher consultation, and peer-mediated interventions. *Journal of Learning Disabilities, 21,* 43–52.

Marston, D. (1987–88). The effectiveness of special education: A time series analysis of reading performance in regular and special education settings. *The Journal of Special Education, 21*(4), 13–26.

McKinney, J. D., & Hocutt, A. M. (1988a). Policy issues in the evaluation of the regular education initiative. *Learning Disabilities Focus, 4*(1), 15–23.

McKinney, J. D., & Hocutt, A. M. (1988b). The need for policy analysis in evaluating the regular education initiative. *Journal of Learning Disabilities, 21,* 12–18.

Mesinger, J. F. (1985). Commentary on "A rationale for the merger of special and regular education" or, Is it now time for the lamb to lie down with the lion? *Exceptional Children, 51,* 510–512.

Miller, J. A. (1989). Bush floats plan to free schools from regulation. *Education Week, 8*(30), 1, 19.

Minarik, J. J. (1988). Family incomes. In I. V. Sawhill (Ed.), *Challenge to leadership: Economic and social issues for the next decade* (pp. 33–66). Washington, DC: Urban Institute Press.

Minow, M. (1987). Learning to live with the dilemma of difference: Bilingual and special education. In K. T. Bartlett & J. W. Wenger (Eds.), *Children with special needs* (pp. 375–429). New Brunswick, NJ: Transaction Books.

National Center on Education and the Economy. (1989). *To secure our future: The federal role in education.* Rochester, NY: Author.

National Commission on Excellence in Education. (1983). *A nation at risk: The imperative for educational reform.* Washington, DC: U.S. Department of Education.

O'Connor, P. D., Stuck, G. B., & Wyne, M. D. (1979). Effects of a short-term intervention resource-room program on task orientation and achievement. *The Journal of Special Education, 13,* 375–385.

Pugach, M. (1987). The national education reports and special education: Implications for teacher preparation. *Exceptional Children, 53,* 308–314.

Pugach, M. (1988). Special education as a constraint on teacher education reform. *Journal of Teacher Education, 39*(3), 52–59.

Reschly, D. J. (1988a). Special education reform: School psychology revolution. *School Psychology Review, 17,* 459–475.

Reschly, D. J. (1988b). Obstacles, starting points, and doldrums notwithstanding: Reform/revolution from outcomes criteria. *School Psychology Review, 17,* 495–501.

Reynolds, M. C., & Wang, M. C. (1983). Restructuring "special" school programs: A position paper. *Policy Studies Review, 2*(1), 189–212.

Reynolds, M. C., Wang, M. C, & Walberg, H. J. (1987). The necessary restructuring of special and regular education. *Exceptional Children, 53,* 391–398.

Robert Wood Johnson Foundation. (1988, December). *Serving handicapped children: A special report.* Princeton, NJ: Author.

Schumaker, J. B., & Deshler, D. D. (1988). Implementing the regular education initiative in secondary schools: A different ball game. *Journal of Learning Disabilities, 21,* 36–42.

Singer, J. D. (1988). Should special education merge with regular education? *Educational Policy, 2,* 409–424.

Singer, J. D., & Butler, J. A. (1987). The Education for All Handicapped Children Act: Schools as agents of social reform. *Harvard Educational Review, 57,* 125–152.

Smith, T. W. D., Jr. (1988). *The regular education initiative: A practitioner's view.* Unpublished doctoral dissertation, University of Virginia, Charlottesville.

Snell, M. E. (1988). Gartner and Lipsky's Beyond Special Education: Toward a Quality System for All Students. *Journal of the Association for Persons with Severe Handicaps, 13,* 137–140.

Stainback, S., & Stainback, W. (1985). The merger of special and regular education: Can it be done? A response to Lieberman and Mesinger. *Exceptional Children, 51,* 517–521.

Stainback, S., & Stainback, W. (1987). Integration versus cooperation: A commentary on "Educating children with learning problems: A shared responsibility." *Exceptional Children, 54,* 66–68.

Stainback, S., & Stainback, W. (1988). Letter to the editor. *Journal of Learning Disabilities, 21,* 452–453.

Stainback, S., & Stainback, W. (1989). No more teachers of students with severe handicaps. *TASH Newsletter, 15*(2), 9.

Stainback, W., & Stainback, S. (1984). A rationale for the merger of special and regular education. *Exceptional Children, 51,* 102–111.

Taylor, S. J. (1988). Caught in the continuum: A critical analysis of the principle of the least restrictive environment. *Journal of the Association for Persons with Severe Handicaps, 13,* 41–53.

Teacher Education Division of the Council for Exceptional Children. (1986). *Message to all TED members concerning The National Inquiry into the Future of Education for Students with Special Needs.* Reston, VA: Author.

Van Houten, R., Axelrod, S., Bailey, J. S., Favel, J. E., Foxx, R. M., Iwata, B. A., & Lovaas, O. I. (1988). The right to effective behavioral treatment. *Journal of Applied Behavior Analysis, 21,* 381–384.

Vergason, G., & Anderegg, M. L. (1989). Save the baby!: An answer to integrating children of the second system. *Phi Delta Kappan, 71,* 61–63.

Verstegen, D. A. (1984). The education block grant: A policy evaluation. *Journal of Educational Equity and Leadership, 4,* 290–303.

Verstegen, D. A. (1985). Redistributing federal aid to education: Chapter 2 of the Education Consolidation and Improvement Act of 1981. *Journal of Education Finance, 10,* 517–523.

Verstegen, D. A. (1987). Two hundred years of federalism: A perspective on national fiscal policy in education. *Journal of Education Finance, 12,* 516–548.

Verstegen, D. A., & Clark, D. L. (1988). The diminution in federal expenditures for education during the Reagan administration. *Phi Delta Kappan, 70,* 134–138.

Viadero, D. (1989). Panel asked to stop "morally wrong" application of special-education law. *Education Week, 8*(25), 26.

Wang, M. C. (1980). Adaptive instruction: Building on diversity. *Theory into Practice, 19*(2), 122–127.

Wang, M. C., & Birch, J. W. (1984). Comparison of a full-time mainstreaming program and a resource room approach. *Exceptional Children, 51,* 33–40.

Wang, M. C., Peverly, S., & Randolph, R. (1984). An investigation of the implementation and effects of a full-time mainstreaming program. *Remedial and Special Education, 5*(6), 21–32.

Wang, M. C., Reynolds, M. C., & Walberg, H. J. (1986). Rethinking special education. *Educational Leadership, 44*(1), 26–31.

Wang, M. C., Reynolds, M. C., & Walberg, H. J. (1988). Integrating the children of the second system. *Phi Delta Kappan, 70,* 248–251.

Wang, M. C., & Walberg, H. J. (1988). Four fallacies of segregationism. *Exceptional Children, 55,* 128–137.

Will, M. C. (1984). Let us pause and reflect—but not too long. *Exceptional Children, 51,* 11–16.

Will, M. C. (1986a). *Educating children with learning problems: A shared responsibility. A report to the secretary.* Washington, DC: U.S. Department of Education.

Will, M. C. (1986b). Educating children with learning problems: A shared responsibility. *Exceptional Children, 52,* 411–415.

Will, M. C. (1988). Educating students with learning problems and the changing role of the school psychologist. *School Psychology Review, 17,* 476–478.

Will, M. C. (1989). Individualization: Is it possible in the regular classroom? *Virginia Journal of Education, 82*(4), 7–12.

Woodring, P. (1989). A new approach to the dropout problem. *Phi Delta Kappan, 70,* 468–469.

Chapter 9

Toward a Comprehensive Delivery System for Special Education

James M. Kauffman and Daniel P. Hallahan

"YOUR DESIGN MUST BE DIRECTED primarily at helping all students meet world class standards in five core subjects."[1] This constraint on designs for a "new generation of American schools" was proposed by the chief executive officer and the chairman of the board of the New American Schools Development Corporation (NASDC). The NASDC was created in response to President Bush's unveiling in April 1991 of his new strategy for American education. Its emphasis on the achievement of world-class standards by all students follows a spate of "system-wide 'crisis rhetoric' "[2] and a rush of calls for "radical reform," "restructuring," and "transformation" of American public education, including appeals for integrating general and special education.[3]

Much of the current language of education reform consists of disparaging commentaries on the failure of American education and calls for inclusiveness (all students) and unity of service delivery structures (integrated, merged). Some researchers have observed that American education does not appear by objective standards to be the miserable failure portrayed by its contemporary critics.[4] In appeals for integration of general and special education the two are frequently described as separate systems, yet one might note the ways in which special education already exists as an integral component of public general education. In this context, we must consider carefully the implications of key concepts in reform rhetoric and the ways in which general and special education have been, are, and should be integrated in a comprehensive delivery system.

Special education evolved as an integral part of public general education in the early twentieth century, as MacMillan and Hendrick explain in Chapter 2.[5] In conception, special education was—and we argue that it remains—a necessary and integral part of a comprehensive general education delivery system. A comprehensive education delivery system addresses the educational needs, but not all the needs, of all children, not merely most. Special education originated because the education designed for most children was not having the desired effect on some. Educators saw that the appropriate education of all children required different instruction (i.e., special education) for a minority.

A central issue in designing a comprehensive education delivery system is the definition of *all,* a word with desultory meanings. More than the rhetorical meaning of *all* is at stake in designing a comprehensive delivery system. What is at stake is (1) whether general education will have a special-purpose branch to serve the exceptional needs of some children and (2) how that branch will be articulated with the trunk program of education. Thus, the varied meanings of *all* in controversies regarding special and general education, and the implications of these meanings for a comprehensive delivery system, are central issues in our discussion.

THE VARIED MEANINGS OF *ALL*

The implicit and explicit meanings of *all* are critical for understanding political and educational dialogue because one typically assumes that the freedoms, rights, and responsibilities addressed in these exchanges are limited, not absolute. The user of the word *all* does not usually intend that it be interpreted literally because either tradition or rational discourse (or both) suggests exceptions, meaning that *all* usually represents only an approximation (and sometimes not a very close approximation) of every individual. *All,* then, is frequently understood to exclude certain individuals, sometimes for reasons that are justifiable and sometimes for reasons that are not. The varied meanings of *all* are therefore of considerable consequence to those who may be tacitly excluded.

Impoverished and Exclusionary Meanings of *All*

The meaning of *all* can be impoverished, either by unintelligible exclusions or by extreme literalness. In today's political rhetoric regarding education, and too often in the speaking and writing of educators, we encounter the cliché "all children can learn" proffered without clarifications that might make it more than a hint of an allusion. One must ask for answers to follow-up questions to this slogan: What can all children learn? At what rate? With what allocation of instructional resources? To what degree of proficiency or mastery? For what purpose? These are particularly important questions when we are considering students who are exceptional—markedly different from their typical age-mates in ways that are directly related to learning and instruction (thinking, communicating, or moving).

One might interpret the hackneyed "all children can learn" to mean that most children can learn what most teachers are supposed to teach at about an average rate and to a generally acceptable degree of mastery. Perhaps it is intended as a reminder that students differ in some ways that are very seldom inherent constraints on teaching and learning (e.g., color, gender, or socioeconomic status) and that teachers have sometimes been guilty of lowered expectations based on these differences that have relatively trivial implications for instruction. But "all children can learn" is a hollow slogan when we consider the full range of child characteristics. It is devoid of meaning because it merely reifies two facts: (1) many students, but not literally all, can learn what we expect of the typical student, and (2) most children, but not literally all, can learn something worthwhile. Historically, users of this slogan have not meant it to include all children with disabilities because some of them cannot learn that which, presumably, "all children" can.

Until the 1970s, many children with disabilities were routinely excluded from public schools. Educating "all children" once meant, in the common parlance of many state legislators and local school officials, something considerably less than teaching every youngster who can learn useful skills. Since enactment in 1975 of the federal legislation known commonly as P.L. 94-142 (now the Individuals with Disabilities Education Act, or IDEA), the courts have interpreted the education of "all handicapped children" to mean the inclusion of literally all, regardless of the nature or severity of their handicaps. The blunt literalness of high court interpretations of federal special education law apparently allows no living child to be found ineducable, meaning that schools must provide a free appropriate public "education" to children with scant cortical function and even to those with no cerebral cortex and no possibility of consciousness.[6] Whether attempting to educate children who are permanently unconscious is a moral imperative or a mockery is an open question for philosophical debate, but legislation and litigation have left no room for educators' clinical judgment on the matter.

We are unable to describe educational needs of permanently unconscious and semicomatose children, although these children have obvious needs for humane treatment. We realize, nonetheless, that what constitutes a sufficient state of consciousness or cortical function to create an educational need is a matter of informed judgment in the individual case. Our point is that *all* can be impoverished of meaning in discussions of education in either of two ways: when it is used glibly and insidiously to exclude children who are not typical in what they can learn or, on the other hand, as a cudgel of literalness that equates inability to learn only with total brain death.

The most extreme cases of cognitive disability and their deliberate inclusion in "all handicapped children" in federal mandates are not merely distracting aberrations for two reasons: (1) they demand that any serious discussion of the inclusion of all children in general education confront the full range of disability without implicit exclusions, and (2) they force us to consider the careless use of *all* and the implications for designing a service delivery system that includes children whose special educational needs are tacitly ignored. The excluded and ignored children often are not only those with such profound intellectual impairments that they arguably have no educational needs but many who have impairments of a far milder form and who can clearly be educated, including children with mild or moderate mental retardation, emotional or behavioral disorders, and learning disabilities.

As efforts to reform, restructure, or "reinvent" American schools have gained momentum, many educators have suggested that schools must become more inclusive of children with diverse educational needs—that schools must serve the needs of all children. Thus we must consider carefully the meanings of *all* in discussions of education reform.

Meanings of *All* in Education Reform

In the language of current education reform, *all* often does not mean literally every student. In fact, it clearly must be interpreted to exclude many students who do not have profound cognitive impairments. The educational goals for the year 2000 set by President

Bush and the states' governors are a case in point. We recognize that many students with disabilities are fully capable of meeting or exceeding the expectations set by the nation's leaders if they are provided appropriate education. Yet the goal that by 2000 "all children will start school ready to learn," for example, is vague in its implications for gifted and handicapped children. To say that "all" students will be ready to learn and be literate is appealing rhetoric, but it renders actual achievement of these goals impossible. We believe that President Bush and the governors are serious in their hope that public education will be improved, but we do not believe that they have considered the ramifications of their goal statements for students with disabilities.

We interpret such goal statements as indicating a lack of awareness of the full range of children's abilities, with the implicit assumption that *all* means, in actuality, "most" or "a somewhat greater percentage." What will children be ready to learn when they start school? What is the meaning of "ready"? At what age will children start school? Clearly, we might expect very dissimilar answers for children with severely limited cognitive abilities, those of near average intelligence, and those with extremely high intellectual abilities. Without answers to these questions, we see *all* in most of the goal statements of education reform as implicitly excluding many exceptional children.

Special education and the problem of constructing a service delivery system that includes exceptional children have been ignored or mentioned only in passing in discussions of general education reform. "The silence about the needs of, or outcomes for, handicapped children in the current reform movement is deafening."[7] The omission may be interpreted in at least two ways. One interpretation is that the needs of exceptional children are considered by most educators not to merit special attention. Accordingly, *all* in the language of reform means those children who are not so different from the norm that the goals established for "all students" are reasonable. Thus, for example, when the president and governors established the goal "By the year 2000 every adult American will be literate and possess the knowledge and skills necessary to compete in a global economy and exercise the rights and responsibilities of citizenship," they were apparently unconcerned about students whose cognitive disabilities preclude their learning to read or to understand concepts such as rights and citizenship and those who can only acquire rudimentary knowledge and skills that will neither make them competitive in a global economy nor enable them to exercise responsibilities of citizenship in meaningful ways. The implication is that special education will be necessary to address the needs of those forgotten in the press to restructure general education.

An alternative interpretation is that the reforms proposed for general education will be (or can be) so sweeping and revolutionary that the need for special education as such will be obviated. In essence, the trunk program of general education should assimilate its special education branch; general education must become special for all students, such that all students are treated with the same care for meeting individual differences, hence without marking any person or service as extraordinary. Special education will, in effect, become "normal" or standard educational practice. Special and general education will be merged into a single entity described in the language of reform as "supple," "flexible,"[8] and even as intended to provide *"an elite education for everyone."*[9] The implication is that restructured general education will provide sufficient safeguards for meeting the needs of exceptional children, an assumption that, we shall show, is untenable.

Even when special education is specifically at issue in discussions of reform, however, *all* is sometimes apparently used with the tacit assumption that no one will ask whether *all* is meant to be taken literally. One widely cited education reform program, known as Success for All[10] and commonly offered by its author as an alternative to special education, clearly does not address the needs of all students.[11] It might more candidly be called "Higher Achievement for Most." Another program widely lauded in the special education reform literature is the Adaptive Learning Environments Model (ALEM) of Wang and her colleagues.[12] Some have stated, "All types of students can be accommodated in ALEM classrooms,"[13] yet it is clear that ALEM has not been demonstrated to meet the needs of all students, particularly not all students with mild or moderate disabilities.[14]

Claims of success for all students in any given program said to be an alternative to special education as it is currently structured are sometimes qualified by explicit exclusions, for example, "those who are retarded or severely emotionally disturbed, as well as those with physical, speech, or language deficits and those with severe learning disabilities."[15] Excluded students are sometimes described as those who are not "judgmentally" handicapped.[16] These exclusions are logical contradictions, namely, that success must be defined as impossible for some students in programs claiming success for all or, on the other hand, that the success of some students must be judged by a different standard from that presumably applicable to all students. We shall return to the problem of these lacunae in the logic of reform.

Candor and prudence in stating goals and making claims for the inclusiveness of educational programs might make innovations and reform proposals less beguiling and create less confusion about what is possible and desirable in public education. Unfortunately, the relentless hyperbole regarding programs said to be alternatives to special education, combined with current political and economic pressures for the reform of both special and general education, have led to much confusion regarding the nature of special programs and their roles in a comprehensive service delivery system designed to meet the educational needs of all students.

THE PRESS FOR SPECIAL EDUCATION REFORM

Extreme unhappiness with American public education is today de rigueur, although many of the bases for its condemnation are questionable.[17] Perhaps dissatisfaction with special education is an indication of the degree to which it is now seen as an integral part of the public education system. Before discussing how we might work toward a comprehensive service delivery system, we examine problems created by current reform rhetoric. Although we recognize that education—special education included—needs substantial improvement, we believe that much of the current press for radical restructuring is based on misrepresentations, tortured ideologies, and conceptual confusion.

Misrepresentations

Part of the press for special education reform and the integration of special with general education has been created by scathing commentaries on educational outcomes for children with disabilities who have received special education and by ardent claims that alternatives to special education are known to produce superior outcomes for all children. Critics of the current system of special and general education charge bluntly that it does not work, provides no benefit, and therefore cannot be justified, whereas restructured programs are highly successful and serve all children well.[18]

Space does not allow us to review the findings here. Suffice to say that research has yielded mixed findings for both prevalent service delivery models and restructured programs. We believe that the conclusions that special education has failed and that restructured programs have not are overgeneralizations. They can be reached only by ignoring substantial findings to the contrary, and they can be maintained only by assiduously avoiding critical analysis of both rhetoric and research.[19] In our view, they are dangerous exaggerations that distort perceptions and create a climate in which research data are devalued in favor of ideologies that, although otherwise defensible, have been twisted into parodies.

Tortured Ideologies

Special education is accurately portrayed as justified in part by two ideologies: civil rights and normalization. Both ideologies have been of considerable value to special education, but both have been invoked inappropriately in attempts to justify proposals that undermine its conceptual foundations.

Civil Rights

Equal protection of law and equal educational opportunity are concepts supporting special education for exceptional students. These same concepts support the integration of diverse ethnic groups in public schools. The educational rights of exceptional children and those of ethnic minorities rest on the same foundation, namely, that children's characteristics must not be used as a justification for unfair treatment (i.e., treatment that denies them equal opportunity to learn). Nevertheless, unfairness in education has historically had very different meanings for ethnic minorities and exceptional children. In the case of ethnic minorities, providing different education for children with the same needs has been seen as creating unfairness; in the case of exceptional children, however, providing the same education for children whose needs are significantly different from others' has been viewed as unfair. When one disregards these differences in the nature of unfairness and applies the same criteria for judging discrimination to exceptionality and ethnicity, civil rights arguments become non sequiturs.

Some calls for radically restructured special and general education assume an isomorphism of ethnicity and disability, which yields the conclusion that separating exceptional children for instruction is as unfairly discriminatory as maintaining schools segregated by ethnicity.[20] Some have used the argument that separate education is inherently and unfairly unequal when children are segregated by skin color or ancestry to justify the conclusion that grouping children for instruction based on their performance is inherently and unfairly unequal, particularly when children differing in performance are instructed in different classrooms. This line of reasoning ignores the fact that racial segregation was the total separation of children for instruction according to the dichotomous and, presumably, instructionally irrelevant variable of skin color, whereas schools separate children into groups for special education for varying amounts of time (a relatively small amount of the school day for most) based on assessment of their academic performance and instructional needs.[21]

Those who have recently proposed to establish special academies for black male students have reversed the argument that separate education is inherently and unfairly unequal when the basis for separation is ethnic identity or gender. In our view, these proposals have merit precisely to the extent that one can make the case that ethnic identity and gender are characteristics determining what or how students can best be taught. Our interpretation of equal educational opportunity is that students must not be grouped for instruction by caprice or by criteria that are irrelevant to their learning and social development but that they must be grouped by criteria directly related to what they are to learn and how they can be taught most effectively.

Normalization

Normalization, the concept on which landmark legislation and litigation in special education has been built, has lost much of its meaning. Rather than a guiding principle for developing services for persons with disabilities, it has become codified as a rule requiring that all students with disabilities be educated in general education classrooms. It has been reduced to a slogan standing for the politically correct position of total integration or inclusion, but it is a much more complex notion than many realize.

Some proponents of educational reform have misconstrued the normalization principle as a rationale for abolishing pullout programs.[22] Wolfensberger has addressed this misconception, stating that normalization and mainstreaming should not be considered synonymous.[23] Today's advocates of total integration have fashioned the meaning of "normalization" for their own purposes. They would certainly have a difficult time reconciling their push for total integration with Wolfensberger's position on the subject. Regarding the misconception that normalization means that people with retardation should *always* work in culturally normative settings, for instance, Wolfensberger has stated, "In fact, I do not recall meeting a single normalization advocate or even zealot who has not recognized the need for at least some type of sheltered work conditions and circumstances for at least some retarded persons."[24]

Furthermore, although favoring small residential arrangements, Wolfensberger is a strong proponent of a variety of different options. For those requiring psychiatric services, for example, he has proposed no less than fifteen different types of models varying in separateness as a function of the characteristics of the clients. Currently, public school programming for students with disabilities appears to be headed in the opposite direction. Instead of multiple service delivery options, the rush toward total integration is reducing the number of alternatives for educational placement.

Although Wolfensberger was not clear on the subject in his earliest formulation of the normalization principle, he later clarified that he did not mean to equate normalization with the statistical norm.[25] His later conceptualization places more importance on the *perceived* value of the means to achieving normalization. Even so, however, one can argue that the most effective treatment methods may not always be those that are most culturally normal or valued. Mulick and Kedesdy, for example, contend that in the case of self-injurious behavior in persons with autism, culturally normative responses worsen the behavior, and some of the most efficacious treatment techniques for self-injurious behavior in persons with autism run counter to normalization principles.[26] The culturally normative response to someone who injures him- or herself is consolation or a response that draws attention to the injured person. Social attention to self-injurious behavior, however, actually leads to increases in self-injury. Techniques that would not be high on a list of cultural normality, such as restraint and punishment, are the ones that researchers have found most effective in reducing self-injury.

A less dramatic, but more common, example of how the best educational techniques are not always culturally normative pertains to the learning problems of children. Placing students in small groups and using a highly teacher-directed, drill-and-practice approach is not the way most children are taught to read, nor is it consistent with current trends in educational reform. Research has documented, however, that just such an approach is the most successful for students with learning disabilities.[27] Such an approach, however, would meet Wolfensberger's later conceptualization of perceived value.

To us, it seems that the almost obsessive concern for normalization promulgated by some advocates of mainstreaming and deinstitutionalization promotes a demeaning attitude toward those with disabilities. There needs to be a balance between focusing on changing the person with a disability to be more "normal," by attending regular schools and classes and being included in the standard curriculum, versus changing society to accept people who have disabilities. As Hauerwas notes,

> We usually associate movements toward justice in our society with the language of equality. We assume to be treated equally is to be treated justly, but on reflection we may discover that is not the case. Often the language of equality only works by reducing us to a common denominator that can be repressive or disrespectful.[28]

Because the originators of the principle of normalization—Bank-Mikkelsen, Nirje, and Wolfensberger—have often written passionately about the validity of the concept, they have probably given present-day normalization proponents justification for imbuing it with status equivalent to one of the Ten Commandments.[29] We note that Wolfensberger describes normalization on the societal level, meaning that society should be more tolerant of the differences of people with disabilities, and that he has stated, "Normalization does not mean that only normative human management tools and methods are used—merely that these be as normal *as feasible*" [italics added].[30]

Advocates of total integration have unfortunately twisted the original intent of the principle of normalization. As a guiding principle, it provides an appropriate rationale for much of what we should be trying to do in educating children with disabilities; as a pretext for total integration or a rationale for wholesale mainstreaming and deinstitutionalization, its meaning is distorted to such an extent that it is in danger of becoming an empty slogan.

Conceptual Confusion

Proposals for integrating special and general education have reflected considerable confusion about basic concepts, including as they do the juxtaposition of incongruous meanings, the use of self-contradictory lines of argument, and antipathy toward critical analysis of purposes and means to achieve them. Such confusion leads inevitably to a circularity of reasoning that thwarts the good intentions of reformers.

Incongruities of Meaning

Much of the language of radical restructuring is peculiarly oxymoronic, containing appeals for common specialness, excellence without exception, and the normalization of exceptionality. Lipsky and Gartner conclude that "it is time to move on to the struggle of changing the educational system to make it both one and special for all students,"[31] ignoring the inherent contradiction of the concepts *same* and *special*. Another example of puzzling disregard of meanings in the reform literature is the statement of the National Center on Education and the Economy that "the challenge is to provide *an elite education for everyone*."[32] These nonsensical "struggles" and "challenges" are similar to others one might construct from combinations of opposite meanings, such as "The challenge is to foster democracy without involving ordinary citizens" or "It is time to move on to the struggle for standards of excellence not derived from comparisons." Perhaps such language has become the norm in the sound bites associated with advertising and political campaigns in which success is based on the assumption that the public will not think critically and analytically, but we hope for a higher level of discourse about educational reform—at least among educators. Language of this type belies any intent to bring intellectual integrity to the tasks of educating children and their teachers,[33] and it carries a peculiar irony when the avowed intent of reform is to promote critical thinking, prepare students to "render critical judgment," and produce students "whose understanding runs deep."[34]

Self-Contradictory Arguments

Lines of arguments offered in support of radical restructuring are often incoherent. One commonly finds self-contradictions in stated assumptions about why special and general education have failed and how their failures can be reversed.

In a paper circulated by the National Center on Education and the Economy, Gartner and Lipsky state that we must abandon the notion that learning problems are inherent in children: "The current practice of special education operates on a deficit model; that is, it identifies something as wrong or missing in the student."[35] Yet one of their recommendations for improving student productivity is "Do not waste time on 'teaching,'" and they go on to say that "the outcome of an education is student learning, [and] it is only the student who can do that learning."[36] On the one hand, they fault special education for identifying something wrong with the student; on the other hand, they argue that students, including those who have failed, hold the keys to their own failure and success.

Criticism of special education is occurring in the larger context of criticism of public education. General education, critics claim, is failing to reach its goals with many students, including those identified as handicapped and many who are not. We agree with Keogh that "it is a strange logic that calls for the regular system to take over responsibility for pupils it has already demonstrated it has failed."[37] MacMillan and Hendrick[38] buttress Singer's observation that "special education was the solution to the regular educator's thorny problem of how to provide supplemental resources to children in need while not shortchanging other students in the class. Nothing else has happened within regular education to solve this problem."[39] We note also that many of the instructional reforms so far implemented in general education and widely favored among general educators (e.g., less explicit, more child-directed, more "developmental" instruction) are those that researchers have found most likely to lead to failure for handicapped and at-risk students.[40]

Critics have characterized special education as a failure,[41] as segregationist,[42] as a way of diminishing children,[43] and as a second-rate system.[44] Yet the same writers have suggested that special education provides a model of what general education should become and that, were special education merged with general education, all students would benefit, none would be diminished, and general education could become first-rate. We do not understand how the alleged failures—general and special education—will be transformed by this fusion, particularly how losing its separate identity will turn special education from evil to good. We understand that reformers propose that purportedly nefarious aspects of special education (e.g., special identities called labels, students taught in places other than their home school or regular classroom) will not be parts of restructured education. But special programs present dilemmas, not the least of which is that when special identities of students are lost, so is the capacity to provide special services,[45] and that stigma and separation can be greater problems in home schools and regular classes than in alternative schools and classes.

Antipathy Toward Analyzing Purposes and Means

As Fuchs and Fuchs have noted, some have presented the goals of restructured general and special education in impressionistic, nonempirical terms.[46] Reformers say that special and general education as they currently exist have failed, and often we read and hear that neither "works."[47] Yet we are not told, except in impressionistic and even surrealistic language, how we should judge that either is "working."[48] The aversion to logical analysis of purposes and means is particularly evident in discussions of performance outcomes and policy (i.e., structure and regulation of access to programs).

What would characterize the distribution of outcomes if general or special education, or both, worked? If all students received an appropriate education, if not the best education possible, would we have fewer or more children who compare unfavorably to the majority on important outcomes? Would the disparities between the achievement of high and low performers become smaller or greater? That is, would we expect education that works to increase or decrease population variance? To us, it is apparent that these and other questions that must be addressed in careful analyses of performance goals have been sidestepped in appeals for reform. If they are not addressed, however, reform proposals are merely bravado, which leaves all of us confused about just what is intended.

Reformers also skirt questions regarding the relationship between special and general education. If special and general education are to become a unitary system, as some suggest,[49] what are the criteria for judging that they are unitary, not separate? What makes a program special or separate? Designated personnel? Special personnel training? Budget lines? Separate professional organizations? What percentage of time must a student be taught in a different curriculum to make a program separate or segregated from that received by others? What physical distance from another group of students constitutes segregation? If a unitary system is to be "supple" and "flexible," what are the criteria for judging that these characteristics have been achieved? Should it contain no option for special classes or schools, no different curricula or goals for different types of students, no "standard" expectations for any group of students? What would a supple, flexible system allow, and what would it disallow? Who will be the arbiters of what is acceptable and what is prohibited in a flexible system?

Given that certain components of a service delivery system are deemed essential, how does one create and maintain the policy structures necessary for their inclusion? Some reform advocates propose a unitary system of service delivery in which current federal regulations are reduced or eliminated.[50] We can think of no case in which important rights and protections are safeguarded without legislation and regulation, human nature being what it is. As Fuchs and Fuchs conclude, the appeal for a unitary, deregulated system is more than an ahistorical, nonempirical perspective; its naiveté invites the neglect of students with disabilities whenever there are competing interests, and there are always competing interests.[51] That a particular school or community appears, at least temporarily, to have gone beyond current regulations in the care of its students must not be interpreted to mean that public policy can be based on the assumption of public goodwill toward children with disabilities or that what is possible in one school is possible in any.

SPECIAL EDUCATION AS PART OF A COMPREHENSIVE SERVICE DELIVERY SYSTEM

To this point we have discussed only problems with the revisionist critique of special education. We acknowledge that special education is beset by substantial problems that must be addressed in any serious effort to improve it. We believe that these problems are primarily a result of inept professional practice and misunderstanding of what special education is. Contrary to the assertion that special education is flawed in its basic conception,[52] we maintain that the basic idea of special education is as sound as the very notion of public education. What is needed is not the reconceptualization or reinvention of special education but a sober look at the postulates on which a comprehensive service delivery system might be based and a careful examination of the extent to which the practice of special education so conceptualized falls short of the ideal. To this end we propose eight postulates and corollaries that might provide the framework for making special education an effective branch of a comprehensive service delivery system.

> **Postulate 1:** Public schooling must serve equitably the educational needs of all children by helping them achieve a level of academic, social, and vocational competence commensurate with their potential.

This postulate reaffirms our belief that public schools must serve more than academic needs and that it must address the full range of students' educational needs, from those of the most talented or educationally gifted to those of students with such severe intellectual impairments that they will be able to learn only simple self-care skills. It recognizes that students have needs that are not educational and acknowledges that some children, though a very few in number, may have no educational needs.

> **Corollary 1a:** Because public education must serve all children who have educational needs, the largest part of general education must be designed for the modal characteristics of students and teachers.

Public education by definition must serve the masses. Like any product or service designed for the public, most of public education must be designed to fit the most common (modal, "standard") characteristics of consumers. Economies of scale require that products and services designed for the general public be structured by the size, shape, and abilities of citizens falling within a limited band of variability around a mean. This does not mean that individuals with characteristics very different from the average cannot be accommodated by services or product lines designed and produced by public agencies; it does mean, however, that the needs of exceptional individuals will not be met by the standard products and services that are appropriate for most persons.

Likewise, education must be structured so that the modal teacher is capable of accomplishing the tasks of education with most students. This does not mean that the performance capability of the average teacher cannot be raised through better training; it does mean, however, that expectations for the performance of most teachers must not outstrip what the average teacher can do with appropriate training.

Corollary 1b: Because public education must address all children's educational needs, it must include explicit structures ensuring the accommodation of exceptional students.

Explicit structures creating differentiation of public services are required to meet extraordinary needs. Exceptional children by definition require extraordinary education—that which is different from the standard education that serves most students well. The structure of education includes goals, lines of authority, roles and responsibilities of personnel, budgets and purchases, allocation of time and space, curriculum, selection and assignment of students to classes, and evaluation. Failure to create and maintain explicit structures accommodating exceptional individuals inevitably results in the neglect of those for whom the core services are inadequate. The necessary explicit structures may become a predictable or required part (a "normal" part) of public services, but without these structures we can predict that exceptional individuals will be ill served.

Dramatic changes in certain school structures—lowering the typical class size to twelve or fewer students or placing two competent teachers in every class of twenty-five students, for example—would allow teachers to accommodate greater variability in student characteristics. Even assuming these desirable (but highly improbable) changes in standard school structures, however, teachers will not be able to accommodate every student within the new, standard structure. No single teaching arrangement is infinitely flexible.

Postulate 2: Exceptional students differ significantly from the modal or typical student in instructionally relevant ways that result in their inevitable failure, given standard educational goals and programs.

Abilities to access and process specific information are directly relevant to instruction. The extreme differences in such abilities of some students preclude their attainment of certain educational goals that are appropriate for most students. Moreover, standard instructional programs that are successful with most students cannot accommodate extreme differences in students' abilities to perceive, organize, store, retrieve, and apply information to the solution of specific problems. Thus, some exceptional students will fail to meet standard educational goals regardless of the instructional program that is provided; others will be able to meet standard educational goals but not with standard instructional programs.

Teachers must not be led down a path of fantasy or intellectual duplicity regarding what is possible and what their moral responsibility is when confronted by students whose needs they have not the resources to meet. Goodlad suggests, "For teacher education programs not to be models of educating is indefensible."[53] He notes, further, that teacher education programs have a moral responsibility to confront their limitations:

> Even supposing it could be argued that all traits are amenable to education, teacher education programs possess neither the resources nor the time to redress severe personality disorders; and they appear ill-equipped to perform much lesser tasks. Consequently, the moral and ethical imperatives of selection require that applicants be counseled out if they fall seriously short in characteristics that are deemed important but for which there are no programmatic provisions. Failure to so counsel is morally wrong, and the consequences are costly.[54]

We believe that the same moral responsibility applies to teachers in our public schools who are aware that they are ill equipped to redress the limitations of their students' ability to learn.

Corollary 2a: The requirements of alternative educational goals and programs must be made explicit for exceptional students.

When standard goals or instructional methods are inappropriate for a student, appropriate alternatives must be available. These alternatives will not be available in all school systems unless they are explicitly required by law and regulation, as public attention and economies of scale are inevitably centered on meeting modal needs. The implicit or explicit assumption that standard educational goals and programs will accommodate the educational needs of all students is not only logically untenable but places the onus of proof on the student when questions regarding an individual student arise. The explicit requirement of alternatives to meet the needs of exceptional students places the burden of proof on the school's service delivery system.

Corollary 2b: Alternative goals and programs must be expressed as alternative curricula and methods for exceptional students.

Educational goals and programs entail instructional materials, teaching procedures, and an array of activities designed to result in the acquisition of specific skills, attitudes, and values. Thus, goals and programs for exceptional students involve alternative curricula or methods, beyond the range of the standard materials, procedures, and activities that produce acceptable outcomes for most students.

Corollary 2c: Alternative curricula and methods sometimes require alternative grouping of students.

It is axiomatic that a teacher cannot teach all things to all students at the same time. Students are necessarily grouped for instruction in specific content according to the teachers' instructional capabilities and the germane pupil characteristics. Moreover, the greater the variability in a group of the students in their characteristics germane to instruction (beyond a base level of manageable variability), the smaller the number of students a teacher is able to instruct successfully. Efficient and effective instruction of nonexceptional students can best be accomplished by forming standard patterns of grouping (i.e., groups designed for instruction of students falling within a band of teachability in specific skills). Effective and efficient instruction of exceptional students sometimes requires nonstandard groupings to facilitate the use of alternative curricula and methods.

Both general and special educators teach heterogeneous groups of students. Teachers observe variability between students on specific characteristics and within individual students in various domains such as academic, social, and vocational skills. Instructional grouping must be designed to limit the heterogeneity of students to facilitate effective and efficient instruction.

We recognize that some categorical groupings do not achieve their intent of substantially reducing the variability among students to be instructed. Moreover, we recognize that it is neither possible nor desirable to reduce the variance of instructionally relevant characteristics in groups of students to near zero. Effective teaching demands the ability to accommodate a tolerable level of student variance. Nevertheless, we assert that, as Goodlad argues for teacher education, a moral commitment to educating children and youth carries with it the clear implication that teachers must recognize the limitations of their ability to accommodate student variance and seek alternative instruction for those whom they are not equipped to serve competently.[55] A further implication is that in a comprehensive service delivery system, the student whose characteristics are judged to be incompatible with those of an instructional group must be included in an alternative group of students for whom alternative instruction is offered. A final implication is that individual instruction in one or more areas of the curriculum may be required for some students.

We note that alternative grouping of students for special education may sometimes be necessary to avoid significant deleterious effects for nonhandicapped students. At times, students with disabilities may be so disruptive or otherwise require so great a proportion of the teacher's resources that the educational needs of other members of the class suffer to a significant degree. We recognize that the degree of interference with the education of other students is a matter of professional judgment, but we think it better that the issue be addressed rather than ignored. We believe that it is the moral responsibility of the teacher to see that all students are receiving a fair chance to succeed. The consequences of failure to make such judgments in education are, as Goodlad points out, costly.[56]

Postulate 3: Exceptional students must have open to them the full range of options for instructional grouping and environments for delivery of educational services. No single curriculum, instructional approach, grouping plan, or learning environment is appropriate for all students.

Given the extreme differences in the instructionally relevant characteristics of children and youth, a very wide range of options for instructional grouping and learning environments is required. It is self-evident that not all kinds of instruction and environmental conditions can be present in one classroom or school at the same time. Recognition of variance in instructional needs, beyond lip service to designing individualized programs, demands recognition of the need for variance in service delivery options. Restriction to one or a few service delivery options increases the rate of poor fits between students and the curricula and methods employed in their instruction.[57]

> **Corollary 3a:** The full range of grouping options ranges from full-time placement in standard educational curricula and groups with special assistance to special residential schools.

We may assume that for educational purposes students are not exceptional if their needs are adequately met in standard educational groups and by standard curricula and methods without supplementary services. Some exceptional students' appropriate education is possible without alternative grouping, so long as they are provided supplementary services (e.g., alternative instructional strategies) not required by modal students. Thus, not all exceptional students need alternative grouping for instruction. Other students, however, are exceedingly unlikely to receive appropriate education without placement in alternative instructional groups or alternative learning environments. The relevant characteristics of some students are so different from those of most students that they require substantially different environments for learning in one or more areas of their curriculum. These different environments may be best constructed in part-time or full-time special classes, alternative day schools, or residential schools.

> **Corollary 3b:** Selection of instructional and grouping options should be guided by the policies and procedures established in IDEA (P.L. 94-142); parents and teachers must together select the least restrictive appropriate option from a full range of alternatives.

In 1975, P.L. 94-142 (now IDEA) established the expectation that appropriate education of children with disabilities will be a part of all schools' service delivery system. The policy represented in this law is that decisions regarding appropriate education and the least restrictive environment will be made jointly by educators and parents of students with disabilities on an individual basis. Procedural protections in the law are designed to ensure that a full range of instructional and grouping options is available and that the environment (placement) option judged least restrictive is chosen from those that are first judged appropriate.

> **Postulate 4:** Alternative goals and instruction needed by exceptional students will not be ensured without explicit, permanent

structures that include them in a comprehensive system of public education.

Public education itself was established by explicit, permanent structures, first those creating public schools, then those involving mandatory school attendance, later those granting equal access to schooling by students of color, and more recently those ensuring accommodations of students with disabilities. In each case, explicit and permanent structures were required to produce the intended benefits to students and the larger society. In the case of special education, the basic structures were provided by IDEA.

Corollary 4a: These structures must include special education as an integral but clearly differentiated part of a comprehensive service delivery system; the structures must include special teachers, administrators, funding mechanisms, and procedures.

IDEA established, within the larger structure of general education, mechanisms designed to require attention to the needs of students with disabilities. These mechanisms include fiscal, administrative, procedural, and instructional requirements that are necessary to ensure the inclusion of special education in school systems' service delivery. Without identifiable special personnel, specific funding channels, and procedural requirements, school systems are unlikely to be held accountable for their accommodation of students with disabilities; without these structures, the burden of proof of failure to accommodate is on the student and parents.

Corollary 4b: Special education structures must be ongoing; they must not be viewed as temporary measures that can be eliminated once their objectives have been achieved and special education is ensconced in public education.

The structures that created public schools, required student attendance, demanded equal access by students regardless of color, and required accommodation of students with disabilities cannot be abandoned under the assumption that once they have accomplished their purpose they are superfluous. Without constant attention to their preservation and maintenance, these structures and the practices they support will inevitably deteriorate and collapse. Special education has become an integral part of public education service delivery, but it will be maintained as such only if its supportive structures are maintained.

Postulate 5: The structures needed to ensure appropriate education of exceptional students require carefully regulated decisions regarding which students shall receive specific educational options.

Special provisions for at least some students with special needs have been "normal" components of the public education service delivery system of most state and local education agencies for two decades or more. Only since 1975, however, has federal education policy set the expectation that special education for all students with disabilities will be a part of the total symmetry of schools. Prior to the enactment of IDEA, the designation of students as having special needs, and therefore as needing special education programs, was not carefully regulated in most states. Consequently, decisions regarding the selection of individual students for specific instructional options were often capricious, and parents were often excluded from participation in the processes of identification and placement of their children.

Students cannot be provided educational options that are substantially different from the standard program without someone's making the decisions regarding which students should receive such options and which students should not. If one argues that no student should receive a "standard" program—that all students' programs should be individualized, and therefore "special"—we can predict that the vast majority of students' programs will be highly similar and hence "special" only in name. That is, it is predictable that a limited range of variability will define what is typical, expected, or unremarkable for students of a given age. Some students, however, will need programs that are remarkable outliers (i.e., very different from most).

The question remains, should the decision that a student needs a substantially different program from that appropriate for most students be regulated, such that special consideration and parental participation are required? One might argue that the same level of care and parental participation should be required in decisions regarding all students' programs. We question whether this argument can be grounded in the realities of public schooling and understanding of the responsibilities of teachers. Moreover, we see this argument as reducing all students' needs to unity, not merely to a common denominator. It is based on the denial of difference, not its recognition. The consequences of educators treating decisions regarding all students' programs with the same level of scrutiny would be predictably disastrous for students with special needs, much as the failure of professionals in other fields (law and medicine come immediately to mind) to discriminate cases requiring a special level of scrutiny would predictably result in grotesque malpractice.

Corollary 5a: Selection of education options is unavoidably judgmental, requiring informed professional and parental judgment of the individual student's abilities and needs.

There are two ways for educators to avoid making difficult judgments about which students should be granted special options. One is to treat all cases the same, which, as we have discussed, is tantamount to malpractice. The other is to set forth criteria based on psychometric data and to make these criteria the sole basis for decisions, which may seem to remove subjectivity from the decision-making process but also leads inevitably to abrogation of professional responsibility.

Education, like every other profession, is inherently judgmental. To speak of the "judgmentally handicapped" is as trite as to speak of the "judgmentally guilty," the "judgmentally ill," or an automobile that is "judgmentally unsafe." When disability or guilt or danger is said to be "obvious," we must ask, "Obvious to whom?" When the consequences are significant for the individual about whom a decision is made, society imposes regulatory mechanisms for making judgments, including procedural and authority structures.

True, there are cases in which most or all casual observers might judge an individual to have a disability—the "obvious" cases. Nevertheless, the great majority of cases of disability are not "obvious" to the casual observer. Moreover, the suggestion that special education should serve only the "obvious" cases or those whose disabilities are "severe" does not make special education nonjudgmental. "Obvious" and "severe" are themselves judgments about which well-informed persons may disagree. A structure is needed, therefore, for decision making in the case of students who may need nonstandard educational options. IDEA and attendant regulations set forth such a structure, which requires that the informed and combined judgment of educators and parents be the basis for the identification of handicapped students and for designing their programs.

Corollary 5b: The procedures for making judgments regarding educational options must be explicit, not covert.

As we have seen, judgments regarding the educational options students are eligible to receive cannot be avoided. All options should be available to all students who need them, but it is obvious that not all students will need all options. How, then, are decisions regarding options to be made? Asserting that general education should be sufficiently "flexible" or "supple" to accommodate all students begs the question; it is a ruse for driving the decision-making process underground, unless the regulatory mechanisms for decision making are explicated. IDEA was enacted in large measure because identification and placement decisions regarding handicapped children were not aboveboard. Moreover, the law was designed precisely to require that public education be flexible, supple, and accommodating of special needs.

When explicit structures for making decisions are not present, decisions regarding selection of curriculum and programming options cannot be monitored effectively.[58] Appeals to deregulate special education eligibility decisions are a direct appeal to abandon the structures—the procedural protections—that are necessary to maintain open and accountable decision making.

> **Corollary 5c:** Judgments regarding educational options must not be made solely on the basis of psychometric data; teachers and parents must be the primary decision makers.

Psychometric assessments may yield useful information for decision making, but they are not sufficient in themselves for determining students' educational needs. Parents and those who are responsible for teaching the student must be the primary decision makers. Their decisions may be imperfect, but they are nevertheless the best equipped to make decisions regarding individual pupils when their judgment is informed by the best available data.[59] This principle is embodied in IDEA.

> **Corollary 5d:** Selection of specific educational options unavoidably results in labeling.

Individuals who receive educational programs (or any other treatment or recognition that others do not) are labeled by whatever language we use to describe them. The labels may not be the traditional ones associated with special education, but they are labels nonetheless.[60] Care must be taken to avoid letting labels turn into abusive epithets, but our choice is clear: Either we label students with disabilities by speaking of their special needs, or we label them only as students, thereby denying the possibility of providing special programs for them.

Furthermore, the suggestion that programs but not students should be labeled[61] is gratuitous, as IDEA requires special education labels only for reporting purposes. The law does not require that students themselves be given labels, nor does it require that students be grouped by traditional special education categories. With regard to labels, the law requires only that programs for students with specific handicapping conditions be available and that students with disabilities be placed in programs designed to meet their special individual needs. The appeal for restructuring that eliminates labeling, then, must be seen for what it is—an appeal based on misrepresentation of the law and one not cognizant of the consequences of ignoring differences.

Postulate 6: Appropriate education of exceptional students depends on adequate preparation of professional personnel.

Teaching exceptional students well requires specialized training as surely as specialized training is required for other professionals who deal with unusual cases. We recognize that basic professional training must prepare the teacher to respond appropriately to a wide range of students. All professions see the need for a core of common training as well as the need for specialized training for those who will serve clients with particular needs.

Corollary 6a: All professional educators must be prepared to accommodate diversity among students and to recognize the need of some students for alternative instruction.

All teachers must be prepared to deal with diversity among the students they teach. It is also axiomatic that all teachers have limitations in the diversity they are able to accommodate. A critical aspect of ethical practice in any profession is recognition of one's limitations of training and expertise. Teachers who are unprepared or unwilling to request consultation from others and to refer a student for possible alternative placement when they are not able to meet the student's needs are in violation of federal special education policy as stated in IDEA. Moreover, they are violating standards of professional conduct.

Corollary 6b: Special educators must be prepared first as general educators and, following a period of successful practice as general educators, receive additional extensive training in specialized instruction.

One of the most substantial problems faced by special education is improving the competence of its classroom practitioners. Our belief is that special education has erred in its preparation of preservice teachers. Special education teachers must have prior training and experience as general educators if their training is to be truly specialized and if they are to collaborate effectively with teachers in general education classrooms. More than a cursory textbook understanding of the conditions and rigors of teaching in general education is required of special teachers who are to be collaborators with general educators.

Corollary 6c: Optimum accommodation of exceptional students depends on preparation of general and special educators to collaborate with other professionals and parents.

Teachers will become effective collaborators only if they are taught the procedures and skills involved in working with professional colleagues. Both general and special educators must receive training in how to work with each other for the benefit of exceptional students, how to work with noneducation professionals whose related services are required for their students, and how to work with parents as partners. The neglect of these procedures and skills in teacher training programs is a serious problem limiting the effectiveness of special education as part of a comprehensive service delivery system.

Postulate 7: The outcomes used to judge the effectiveness of general education are not always appropriate as criteria for judging the effectiveness of special education.

Special education is sometimes assessed by noting discrepancies between the performance of students with disabilities and that of the general population of students. Predictably, special education so weighed is found wanting, as the measure of success is inappropriate. Many students with disabilities can, if they are provided appropriate education, be expected to achieve outcomes similar to those of their nondisabled peers. It is predictable, however, that the rate of failure by those standards (e.g., graduation rate, number of passing grades, transition to higher education, successful employment) will be higher for students with disabilities than among students without disabilities, given equally appropriate education for the two groups. Special education must be conceptualized as a continuing support system for students who cannot be enabled to participate in programs appropriate for modal students as well as a means of addressing academic and social deficits that are remediable.

Corollary 7a: Appropriate education for exceptional students will not necessarily result in their performance within the range deemed adequate, expected, or "normal" for nonexceptional students.

The expectation of a "cure" for educational disabilities—enabling all disabled students to function as if their disabilities no longer existed—is not realistic. If appropriate education is assumed to be only that which allows the student to achieve "normal" educational progress, then many exceptional students, their teachers, their parents, and the public face uninterrupted failure and censure.

Corollary 7b: The informed, ethical behavior of practitioners is an important criterion for evaluating the appropriateness of special education and evaluating its practices.

The extent to which special education improves students' performance over what they would otherwise achieve is an important criterion for evaluating its practice, but it must not be the sole criterion. As is the case in other professions, the outcome of individual cases must be evaluated in the light of the best professional practices under the circumstances. The extent to which procedures designed to protect the interests of the involved parties were followed and the extent to which the behavior of professional practitioners was informed and ethical must be weighed in the balance.

Postulate 8: Special education may not be the only special compensatory program serving students who have difficulty in school, but it must be maintained as a branch of general education having special identity and articulation with other programs.

It is a truism that many students have difficulty in school. Nevertheless, we can safely assume that the effective education of all students will not eliminate variance in the desired performance outcomes of the student population. In fact, we venture that a uniform degree of improvement in the education offered every student would increase the population variance in such outcomes, which would make the educationally "disadvantaged" even more so. This is one of the reasons we believe compensatory education programs are necessary for students who perform poorly; such programs are a means of "leveling the playing field" somewhat in the interests of fairness and human compassion as well as the eventual economic benefits of the habilitation of those who are given special assistance.

All compensatory programs are by definition failure-driven; they are intended to compensate for conditions producing actual or predicted failure of individuals. Access to compensatory programs is knowingly granted only to individuals judged to be in jeopardy, and for good reason: Access by all squanders the resources intended for those "at risk" and, predictably, quickly bankrupts the program. When the risk factors that predict failure are complex, poorly understood, and pandemic, as they are in many schools, extraordinary care must be taken to protect the interests of specific groups through special allocations of compensatory resources. Attention to either prevention or remediation alone is insufficient; special resources must be allocated both to programs designed to avoid failure and to those designed to cope with the reality of failure.

> **Corollary 8a:** An array of special programs with specific eligibility criteria for participation is an appropriate means of creating a comprehensive service delivery of general education.

Given the range of educational needs in most school systems, it is not reasonable to believe that one compensatory program will be sufficient to provide the comprehensive services necessary. Even those who argue passionately for restructuring to eliminate special program authority recognize the need for an array of special programs for selected students. One can imagine a school situation that has programs such as the following (Reynolds's list includes five more):[62]

- The Braille Reading Program
- The Reading Recovery Program
- The Intensive Basic Skills Program
- The Social Skills Program
- The White Cane and Mobility Program

As we have seen, the issue of eligibility for special programs cannot be avoided. The criteria and procedures for determining individual students' eligibility for specific programs must be regulated explicitly. Otherwise, eligibility will be covertly determined, the reasons and processes for program selection being matters one cannot monitor effectively.

> **Corollary 8b:** Efforts to marginalize or disable special education by obscuring its identity through its assimilation into general education must be resisted.

To flourish, a program of education must enjoy visibility, status, budget, and personnel—those things that give it borders and identity. Without these, the program inevitably becomes increasingly derelict in both intent and accomplishment. Goodlad describes the unhappy situation of teacher education:

> First, the farther down in a university's organizational structure teacher education finds itself, the less chance it has to obtain the conditions necessary to a healthy, dynamic existence. Second, the farther down in the hierarchy teacher education finds itself, the less likely it is that it will enjoy the tender loving care of those tenure-line faculty members universities strive so hard to recruit. Who, then, speaks for teacher education? Who speaks for those who would become teachers?[63]

We might substitute *special education* for *teacher education* in this statement. Goodlad goes on to suggest the minimum essentials for making teacher education "[fit] comfortably into the context of a college or university":

1. A school or center of pedagogy with a sole commitment to teaching

2. "Its own budget, determined in negotiation at the highest level of budget approvals, and this budget must be immune to erosion by competing interests"

3. Authority and responsibility for student selection and personnel

4. A full complement of faculty

5. Control over specification of prerequisites for admission[64]

We suggest that the same minimum essentials are necessary for special education to fit comfortably into the context of the public school. Those who encourage general education to assimilate special education fully or urge special education to merge with general education cannot be both aware of the realities of educational organizations and concerned for special education's viability.

CONCLUSION

The capacity of American public education to respond humanely and effectively to variance among students should be expanded, but this can be accomplished only by maintaining and strengthening the essential structures on which a comprehensive delivery system is based. Although general and special education are now distinctive parts of an integrated system, their interface needs more attention.

Many of the suggestions for restructuring or integrating special and general education, however, are based on notions that have a highly charming surface appeal but are the antitheses of a reflective, analytical approach to the problems of designing a comprehensive service delivery system of education to serve an extremely diverse student body. They suppose a world in which one never need take a hard look at realities, one in which inspirational rhetoric and the callousness of policymakers in the Reagan-Bush era to the plight of the socially, economically, and educationally disinherited will carry the day. We return to Goodlad's observations on the conditions of renewal in teacher education. He calls for substantially increased resources to conduct the enterprise.

> And these resources must be made secure for the purposes intended. That is, they must be earmarked for and assigned to a unit with clear borders, a specified number of students with a common purpose, and a roster of largely full-time faculty requisite to the formal and informal socialization of these students into teaching. Put negatively, these resources must not go to the larger, multipurpose unit of which teacher education is a part; there they run the danger of being impounded by entrepreneurial program heads and faculty members.[65]

The people responsible for teacher education, suggests Goodlad, must have clear focus, identity, and authority. His prediction of the alternative: "Otherwise, teacher education will remain an orphan, dependent on charity and goodwill."[66] We believe that the same is true for special education if its mission is to be taken seriously. Special education once was what Goodlad describes as the inevitable consequence of lack of focus, identity, and authority—an orphan, dependent on charity and goodwill in a larger, multipurpose unit, its resources constantly in danger of impoundment by competing interests. The interests now competing most overtly for special education's resources are (1) concern for underachieving students who are at risk for greater failure and (2) pursuit of the higher performance of "all" students out of concern for America's economic competitiveness. These interests will, of course, seek to attach special education's resources by arguing that these assets must not be protected from infringement because their reallocation or redistribution can serve not only children with disabilities but the common good as well.

After a long period of struggle, special education has finally achieved the status of a normal part of public general education and been integrated into the fabric of our thinking about students' special needs. It has done so only by recognizing the realities of which Goodlad speaks, and it will remain such only if it is successful in fending off the entrepreneurial interests and irresponsible attacks that threaten its hard-won position.

AUTHORS' NOTE

Preparation of this manuscript was supported in part by the Commonwealth Center for the Education of Teachers, Curry School of Education, 405 Emmet Street, University of Virginia, Charlottesville, VA 22903. We are grateful to Doug Fuchs for his helpful comments on an earlier version of this chapter.

NOTES

1. William F. Blount and Thomas H. Kean, *Designs for a New Generation of American Schools: A Request for Proposals* (Arlington, VA: New American Schools Development Corporation, 1991), 3.
2. C. C. Carson, R. M. Huelskamp, and T. D. Woodall, *Perspectives on Education in America: Annotated Briefing—Third Draft* (Albuquerque: Systems Analysis Department, Sandia National Laboratories, 1991), p. 172.
3. See also John W. Lloyd, Alan C. Repp, and Nirbhay N. Singh, eds., *The Regular Education Initiative: Alternative Perspectives on Concepts, Issues, and Models* (Sycamore, IL: Sycamore, 1991).
4. Gerald W. Bracey, "Why Can't They Be Like We Were?" *Phi Delta Kappan* 73 (1991): 104–17. See also Carson et al., *Perspectives on Education.*
5. See also Irving G. Hendrick and Donald L. MacMillan, "Selecting Children for Special Education in New York City: William Maxwell, Elizabeth Farrell, and the Development of Upgraded Classes, 1900–1920," *Journal of Special Education* 22 (1989): 395–417.
6. *Timothy W. v. Rochester, New Hampshire School District,* 875 F.2d 954 (1st Cir. 1989), cert. denied, 110 S. Ct. 519 (1989). See also Martha M. McCarthy, "Severely Disabled Children: Who Pays?" *Phi Delta Kappan* 73, no. 1 (Sept. 1991): 66–71.
7. Anne M. Hocutt, Edwin W. Martin, and James D. McKinney, "Historical and Legal Context of Mainstreaming" in *The Regular Education Initiative,* 24.

8. Dorothy K. Lipsky and Alan Gartner, "Capable of Achievement and Worthy of Respect: Education for Handicapped Students as If They Were Full-fledged Human Beings," *Exceptional Children 54* (1987): 69–74.

9. National Center on Education and the Economy (NCEE), *To Secure Our Future* (Rochester, NY: National Center on Education and the Economy, 1989), 9.

10. See Robert E. Slavin, "General Education under the Regular Education Initiative: How Must It Change?" *Remedial and Special Education 11,* no. 3 (1990): 40–50; Robert E. Slavin et al., "Neverstreaming: Prevention and Early Intervention as an Alternative to Special Education," *Journal of Learning Disabilities 24* (1991): 373–78.

11. See Melvyn I. Semmel and Michael M. Gerber, "If at First You Don't Succeed, Bye, Bye Again: A Response to General Educators' Views on the REI," *Remedial and Special Education 11,* no. 4 (1990): 53–59; Robert E. Slavin, "On Success for All: Defining 'Success,' Defining 'All,'" *Remedial and Special Education 11,* no. 4 (1990): 60–61.

12. For example, see Margaret C. Wang, Maynard C. Reynolds, and Herbert J. Walberg, "Rethinking Special Education," *Educational Leadership 44,* no. 1 (1986): 26–31; Margaret C. Wang, Maynard C. Reynolds, and Herbert J. Walberg, "Integrating the Children of the Second System," *Phi Delta Kappan 70* (1988): 248–51; Margaret C. Wang and Nancy J. Zollers, "Adaptive Instruction: An Alternative Service Delivery Approach," *Remedial and Special Education 11,* no. 1 (1990): 7–21.

13. Douglas Biklen and Nancy Zollers, "The Focus of Advocacy in the LD Field," *Journal of Learning Disabilities 19* (1986): 583.

14. James H. Bryan and Tanis H. Bryan, "Where's the Beef? A Review of Published Research on the Adaptive Learning Environment Model," *Learning Disabilities Focus 4,* no. 1 (1988): 9–14; Douglas Fuchs and Lynn S. Fuchs, "An Evaluation of the Adaptive Learning Environments Model," *Exceptional Children 55* (1988): 115–27.

15. Slavin et al., "Neverstreaming," 377.

16. Maynard C. Reynolds, Margaret C. Wang, and Herbert J. Walberg, "The Necessary Restructuring of Special and Regular Education," *Exceptional Children 53* (1987): 391–98.

17. Carson et al., *Perspectives on Education.*

18. Biklen and Zollers, "The Focus of Advocacy"; Alan Gartner and Dorothy K. Lipsky, *The Yoke of Special Education: How to Break It* (Rochester, NY: National Center on Education and the Economy, 1989); Dorothy K. Lipsky and Alan Gartner, "Restructuring for Quality" in *The Regular Education Initiative,* 43–57; Maynard C. Reynolds, "An Historical Perspective: The Delivery of Special Education to Mildly Disabled and At-risk Students," *Remedial and Special Education 10,* no. 6 (1989): 7–11.

19. Douglas Fuchs and Lynn S. Fuchs, "Framing the REI Debate: Abolitionists Versus Conservationists" in *The Regular Education Initiative,* 241–55; Daniel P. Hallahan, James M. Kauffman, John W. Lloyd, and James D. McKinney, eds., "Questions about the Regular Education Initiative," *Journal of Learning Disabilities 21,* no. 1, special issue (1988); James M. Kauffman, "The Regular Education Initiative as Reagan-Bush Education Policy: A Trickle-Down Theory of Education of the Hard-to-Teach," *Journal of Special Education 23* (1989): 256–78; James M. Kauffman,

"Restructuring in Sociopolitical Context: Reservations about the Effects of Current Reform Proposals on Students with Disabilities" in *The Regular Education Initiative*, 57–66; James M. Kauffman and Daniel P. Hallahan, "What We Want for Children: A Rejoinder to REI Proponents," *Journal of Special Education 24* (1990): 340–45; James M. Kauffman and Patricia L. Pullen, "An Historical Perspective: A Personal Perspective on Our History of Service to Mildly Handicapped and At-risk Students," *Remedial and Special Education 10*, no. 6 (1989): 12–14.

20. Lipsky and Gartner, "Capable of Achievement"; William Stainback and Susan Stainback, "A Rationale for Integration and Restructuring: A Synopsis" in *The Regular Education Initiative*, 225–39; Madeleine C. Will, "Let Us Pause and Reflect—But Not Too Long," *Exceptional Children 51* (1984): 11–16.

21. Kauffman, "The Regular Education Initiative"; Kauffman and Hallahan, "What We Want for Children."

22. For example, Alan Gartner and Dorothy K. Lipsky, "Beyond Special Education: Toward a Quality System for All Students," *Harvard Educational Review 57* (1987): 367–95.

23. Wolf Wolfensberger, "The Definition of Normalization: Update, Problems, Disagreements, and Misunderstandings" in *Normalization, Social Integration, and Community Services*, ed. R. J. Flynn and K. E. Nitsch (Baltimore: University Park Press, 1980), 71–115.

24. Ibid., 98.

25. Ibid.

26. James A. Mulick, and Jurgen H. Kedesdy, "Self-injurious Behavior, Its Treatment, and Normalization," *Mental Retardation 26*, no. 4 (1988): 223–29.

27. W. A. T. White, "A Meta-analysis of the Effects of Direct Instruction in Special Education," *Education and Treatment of Children 11*, no. 4 (1988): 364–74.

28. Stanley Hauerwas, *Suffering Presence: Theological Reflections on Medicine, the Mentally Handicapped, and the Church* (Notre Dame, IN: University of Notre Dame Press, 1986), 213.

29. See N. E. Bank-Mikkelsen, "A Metropolitan Area in Denmark: Copenhagen" in *Changing Patterns of Residential Services for the Mentally Retarded*, ed. Robert B. Kugel and Wolf Wolfensberger (Washington, D.C.: President's Committee on Mental Retardation, 1969), 227–54; B. Nirje, "The Normalization Principle and Its Human Management Implications" in *Changing Patterns in Residential Services*, 179–95; Wolfensberger, "The Definition of Normalization."

30. Wolf Wolfensberger, *Normalization* (Toronto: National Institute on Mental Retardation, 1972), 238.

31. Lipsky and Gartner, "Capable of Achievement," 73.

32. NCEE, *To Secure Our Future*, 9.

33. See John I. Goodlad, *Teachers for Our Nation's Schools* (San Francisco: Jossey-Bass, 1990).

34. Carnegie Forum on Education and the Economy, *A Nation Prepared: Teachers for the 21st Century* (New York: Carnegie Foundation, 1986), 20.

35. Gartner and Lipsky, *The Yoke of Special Education*, 20.

36. Ibid., 28.

37. Barbara K. Keogh, "Improving Services for Problem Learners: Rethinking and Restructuring," *Journal of Learning Disabilities 21* (1988): 20.

38. Chap. 2 in this book; see also Hendrick and MacMillan, "Selecting Children for Special Education."

39. Judith D. Singer, "Should Special Education Merge with Regular Education?" *Educational Policy 2* (1988): 416.

40. Douglas Carnine, "Increasing the Amount and Quality of Learning through Direct Instruction: Implications for Mathematics" in *The Regular Education Initiative,* 163–75; Douglas Carnine and Edward Kameenui, "The Regular Education Initiative and Children with Special Needs: A False Dilemma in the Face of True Problems," *Journal of Learning Disabilities 23* (1990): 141–44.

41. Lipsky and Gartner, "Restructuring for Quality."

42. Stainback and Stainback, "A Rationale for Integration and Restructuring."

43. Lipsky and Gartner, "Capable of Achievement."

44. Wang et al., "Rethinking Special Education"; Wang et al., "Integrating the Children of the Second System."

45. See Martha Minow, "Learning to Live with the Dilemma of Difference: Bilingual and Special Education" in *Children with Special Needs,* ed. Katharine T. Bartlett and Judith W. Wenger (New Brunswick, NJ: Transaction Books, 1987), 375–429.

46. Fuchs and Fuchs, "Framing the REI Debate."

47. For example, Lipsky and Gartner, "Restructuring for Quality."

48. James M. Kauffman, "What Happens When Special Education Works? The Sociopolitical Context of Special Education Research in the 1990s," invited address, Special Interest Group: Special Education Research (Boston: Annual Meeting of the American Educational Research Association, April 1990).

49. For example, Dorothy K. Lipsky and Alan Gartner, "Restructuring for Quality"; Stainback and Stainback, "A Rationale for Integration and Restructuring."

50. For example, Gartner and Lipsky, *The Yoke of Special Education;* NCEE, *To Secure Our Future.*

51. Fuchs and Fuchs, "Framing the REI Debate." See also Hocutt et al., "Historical and Legal Context of Mainstreaming."

52. Lipsky and Gartner, "Restructuring for Quality."

53. Goodlad, *Teachers for Our Nation's Schools,* 59.

54. Ibid., 284.

55. Ibid.

56. Ibid.

57. See James M. Kauffman and Stanley C. Trent, "Issues in Service Delivery for Students with Learning Disabilities" in *Learning about Learning Disabilities,* ed. Bernice Y. L. Wong (New York: Academic Press, 1991), 465–81, for comments regarding learning disabilities.

58. Catherine A. Feniak, "Labelling in Special Education: A Problematic Issue in England and Wales," *International Journal of Special Education 3* (1988): 117–24.

59. Michael M. Gerber and Melvyn I. Semmel, "Teacher as Imperfect Test: Reconceptualizing the Referral Process," *Educational Psychologist 19* (1984): 137–48.

60. See Feniak, "Labelling in Special Education"; Martha Minow, "Learning to Live with the Dilemma of Difference."

61. Maynard C. Reynolds, "Classification and Labeling" in *The Regular Education Initiative,* 29–41; see also Stainback and Stainback, "A Rationale for Integration and Restructuring."

62. Reynolds, "Classification and Labeling," 35.

63. Goodlad, *Teachers for Our Nation's Schools,* 277.

64. Ibid., 278.

65. Ibid., 152.

66. Ibid., 153.

Chapter 10

How We Might Achieve the Radical Reform of Special Education

James M. Kauffman

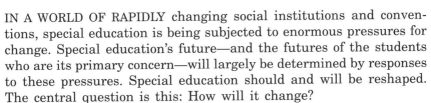

IN A WORLD OF RAPIDLY changing social institutions and conventions, special education is being subjected to enormous pressures for change. Special education's future—and the futures of the students who are its primary concern—will largely be determined by responses to these pressures. Special education should and will be reshaped. The central question is this: How will it change?

Those who are skeptical of proposed reforms are typically depicted as defenders of the status quo. An alternative perspective is that the status quo in education has been a succession of reforms, many of which were not based on careful analyses of the problems or tools of teaching or of the policies that constrain practice. Most reform movements in education have led to disappointment and a predictable reversal of direction, rather than to progress—the familiar phenomenon described as a cycle, pendulum, or wave (cf. Carnine, 1992; Cuban, 1990; Sarason, 1990; Zigler, Hodapp, & Edison, 1990).

The current reform movement in both general and special education appears to be weakly linked to logical or empirical analyses and largely unmindful of history. Special education, however, may have the means to achieve the substantive reforms that are needed to

Reprinted from "How we might achieve the radical reform of special education" by James M. Kauffman, *Exceptional Children*, Vol. 60, 1993, 6–16. Copyright © 1993 by The Council for Exceptional Children. Reprinted by permission.

advance its practice. The profession could confront its problems in ways likely to bring truly substantive, lasting change—reform that is radical in that its failure is not highly predictable.

Much commentary about special education reform from both sides of the issue has been clangorous and rancorous, perhaps diverting attention from more important issues (e.g., Gartner & Lipsky, 1989; Kauffman, 1989, 1991, 1992a; Lipsky & Gartner, 1987, 1991; Wang & Walberg, 1988). Recognizing consensus is at least as important as emphasizing differences. Raspberry (1992) noted the importance of distinguishing between enemies and problems. Problems persist after enemies are vanquished, and diverting energy into battles with real or imagined enemies often prevents or delays solutions.

Significant agreements can be found among most educators, researchers, and parents committed to the appropriate education of students with disabilities, regardless of their views on current reform. Nearly all advocates for students with disabilities want effective instruction in academic and social skills, appropriate education in the least restrictive environment, public education that accommodates students with special problems, labels that carry the least possible social stigma, parental participation in decisions to provide special services, and collaboration among all services providers. There probably are many other points of agreement, and these could provide leverage for reform.

Many of special education's problems will persist whether the current calls for restructuring are answered or ignored. A central problem is that too many students are poorly served by special education because their programs are not really special—no more appropriate than the programs they would receive in general education. For these students, special education does little to enhance academic or social learning or prepare them for life after school. This problem may be largely a function of inadequate training and support of special education teachers, not other structural weaknesses. No structural change is likely to make much difference unless it improves the teacher–student interactions that constitute academic instruction and behavior management. One can recite a litany of other problems, all of which critics have listed and reiterated. However, many problems cited by proponents of restructuring are relatively superficial; the proposed changes are primarily alterations of image, location, and administrative structure, not the learner–teacher interactions that are at the core of effective instruction. The issue, then, is how to achieve reform that will make a substantive, lasting difference in what special education does for students, not a cosmetic, temporary change in structure.

In his reflections on school reform and its predictable failure, Sarason (1990) suggested that attempts to reform education will make little difference until reformers understand that schools must exist as much for teachers as for students. Put another way, schools will be successful in nurturing the intellectual, social, and moral development of children only to the extent that they also nurture such development of teachers. The notion that what is good for students is also good for teachers applies not only to the conditions under which they work but also to the way they approach problems. That is, Sarason's basic premise suggests that special educators will approach problems successfully only if they use the same problem-solving strategies that they recommend for students: careful logical analysis of problems and proposed solutions, meticulous evaluation of data, recognition and appreciation of complexity, tolerance of necessary ambiguity, mindfulness of history, clear communication of ideas, and devotion to ethical decision making. Perhaps special education could achieve radical reform were these strategies faithfully employed in approaching immediate and long-term problems.

THREE IMMEDIATE TASKS

Special education is faced with three immediate, critical, and inter-related tasks in responding to current proposals for reform: keeping the issue of the place of education in proper perspective, choosing idea over image, and avoiding fanaticism. Place, image, and fanaticism are important partly because they appeal so powerfully to emotion; they are interconnected because place has become the central issue in discussion of special education reform, an issue pressed largely on the basis of image and sometimes carried to the point of fanaticism.

Keeping Place in Perspective

Place has varied literal and metaphorical meanings, including location, perspective, status, and power. The issue of where students are taught has been at the center of efforts to restructure special education. Physical place has been the hub of controversy because it clearly defines proximity to age peers with certain characteristics. A student's being in the same location as others has been assumed to be a necessary if not sufficient condition for receiving equal educational opportunity. Physical place can be measured easily, can be reduced to simple images, and has immediate and deep emotional overtones; thus it is fertile ground for fanaticism.

A sense of physical place—location in space, where things are, and where things happen—is basic to human thought. Place, as a set of coordinates in the physical world, is a central issue in identity or belonging. It is the basis for many ethnic, tribal, national, and religious conflicts. Every society is structured by assumptions and rules about what is appropriate behavior in certain locations and by the observation that some events or outcomes are probable or possible in some places but improbable or impossible in others (cf. Goffman, 1973). What is assumed to be possible, probable, desirable, or permissible in certain places may change, either because of empirical findings or because social values change, or both. Small wonder that physical place is a pervasive and highly emotional topic in education.

One might assume that what is likely to happen socially and academically in one place cannot be assumed to be equally probable in any place. Nevertheless, we understand relatively little about how students' placement determines what is possible and what is probable as far as instruction and its outcomes are concerned. There is a lot of "noise," or unexplained variance, in the available data regarding place. In any given study, the "noise" might be an artifact of outcome measures, a confound of place with what actually happens instructionally and socially in various places, a function of the heterogeneity of student characteristics, or some combination of these and other factors (cf. Gottlieb, Alter, & Gottlieb, 1991; MacMillan & Hendrick, 1993; Walker & Bullis, 1991; Zigler et al., 1990).

Some have suggested that where students with disabilities are taught is the variable largely responsible for our disappointment in what students learn and how they perceive themselves. This belief has sometimes been promulgated by those critical of teaching students in locations other than regular classrooms, who have argued that we now have the means to transform the mainstream of public education so that all students with disabilities can be taught in regular schools and classes (e.g., Gartner & Lipsky, 1989; Lipsky & Gartner, 1991; Stainback & Stainback, 1991). Blackman (1992) has articulated this position:

> *There is nothing pervasively wrong with special education.* What is being questioned is not the interventions and knowledge that has been acquired through special education training and research. Rather, what is being challenged is the location where these supports are being provided to students with disabilities.
>
> Special education needs to be reconceptualized as a support to the regular education classroom, rather than as "another place to go." Recent research suggests that what is so wrong about special

education is the stigma and isolation that result from being removed from the regular education class for so long. We now have the effective strategies to bring help to the student rather than removing the student from the enriching setting of the regular education class. (p. 29)

Neither the history of special education (e.g., MacMillan & Hendrick, 1993; Zigler et al., 1990) nor reviews of the effects of placement (e.g., Gottlieb et al., 1991; Hallahan, Keller, McKinney, Lloyd, & Bryan, 1988) suggest that the location of supports is the key to improvement of special education outcomes. Furthermore, recent empirical evidence does not indicate that we currently have effective and reliable strategies for improving and sustaining outcomes for *all* students in regular classrooms (e.g., Fuchs, Fuchs, & Fernstrom, 1993; Jenkins, Jewell, Leicester, Jenkins, & Troutner, 1991; Jenkins, Zigmond, Fuchs, Fuchs, & Deno, 1993). Moreover, studies of the social status of children with disabilities do not show that the stigma and isolation they feel is necessarily a result of their being taught outside the regular classroom (e.g., Bear, Clever, & Proctor, 1991; Patterson, Kupersmidt, & Griesler, 1988). There is some evidence that not all children with disabilities would prefer to receive special services in the regular classroom (e.g., Jenkins & Heinen, 1989).

The intimation that special education is now conceptualized as "another place to go" is a misrepresentation of the conceptual foundations of the field (cf., Bateman, 1992; Deno, 1970) and is at odds with the language of the Individuals with Disabilities Education Act (IDEA). IDEA codified the conceptualization that special education includes, but is not limited to, supports for children and teachers in regular classrooms.

Complex social and interpersonal issues seldom yield to broad generalizations. Goodman (1992a) suggested that in thinking about the moral implications of single motherhood "we understand lives one by one," not an aggregate of lives. The issue of where students should be taught demands no less attention to individual lives. Student-by-student decisions regarding placement require attention to subtleties, ambiguities, realities, and interconnections among ideas; and these requirements are not prominent features of today's education reform movement. Making individual decisions necessitates weighing options and understanding that a given environment may have advantages and disadvantages for teaching specific skills. Case-by-case placement decisions are consistent with a fundamental idea underlying special education—rejection of overgeneralizations that allow the tacit exclusion of students from appropriate education for the sake of keeping all students in regular classrooms. A view from New Zealand is apropos to other countries: "For students with learning difficulties, whose needs have barely been met, inclusion in the mainstream seems like exclusion from remedial assistance" (Chapman, 1992, p. 369).

Place is a critical consideration in both general and special education. Perhaps it should not be the only or even the most important consideration. Keeping it in perspective requires attention to the idea of special education.

Choosing Idea Over Image

The *where* of education (place) is related to its *what* (content and outcomes) in complex ways that demand careful analysis of ideas and their relationships. Unfortunately, much current reform rhetoric is centered on simplisms intended to convey appealing images, rather than a complex and compelling set of ideas. For example, the national education goals drafted by the nation's governors and President Bush—as well as much of the rhetoric surrounding these goal statements—are misleading and jingoistic, designed to address issues that appeal to suspicions and fears rather than real problems and focused on America's being first in international competition (cf. Berliner, 1992). Goals and programs purportedly for *all* (e.g., "By the year 2000 every adult American will be literate and possess the knowledge and skills necessary to compete in a global economy and exercise the rights and responsibilities of citizenship") reflect simplistic conceptualizations and images that ignore the capacities and needs of many students (see Kauffman & Hallahan, 1993, for further discussion). As Eisner (1992) put it, what many policymakers are saying about education "replaces serious analyses with slogans" (p. 723).

The level of discourse in proposals for reforming special education has not been perceptibly higher than that in proposals for reforming general education. Fuchs and Fuchs (1991) noted the aversion of many special education reformers to careful scrutiny of their rhetoric and interpretation of data. The National Joint Committee on Learning Disabilities (1992) has also observed that reform proponents have failed to address even the most obvious questions regarding the effects of their proposals on students with learning disabilities.

The debasement of language is an effective way of oversimplifying complex ideas, eliminating ambiguity, and constructing powerful images (cf. Cohen, 1993). Special education is demeaned by language that conveys negative imagery, primarily images involving place defined literally as location or metaphorically as power: for example, "segregation" (e.g., Stainback & Stainback, 1991; Wang & Walberg, 1988) and treatment of children as if they are not "capable of achievement and worthy of respect" or "full-fledged human beings" (Lipsky & Gartner, 1987).

Today in special education, as in many other aspects of our lives, image is replacing idea; image is becoming the measure of truth. The substitution of image for idea was described brilliantly by Kundera (1990), who used the term *imagology* in his description of how ideas are being replaced by images.

> [Imagology] finally lets us put under one roof something that goes by so many names: advertising agencies; political campaign managers; designers who devise the shape of everything from cars to gym equipment; fashion stylists; barbers; show-business stars dictating norms of physical beauty that all branches of imagology obey. (p. 114)

Kundera has helped us understand the power of images in contemporary life and has cautioned that preserving ideas in discourse will require great effort. In fact, he was not optimistic about the future of ideology: "We can rightfully talk of a gradual, general, planetary transformation of ideology into imagology" (Kundera, 1990, p. 114). Kundera concluded that dealing competently with ideas demands confronting reality and that "for contemporary man reality is a continent visited less and less often and, besides, justifiably disliked" (p. 115). Goodman (1992b) also noted the difficulty in discerning the difference between news and counternews, the television commercials that provide images opposite those of the realities of the actual news. She described "our longing for any answer and our discomfort with the ambiguous and the uncertain," those real-world qualities that get in the way of impatience for simple answers to complex problems.

The imagology and evasion of reality that Kundera and Goodman described so pungently are common problems that pose serious dangers for special education. Yet, choosing idea over image is likely to make one unpopular with many proponents of restructuring because it means pressing for answers to questions about how reform will be operationalized and how evidence of special education's failures and successes will be weighed. Maintaining a focus on ideas also demands constant self-examination, searching for answers when challenged, and articulating a coherent set of propositions about educating children with disabilities.

Ideas will serve special educators more reliably than images when the goal is to improve what actually happens to students in school. Ideas are the hard currency of cognitive development and intelligent discourse. Still, an idea can be dangerous when it becomes a conviction too tightly held.

Avoiding Fanaticism

Nobel Peace Prize–winner Elie Wiesel (1992) suggested that fanaticism is nothing more than a conviction pushed to excess, passion that has become dangerous: "I would say that an idea becomes fanatical the moment it minimizes or excludes all the ideas that confront or oppose it" (p. 20). He explained, "A fanatic has answers, not questions; certainties, not hesitations"; and he quoted Friedrich Nietzsche: *"Madness is the result not of uncertainty but certainty"* (Wiesel, p. 21). Recognizing fanaticism and countering it in any area of our lives is extremely important, Wiesel counseled, because it is a distortion of truth that inevitably destroys human freedom and produces hatred.

Few statements about special education reform clearly reflect fanatical certainty. Nevertheless, we might take special note of those that do, given the danger fanaticism poses to any important social enterprise. Perhaps fanatical commitment to placement in the neighborhood school is reflected in the following:

> Three generations of children subject to LRE [least restrictive environment] are enough. Just as some institution managers and their organizations—both overt and covert—seek refuge in the continuum and LRE regional, intermediate unit, and special school administrators and their organizations will continue to defend the traditional and professionally pliable notion of LRE. The continuum is real and represents the status quo. However, the morass created by it can be avoided in the design and implementation of reformed systems by focusing all placement decisions on the local school and routinely insisting on the home school as an absolute and universal requirement. In terms of placement, the home-school focus renders LRE irrelevant and the continuum moot. (Laski, 1991, p. 413)

Fortunately, the rights granted by IDEA and by the U.S. Constitution's Bill of Rights are "professionally pliable," not absolute or universal. Their pliability, in fact, is their best protection against their destruction by fanatics. Justice is sometimes served by purposeful ambiguity (Statsky, 1984).

Perhaps fanatical certainty has been expressed also in a widely shown videotape, *Regular Lives* (Goodwin, Wurzburg, & Biklen, 1987). In a closing commentary on the practice of including all students with disabilities in their home schools and regular classrooms, the speaker said, "It really doesn't matter whether or not it works. It does work, and that's great. But even if it didn't work it would still be the thing to do, because it's right."

The conclusion that inclusion is right even if it doesn't work is reminiscent of another moral certitude about place per se: "My country, right or wrong, but my country." The problem with this kind of thinking is that it starts with a moral certainty that is assumed to be beyond rational analysis or evaluation by empirical means (cf. Kauffman, 1992b). Wiesel (1992) suggested that it is a way of hiding from true debate, alienating oneself from dialogue, fearing pluralism and diversity, abhorring learning, and speaking only in monologue. It is the antithesis of ethical deliberation in special education (cf. Howe & Miramontes, 1992). It transforms an idea that is often a good one—students with disabilities being in the same place as those without disabilities—into a tyrannical idea. It merely replaces the tyranny of placing all in institutions with the tyranny of placing all in neighborhood schools and regular classrooms.

Perhaps the ultimate degradation of special education is a fanatical allegiance to place—even if it doesn't work. The fanatical idea might be expressed this way: We know where all students with disabilities belong, and that is in _____ , because it's right. As Laski (1991) stated: "All children with learning problems, whether they be 'special education' students, 'at-risk' students, or otherwise regarded as disadvantaged in schooling, belong in regular classroom environments" (p. 412). At other times in our history, we have filled the blank with "institutions" or "special classes." Fanatics often form bandwagons, and Blatt (1979) described the destination of processions so led: "Bandwagons also go to funerals."

THREE LONG-TERM STRATEGIES FOR ACHIEVING SUBSTANTIVE REFORM

Popular reform rhetoric in general and special education calls for sweeping change: "break the mold," "revolution," "paradigm shift," "fundamental reconceptualization," "radical restructuring," and similar terms suggesting a dramatic shift in theory and practice. Perhaps none of these idioms of school reform suggests a strategy that will, in fact, produce substantive, lasting reform. Santayana's (1911) commentary on flux and constancy in human affairs suggests that progress requires retaining knowledge of the past and making change in measured steps:

Progress, far from consisting in change, depends on retentiveness. When change is absolute ... and when experience is not retained ... infancy is perpetual. Those who cannot remember the past are condemned to repeat it.... Retentiveness, we repeat, is the condition of progress. (pp. 284–286)

Progress in special education might be achieved by three modest and perhaps mundane strategies grounded in memory of the past: disaggregating special education populations, repairing and elaborating special education's conceptual foundations, and strengthening special education's empirical base. These strategies call for the patient, deliberate, persistent course of action we urge students to adopt when faced with complex and seemingly intractable problems.

Disaggregating Special Education Populations

The current reform movement emphasizes the presumptive "all children" without acknowledging special education's first premise: Disaggregation of students is necessary to ensure the appropriateness of education for all. Some reform proposals are quite explicit about retrenching special education in the interests of better serving "all" (e.g., National Association of State Boards of Education, 1992). What has been lost is the memory that special education was created to help schools serve all children better—to help teachers deal with the diversity of students. The problems that brought special education into being remain features of general education, and merging special education into general education will not alter those realities (MacMillan & Hendrick, 1993; Singer, 1988).

Education is an extremely diverse enterprise—diverse in its clients, problems, methods, and objectives. This diversity requires attention to what is known and to what is possible, probable, or desirable for particular groups of students (DeStefano & Wagner, 1991; Gottlieb et al., 1991; Walker & Bullis, 1991). Disaggregating general from special education is not sufficient; students with disabilities must be disaggregated. As Walker and Bullis noted, proposed restructuring "does not apply uniformly across handicapping conditions" (p. 76).

A major problem in discussions of the reform of special education is the failure to recognize the different constituencies supporting various proposals and strategies (Fuchs & Fuchs, 1991). Furthermore, "disaggregating the population of youth with disabilities by type of disability adds greatly to an understanding of outcomes" (DeStefano & Wagner, 1991, p. 14). Yet in many critiques of special education and its outcomes and in many proposals for change, no attempt is made to disaggregate the population of students with disabilities (e.g., Blackman, 1992; Gartner & Lipsky, 1989; Lipsky & Gartner, 1991; Stainback & Stainback, 1991).

Diversity among students is often described as something to be celebrated. If diversity of students is to be celebrated, then perhaps the diversity of services, programs, and environments providing appropriate education and habilitation should also prompt celebration. Special education is built on the premise that "all children" is a suspect phrase, often used to rationalize the tacit denial of special needs, which are not shared by all (Kauffman & Hallahan, 1993). Universal remedies are delusions.

> Unfortunately, there is no single answer to the question "What works?" because of the tremendous and growing diversity of students attending schools today. Cultural and language diversity in the classroom, for example, means that no single mode of teacher–student relating and no single pedagogical style is likely to be effective for all children in that classroom. Among students with disabilities, too, the great variation in their abilities and disabilities underscores the critical importance of the individualized programs that are one of the hallmarks of special education, as required by law. (U.S. Department of Education, 1992, p. 102)

Repairing and Elaborating Special Education's Conceptual Foundations

Special education is sometimes criticized because it does not "work." Nevertheless, virtually everyone agrees that special education "works" in some ways, but not well enough. Although most agree on a few general goals of special education, relatively little attention has been given to building the conceptual foundations of special education that allow clear definition of what "it works" means (Kauffman, 1990).

Special education's conceptual foundations are weakened by discussion of critical issues that will not withstand critical analysis. Conceptual advances in special education are exciting, but "reconceptualizations" that do not yield to critical analysis are disconcerting. Certainly, new conceptualizations—new conceptual models of how special and general education might work—should be encouraged. But it is important to discriminate indecipherable statements and earnest platitudes from new conceptualizations and to understand the implications of decipherable statements about reform. The meaning of some statements about conceptualizing or reconceptualizing special education is, at best, obscure; the implications of some appear to be that special education should be abandoned. For example, the following statements are offered in a discussion of the purpose of special education and the need for reform.

> The human service practices that cause providers to believe that clients (students) have inadequacies, shortcomings, failures, or faults that must be corrected or controlled by specially trained professionals must be replaced by conceptions that people with disabilities are capable of setting their own goals and achieving or not. Watered-down curricula, alternative grading practices, special competency standards, and other "treat them differently" practices used with "special" students must be replaced with school experiences exactly like those used with "regular" students. (Ysseldyke, Algozzine, & Thurlow, 1992, p. 64)

One might ask whether the meaning of these sentences can be unraveled; and, if it can, whether these statements come full circle, promising to recreate the conditions that prompted the founding of The Council for Exceptional Children in 1922.

Strong conceptual work in special education can be found. The conceptual foundations of special education have been strengthened significantly, for example, by the explanation of how to write legally correct and educationally useful Individualized Education Programs (IEPs) (Bateman, 1992), the development of an empirically derived theory of instruction (Englemann & Carnine, 1982), analysis of proposed policy changes (Singer, 1988), and a treatise on the ethics of special education (Howe & Miramontes, 1992). Special education's lasting reform would be furthered by more such carefully honed and coherent statements about its meaning and practice.

Strengthening Special Education's Empirical Base

Reliable quantitative and qualitative research data are needed to judge the extent to which special education is having its intended results. The research necessary to strengthen the empirical base of special education can be obtained neither quickly nor easily. Special education deals primarily with residual problems of learning—the tasks remaining when good general education does not have or can be predicted not to have its intended effects. Researching what "works" is thus difficult and produces many false starts and persistent ambiguities, particularly so because special education may be broadly defined to include preventative work in general education.

Perhaps the most effective way of improving and evaluating the education of students with disabilities is through experimentation with new programs, strategies, and policies. Experiments can lead to significant improvements if they are scientific assays, but not if they are merely episodes of doing something unfamiliar. That is, experimentation will facilitate progress only if its effects are evaluated rigorously and if caution is used in extrapolating findings. Giving experimental programs or policies a measure of relief from scrutiny regarding the empirical evidence of their immediate and long-term effects is a seductive strategy; it may nurture creativity and innovation, and this benefit is highly desirable. One must not, however, be beguiled into lowering the standard of evidence for dissemination. When this temptation is yielded to, the outcome is eventually found to be no better, perhaps even worse, than before. One disappointment is exchanged for another, further eroding the belief that special education can "work."

Consider two currently popular (some might say "hot") approaches that, although widely disseminated and supported by much personal testimony, have received virtually no confirmation from empirical studies or little empirical scrutiny at all—facilitated communication and total quality education. Facilitated communication is a method of augmentative communication in which someone physically assists a disabled individual, who ostensibly communicates through typing (e.g., Biklen, 1990, 1992; Biklen & Schubert, 1991). Although this alternative method of attempting to enable people with severe disabilities to communicate has been widely touted as a breakthrough and is being disseminated aggressively on an international scale, careful empirical studies indicate that the facilitator, not the disabled individual, is the communicator in all but a very small number of cases (e.g., Green, 1992; Mulick, Jacobson, & Kobe, 1993; Thompson, 1993). "Total quality education," an adaptation of an approach to business management, has been described with great enthusiasm as a way of correcting special education's ills and ensuring that all students are well served (e.g., Audette & Algozzine, 1992). Yet, reliable empirical studies of the effects of this approach to education are apparently nonexistent, and the frequent failure of the total quality fad in business is widely known (e.g., Mathews, 1993). Perhaps these approaches could be justified as experiments, but their widespread implementation prior to careful empirical scrutiny is an invitation to eventual ridicule.

Established programs and policies and those proposed as trustworthy alternatives carry equal burdens of proof of their effectiveness; the different demands no special grace when it is said to be an improvement over the extant (Fuchs & Fuchs, 1988). Betting on relatively low odds may make sense for individual experiments, but not for generalizing or writing policy. Perhaps the too-ready bet on low odds in making generalizations and policy decisions is one of the reasons people often say that we do not learn from history and that the more things change the more they stay the same. An example of betting on low odds in making generalizations about educational reform is the suggestion that "total quality" principles represent a "paradigm shift" in the business world and that by embracing these principles, special and general education can be transformed into a more effective enterprise (Audette & Algozzine, 1992). An example of betting on low odds in formulating policy is a joint resolution of the House of Delegates and Senate of Virginia that information regarding facilitated communication be made available throughout the state (Department of Rehabilitative Services, 1992). Both facilitated communication and total quality business principles applied to education appear to be extremely long-odds approaches, neither having any substantial foundation in reliable research. Like the lottery, they foster unrealistic hopes against formidable odds but, nevertheless, capture the imagination of the masses, the enthusiastic participation of many, and recompense for very, very few.

Moynihan (1993) describes how deinstitutionalization was given impetus by people with altruistic motives, but people whose rhetoric about psychotropic medications and the practice of community treatment got far ahead of actual knowledge. Others with opportunistic motives, looking for ways to keep mental health expenditures low, found those with altruistic motives convenient and effective allies in the movement to reduce institutional populations. Community mental health services were never made widely available; and where they were, the results were disappointing. The misrepresentation of knowledge about community mental health care and the exploitation of liberal rhetoric for conservative ends contributed to today's extremely high rates of incarceration and homelessness of the mentally ill. Where altruism meets opportunism there are dangerous currents for policymakers, including those with the best of intentions. There may be a lesson here for today's special education, in which advocacy for new strategies and practices is very far ahead of reliable data.

Obtaining a stronger empirical base is painstaking and, in the opinion of some, a prosaic task little connected to reform. It requires dogged pursuit of reliable answers to research questions and protracted public scrutiny of one's data and their interpretation. However, decades of programmatic research have brought significant advances in knowledge of some aspects of disability and special education, including, for example, conduct disorder (e.g., Patterson, Reid, & Dishion, 1992), autism (e.g., Lovaas, 1987), direct instruction (e.g., Engelmann & Carnine, 1982), and assessment of behavioral disorders in school (e.g., Walker & Severson, 1990). These advances and others like them are key to the substantive reform of special education—changing the way we deal with exceptional children in the light of meticulously accumulated evidence about the nature of disability and how we can identify and ameliorate it.

CONCLUSION

The approach I have suggested for achieving reform will not grab headlines, capture the imagination of the public, or foster the image of radical change. It will be criticized by some as lacking originality, the "punch" needed to spark radical restructuring, revolution, or total systems change. But total systems change and its synonyms will not necessarily bring progress. We tell our students that progress typically comes through everyday activities that may at times seem dull but are necessary to obtain long-term gratification. These mundane activities include self-questioning, reflection, practice, persistence, attention to detail, and mindfulness of the past. The best guarantee of progress in special education may be to practice what we teach. Were we to change our customary ways of responding to educational problems—dramatic gestures, ill-conceived propositions, overgeneralizations, decisions based on image, and disregard for history— we might, just might, achieve truly radical reform.

AUTHOR'S NOTE

Preparation of this article was supported in part by the Commonwealth Center for the Education of Teachers, Curry School of Education, University of Virginia. Portions of this manuscript were included in a keynote presentation at the national conference of the Australian Association of Special Education in Perth, Western Australia, in October 1992 and appeared in *The Australasian Journal of Special Education*. Terry A. Astuto, Eugene Edgar, Douglas Fuchs, Daniel P. Hallahan, and three anonymous reviewers provided helpful comments on earlier drafts of the manuscript.

REFERENCES

Audette, B., & Algozzine, B. (1992). Free and appropriate education for all students: Total quality and the transformation of American public education. *Remedial and Special Education, 13*(6), 8–18.

Bateman, B. D. (1992). *Better IEPs.* Creswell, OR: Otter Ink.

Bear, G. G., Clever, A., & Proctor, W. A. (1991). Self-perceptions of nonhandicapped children and children with learning disabilities in integrated classes. *Journal of Special Education, 24,* 409–426.

Berliner, D. C. (1992, February). *Educational reform in an era of disinformation.* Paper presented at the meeting of the American Association of Colleges for Teacher Education, San Antonio, TX.

Biklen, D. (1990). Communication unbound: Autism and praxis. *Harvard Educational Review, 60,* 291–314.

Biklen, D. (1992). Typing to talk: Facilitated communication. *American Journal of Speech-Language Pathology, 1*(2), 15–17.

Biklen, D., & Schubert, A. (1991). New words: The communication of students with autism. *Remedial and Special Education, 12*(6), 46–57.

Blackman, H. P. (1992). Surmounting the disability of isolation. *The School Administrator, 49*(2), 28–29.

Blatt, B. (1979). Bandwagons also go to funerals: Unmailed letters 1 and 2. *Journal of Learning Disabilities, 12*(4), 17–19.

Carnine, D. (1992). *Untested tools deprive special education students of an effective education.* Eugene, OR: National Center to Improve the Tools of Educators.

Chapman, J. W. (1992). Learning disabilities in New Zealand: Where kiwis and kids with LD can't fly. *Journal of Learning Disabilities, 25,* 362–370.

Cohen, R. (1993, March 16). Killing words. *The Washington Post,* p. A17.

Cuban, L. (1990). Reforming again, again, and again. *Educational Researcher, 19*(1), 3–13.

Deno, E. (1970). Special education as developmental capital. *Exceptional Children, 37,* 229–237.

Department of Rehabilitative Services and the Department of Mental Health, Mental Retardation, and Substance Abuse Services. (1992, November). *House Joint Resolution 38: A study of facilitated communication in Virginia.* Richmond, VA: Author.

DeStefano, L., & Wagner, M. (1991). *Outcome assessment in special education: Lessons learned.* Menlo Park, CA: SRI International.

Eisner, E. W. (1992). The federal reform of schools: Looking for the silver bullet. *Phi Delta Kappan, 73,* 722–723.

Engelmann, S., & Carnine, D. (1982). *Theory of instruction: Principles and applications.* New York: Irvington.

Fuchs, D., & Fuchs, L. S. (1988). Response to Wang and Walberg. *Exceptional Children, 55,* 138–146.

Fuchs, D., & Fuchs, L. S. (1991). Framing the REI debate: Abolitionists versus conservationists. In J. W. Lloyd, N. N. Singh, & A. C. Repp (Eds.), *The regular education initiative: Alternative perspectives on concepts, issues, and models* (pp. 241–255). Sycamore, IL: Sycamore.

Fuchs, D., Fuchs, L. S., & Fernstrom, P. (1993). A conservative approach to special education reform: Mainstreaming through transenvironmental programming and curriculum-based measurement. *American Educational Research Journal, 30,* 149–177.

Gartner, A., & Lipsky, D. K. (1989). *The yoke of special education: How to break it.* Rochester, NY: National Center on Education and the Economy.

Goffman, E. (1973). *The presentation of self in everyday life.* New York: Overlook Press.

Goodman, E. (1992a, May 23). Single mothers, many values. *The Washington Post,* p. A31.

Goodman, E. (1992b, June 16). It pays to discover how viewers are being doused by ad "news." *The Charlottesville Daily Progress,* p. A4.

Goodwin, T., Wurzburg, G. (Producers and Directors), & Biklen, D. (Executive Producer). (1987). *Regular lives.* [Video Cassette]. Syracuse, NY: Syracuse University.

Gottlieb, J., Alter, M., & Gottlieb, B. W. (1991). Mainstreaming academically handicapped children in urban schools. In J. W. Lloyd, N. N. Singh, & A. C. Repp (Eds.), *The regular education initiative: Alternative perspectives on concepts, issues, and models* (pp. 95–112). Sycamore, IL: Sycamore.

Green, G. (1992, October). *Facilitated communication: Scientific and ethical issues.* Paper presented at the E. K. Shriver Center, Northeastern University, Waltham, MA.

Hallahan, D. P., Keller, C. E., McKinney, J. D., Lloyd, J. W., & Bryan, T. (1988). Examining the research base of the regular education initiative: Efficacy studies and the adaptive learning environments model. *Journal of Learning Disabilities, 21,* 29–35.

Howe, K. R., & Miramontes, O. B. (1992). *The ethics of special education.* New York: Teachers College Press.

Jenkins, J. R., & Heinen, A. (1989). Students' preferences for service delivery: Pull-out, in-class, or integrated models. *Exceptional Children, 55,* 516–523.

Jenkins, J. R., Jewell, M., Leicester, N., Jenkins, L., & Troutner, N. M. (1991). Development of a school building model for educating students with handicaps and at-risk students in general education classrooms. *Journal of Learning Disabilities, 24,* 311–320.

Jenkins, J., Zigmond, N., Fuchs, L., Fuchs, D., & Deno, S. (1993). *Special education in restructured schools: Findings from three multi-year studies.* Manuscript in preparation.

Kauffman, J. M. (1989). The regular education initiative as Reagan-Bush education policy: A trickle-down theory of education of the hard-to-teach. *Journal of Special Education, 23,* 256–278.

Kauffman, J. M. (1990, April). *What happens when special education works? The sociopolitical context of special education research in the 1990s.* Invited address, Special Interest Group: Special Education Research, annual meeting of the American Educational Research Association, Boston.

Kauffman, J. M. (1991). Restructuring in sociopolitical context: Reservations about the effects of current reform proposals on students with disabilities. In J. W. Lloyd, N. N. Singh, & A. C. Repp (Eds.), *The regular education initiative: Alternative perspectives on concepts, issues, and models* (pp. 57–66). Sycamore, IL: Sycamore.

Kauffman, J. M. (1992a). School reform disorder: Alternative responses to nonsense. *Journal of Behavioral Education, 2,* 157–174.

Kauffman, J. M. (1992b). Foreword. In K. R. Howe & O. B. Miramontes, *The ethics of special education* (pp. xi–xvii). New York: Teachers College Press.

Kauffman, J. M., & Hallahan, D. P. (1993). Toward a comprehensive service delivery system. In J. I. Goodlad & T. C. Lovitt (Eds.), *Integrating general and special education* (pp. 73–102). Columbus, OH: Merrill/Macmillan.

Kundera, M. (1990). *Immortality* [translated by Peter Kussi]. New York: Grove Weidenfeld.

Laski, F. J. (1991). Achieving integration during the second revolution. In L. H. Meyer, C. A. Peck, & L. Brown (Eds.), *Critical issues in the lives of people with severe disabilities* (pp. 409–421). Baltimore: Paul H. Brookes.

Lipsky, D. K., & Gartner, A. (1987). Capable of achievement and worthy of respect: Education for handicapped students as if they were full-fledged human beings. *Exceptional Children, 54,* 69–74.

Lipsky, D. K., & Gartner, A. (1991). Restructuring for quality. In J. W. Lloyd, N. N. Singh, & A. C. Repp (Eds.), *The regular education initiative: Alternative perspectives on concepts, issues, and models* (pp. 43–57). Sycamore, IL: Sycamore.

Lovaas, O. I. (1987). Behavioral treatment and normal educational and intellectual functioning in young autistic children. *Journal of Consulting and Clinical Psychology, 55,* 3–9.

MacMillan, D. L., & Hendrick, I. G. (1993). Evolution and legacies. In J. I. Goodlad & T. C. Lovitt (Eds.), *Integrating general and special education* (pp. 23–48). Columbus, OH: Merrill/Macmillan.

Mathews, J. (1993, June 6). Totaled quality management: Consultants flourish helping firms repair the results of a business fad. *The Washington Post,* pp. H1, H16.

Moynihan, D. P. (1993). Defining deviancy down. *American Scholar, 62*(1), 17–30.

Mulick, J. A., Jacobson, J. W., & Kobe, F. H. (1993). Anguished silence and helping hands: Autism and facilitated communication. *Skeptical Inquirer, 17,* 270–287.

National Association of State Boards of Education. (1992, October). *Winners all: A call for inclusive schools.* Alexandria, VA: Author.

National Joint Committee on Learning Disabilities. (1992). School reform: Opportunities for excellence and equity for individuals with learning disabilities. *Journal of Learning Disabilities, 25,* 276–280.

Patterson, C. J., Kupersmidt, J. B., & Griesler, P. C. (1988). *Self-concepts of children in regular education and special education classes.* Unpublished manuscript, University of Virginia, Virginia Behavior Disorders Project, Charlottesville.

Patterson, G. R., Reid, J. B., & Dishion, T. J. (1992). *Antisocial boys.* Eugene, OR: Castalia.

Raspberry, W. (1992, May 24). Address at the First Annual Invitational Team Case Competition, University of Virginia, Charlottesville.

Santayana, G. (1911). *The life of reason: Or the phases of human progress* (Vol. 1). New York: Charles Scribner's Sons.

Sarason, S. B. (1990). *The predictable failure of educational reform: Can we change course before it's too late?* San Francisco: Jossey-Bass.

Singer, J. D. (1988). Should special education merge with regular education? *Educational Policy, 2,* 409–424.

Stainback, W., & Stainback, S. (1991). A rationale for integration and restructuring: A synopsis. In J. W. Lloyd, N. N. Singh, & A. C. Repp (Eds.), *The regular education initiative: Alternative perspectives on concepts, issues, and models* (pp. 226–239). Sycamore, IL: Sycamore.

Statsky, W. P. (1984). *Legislative analysis and drafting* (2nd ed.). St. Paul, MN: West Publishing.

Thompson, T. (1993, January). A reign of error: Facilitated communication. *Kennedy Center News,* No. 22.

U.S. Department of Education. (1992). *Fourteenth annual report to Congress on the implementation of the Individuals with Disabilities Education Act.* Washington, DC: Author.

Walker, H. M., & Bullis, M. (1991). Behavior disorders and the social context of regular class integration: A conceptual dilemma? In J. W. Lloyd, N. N. Singh, & A. C. Repp (Eds.), *The regular education initiative: Alternative perspectives on concepts, issues, and models* (pp. 75–93). Sycamore, IL: Sycamore.

Walker, H. M., & Severson, H. H. (1990). *Systematic Screening for Behavior Disorders (SSBD): A Multiple Gating Procedure.* Longmont, CO: Sopris West.

Wang, M. C., & Walberg, H. J. (1988). Four fallacies of segregationism. *Exceptional Children, 55,* 128–137.

Wiesel, E. (1992, April 19). When passion is dangerous. *Parade Magazine,* pp. 20–21.

Ysseldyke, J. E., Algozzine, B., & Thurlow, M. L. (1992). *Critical issues in special education* (2nd ed.). Boston: Houghton Mifflin.

Zigler, E., Hodapp, R. M., & Edison, M. R. (1990). From theory to practice in the care and education of mentally retarded individuals. *American Journal on Mental Retardation, 95,* 1–12.

Chapter 11

Inclusive Schools Movement and the Radicalization of Special Education Reform

Douglas Fuchs and Lynn S. Fuchs

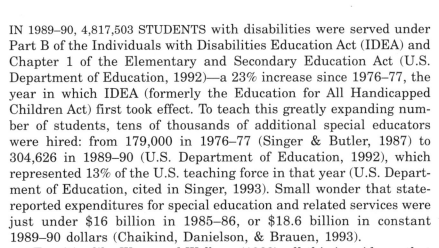

IN 1989–90, 4,817,503 STUDENTS with disabilities were served under Part B of the Individuals with Disabilities Education Act (IDEA) and Chapter 1 of the Elementary and Secondary Education Act (U.S. Department of Education, 1992)—a 23% increase since 1976–77, the year in which IDEA (formerly the Education for All Handicapped Children Act) first took effect. To teach this greatly expanding number of students, tens of thousands of additional special educators were hired: from 179,000 in 1976–77 (Singer & Butler, 1987) to 304,626 in 1989–90 (U.S. Department of Education, 1992), which represented 13% of the U.S. teaching force in that year (U.S. Department of Education, cited in Singer, 1993). Small wonder that state-reported expenditures for special education and related services were just under $16 billion in 1985–86, or $18.6 billion in constant 1989–90 dollars (Chaikind, Danielson, & Brauen, 1993).

To critics like Wang and Walberg (1988), all this is evidence that the leadership in special education is interested more in empire building than in effective teaching: More students eventually lead to more teachers, which, in turn, engender more programs, dollars, and power for special education. Those with a more benign view explain the field's swelling enrollments in terms of special educators' pre-

Reprinted from "Inclusive schools movement and the radicalization of special education reform" by D. Fuchs and L. Fuchs, *Exceptional Children*, Vol. 60, 1994, 294–309. Copyright © 1994 by The Council for Exceptional Children. Reprinted by permission.

sumed bleeding-heart, Statue-of-Liberty ("Give me your tired, your poor, your huddled masses") mentality. Regardless of the motives imputed, it is increasingly obvious that burgeoning enrollments and crowded classrooms in many places (see Algozzine, Christenson, & Ysseldyke, 1982; Buttram & Kershner, 1988, Tables B-1 and I-2) are making a mockery of special education's historic and noble intent to differentiate and enhance instruction for students with disabilities.

Moreover, faced with this and other problems bedeviling its programs, such as the infrequency with which it marshals evidence to support its effectiveness, special education appears reluctant to help itself. After all, reform strategies have been outlined in white papers (e.g., Will, 1986), and exhortations and admonishments have been offered by blue-ribbon committees (e.g., Heller, Holtzman, & Messick, 1982)—but little has changed. Whereas this inaction (some would say paralysis) might be explained in terms of widespread complacency or weak leadership, some critics argue that even if the field were to become a whirling dervish of activity, its reform making would fail because of a fundamentally incorrect conception of itself, a self-image warped by its own success, if "success" may be defined narrowly in terms of an increasing number of children served. More specifically, goes this critique, as special education has grown pell-mell in the past 2 decades, it has evolved into a second system (Wang, Reynolds, & Walberg, 1988) complete with its own teachers, administrators, credentialing process, programs, and budgets. At the same time, it has developed a sense of independence and autonomy (some would say hubris), a penchant for doing things unilaterally even when issues and problems seem to demand bilateral action. Special education's failure to mend itself, say the critics, is due partly to its organizational, physical, and psychological separation from the source of its problems—general education (e.g., Skrtic, 1987).

Whereas many special educators reject all or part of this "second-system" analysis (e.g., Vergason & Anderegg, 1989), recognition grows that a meaningful connection with general education is necessary; that a "Lone Ranger" strategy for special education is self-defeating. More and more special educators are resonating to a view first expressed by Dunn (1968) more than 25 years ago. To wit: Special education is not a Nantucket or Martha's Vineyard, but a town on the mainland, and its students and teachers are served better when its business is coordinated closely with mainland business (see Behrmann, 1992; Hales & Carlson, 1992).

Applied to special education's high pupil–teacher ratios, this recrudescent Dunnian view holds that the problem is caused by general education's lack of will and capacity to accommodate more of its students. General education must be fortified through fundamental changes in its teaching and learning processes. It must draw on the talents and energies of building-based special educators, Chapter 1 and bilingual teachers, and other professionals working with general educators to fashion a smarter, more supple, coordinated school program responsive to fast and slow learners alike. According to this view, only when all teachers and support staff are working together will general education become sufficiently competent and confident to grant special educators small enough caseloads so they may work intensively with most-deserving students.

But how likely is this partnership? During the 1980s, proponents of the regular education initiative (REI) tried to interest general education in special education concerns. As documented by Pugach and Sapon-Shevin (1987), general education took little notice, prompting Lieberman (1985) to quip that general education was like the uninvited bride for a wedding thrown together by special educators. And whereas REI-inspired activity in the 1980s changed special education in places like Utah (Kukic, 1993), such reform making tended to parallel rather than converge with general education's renewal efforts (McLaughlin & Warren, 1992; Miller, 1990; Pugach & Sapon-Shevin, 1987).

The rallying cry today is "inclusive schools," but the basic question remains: How likely is this new movement to bring special and general education into synergistic alignment? Some are optimistic. They point to much-publicized position papers of the Association for Supervision and Curriculum Development (cited in The Association for Persons with Severe Handicaps newsletter, 1992), Council of Chief State School Officers (1992), and National Association of State Boards of Education (1992) as evidence that general education now appears more interested in special education. But as general education finally may be turning an ear, special education's reformist message is changing. In this article, we examine inclusive school proposals and compare them to those of the REI. After contrasting the movements' respective advocates, goals, tactics, and understanding of and links to general education, we argue that the field's rhetoric has become increasingly strident and its perspective increasingly insular and disassociated from general education's concerns. We offer a rather pessimistic prediction about the current movement's success in forging a productive alliance with general education.

Before proceeding, we must make two more points. By focusing on the REI and inclusive schools movement, we give short shrift to those who view some reformers' characterizations of special education as distorted and unfair. Writing in support of a strong, independent special education, many researchers and advocates have claimed that general education cannot be trusted always to respect the needs of special needs children (e.g., Braaten, Kauffman, Braaten, Polsgrove, & Nelson, 1988; Hallahan, Keller, McKinney, Lloyd, & Bryan, 1988; Kauffman, 1989; Kauffman, Gerber, & Semmel, 1988; Keogh, 1988a, 1988b; Megivern, 1987; Singer, 1988; Vergason & Anderegg, 1989; Walker & Bullis, 1991). Evidence from surveys of parents of students with disabilities (Harris, cited in Kauffman, 1991) and recent policy statements from several special and general education professional organizations (e.g., Commission on the Education of the Deaf, 1988; The Council for Exceptional Children, 1993; Learning Disabilities Association, 1993; National Education Association, 1992) also indicate support for a strong multifaceted special education system. Thus, many in special education hold reservations about at least some of the principles and ideas discussed here.

Second, if harboring a biased view on inclusion is a sin, then we admit our guilt. However, we have little interest in browbeating or proselytizing. Our primary aim is to explain how the field's reformist impulse has been radicalized and why we believe this is undesirable. In the interest of fairness and scholarship, we try to distinguish between facts and beliefs.

REGULAR EDUCATION INITIATIVE

Who Were the Advocates?

"High-Incidence" Group

Two distinct groups advocated for the REI. The larger of the two included those with interest in students with learning disabilities, behavior disorders, and "mild/moderate" mental retardation (e.g., Algozzine, Maheady, Sacca, O'Shea, & O'Shea, 1990; Gersten & Woodward, 1990; Gottlieb, Alter, & Gottlieb, 1991; Jenkins, Pious, & Peterson, 1988; Lilly, 1987; Pugach & Lilly, 1984; Reynolds, 1988, 1989, 1991), the so-called "high-incidence" group of students. This first group also included nonspecial educators like Wang (e.g., Wang, Rubenstein, & Reynolds, 1985), McGill-Franzen (1987), and Slavin (e.g., Slavin et al., 1991), who approached special education reform from the perspective of advocacy for at-risk students without disabilities. At least two characteristics united these REI supporters:

first, a willingness to offer a no-holds-barred critique of special education, and second, a belief that the field must recognize that it is part of a larger system, not a separate order; that it must coordinate and collaborate with general education (e.g., Allington & McGill-Franzen, 1989); and that a stronger general education means a stronger special education.

"Low-Incidence" Group

The second group of REI proponents consisted of advocates for students with severe intellectual disabilities (e.g., Biklen, 1985; Biklen, Lehr, Searl, & Taylor, 1987; Snell, 1988; S. Stainback & W. Stainback, 1985). Members of this second group and the first group sometimes coordinated similar-sounding critiques of special education and even met, on occasion, to coordinate tactics (e.g., a December 6, 1988, meeting at Temple University). Nevertheless, the rather exclusive concern of the second group was to help integrate children with severe intellectual disabilities into neighborhood schools. The positions of many proponents seemed synchronous with the view expressed by Allington and McGill-Franzen (1989) that special education should coordinate and collaborate with general education (e.g., Gartner & Lipsky, 1987; S. Stainback & W. Stainback, 1985; W. Stainback & S. Stainback, 1984); a few, however, argued against the moderation implicit in such a position, choosing instead to push for the elimination of special education altogether (e.g., Taylor, 1988).

This rather disparate, "low-incidence" group proceeded parallel to, rather than under the banner of, the REI. Most were not enthusiastic supporters because they saw it as a policy initiative for children with "high incidence" disabilities. Nevertheless, they gave it their tacit approval because its goals, though different from their own, meshed with their overall strategy. They understood that the central issue for Reynolds, Wang, and others was to achieve a restructuring whereby most students with mild and moderate disabilities would be transferred on a full-time basis to mainstream settings. By contrast, during the middle to late 1980s, most members of their own group were thinking "neighborhood schools," not "mainstream" (e.g., Biklen, 1985; S. Stainback & W. Stainback, 1985; W. Stainback & S. Stainback, 1984). Thus, we infer that many in the "low-incidence" group had the following strategy: "Let the REI folks get the 'high-incidence' students into the mainstream. This will make room for our children in self-contained and resource settings in the neighborhood school."

REI Leadership

Those speaking for students with "high-incidence" disabilities set the goals for the movement and the tone of the debate. There were several reasons for this. First, Assistant Secretary of Education Madeleine Will (1986) wrote an influential paper that focused on children with mild and moderate disabilities; second, Reynolds and Wang assumed high-profile roles by writing frequently in visible journals and organizing prestigious conferences; and third, the low-incidence group viewed the REI as a secondary concern.

Goals: Restructuring and Large-Scale Mainstreaming

REI leaders had several distinguishable goals. The first was to merge special and general education into one inclusive system. Although some proponents objected to the term *merger*, preferring phrases like "shared responsibilities" and "inclusive educational arrangements" (Wang & Walberg, 1988, p. 128), they in fact were describing a fundamental restructuring of the relationship between general and special education. This reconfiguration would unite a balkanized education system. It also would circumvent the need for an eligibility process that purportedly depends on invalid test instruments and psychologically harmful labels, only to pigeonhole children into educationally questionable classifications (e.g., Reynolds, Wang, & Walberg, 1987; Reynolds, Zetlin, & Wang, 1993; Ysseldyke, Algozzine, & Epps, 1983).

The second goal was to increase dramatically the number of children with disabilities in mainstream classrooms by use of large-scale, full-time mainstreaming (e.g., Slavin & Stevens, 1991; Wang & Birch, 1984) as opposed to the more traditional case-by-case approach (e.g., Anderson-Inman, Walker, & Purcell, 1984; Brown et al., 1979; Fuchs, Fuchs, & Fernstrom, 1993). The third goal, implicit in the first two, was to strengthen the academic achievement of students with mild and moderate disabilities, as well as that of underachievers without disabilities. To wit: "Local schools should be encouraged to experiment and evaluate the effectiveness of a variety of educational approaches in solving the widespread persistent problem of how to achieve more productive learning for all students" (Wang, 1987, p. 27).

Tactics

REI supporters generated a handful of tactics to restructure the special education–general education relationship and to move greater numbers of students with disabilities into mainstream classrooms. Some of these strategies were downright ingenious, others irritatingly vague or inconsistent. Several were cleverly aimed to curry favor with both special and general education communities.

Waivers for Restructuring

Waivers constituted a principal means of realizing a merger. Waivers from state and federal rules and regulations were sought, granting school districts increased flexibility to use special education resources in different, and presumably more imaginative and adaptive, ways (e.g., Reynolds, Wang, & Walberg, 1987; Wang & Reynolds, 1985). For example, a district might ask for a waiver to lower special educators' direct-service caseloads with no corresponding decrease in the reimbursement it received from its state department of education. With fewer children to serve in resource rooms, the special educators would be expected to spend more time in the mainstream working with general educators and helping not only mainstreamed students with disabilities but also underachievers without disabilities. In return for such waivers, REI supporters promised accountability to determine the effectiveness of the new administrative arrangements and professional roles engendered by them. Reynolds et al. (1987) called this quid pro quo, "waivers for performance" (p. 394).

Modifying the Continuum

Another tactic for achieving a special education–general education merger, as well as for instigating more aggressive forms of mainstreaming, was to modify the nature of the continuum of services. Many writers advanced suggestions in this vein. Sometimes the same individuals advocated different and conflicting solutions. Wang and Reynolds (1985), for example, proposed a form of merger and greater mainstreaming with no change in the existing continuum of services: "Funding formulae should support a full continuum of services" (p. 501). At other points, however, their plans indicated an opposite strategy, as when Wang (1981) called for an elimination of the entire continuum: "The term 'mainstreaming' is used here to mean the integration of regular and exceptional children in a school setting where *all* children share the same resources and opportunities for learning on a full-time basis" (p. 196, emphasis added).

Yet another solution called for an elimination of the bottom of the continuum; that is, closing residential and day schools. Children in these settings would move into self-contained classes and resource rooms in neighborhood schools, while the children previously served in these settings would be mainstreamed (Reynolds, 1989). And, finally, it was proposed that mainstreaming should be accomplished by eliminating not the bottom, but the near-top of the continuum of services (i.e., resource and self-contained classes). Wang's Adaptive Learning Environments Model (ALEM), for example, was developed to replace pullout in regular schools, especially resource rooms and compensatory education programs (e.g., Wang & Birch, 1984). Similarly, Reynolds et al. (1987) stated: "Our remarks [about reform] refer to programs for 'mildly' or 'judgmentally' handicapped children . . . but not to programs for children who are deaf, blind, severely disturbed, or deeply retarded in cognitive development" (p. 391). This wide swing in choice of strategies, and differing views of the viability of the continuum, caused confusion, which, in turn, reinforced critics' fears that REI proponents wanted dramatic change without a carefully conceptualized blueprint (e.g., McKinney & Hocutt, 1988).

Large-Scale Mainstreaming

REI backers advocated two basic ways of transforming general education classrooms into more academically and socially responsive settings for most students with disabilities. The first was to individualize instruction for all students, illustrated by the ALEM. The second was cooperative learning (e.g., Slavin & Stevens, 1991). Whereas a number of differences separate these two classroom reorganization strategies, both claim a strong academic focus. The ALEM's overall goal, for example, is to "provide effective school environments that maximize the outcomes of learning for individual children—environments where each child can effectively master basic skills in academic subjects . . . while becoming confident in his or her ability to learn and to cope with the social and physical classroom" (Wang, 1980, p. 126). Cooperative learning methods are defined by Slavin and Stevens (1991) as "instructional techniques in which students work in heterogeneous learning teams to help one another learn academic material" (p. 177).

In addition, both large-scale mainstreaming strategies depend on extant curricula, either chosen by the teacher (ALEM) or by the developers (Slavin & Stevens, 1991), and they are directive. For example, the ALEM includes a prescriptive learning component that comprises a series of hierarchically organized curricula for basic skills development; a more open-ended exploratory learning component; and classroom management procedures to facilitate implementation of the prescriptive and exploratory components (see Wang, 1980). Slavin and colleagues' Team-Assisted Individualization (TAI) combines programmed mathematics instruction with cooperative learning. TAI's principal features include teams, placement tests, curriculum materials, teaching groups, team study methods, team scores and team recognition procedures, facts tests, and whole-class units (see Slavin & Stevens, 1991). The curricular focus and prescriptive nature of these mainstreaming strategies are points to which we will return when we discuss "full-inclusionist" approaches to restructuring.

The Big Tent

REI leaders recognized the importance of building bridges to various constituencies, of developing broad-based support for REI ideas and proposals. They were loathe, for example, to alienate special education's teachers and administrators. Despite calls for waivers, modifications of the continuum of services, and a reorganization of mainstream classrooms, most REI leaders did not advocate an end to special education. "The REI," wrote Wang and Walberg (1988), "is *not* aimed at eliminating or subordinating special education services" (p. 23, emphasis in original). REI-inspired reforms usually were explicit about a role—albeit a different role—for special educators:

> We need to move special teachers [of students with mild disabilities] into mainstream structures as co-teachers with general teaching staff where both groups share in the instruction. The special education teachers can . . . lead in such matters as child study, working with parents, and offering individualized, highly intensive instruction to students who have not been progressing well. (Reynolds, 1989, p. 10)

There was equal interest in courting those in higher education and elsewhere who argued that reforms must be based partly on data and accountability. To make waivers and large-scale mainstreaming more credible, REI supporters appealed to federal officials for monies to underwrite efforts by the special and general education research communities to develop mainstream instructional environments more responsive to greater student diversity. REI proponents went on record both as supporting a data-driven reform effort and as admitting that no one had the proverbial silver-bullet solution (Wang, Rubenstein, & Reynolds, 1985). They also tried (unsuccessfully) to organize a pooling of data on experimental programs at the Office of Special Education Programs/The Council for Exceptional Children's jointly sponsored Project Directors' Meeting in summer 1988, and to undertake (successfully) an ambitious compilation of reviews of the literature on the conceptual and empirical validity of special education (see Wang, Reynolds, & Walberg, 1987).

Impact on Special and General Education Reform

One would have thought REI goals to be attractive to the leaders of general education reform. REI supporters' intention to strengthen regular classrooms' teaching and learning processes by an infusion of special education resources, thereby making such settings more responsive to student diversity, seemed consonant with, if not inspired by, reports from the Carnegie Council for Adolescent Development (1989), the Carnegie Forum on Education and the Economy (1986), the Holmes Group (1986), the National Commission on Excellence in Education (1983), and the National Governors' Association (1986). But general education was uninterested in the REI (Lieberman, 1985; McLaughlin & Warren, n.d.; National Council on Disability, 1989; Pugach & Sapon-Shevin, 1987). Perhaps this was because special education was viewed nationally as a separate concern; maybe because of general educators' greater interest in excellence than equity (National Council on Disability, 1989; Sapon-Shevin, 1987). In any case, at its most effective, the REI was a *special* education initiative. In Colorado, Pennsylvania, Utah, and Washington, special education was reorganized at the state or local levels, but with little concomitant change in general education programs like Chapter 1, or with respect to issues like personnel preparation. Exceptions to this pattern of change may be states such as Vermont and Kentucky (McLaughlin, personal communication, February 1993; Thousand & Villa, 1990).

INCLUSIVE SCHOOLS MOVEMENT

Increasingly, special education reform is symbolized by the term *inclusive schools*. Like the REI, which grabbed the field's attention nearly a decade ago, the newer term seems to defy straightforward interpretation. And like the REI, this is partly because "inclusion" means different things to people who wish different things from it. For the group that wants least, it is old wine in a new bottle, a subtle form of co-opting reformist impulses to maintain the status quo. To those who want more, it means decentralization of power and the concomitant empowerment of teachers and building-level administrators; a fundamental reorganization of the teaching and learning process through innovations like cooperative learning and thematic teaching; and the redefinition of professional relationships within buildings (e.g., The Board of Education for the City of Toronto, 1989; The Council for Exceptional Children, 1993). Such objectives are neither dissimilar from those of the REI, nor inherently inimical to special education or its continuum of services. (See McLaughlin & Warren's [1992] description of inclusive schools, pp. 34–37). But to yet a third group, those who currently lead the inclusive schools movement, "special education reform" is an oxymoron: No meaningful transformation can occur unless and until special education and its continuum of placements are eliminated altogether. The "inclusive school" denotes a place rid of special educators, where *full* inclusion reigns (e.g., S. Stainback & W. Stainback, 1992).

Who Are the Advocates?

TASH Takes Control

In the past several years, there has been an important change in leadership of the special education reform movement, a rather abrupt replacement of the heterogeneous, special education–general education, "high-incidence/low-incidence" crowd, with a group primarily concerned about the rights and well-being of children and adults with severe intellectual disabilities. How did this come about? First, many REI supporters became disillusioned and devitalized by general education's lack of interest in special education and by many special education organizations' hostility, often masked by an official neutrality. Second, and relatedly, these special education organizations were slow to take a stand on reform and remained on the periphery of the policy skirmishes. Not so the leadership of The Association of Persons with Severe Handicaps (TASH). In our view, they took the field by storm; they rushed into a vacuum created by others' inaction, no doubt intimidating by their vigor alone many who disagreed with their radical message.

TASH spokespersons, in alliance with some parents of children and adults with severe intellectual disabilities, appear disciplined, well organized, articulate, and politically connected. They tend to focus on a single issue, identify with a precisely defined constituency, and use rhetoric effectively. Their inspiration is the "normalization principle," defined by Nirje as "making available to the mentally retarded patterns and conditions of everyday life which are as close as possible to the norms and patterns of the mainstream society" (cited by Biklen, 1985, p. 6). Their faith and optimism are obvious. Both seem based on a presumed historical imperative that "the whole history of education can be told in terms of one steady trend that can be described as progressive inclusion" (Reynolds & Birch, 1977, p. 22).

And there can be no doubt about TASH's profound impact on the policy environment. Its positions have influenced special education policy in states like New Mexico (New Mexico State Department of Education, 1991) and Michigan (Michigan Department of Education, 1992), and in more than a handful of local school districts. Its imprint may be seen on recent special education-related statements made by such powerful groups as the Council of Chief State School Officers (1992) and the National Association of School Boards of Education (1992). Directly or indirectly, it helped shape several of the Office of Special Education Programs' funding initiatives, such as the technical assistance the agency underwrites states to help integrate students with severe disabilities (California Research Institute, 1990). TASH's activity was an important catalyst in the formation of The Council for Exceptional Children's President's Panel on Special Education Reform and Integration, which drafted a statement on inclusive schools that was ratified during the 1993 convention in San Antonio.

TASH leaders' position on integration also has attracted major media attention. In April 1993, the film *Educating Peter* won the year's Academy Award for Best Achievement in Documentary Short Subjects. The half-hour film captured the challenges and rewards of including Peter Gwazdauskas, a 10-year-old with Down syndrome, in a 3rd-grade classroom at the Gilbert Linkous Elementary School in Blacksburg, Virginia. In accepting the award on national TV, the film's co-producer, Gerardine Wurzburg, concluded, "I'd like to say for the advocates of full inclusion for people with disabilities in our society, let us please move forward." *Educating Peter* aired nationwide on HBO five times between May 11 and May 27, 1993. And on May 19, 1993, the *New York Times* ran a front-page story entitled, "When Disabled Students Enter Regular Classrooms" (Chira, 1993).

Reformist Rhetoric Hardens

As the TASH leadership seized control of the reform movement, prevalent reformist opinion about special education and the continuum of services made an important about-face—that is, from a belief in the desirability of placement options, represented by the continuum, to the view that the continuum has outlived its usefulness and should be eliminated. This radical transformation was reflected in the changing rhetoric of several visible advocates of inclusion. In the mid-1980s, the Stainbacks favored special education options in home schools: "While heterogeneous educational arrangements should be encouraged wherever possible, students would still need to be grouped, in some instances, into specific courses or classes according to their instructional needs" (W. Stainback & S. Stainback, 1984, p. 108). Eight years later, the same authors argued for the elimination of the continuum:

> An inclusive school or classroom educates all students in the mainstream. No students, including those with disabilities, are relegated to the fringes of the school by placement in segregated wings, trailers, or special classes. (S. Stainback & W. Stainback, 1992, p. 34)

Gartner and Lipsky have demonstrated a similar transmutation. In the late 1980s, they defined integration for students with severe disabilities partly as "placement of [special] classes in general school buildings which are the chronologically age-appropriate sites for the students" and "participation . . . in all non-academic activities of the school" and "implementation of a functional life-skills curriculum" (1987, p. 386). Five years later, they wrote, "The concepts of Least Restrictive Environment—a continuum of placements, and a cascade of services—were progressive when developed but do not today promote the *full* inclusion of *all* persons with disabilities in *all* aspects of societal life" (Lipsky & Gartner, 1991, p. 52, emphasis in original).

For Whom Do TASH Leaders Speak?

The TASH leadership presumes to speak for all students with disabilities. But its position differs markedly from the official views of many advocacy and professional groups, evidenced by the recent position statements of The Council for Exceptional Children (1993), the Commission on the Education of the Deaf (1988), a consortium of national organizations of the blind (American Council on the Blind et al., n.d.), the Learning Disabilities Association (1993), and the National Joint Committee on Learning Disabilities (1993). Nor does the TASH leadership necessarily represent the views of all or even many members of its own organization. This possibility is suggested by W. Stainback, S. Stainback, and Moravec's (1992) forceful rejection of Brown and colleagues' (1991) carefully reasoned position that students with severe intellectual disabilities should spend some time outside general education classrooms. In other words, the TASH leadership, although enjoying success in shaping state and national policy, is a relatively small and insular group that advocates primarily, if not exclusively, for children with severe intellectual disabilities—smaller and considerably more homogeneous than the REI supporters of 5 to 10 years ago.

Goals: Abolishing Special Education and Promoting Social Competence

Eliminating the Continuum of Services

Biklen (1985); Biklen et al. (1987); Giangreco, Dennis, Cloninger, Edelman, and Schattman (1993); Lipsky and Gartner (1989, 1991); W. Stainback and S. Stainback (1991); S. Stainback and W. Stainback (1992); Taylor (1988); Thousand and Villa (1990); York and Vandercook (1991) and other leaders of the inclusive schools movement are attempting to deconstruct special education on two levels: to demythologize the construct of "special education" and to abolish its organization and structure, ridding the education landscape of professionals called "special educators." That is, they wish to eliminate not just the very bottom or near-top of the cascade, as advocated by REI supporters (e.g., Gersten & Woodward, 1990; Jenkins et al., 1988; Pugach & Lilly, 1984; Reynolds et al., 1987), but virtually the entire range of options represented by the continuum. To wit: "The inclusion option signifies the end of labeling, special education, and special classes, but not the end of necessary supports and services . . . in the integrated classroom" (Pearpoint & Forest, 1992, p. xvi).

As illustrated by the Pearpoint and Forest quotation, proponents of eliminating the continuum are quick to point out that, whereas they wish to see an end to special education teachers and students, they are not advocating "dumping," or moving children with disabilities into general education classrooms without appropriate support. Specialists of all types, they say, would follow the children into the mainstream, where services would be available to any student, previously labeled or not, who may be in need.

Focus on Social Competence and Friendships

Whereas the first goal of many inclusionists is to abolish special education, a second is to enhance students' social competence and to change the attitudes of teachers and students without disabilities who, some day, will become parents, taxpayers, and service providers (e.g., Gartner & Lipsky, 1987; S. Stainback & W. Stainback, 1985).

Although the first goal has received the publicity, the second is the advocates' end goal. As explained by Gartner & Lipsky (1987): "The rationale for educating students with severe disabilities in integrated settings is to ensure their normalized community participation by providing them with systematic instruction in the skills that are essential to their success in the social and environmental contexts in which they will ultimately use these skills" (p. 386). Snell (1991) stated, "Probably the three most important and reciprocal benefits from integration . . . are (a) the development of social skills . . . across all school age groups, (b) the improvements in the attitudes that nondisabled peers have for their peers with disabilities, and (c) the development of positive relationships and friendships between peers as a result of integration" (pp. 137–138). (Also see Vandercook, Fleetham, Sinclair, & Tettie, cited in W. Stainback & S. Stainback, 1991.)

In sharp contrast to this focus on socialization skills, attitude change, and positive peer relations, REI advocates' primary concern was strengthening the academic performance of students with disabilities and those at risk for school failure. Put another way, whereas full inclusionists would appear to measure integration success in terms of social acceptance, REI proponents' bottom line tended to index academic competence/success. This reflects the fact that whereas full inclusionists advocate primarily for children with severe intellectual disabilities, REI supporters often were working on behalf of students for whom relatively ambitious academic goals had been established (Fuchs & Fuchs, 1991).

Tactics

Full Inclusion

Why do leaders of the inclusive schools movement adhere to the uncompromising position of *no* special education and *all* children with disabilities in regular classrooms? Quite simply, they view special education as the root cause of much that is wrong with general education. S. Stainback and W. Stainback (1992) stated: "Because . . . 'special' education has operated for so long, many schools unfortunately do not know . . . how to adapt and modify the curriculum and instructional programs to meet diverse student needs" (p. 40). To at least some full inclusionists, then, special education's very existence is responsible for general education's failure to accommodate the needs of many students, because it has served as a "dumping ground" that has made it easy for general education to rid itself of its "undesirables" and "unteachables." Moreover, some critics contend, if providing the mainstream with a dumping ground were not complicity enough, special education's tendency to locate students' learning and behavior problems within the child (see S. Stainback & W. Stainback, 1992, p. 32) has absolved general educators of responsibility for the children they have removed from their system. Eliminating special education, say the full inclusionists, will force general educators both to deal with the children it heretofore had avoided and, in the process, to transform itself into a more responsive, resourceful, humane system.

Lieberman (1992) and others have noted similarities between the policies of full inclusion and the deinstitutionalization of persons with mental illness. According to a study conducted by the Public Citizen Health Research Group and the National Alliance for the Mentally Ill (cited in Hilts, 1990), deinstitutionalization has caused more than 250,000 people with schizophrenia or manic-depressive illness to live in shelters, on the streets, or in jails. Begun in the 1960s, its failure became so obvious, pervasive, and devastating that Seymour Kaplan, the late psychiatrist who pioneered the movement in New York State, was often heard to remark that it was the gravest error he had ever made (Sacks, 1991).

Deinstitutionalization's failure (also see Bachrach, 1986) prompts these questions: Why do full inclusionists believe general education can respond appropriately to all students heretofore receiving special education (as well as Chapter 1 and English as a second language [ESL] instruction)? How can the mainstream improve so dramatically to incorporate an increase in diversity when it has such obvious difficulty accommodating the student diversity it already has (see Baker & Zigmond, 1990; L. Fuchs, D. Fuchs, & Bishop, 1992; McIntosh, Vaughn, Schumm, Haager, & Lee, 1993)? The infusion of specialists, bought with dollars saved from the dismantling of special education, would be a start; but nearly all agree it would be only a start. Fundamental changes in mainstream classes would seem necessary. And some full inclusionists believe they have the answer. Their solution, we believe, reveals how poorly they understand general education and how shaky the ground is on which their movement is being built.

The Curriculum Is Out, Process Is In: An Open-School Revival

Many an inclusionist's vision of restructured schooling prominently features a deemphasis, if not the outright rejection, of standard curricula (see S. Stainback & W. Stainback, 1992). W. Stainback et al. (1992), for example, offered three reasons for their dislike of standard, or "predefined," curricula. First, they claimed, there is no intellectual basis for textbook knowledge: "There is no longer (if there ever was) a single, discrete, stagnant [sic] body of information" (p. 69). Second, the standard curriculum "does not accommodate the inherent diversity in background experiences, learning needs, styles, and interests of all students" (p. 69). Third, it and related instruction are "boring, uninteresting, and lacking in meaning or purposefulness for many students" (p. 69).

There is another, and less explicit, reason for this antipathy. A standard curriculum typically becomes a focal point for the teaching and learning process: Teachers feel obligated to teach it, and students are held accountable for learning it. For most children with severe intellectual disabilities, it is usually unattainable. This means that mainstream teachers attempting to accommodate a wide diversity of students must orchestrate a greater number of activities and materials, substantially complicating their job. Further, these different activities and materials tend to separate students with and without disabilities, reducing the amount and quality of social interaction between them. In short, the standard curriculum is anathema to many inclusionists because it creates de facto segregation within the mainstream and requires more planning which, for some teachers, can become reason enough to turn their backs on the inclusion concept.

Whereas at least some full inclusionists eschew the standard curriculum and knowledge for knowledge's sake, they enthusiastically embrace a process approach to education. W. Stainback et al. (1992) have stated:

> From a holistic, constructivist perspective, all children simply engage in a process of learning as much as they can in a particular subject area; how much and exactly what they learn will depend upon their backgrounds, interests, and abilities. (p. 72)

> The teacher may share his or her knowledge of "tricks of the trade" with students through "mini-lessons" or by other means, but the focus is on facilitating students to become actively engaged in their own learning. . . . The classroom is often filled with real-life, purposeful projects and activities. There is little focus on practicing skills such as punctuation, capitalization, or noun-verb identification in isolated ways—these are learned in the context of writing activities. (p. 70)

> There is little or no focus on remediating deficits and weaknesses—
> these are addressed or compensated for as children become excited
> about learning and engage in real-life, purposeful projects and
> activities. (p. 70)

These descriptions have the same romantic appeal as Weber's (1971)
and Featherstone's (1971) charming portraits of the British Infant
Schools and Rathbone's (1971) descriptions of open education, an
American movement based on the British Infant Schools that both
bloomed and withered in the early 1970s, thirsting for sufficient
parent support and teacher training (see Myers, 1974). But, more
important, the W. Stainback et al. descriptions reveal an offbeat view
of schooling, an understanding of general education that clashes with
what currently is being written and advocated by many reformers,
policy makers, and researchers.

Consider, for example, the oil-and-water mix of W. Stainback
et al.'s (1992) approach with Cooperative Integrated Reading and
Composition (Stevens, Madden, Slavin, & Farnish, 1987) and Team-
Assisted Individualization (Slavin, 1984), two programs that claim a
strong academic focus, are curriculum driven, and use relatively
explicit teaching strategies. The same may be said for Wang's ALEM
and Reading Recovery (e.g., Pinnell, DeFord, & Lyons, 1988). It would
seem that full inclusionists like the Stainbacks would reject the very
approaches to reform that REI proponents championed. Judging from
W. Stainback et al.'s (1992) nonchalance toward students in academic difficulty (in their third passage), we would expect them also
to reject the intensive remedial activity described by Oakes and
Lipton (1992) in successfully "detracked" schools, or schools that have
eliminated (or nearly eliminated) grouping for instruction by ability:

> In some schools, students . . . having difficulty keeping up in hetero-
> geneous academic classes are enrolled in a support or booster class
> where they receive additional instruction; in others, peer- or cross-
> age tutoring programs offer after-school help. Some schools make
> reading assignments available on cassette tapes so that less accom-
> plished readers can participate fully. (pp. 450–451)

Finally, compare the devaluation of student and teacher accountability and, by implication, the deemphasis on academic standards
that suffuses the three passages from W. Stainback et al. (1992) with
the following statements of two recent Secretaries of Education and
the President of the American Federation of Teachers:

> We urgently need a nationwide system of assessment that covers
> every school district . . . in the U.S. The next President must rally

parents, community leaders, the media, and corporate America . . . to bring all U.S. residents to a high level of literacy and of skilled and productive intelligences. (Bell, 1988, p. 10)

The critical public mission in education is to set tough, clear standards of achievement and insure that those who educate our children are accountable for meeting them. (Lamar Alexander at the Republican National Convention, cited in "Excerpts from the Texts of Education-Related Planks," 1992, p. 33)

[Education reform] includes defining what students should know and be able to do; assessments that tell us who is or isn't making it; and consequences. The last are designed to get students to work as hard as they do in other countries because they know something important—like college admissions or access to a good job—is at stake. (Shanker, 1993)

"All Children"

Why are at least some full inclusionists out of step with general education's steady drumbeat? Because as zealous advocates of children with severe intellectual disabilities, they march to a beat of their own. Despite their slogan of "all children," they are concerned primarily about their own children. Their plan for school reform is driven by the concern, "What type of school will be best for our children?" and by a related presumption that "What's best for our kids is good for all kids." The academic needs of low-, average-, and above-average-achieving students, as well as those with varying disabilities, typically are ignored.

Full inclusionists appear unmoved by the well-publicized statements of the Learning Disabilities Association (1993) and the National Joint Committee on Learning Disabilities (1993), which have claimed that students with learning disabilities sometimes require an intensity and systematicity of instruction uncommon to general education classrooms. Nor are they swayed by advocates of children with hearing and visual impairments, many of whom fiercely support special schools on grounds that general education cannot be trusted always to provide specialized services to their children, and that it deprives many students of necessary cultural and socialization experiences (e.g., American Council on the Blind et al., n.d.; De Witt, 1991; National Council on Disability, 1989). There is an inconsistency in the TASH leadership's apparent unresponsiveness to advocates of deaf and blind students. The leadership wants an end to the continuum of services primarily because it precludes desirable socialization experiences for students with severe intellectual disabilities. But the leadership turns its back on the very same argument when used by advocates for those with hearing and visual impairments wishing to preserve the continuum.

TASH leaders' use of the phrase "all children," then, is presumptive and misleading. It is ironic, too, because, rhetoric aside, their goals and tactics reflect an exclusionary, not inclusionary, mindset: Their writings suggest little interest in others' points of view (see Kauffman, 1993); manifest scant recognition that many special and general educators and administrators, as well as academics, have concerns about their positions (e.g., Coates, 1989; Houck & Rogers, in press; Knoff, 1985; Pedhazur-Schmelkin, 1981; Semmel, Abernathy, Butera, & Lesar, 1991; Stephens & Braun, 1980); and generally give the impression that they see accommodation as a compromise of principles and a capitulation—that only a purist's perspective is honorable and permissible. (Apropos, the newest variant of the phrase "full inclusion," heard at TASH's 1993 annual meeting in Chicago, is "uncompromised inclusion"—as in "Please join friends and colleagues who stand for uncompromised inclusion and for honesty in broadcasting," this from an announcement written by the organization publicizing a press conference to object to how a PBS TV program, *Frontline,* treated facilitated communication.) Full inclusionists' romanticism, insularity, and willingness to speak for all is markedly different from REI supporters' pragmatism, big-tent philosophy and reluctance to speak for all.

Impact on Special and General Education Reform

Success Story?

"Radical" is defined as "favoring extreme social changes or reforms." The TASH leadership has radicalized reform making in special education: Whereas the signature phrase of REI advocates was "cooperation between special and general education," the full-inclusionist mantra is "eliminate special education." Despite their extremist position, and although small in number, full inclusionists are shaping special education policy and practice in a handful of state agencies and in more than a few local school districts. Moreover, after ignoring special education for a decade or more, general education is giving evidence of listening, finally, just in time to hear special educators talk of dismantling the continuum and refashioning mainstream classes—calls for change guided by radical constructivist blueprints unsubstantiated by research.

The power to influence must be heady stuff for the leaders of full inclusion. Few others, after all, can claim to inspire policy making in the states of Michigan and New Mexico, or see their ideas incorporated in a National Association of State Boards of Education white paper, or hear their movement celebrated during the nationally televised Academy Awards. The sun surely is shining on the current movers and shakers of special education reform. But if clear skies are overhead, black clouds may be crowding for room on the horizon.

We predict that if the full inclusionists adhere to their no-optional-placement strategy, opposition to their movement will become increasingly vocal, especially now that prominent professional and parent groups have produced position papers rejecting full inclusion and supporting the continuum of services. Likewise, if TASH leaders cling to a vision of regular education that emphasizes a radical constructivist approach to teaching and learning and that deemphasizes curriculum, academic standards, and student and teacher accountability, general education will lose interest in special education as a partner in reform making.

Gratuitous Advice

To the leaders of full inclusion we offer the following message, which we suspect is on the tip of many tongues: For years we've been impressed by arguments for the inclusion of children with severe intellectual disabilities in regular schools and classrooms. Fix your attention on these children and permit the parents and professional advocates of children with severe behavior problems, hearing impairments, learning disabilities, and so forth to speak on behalf of the children *they* know best. Recognize that they are for the most part steadfast and united in their support of special-education options. Recognize, too, that you're probably at the apex of your power. Use it to build bridges. Choose compromise over principles. By doing this, you will transform adversaries into allies willing to help you secure the inclusion, not of all children, but of those who are the touchstone of your work and dreams.

Will full inclusionists heed such advice? We hope so because, if not, their continued provocative rhetoric will polarize a field already agitated. A troubling sign that special education is in the process of dividing into opposite camps is the emergence of a new extremist group to which the full inclusionists inadvertently gave life; namely, the reactionaries who champion the status quo and all but rule out thoughtful self-criticism that can lead to constructive adaptations. Lest readers think that this group is little more than feverish imagining, we suggest they speak to colleagues who listened to discussions on the floor of the Delegate Assembly at The Council for Exceptional Children's 1993 convention in San Antonio.

LOOKING FOR PRAGMATISTS

Special education has big problems, not least of which is that it must redefine its relationship with general education. Now is the time to hear from inventive pragmatists, not extremists on the right or the left. Now is the time for leadership that recognizes the need for change; appreciates the importance of consensus building; looks at general education with a sense of what is possible; respects special education traditions and values and the law that undergirds them; and seeks to strengthen the mainstream, as well as other educational options that can provide more intensive services, to enhance the learning and lives of all children.

AUTHORS' NOTES

Preparation of this article was supported in part by the Office of Special Education Programs, U.S. Department of Education (Grant H023C10086-92), and by the National Institute of Child Health and Human Development (Core Grant HD 15052). The article does not necessarily reflect the position or policy of the funding agencies, and no official endorsement by them should be inferred.

We thank Jim Kauffman, Maggie McLaughlin, and Helen Thornton (as well as three anonymous reviewers) for their helpful comments on an earlier draft of the manuscript. Their willingness to provide us with feedback should not be construed as support for the position we have taken. A small portion of the article is based on a book review in press with the *American Journal on Mental Retardation*.

REFERENCES

Algozzine, B., Christenson, S., & Ysseldyke, J. E. (1982). An analysis of the incidence of special class placement: The masses are burgeoning. *The Journal of Special Education, 17,* 141–147.

Algozzine, B., Maheady, L., Sacca, K. C., O'Shea, L., & O'Shea, D. (1990). Sometimes patent medicine works: A reply to Braaten, Kauffman, Braaten, Polsgrove, and Nelson. *Exceptional Children, 56,* 552–557.

Allington, R. L., & McGill-Franzen, A. (1989). Different programs, indifferent instruction. In D. K. Lipsky & A. Gartner (Eds.), *Beyond separate education: Quality education for all* (pp. 75–97). Baltimore: Brookes.

American Council on the Blind et al. (n.d.). *Full inclusion of students who are blind and visually impaired: A position statement.* Washington, DC: Author.

Anderson-Inman, L., Walker, H. M., & Purcell, J. (1984). Promoting the transfer of skills across settings: Transenvironmental programming for handicapped students in the mainstream. In W. L. Heward, T. E. Heron, D. S. Hill, & J. Trap-Porter (Eds.), *Focus on behavior analysis in education* (pp. 17–35). Columbus, OH: Merrill.

The Association for Persons with Severe Handicaps. (1992, July). CEC slips back; ASCD steps forward. *TASH Newsletter, 18,* 1.

Bachrach, L. L. (1986). Deinstitutionalization: What do the numbers mean? *Hospital and Community Psychiatry, 37,* 118–119, 121.

Baker, J., & Zigmond, N. (1990). Are regular education classes equipped to accommodate students with learning disabilities? *Exceptional Children, 56,* 515–526.

Behrmann, J. (1992). All must collaborate to serve children with disabilities. *Counterpoint, 13,* 1, 9.

Bell, T. H. (1988). On the need for national leadership to make American education work. *Phi Delta Kappan, 70,* 8–10.

Biklen, D. (1985). *Achieving the complete school.* New York: Teachers College.

Biklen, D., Lehr, S., Searl, S. J., & Taylor, S. J. (1987). *Purposeful integration . . . inherently equal* [Manual prepared by the Center on Human Policy, Syracuse University.] (Available from Technical Assistance for Parent Programs Project, 312 Stuart Street, Boston, MA 02116)

The Board of Education for the City of Toronto. (1989). *A report to the Minister of Education on the provision of special education programs and special education services for the city of Toronto.* Toronto: Author.

Braaten, S., Kauffman, J. M., Braaten, B., Polsgrove, L., & Nelson, C. M. (1988). The Regular Education Initiative: Patent medicine for behavioral disorders. *Exceptional Children, 55,* 21–27.

Brown, L., Branston-McClean, M., Baumgart, D., Vincent, L., Falvey, M., & Schroeder, J. (1979). Using the characteristics of current and subsequent least restrictive environments in the development of curricular content for severely handicapped students. *AAESPH Review, 4,* 407–424.

Brown, L., Schwarz, P., Udvari-Solner, A., Kampschroer, E., Johnson, F., Jorgensen, J., & Gruenewald, L. (1991). How much time should students with severe intellectual disabilities spend in regular classrooms and elsewhere? *JASH, 16,* 39–47.

Buttram, J. L., & Kershner, K. M. (1988). *Special education in America's cities: A descriptive study.* Philadelphia: Research for Better Schools. (ERIC Document Reproduction Service No. ED 319 187)

California Research Institute. (1990). Strategies on the integration of students with severe disabilities. *TASH Newsletter, 16,* pp. 1–4 (inset).

Carnegie Council for Adolescent Development. (1989). *Turning points.* Washington, DC: Author, (ERIC Document Reproduction Service No. ED 312 322)

Carnegie Forum on Education and the Economy. (1986). *A nation prepared: Teachers for the 21st century.* Washington, DC: Author. (ERIC Document Reproduction Service No. ED 268 120)

Chaikind, S., Danielson, L. C., & Brauen, M. L. (1993). What do we know about the costs of special education? A selected review. *The Journal of Special Education, 26,* 344–370.

Chira, S. (1993, May 19). When disabled students enter regular classrooms. *The New York Times,* pp. 1, 17.

Coates, R. D. (1989). The Regular Education Initiative and opinions of regular classroom teachers. *Journal of Learning Disabilities, 22,* 532–536.

Commission on the Education of the Deaf. (1988, February). *Toward equality: Education of the deaf.* Washington, DC: U.S. Government Printing Office. (ERIC Document Reproduction Service No. ED 303 932)

Council of Chief State School Officers. (1992, March). Special education and school restructuring. *Concerns, 35,* 1–7.

The Council for Exceptional Children. (1993, April). *Statement on inclusive schools and communities.* Reston, VA: Author.

De Witt, K. (1991, May 12). How best to teach the blind: A growing battle over braille. *The New York Times,* pp. 1, 12.

Dunn, L. M. (1968). Special education for the mildly retarded: Is much of it justifiable? *Exceptional Children, 34,* 5–22.

Excerpts from text of education-related planks in Republican party platform. (1992). *The Chronicle of Higher Education, 39*(2), 32–33.

Featherstone, J. (1971). *Schools where children learn.* New York: Liveright.

Fuchs, D., & Fuchs, L. S. (1991). Framing the REI debate: Abolitionists versus conservationists. In J. W. Lloyd, A. C. Repp, & N. N. Singh (Eds.), *The Regular Education Initiative: Alternative perspectives on concepts, issues, and models* (pp. 241–255). Sycamore, IL: Sycamore.

Fuchs, D., Fuchs, L. S., & Fernstrom, P. (1993). A conservative approach to special education reform: Mainstreaming through transenvironmental programming and curriculum-based measurement. *American Educational Research Journal, 30,* 149–177.

Fuchs, L. S., Fuchs, D., & Bishop, N. (1992). Teacher planning for students with learning disabilities: Differences between general and special educators. *Learning Disabilities Research and Practice, 7,* 120–128.

Gartner, A., & Lipsky, D. K. (1987). Beyond special education: Toward a quality system for all students. *Harvard Educational Review, 57,* 367–395.

Gersten, R., & Woodward, J. (1990). Rethinking the Regular Education Initiative: Focus on the classroom teacher. *Remedial and Special Education, 11,* 7–16.

Giangreco, M. F., Dennis, R., Cloninger, C., Edelman, S., & Schattman, R. (1993). "I've counted Jon": Transformational experiences of teachers educating students with disabilities. *Exceptional Children, 59,* 359–372.

Gottlieb, J., Alter, M., & Gottlieb, B. W. (1991). Mainstreaming academically handicapped children in urban schools. In J. W. Lloyd, A. C. Repp,

& N. N. Singh (Eds.), *The Regular Education Initiative: Alternative perspectives on concepts, issues, and models* (pp. 95–112). Sycamore, IL: Sycamore.

Hales, R. M., & Carlson, L. B. (1992). *Issues and trends in special education.* Lexington: Federal Resource Center for Special Education, University of Kentucky. (ERIC Document Reproduction Service No. ED 349 753)

Hallahan, D. P., Keller, C. E., McKinney, J. D., Lloyd, J. W., & Bryan, T. (1988). Examining the research base of the Regular Education Initiative: Efficacy studies and the Adaptive Learning Environments Model. *Journal of Learning Disabilities, 21,* 29–35.

Heller, K. A., Holtzman, W. H., & Messick, S. (Eds.). (1982). *Placing children in special education: A strategy for equity.* Washington, D.C.: National Academy Press.

Hilts, P. J. (1990, September 12). U.S. care of mentally ill is assailed in a report. *The New York Times,* p. 14.

Holmes Group. (1986, April). *Tomorrow's teachers.* East Lansing, MI: Author.

Houck, C. K., & Rogers, C. (in press). The special/general education initiative for students with specific learning disabilities: Program status and input. *Journal of Learning Disabilities.*

Jenkins, J. R., Pious, C. G., & Peterson, D. L. (1988). Categorical programs for remedial and handicapped students: Issues of validity. *Exceptional Children, 55,* 147–158.

Kauffman, J. M. (1989). The Regular Education Initiative as Reagan-Bush education policy: A trickle-down theory of education of the hard to teach. *The Journal of Special Education, 23,* 256–278.

Kauffman, J. M. (1991). Restructuring in sociopolitical context: Reservations about the effects of current reform proposals on students with disabilities. In J. W. Lloyd, A. C. Repp, & N. N. Singh (Eds.), *The Regular Education Initiative: Alternative perspectives on concepts, issues, and models* (pp. 57–66). Sycamore, IL: Sycamore.

Kauffman, J. M. (1993). How we might achieve the radical reform of special education. *Exceptional Children, 60,* 6–16.

Kauffman, J. M., Gerber, M. M., & Semmel, M. I. (1988). Arguable assumptions underlying the Regular Education Initiative. *Journal of Learning Disabilities, 21,* 6–11.

Keogh, B. K. (1988a). Improving services for problem learners: Rethinking and restructuring. *Journal of Learning Disabilities, 21,* 19–22.

Keogh, B. K. (1988b). Perspectives on the Regular Education Initiative. *Learning Disabilities Focus, 4,* 3–5.

Knoff, H. M. (1985). Attitudes toward mainstreaming: A status report and comparison of regular and special educators in New York and Massachusetts. *Psychology in the Schools, 22,* 411–418.

Kukic, S. (1993, March). *Report on the development of a national agenda for achieving better results for children and youth with disabilities.* Paper presented at a meeting of the CEC President's Panel on Reform and Integration in Special Education, Logan, Utah.

Learning Disabilities Association. (1993, January). *Position paper on full inclusion of all students with learning disabilities in the regular education classroom.* Pittsburgh, PA: Author.

Lieberman, L. M. (1985). Special education and regular education: A merger made in heaven? *Exceptional Children, 51,* 513–516.

Lieberman, L. M. (1992). Preserving special education . . . for those who need it. In W. Stainback & S. Stainback (Eds.), *Controversial issues confronting special education* (pp. 13–25). Boston: Allyn & Bacon.

Lilly, M. S. (1987). Lack of focus on special education in literature on educational reform. *Exceptional Children, 53,* 325–326.

Lipsky, D. K., & Gartner, A. (1989). *Beyond separate education: Quality education for all.* Baltimore: Paul Brookes.

Lipsky, D. K., & Gartner, A. (1991). Restructuring for quality. In J. W. Lloyd, A. C. Repp, & N. N. Singh (Eds.), *The Regular Education Initiative: Alternative perspectives on concepts, issues, and models* (pp. 43–56). Sycamore, IL: Sycamore.

McGill-Franzen, A. (1987). Failure to learn to read: Formulating a policy problem. *Reading Research Quarterly, 22,* 475–490.

McIntosh, R., Vaughn, S., Schumm, J. S., Haager, D., & Lee, O. (1993). Observations of students with learning disabilities in general education classrooms. *Exceptional Children, 60,* 249–261.

McKinney, J. D., & Hocutt, A. M. (1988). Policy issues in the evaluation of the Regular Education Initiative. *Learning Disabilities Focus, 4,* 15–23.

McLaughlin, M., & Warren, S. (n.d.). *The restructuring of special education.* Unpublished document. College Park, MD: The Center for Policy Options in Special Education, University of Maryland.

McLaughlin, M., & Warren, S. (1992, September). *Issues and options in restructuring schools and special education programs.* College Park, MD: The Center for Policy Options in Special Education, University of Maryland. (ERIC Document Reproduction Service No. ED 350 774)

Megivern, K. (1987). The war within. *Yearbook of the Association for Education and Rehabilitation of the Blind and Visually Impaired, 5,* 29–32.

Michigan Department of Education and State Board of Education. (1992, February). *Inclusive education: Position statement.* Lansing, MI: Author.

Miller, L. (1990). The Regular Education Initiative and school reform: Lessons from the mainstream. *Remedial and Special Education, 11,* 17–22.

Myers, D. A. (1974). Why open education died. *Journal of Research and Development in Education, 8,* 60–67.

National Association of State Boards of Education. (1992, October). *Winners all: A call for inclusive schools.* Washington, DC: Author.

National Commission on Excellence in Education. (1983, April). *A nation at risk: The imperative of educational reform.* Washington, DC: U.S. Government Printing Office.

National Council on Disability. (1989, September). *The education of students with disabilities: Where do we stand?* Washington, DC: Author. (ERIC Document Reproduction Service No. ED 315 961)

National Education Association. (1992). *Resolution B-20: Education for all students with disabilities.* Washington, DC: Author.

National Governors' Association. (1986). *Time for results.* Washington, DC: Author. (ERIC Document Reproduction Service No. ED 279 609)

The National Joint Committee on Learning Disabilities. (1993, January). *A reaction to "full inclusion": A reaffirmation of the right of students with learning disabilities to a continuum of services.* Author.

New Mexico State Department of Education. (1991). *Administrative policy on full inclusion.* Santa Fe, NM: Author.

Oakes, J., & Lipton, M. (1992). Detracking schools: Early lessons from the field. *Phi Delta Kappan, 73,* 448–454.

Pearpoint, J., & Forest, M. (1992). Foreword. In S. Stainback & W. Stainback (Eds.), *Curriculum considerations in inclusive classrooms: Facilitating learning for all students* (pp. xv–xviii). Baltimore: Paul Brookes.

Pedhazur-Schmelkin, L. (1981). Teachers' and nonteachers' attitudes toward mainstreaming. *Exceptional Children, 48,* 42–47.

Peterson, P. L., & Clark, C. M. (1978). Teachers' reports of their cognitive process during teaching. *American Educational Research Journal, 15,* 417–432.

Pinnell, G. S., DeFord, D. E., & Lyons, C. A. (1988). *Reading recovery: Early intervention for at-risk first graders.* Arlington, VA: Educational Research Services. (ERIC Document Reproduction Service No. ED 303 790)

Pugach, M., & Lilly, S. M. (1984). Reconceptualizing support services for classroom teachers: Implications for teacher education. *Journal of Teacher Education, 35,* 48–55.

Pugach, M., & Sapon-Shevin, M. (1987). New agendas for special education policy: What the national reports haven't said. *Exceptional Children, 53,* 295–299.

Rathbone, C. H. (1971). The implicit rationale of the open education classroom. In C. H. Rathbone (Ed.), *Open education: The informal classroom* (pp. 99–116). New York: Citation.

Reynolds, M. C. (1988). Reaction to the JLD special series on the Regular Education Initiative. *Journal of Learning Disabilities, 21,* 352–356.

Reynolds, M. C. (1989). An historical perspective: The delivery of special education to mildly disabled and at-risk students. *Remedial and Special Education, 10,* 7–11.

Reynolds, M. C. (1991). Classification and labeling. In J. W. Lloyd, A. C. Repp, & N. N. Singh (Eds.), *The Regular Education Initiative: Alternative perspectives on concepts, issues, and models* (pp. 29–41). Sycamore, IL: Sycamore.

Reynolds, M. C., & Birch, J. W. (1977). *Teaching exceptional children in all America's schools.* Reston, VA: The Council for Exceptional Children.

Reynolds, M. C., Wang, M. C., & Walberg, H. J. (1987). The necessary restructuring of special and regular education. *Exceptional Children, 53,* 391–398.

Reynolds, M. C., Zetlin, A. G., & Wang, M. C. (1993). 20/20 analysis: Taking a close look at the margins. *Exceptional Children, 59,* 294–300.

Sacks, O. (1991, February 13). Forsaking the mentally ill. *The New York Times* (OpEd), p. 23.

Sapon-Shevin, M. (1987). The national education reports and special education: Implications for students. *Exceptional Children, 53,* 300–306.

Semmel, M. I., Abernathy, T. V., Butera, G., & Lesar, S. (1991). Teacher perceptions of the Regular Education Initiative. *Exceptional Children, 58,* 9–23.

Shanker, A. (1993, May 30). Where we stand: Opportunity to learn. *The New York Times,* p. E-7.

Singer, J. D. (1988). Should special education merge with regular education? *Educational Policy, 2,* 409–424.

Singer, J. D. (1993). Once is not enough: Former special educators who return to teaching. *Exceptional Children, 60,* 58–72.

Singer, J. D., & Butler, J. B. (1987). The Education for All Handicapped Children Act: Schools as agents of social reform. *Harvard Educational Review, 57,* 125–152.

Skrtic, T. (1987). Preconditions for merger: An organizational analysis of special education reform. In M. Semmel (Chair), *Prenuptial agreements necessary for wedding special education and general education.* Symposium presented at the annual meeting of the American Educational Research Association, Washington, DC. (ERIC Document Reproduction Service No. ED 291 177)

Slavin, R. E. (1984). Team Assisted Individualization: Cooperative learning and individualized instruction in the mainstreamed classroom. *Remedial and Special Education, 5,* 33–42.

Slavin, R. E., Madden, N. A., Karweit, N. L., Dolan, L., Wasik, B. A., Shaw, A., Mainzer, K. L., & Haxby, B. (1991). Neverstreaming: Prevention and early intervention as an alternative to special education. *Journal of Learning Disabilities, 24,* 373–378.

Slavin, R. E., & Stevens, R. J. (1991). Cooperative learning and mainstreaming. In J. W. Lloyd, A. C. Repp, & N. N. Singh (Eds.), *The Regular Education Initiative: Alternative perspectives on concepts, issues, and models* (pp. 177–191). Sycamore, IL: Sycamore.

Snell, M. E. (1988). Gartner and Lipsky's "Beyond special education: Toward a quality system for all students." *Journal of the Association for Persons with Severe Handicaps, 13,* 137–140.

Snell, M. E. (1991). Schools are for all kids: The importance of integration for students with severe disabilities and their peers. In J. W. Lloyd, A. C. Repp, & N. N. Singh (Eds.), *The Regular Education Initiative: Alternative perspectives on concepts, issues, and models* (pp. 133–148). Sycamore, IL: Sycamore.

Stainback, S., & Stainback, W. (1985). *Integration of students with severe handicaps into regular schools.* Reston, VA: The Council for Exceptional Children. (ERIC Document Reproduction Service No. ED 255 009)

Stainback, S., & Stainback, W. (1992). *Curriculum considerations in inclusive classrooms: Facilitating learning for all students.* Baltimore: Brookes.

Stainback, W., & Stainback, S. (1984). A rationale for the merger of special and regular education. *Exceptional Children, 51,* 102–111.

Stainback, W., & Stainback, S. (1991). Rationale for integration and restructuring: A synopsis. In J. W. Lloyd, A. C. Repp, & N. N. Singh (Eds.), *The Regular Education Initiative: Alternative perspectives on concepts, issues, and models* (pp. 225–239). Sycamore, IL: Sycamore.

Stainback, W., Stainback, S., & Moravec, J. (1992). Using curriculum to build inclusive classrooms. In S. Stainback & W. Stainback (Eds.), *Curriculum considerations in inclusive classrooms: Facilitating learning for all students* (pp. 65–84). Baltimore: Paul Brookes.

Stephens, T. M., & Braun, B. J. (1980). Measures of regular classroom teachers' attitudes toward handicapped children. *Exceptional Children, 46,* 292–294.

Stevens, R. J., Madden, N. A., Slavin, R. E., & Farnish, A. M. (1987). Cooperative integrated reading and composition: Two field experiments. *Reading Research Quarterly, 22,* 433–454.

Taylor, S. J. (1988). Caught in the continuum: A critical analysis of the principle of least restrictive environment. *Journal of the Association of Persons with Severe Handicaps, 13,* 41–53.

Thousand, J. S., & Villa, R. A. (1990). Strategies for educating learners with severe disabilities within their local home schools and communities. *Focus on Exceptional Children, 23,* 1–24.

U.S. Department of Education, Special Education Programs. (1992). *Fourteenth annual report to Congress on the implementation of the Individuals with Disabilities Education Act.* Washington, DC: Author. (ERIC Document Reproduction Service No. ED 347 779)

Vergason, G. A., & Anderegg, M. L. (1989). Save the baby! A response to "Integrating the children of the second system." *Phi Delta Kappan, 71,* 61–63.

Walker, H. M., & Bullis, M. (1991). Behavior disorders and the social context of regular class integration: A conceptual dilemma? In J. W. Lloyd, A. C. Repp, & N. N. Singh (Eds.), *The Regular Education Initiative: Alternative perspectives on concepts, issues, and models* (pp. 75–93). Sycamore, IL: Sycamore.

Wang, M. C. (1980). Adaptive instruction: Building on diversity. *Theory Into Practice, 19,* 122–128.

Wang, M. C. (1981). Mainstreaming exceptional children: Some instructional design and implementation considerations. *Elementary School Journal, 81,* 195–221.

Wang, M. C. (1987). Toward achieving educational excellence for all students: Program design and student outcomes. *Remedial and Special Education, 8,* 25–34.

Wang, M. C., & Birch, J. W. (1984). Comparison of a full-time mainstreaming program and a resource room approach. *Exceptional Children, 51,* 33–40.

Wang, M. C., & Reynolds, M. C. (1985). Avoiding the "Catch 22" in special education reform. *Exceptional Children, 51,* 497–502.

Wang, M. C., Reynolds, M. C., & Walberg, H. J. (Eds.). (1987). *Handbook of special education: Research and practice* (Vol. 1). Oxford: Pergamon.

Wang, M. C., Reynolds, M. C., & Walberg, H. J. (1988). Integrating the children of the second system. *Phi Delta Kappan, 70,* 248–251.

Wang, M. C., Rubenstein, J. L., & Reynolds, M. C. (1985). Clearing the road to success for students with special needs. *Educational Leadership, 43,* 62–67.

Wang, M. C., & Walberg, H. J. (1988). Four fallacies of segregationism. *Exceptional Children, 55,* 128–137.

Weber, L. (1971). *The English Infant School and informal education.* Englewood Cliffs, NJ: Prentice-Hall.

Will, M. (1986). Educating children with learning problems: A shared responsibility. *Exceptional Children, 52,* 411–415.

York, J., & Vandercook, T. (1991). Designing an integrated program for learners with severe disabilities. *TEACHING Exceptional Children, 23,* 22–28.

Ysseldyke, J. E., Algozzine, B., & Epps, S. (1983). A logical and empirical analysis of current practice in classifying students as handicapped. *Exceptional Children, 50,* 160–166.

Part III

Disability-Specific Issues

s noted in the final essay in Part II by Fuchs and Fuchs, the inclusion movement has been driven at different times in the recent history of special education by the agendas of different constituencies. The advocates for students with severe disabilities, however, have propelled the full inclusion movement into the position that placement must be the primary issue and that placement alternatives must be severely truncated or eliminated altogether for all students. Part III contains essays highlighting the perspectives and concerns expressed by advocates other than The Association for Persons with Severe Handicaps (TASH) for students with a variety of disabilities. The authors of these essays caution that the rigidity of the full inclusion movement's insistence that regular schools and regular classrooms are the appropriate and least restrictive environment for all students is, for some, demeaning and debilitating.

The essays in Part III refocus our attention on the necessity of making both programming and placement decisions on an individual basis. They argue for maintaining a full continuum of alternative placements and for renewing our commitment to making all these alternatives what they should be—places in which students learn critical skills, are treated with kindness and respect for their individuality, and are helped to become productive and fulfilled members of supportive communities.

Chapter 12

Special Education and the Great God, Inclusion

Stanley C. Diamond

THE CURRENT BUZZWORDS OF CHANGE in the world of special education are integration, least restrictive environment, mainstreaming, the regular education initiative, and, most recently, inclusion. The future implies the existence of a total program for all kinds and degrees of emotional, physical and intellectually handicapped youngsters within the public school systems of our country. One can reach no other conclusion listening to the oracles from the federal to the state to the local levels of educational bureaucracy extol the virtues of this approach, reading the multitude of articles in the educational press which explain how this feat is to be accomplished,[1] and noting the titles of workshops and presentations at the councils and conferences for educators of special children. The handwriting on the wall could not be clearer.

The current thrust to serve all of our students with special needs and its hopeful promise to our children is more than commendable; it is essential. No person who cares about exceptional youngsters would ever want to return to the days before public laws were passed that ensured attention and services to this population, especially P.L. 94-142, the Education of All Handicapped Act. This law and related legislation were directed toward remedying the inclination of the

Reprinted from "Special education and the great god, inclusion" by Stanley C. Diamond, *Beyond Behavior,* Vol. 4, No. 2, 1993, 3–6. Copyright © 1993 by CCBD Publications. Reprinted by permission.

public schools to consider many youngsters ineducable within their setting, or perhaps requiring an unrealistic investment for the assumed benefits to an individual to be justified. That point of view was always inconsistent with the notion that public education was to be responsible for the education of every child in our country.

In the absence of a commitment by the public sector to provide brain-injured, seriously emotionally disturbed, multiply handicapped and other such challenging youngsters a productive educational opportunity, a host of private programs sprang up throughout the country addressed to the particular needs of one or other of these groups. The most well-known of such schools were those founded to teach the deaf and blind populations and many such programs were the recipients of significant grants and charters by the states in which they were established. The private schools developed a rich variety of options for handicapped children through innovation, dedi-'cation, training of teachers, and a willingness to try anything to work effectively with a child who was severely debilitated education-ally; their results contributed enormously to the research and meth-odology that now undergirds theory and defines methodologies in special education.

One important component of educational law regarding handi-capped children is the notion that such children should be in the most natural and unrestricted setting possible so that they can feel less special and less isolated, so that they can be with a greater variety of peers and so that they can be in a setting which more closely simulates the realities of the world that they may enter in future education or vocation. What an unambiguous concept! Who could argue with such a notion; who could hesitate for a moment in pursuing its obviously positive and helpful goal for the children involved? Yet one significant problem persists for the exponents of this idea, defining the *least* restrictive setting for a particular young-ster. With all the benefits that accrue in a classroom or school which contains both handicapped and nonhandicapped students for both groups of children—surely not a matter for serious dispute—are there still reasons for the "segregation" of certain youngsters for some period of their education, if not its entirety? I believe that this is an essential question in special education at this time and that its con-sideration is not being dealt with honestly and seriously by many influential people in the field. The answer is: Of course, there are youngsters that can not be accommodated in our current public edu-cational systems and who would either be ineffectively instructed in such settings or be so disruptive that their inclusion would be det-rimental to other children. Is this a discredited notion? Surely not in real life, practical situations.

As one who works primarily with seriously disturbed adolescents, my daily experience is with but a single segment of the total special education population and I am well aware of the danger of overgeneralizing from this rather limited experience, but it is quite instructive to *be* working with such youngsters during the time of the thrust toward what has become known as "inclusionism" in education. My understanding of this term is that it describes a belief that all children *can* and *should* be educated in the public school setting. Needless to note, this is surely the most extreme interpretation of the desirability of placing students in the least restrictive environment that has been forwarded since we belatedly discovered that many children were not being serviced at all.

As with most extreme positions, it often does not coincide with the reality of the needs of many of the youngsters it is supposed to help. By reducing the variety of options for such youngsters and by narrowing the continuum of services, it is actually quite detrimental in planning for the education of the students with whom I work. This observation is in fact so clear to me that I believe many protagonists of "inclusionism" are driven not by ideas but rather misguided by some assumed economic advantages to their approach.

At a recent conference of the National Association of Private Schools for Exceptional Children (NAPSEC, 1992), I heard Brian McNulty, the executive director of the Colorado Department of Education, extol the changes he has introduced to his state through the elimination of private programs and the integration of almost *all* students into the public system. He cited letters of joy and appreciation from parents who would normally not have expected the positive results that were obtained by this transition. I heard Jeffry Champagne (1992), the Chief Counsel to the Pennsylvania Department of Education explain the beneficial effects of the movement in that state toward placing even the most difficult to manage students in classes with "normal" kids. How wonderful sounding the gospel of inclusion appeared to be. All students sitting among peers of all abilities, sharing social experiences, having their educational needs adapted for them individually in hundreds of enriched classrooms, receiving therapies supportive of their needs, feeling part of the mainstream. And in entire states no less.

My mind raced backward through a host of related experiences, the most recent being the 20th reunion celebration at Mill Creek School, the program I direct for disturbed adolescents. I remembered the words of the former students who addressed the gathering, the gratitude they expressed for the chance they were given to get on with their lives, the affection they felt for those who had helped them have that opportunity. I remembered the attendance of students from *every* class of the school during those twenty years. We spoke of the colleges they had gone to after Mill Creek, the jobs they held, the spouses and children that were enriching their lives. They talked about the experiences they had that enabled them to *integrate* themselves at their own pace and in their own way after they outgrew the need for Mill Creek. Not one denied the value of their very rich and relatively segregated experience with us. We had as many letters and words of appreciation as had been assembled by Brian McNulty just in that room among 200 or so ex-students who were busy going on with their lives and planning an even more satisfying future.

I thought also about the multitude of calls that I receive from parents, from school counselors and special education administrators seeking a placement for a student for whom they find no proper place in their available school programs. When we can help, there is usually a sigh of relief, a statement of deep appreciation. When we can't there is customarily a request for advice about alternatives. There are few to suggest.

I remembered those students who could not come to us that we deemed appropriate and wondered what happened to them or their peers whose support for placement with us was withdrawn for bureaucratic or financial reasons. Many of them we discovered had dropped out of school; others had self-destructed in some more dramatic way; still others struggled far more painfully than they would have otherwise and for a considerably longer time, but at least they did experience integration.

I recalled the passage from *America 2000* (1991) which described the lives of some of our students in the following way:

> For too many of our children, the family that should be their protector, advocate, and moral anchor is itself in a state of deterioration . . . for too many of our children, such a family never existed. . . . For too many of our children, the neighborhood is a place of menace, the street a place of violence . . .

One may argue some of the assumptions and recommendations of that report, but the facts are indisputable and accurate in this instance. The conclusion that we must be compelled to solve such extreme human problems and crises within what are already frayed and fragile public school structures requires a leap of faith that defies most of what we know about our schools today.

My temptation at this point is to cite a multitude of cases to illustrate the notion that there need to be many options available to accommodate the vast variety of needs of the kinds of students with whom we work. I know of Mill Creek students who succeeded with us who would otherwise have clearly dropped out of school, perhaps winding up on the street or in jail or even dead. At the very best, they would live unfulfilled and unproductive lives. Those I think of are the very students who could not even walk onto the grounds of a public school, or if they did, would withdraw into themselves so dramatically that they were not only segregated but poignantly alone. Others are those who would have forced the schools to respond to them by segregating them in inappropriately separate facilities that addressed their public behavior rather than their private terror and chaos. Can such students be programmed for inclusion in the public school setting? Some yes but others no. If we regard inclusion as a religious principle, if we disregard the differences among the students we consider disabled, if we continue to insist that the least restrictive environment is some absolute standard rather than a continuum of variability that has truth only for each individual in question, we will lose some of the most valuable and creative and lovable citizens in our community. We will waste those who are difficult to program for and those who require the utmost patience and inventiveness.

There is little question in my mind that Bill, who had not gone to school for two years before he came to Mill Creek would have dropped out, become part of a system that would destroy him and would have never had reason to reevaluate his life and change direction but for the circumstance of his finding his way to us. I know that Mary would not have found the strength to return to success in school and eventually return to a public setting on her way to a scholarship at a fine university had she not had a year to work with her fears in a highly personalized, unthreatening, caring setting that was not available outside of a program like ours. Jack would not have given up his drug abuse without a separation from the forces that continually undid him in his neighborhood and school setting. He might never have learned who he was without drugs nor have imagined his survival being so possible and so rewarding.

I could go on and on. We have failures also but that is inevitable when one works with such difficult young people. No program or programs will ever exist to save all those who need help in our educational systems. The public schools are truly the hope of our country. They deserve all the support we can muster as a community. They should clearly be able to serve all but the most exceptional of our youth. But let us not discard the few exceptions as we move toward making the public school system more responsive to those who should be accommodated in it. Jeff Champagne (1992) is correct in making the following observation: "Writers, including judges, often use the phrase 'least restrictive environment' incorrectly. For example, it is not unusual to read that 'A segregated institution is the least restrictive environment for this student.' This is a logical impossibility because a segregated environment by definition cannot provide the most opportunity for proximity to and communication with ordinary students. It is entirely possible, however, that 'A segregated institution is the least restrictive environment *in which a particular student's needs can be met.*'"

Those are the words of a spokesman for the notion of inclusion. In apparent agreement, a group of private special education schools share the view that "All students with disabilities have access to the full continuum of special education services provided in both public and private settings. Appropriate education based upon individual needs cannot occur without options . . ."

(NAPSEC) The Study Group on Special Education (1991) was also accurate when it issued the following opinions:

> To the maximum extent possible, students with special needs should be integrated into the regular education program. . . . Students must learn to function in the 'real world' if they are to be productive, well-adjusted citizens after graduation . . . *but:* A situation in which every child is integrated and there are no choices for separate programming is as unacceptable as one in which every child is segregated and there are no choices for integration. The important issue is . . . whether the student is learning.

We absolutely must safeguard our most needy children. In my work with emotionally disturbed youth, I find that they require a level of faith, imagination, and commitment on the part of the staff working with them and the system that supports them that is truly exceptional. But the most salient fact about such youngsters is that their very life and their future is on the line. As desirable as a more integrated setting may seem, it is no more feasible than placing an ICU patient in a general ward for either ideological or economic reasons. It might make more services available, provide a cheerier setting and support the illusion of normalcy, but that will mean little if the patient dies. I am afraid that extremists who regard the "least restrictive environment" to be only a classroom in the neighborhood school will condemn some of our most precious young people to a dead end, educationally and personally.

We need to keep the choices alive that have enabled many students to move a pace toward integration that suits their abilities and needs and not our ideas of what their progress should be. While we work to improve the programs in our public schools for such students, let us not bite off the hands of special schools that have fed them ideas and training and provided hope for the few who do not fit.

Over the past two decades, the changes in special education have been revolutionary in methodology, public policy and the attitudes of educators toward exceptional children. Nothing should interfere with the profound progress being made in this area. At the same time, let us make sure at every turn that each child gets the program that will most likely help him or her succeed and find fulfillment and happiness to the greatest extent possible. Danger exists from overly dogmatic notions and approaches. There is currently a sound array of options for educating special children, including the separate programs that have a history of much success with certain of these children at crucial phases of their lives. It would be unwise to eliminate those placements at a juncture which does not provide for all children and with knowledge that fails to indicate that every need can be accommodated in a public school, integrated setting. If we unwittingly cause the valuable private special education schools to disappear, the price will be paid by relatively few educators but the cost will be enormous for a generation of exceptional young people who deserve our very best.

NOTE

1. For example, in the Spring 1992 publication of *Exceptional Children,* a magazine for classroom teachers, three out of the ten articles were devoted to aspects of integrating special education students into the regular classroom ("Integrating Elementary Students with Multiple Disabilities into Supported Regular Classes: Challenges and Solutions," "Promoting Integration and Cooperation: The Friendship Games," and "Adapting Textbooks for Children with Learning Disabilities in Mainstreamed Classrooms."

REFERENCES

"America 2000: An Education Strategy," U.S. Department of Education, 1991, p. 10.

Champagne, Jeff. "LRE: Decisions in Sequence," NAPSEC Annual Conference: January, 1992.

NASBE Special Education Study Group, *Newsletter of Pennsylvania Federation, Council for Exceptional Children,* January, 1992.

"Private Special Education and the Least Restrictive Environment LRE," National Association of Private Schools for Exceptional Children, 1991.

Teaching Exceptional Children, Volume 24, Number 3, Spring, 1992.

York, Jennifer, et al., "Feedback about Integrating Middle-School Students with Severe Disabilities in General Education Classes." *Exceptional Children,* Dec.–Jan., 1992.

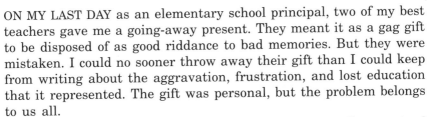

Chapter 13

Swimming Against the Mainstream

Peter Idstein

ON MY LAST DAY as an elementary school principal, two of my best teachers gave me a going-away present. They meant it as a gag gift to be disposed of as good riddance to bad memories. But they were mistaken. I could no sooner throw away their gift than I could keep from writing about the aggravation, frustration, and lost education that it represented. The gift was personal, but the problem belongs to us all.

My "present" came housed in a box that had originally contained 500 envelopes but now contained only three thick folders. These folders were bulging with the documentation that had been required for us to navigate one student through the shoals of a special education bureaucracy to a higher level of service.

Moving this student to a "more restrictive environment" took almost nine months, hundreds of hours of work, and thousands of dollars to achieve. If the district had hired an aide to do nothing but teach this one child, it might have saved money.

As significant as the financial cost was, it remains secondary to the hours of instruction that were stolen from the other 31 students in the classroom. If we accept the relationship between time on task and student learning that is posited by the literature on effective teaching, then this lost instructional time translates directly into education that was stolen from these other youngsters. Most of them were neither special education students nor gifted students; they were the usual mix of children who form the bulk of our student population and who stand without advocate in the political arenas of education.

The claims I make here come from 15 years as a public school administrator, the last five of which were spent as a building principal. In addition, I have spoken with colleagues across the nation about the issue. And while they have not been unanimous in their agreement, the overwhelming majority have echoed my concern and encouraged me to write about the matter.

Let me first say that my argument is not with the spirit of the federal law that is now known as the Individuals with Disabilities Education Act (IDEA). It may not even be with the letter of the law. My problem no doubt lies in the cumbersome implementation of a law that has magnified the concept of due process to the point that it overshadows other school-based concerns, such as instruction and learning.

I believe that the majority of students who are mainstreamed under the IDEA are properly placed and are benefiting greatly from that placement. I further believe that the need to protect these children from an instructionally segregated environment is genuine and has been addressed through this legislation. The concept of "least restrictive environment" however, has created a gate through which students generally move in one direction only. Trying to move a student to a *more* restrictive environment clearly involves swimming against the mainstream.

Critics will be quick to point out that there is no provision in the law that prohibits movement of a student to a more restrictive environment. True as this may be, it doesn't make swimming against the mainstream any easier. Let's look at why one such move cost my school and district so much time, effort, and money.

Ronald Doe was a second-grader with above-average intelligence as measured by the Wechsler Intelligence Scale for Children. However, his behavior was severe enough to warrant placement in a Level 1 special education classroom at the start of the year. Our Level 1 classrooms represented a true mainstreaming situation. One-third of the students in these classrooms had been identified as needing special education, and two-thirds of the students were from the general population, including top students. The case for Ronald's placement had been made the previous year at a cost in time and money similar to that incurred in the current saga.

Less than a month into the school year, Ronald started exhibiting behaviors that made him stand out from all the other students in the classroom. At first it was only the intensity of his behavior that was salient. He would scream, throw furniture, talk to himself, and hit other children with unmatched fervor. The classroom discipline plan called for consequences for each of these behaviors, and they were administered unemotionally by two exceptional teachers.

As this behavior developed, both of the teachers and their instructional aide watched Ronald closely in a heroic effort to catch him being good. When they did, they heaped praise and sometimes tangible rewards upon him. While he obviously enjoyed this positive attention, it did not suffice to maintain the good behavior, despite the fact that he was being reinforced almost continuously. It was as if there were another mechanism at work in his brain, saying, "I'll see your systematic efforts at behavior control and raise you random responses." We ended up enforcing the classroom discipline plan more as a model for the other children in the classroom than in the hope of changing Ronald's behavior.

As principal, I was called in almost daily to remove Ronald from the room to protect the other children. One of the three adults in the classroom was usually forced to deal with Ronald on an individual basis. Simple arithmetic would indicate that the mean instructional time per student was significantly affected by this fact alone. Add in the time it took for the teachers to keep a daily log of his behavior, write an individual behavioral contract, and meet with his mother and me to agree on appropriate rewards and punishments, and the loss of instructional time was even greater.

One of the most frustrating features of this process was that we had to take each step in its prescribed sequence. It wasn't enough simply to be reinforcing, because we *might* just be missing the "proper" reinforcer. So we found ourselves charting beginning behavior, establishing consequences, removing consequences, establishing other consequences, and so on. Indeed, sometimes it seemed we did these things as much for the purposes of "building a case" as for modifying Ronald's behavior. I realize that saying such things will raise the hackles of many special education supervisors and professors of special education. My response is to ask, "How many classroom teachers see this as an honest statement of the reality they and their principals face daily?"

Ronald was duly unimpressed with the best-laid plans of Skinner's mice and men. He proceeded to escalate his assault on the instructional environment in predictable fashion. It continually amazed me how limited the repertoire of available disruptive behaviors is. As I talked to my friends and colleagues about Ronald's conduct, they said such things as, "Oh yes, we see that, too. By the way, has he started licking other students' faces yet?" He had.

He had also rolled around on the floor, thereby delaying recess or lunch. He had eaten paste, paper clips, staples, and various other binding materials and had repeatedly stabbed himself in the arm with pencils. He had alternated between screaming and laughing raucously. In general, he pushed every button he could think of to make his teachers push the button on the wall that would summon me to come to the rescue.

When I removed him from his classroom, I would isolate him in the conference room next to my office, if it was available. If not there, I would place him in the speech room; if not there, then the *bench*. He did not seem to like to be isolated in these ways and would cry and moan and eventually fall asleep. Yet his behavior did not change. I kept Ronald in supervised isolation only long enough to locate his mother, who lacked a home phone, and let her know that I was bringing him home.

I could continue this account, detailing how his teachers and I visited his home on several occasions in an effort to make him feel good about himself or how we provided transportation for his mother to make it easier for her to attend meetings with teachers. Food and gifts were provided anonymously during the holidays, and I even delivered a full set of the *World Book Encyclopedia* to his home for Christmas, compliments of our *World Book* sales representative. In short, we went *more than* a few extra miles in an effort to help Ronald fit in and feel a part of school.

During this same period, we met weekly with the "Student Success Committee" in our building and implemented the committee's suggestions, many of which I have reported above. The day arrived, however, when we said, "Enough is enough." We felt that the time had come to seek a higher level of service for Ronald.

The first step in this process was to take the case to the Multi-Disciplinary Team (MDT) in our building. This team was made up of the school psychologist, the educational diagnostician, the speech therapist, the classroom teachers involved, and me. A student's parents or guardians are also invited to MDT meetings.

At a typical MDT meeting, the teachers present their reasons for requesting a higher level of service, including the documentation of their efforts in the classroom. I add comments regarding my role with the child and relate what has gone on between the home and the school in an effort to help the child. The members of the MDT then suggest interventions to be tried in the classroom before proceeding. Typically, two such interventions, along with baseline data and sufficient time to determine their effectiveness, are to follow the MDT meeting. Time can sometimes be saved when the suggested interventions have already been tried and documented through the efforts of our school's Student Success Committee.

The next step, if approved by the MDT, is to take the case to the school district's Individual Placement Review Decision (IPRD) committee. This committee includes several school psychologists, speech pathologists, educational diagnosticians, cluster coordinators, the director of special services, and, occasionally, the principals of the sending and receiving schools. Parents or guardians are invited and often attend, and they may also bring formal representation. There is frequently more than one such meeting.

At these meetings documentation and motives are questioned, and parents, who are often opposed to having their children moved to another building, have a chance to make their case. After the technical issues of compliance with federal law have been resolved, the issue of developing parental support for the proposed move is addressed. This typically involves a full-scale campaign that includes arranging for the parents to visit the new school, meet with teachers and the principal, and observe classes in session.

All of this is done to obtain the parents' permission to let us provide more resources for their child. Our track record with students who have been moved to more restrictive environments has been exceptional. Every student who was so moved during my five-year tenure as principal settled into his or her new academic environment after a very short period of adjustment and coped extremely well in the new setting. The academic performance of these students improved—and, in several instances, they were moved back into Level 1 settings within a year or two.

Despite this track record, most parents remain resistant to a move. And unless the parent consents, the child cannot be moved without going to court. While it may have happened, I know of no case in which our district was willing to go to court under these circumstances.

In Ronald's case, these procedures took even longer than usual because his mother missed meetings and charged us with incompetence, neglect, and racism. In general, we found our progress thwarted at every turn. However, we persisted, and his mother finally did visit the new school in question. She found that it was a humane place, peopled by happy children, caring teachers, and sensitive administrators. It was also well staffed with psychologists and other support personnel. In general, she found it to be everything we had been telling her it would be.

Once Ronald's mother granted permission for the move, we had to update the psychological and educational testing that had been done on Ronald, and this further testing was also delayed pending his mother's permission. The final obstacle involved transportation arrangements. Since Ronald did not live in the attendance area served by the new school, a special bus had to be dispatched to pick him up at home and return him after school.

Given the time taken from teachers, principals, psychologists, educational diagnosticians, speech pathologists, the director of special services, and the transportation division over the 9 months it took to obtain this placement, it is not difficult to see how the cost of this move mounted. Readers might think that, in order to make my point, I chose the most difficult, cumbersome, and time-consuming case in our files. But the unfortunate truth is that Ronald's case was *typical*. It was not our most difficult or our most time-consuming or our most frustrating case. And in its very representativeness lies the real problem. No amount of explication on my part can ever do justice to the frustration, sense of abandonment, and feeling of demoralization that such cases bring to teachers.

In the case described here, the teachers and the paraprofessional involved were, indeed, the best and the brightest. They were extremely competent, dedicated, conscientious, warm, loving, and caring people who wanted nothing more than to practice their profession and help the children in their charge to learn and to grow. Their efforts were rewarded with nothing less than a full-scale attack on the orderly educational environment that they sought to establish in their classrooms. Their calls for help were answered with as cumbersome a bureaucracy as has been mustered in the history of educational bureaucracies.

Please understand that I do believe that the students who are protected by this bureaucracy have every right to that protection. But the other students in our classrooms have rights too. They have the right to a safe, orderly classroom. They have the right to a teacher's attention when *they* need help. They have the right to a teacher who is fresh and energetic enough to plan for *them*. They have a right to a teacher who feels respected and supported.

The issues involved here are not simple. Certainly there are cases in which a teacher does not have the skill to handle an individual child or group of children. Such children may, indeed, be misplaced in more restrictive environments, when a different teacher or a different setting in the mainstream would best meet their needs. When such students are placed in more restrictive settings, it is a tragedy that can and should be corrected. It seems that we could certainly shift some of the resources consumed by the long and cumbersome identification process to a more careful monitoring of students in more restrictive settings for the purposes of moving them back into the mainstream *when appropriate.*

We also have to acknowledge and confront the racial issue inherent in discussions such as these. Minority students *are* disproportionately represented in special education classrooms, and we must muster the integrity and the courage to confront such issues squarely and to seek answers.

Above all, we have to let our teachers know that we understand and appreciate the incredible pressure that they feel when forced to work with students who remain impervious to their best efforts. We also have to let the parents of students in the general population know that we are at least *equally* concerned about the education of *their* children and that we are taking *their* needs into consideration as we try to devise classroom structures and design classroom strategies. If this means that we must sometimes swim against the mainstream, then so be it.

Chapter 14

A Mother's Thoughts on Inclusion

Margaret N. Carr

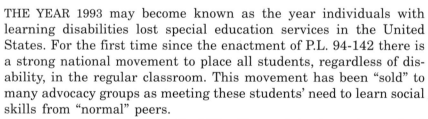

THE YEAR 1993 may become known as the year individuals with learning disabilities lost special education services in the United States. For the first time since the enactment of P.L. 94-142 there is a strong national movement to place all students, regardless of disability, in the regular classroom. This movement has been "sold" to many advocacy groups as meeting these students' need to learn social skills from "normal" peers.

My son has a learning disability. He went to elementary school in a time before students with learning disabilities (LD) were identified. I remember his coming home from first grade and crying over his reader. He could not decode! The only way he managed to get through first grade was to memorize the readers he brought home. He accomplished this by going over and over them with me. I don't think his teacher was ever aware that he memorized.

The texts in second grade were longer; we had to labor over the stories together many times each night. In the spring of his second year our family was transferred for a short period to New York. My son was accepted at his father's old private school, where he finally learned to read. He read slowly, but he was reading.

Spelling was another matter. Try though he might, he simply could not hear the vowel sounds. They all sounded alike to him. His

Reprinted from "A mother's thoughts on inclusion," by Margaret N. Carr, *Journal of Learning Disabilities,* Vol. 26, 1993, 590–592. Copyright © 1993 by PRO-ED, Inc.

visual memory was also unreliable. I kept one of the science papers he wrote in second grade. It was all about how "gravy" held people on earth.

Teacher comments were predictable. "He is immature." "He could do it if he would just try." "He's just sloppy because he rushes through his work." "He's just lazy." If they had only been with him night after night as he cried over his homework!

My son was lucky. I continued to work with him. As he grew older, he learned to compensate somewhat. He typically avoided classes that required much writing. I typed and edited most of his papers for him. By his sheer determination he made it through school, college, and eventually law school.

I shudder to think what would have happened had we been unable to go to New York his second year. The children of many of my friends were not so lucky. They became so frustrated with school that their only solution was to drop out.

I became active in the Learning Disabilities Association of America (LDA); there I discovered many youngsters like my son— many of whom *never* learned to read. I began to advocate for those students in order for them to get the specialized instruction they required to make sense of the printed word.

In my past 22 years as a professional educator, I have seen many panaceas for educating students with learning disabilities be discovered, only to be discarded. When I first became a teacher, children with LD were placed in "minimal brain injured" classes, where they were taught to walk on balance beams, trace lines, and the like. Brain-injured children looked like everyone else, but they attended separate classes.

"Resource rooms" began to replace the brain-injured classes. In resource rooms, children with LD, if they had a knowledgeable teacher, could learn those skills that had eluded them in the regular classroom. Many students were in extremely successful resource programs. In those resource rooms where the special education teacher worked and planned with the regular teacher, students experienced success. Many special education teachers realized that students learn to read by reading! They provided assistance, strategies for coping, and methods that would enable the students to make sense from printed text. They worked with the regular classroom teacher to be sure that the students learned science and social studies vocabularies. The special teachers provided regular classroom teachers with taped texts and ways to modify assignments. They informed the regular classroom teachers about the unique needs of their students with LD and taught them ways to teach successfully.

Resource rooms, however, were not the panacea. Not all resource programs were successful. Some resource teachers operated in isolation not only from regular classroom teachers, but also from other special educators. Some resource students might have "sight–say" reading 1 year and "multisensory phonics" the next. As some regular educators learned to refer students who did not fit the "norm" in their classrooms, they divorced themselves from special educators and from students with special needs.

One of the by-products of the resource movement was a lot of talk about teacher preparation, both special and regular. With the enactment of P.L. 94-142, wholesale teacher training was promised in our state. Every teacher was to be trained to work with all special children, to modify curricula, to teach to different modalities, to make all children successful. Alas, like so many promises, this one was never realized.

In recent years there has been a trend toward so-called "content mastery" programs. Content mastery programs save scarce funds by increasing the number of students "serviced" by a single teacher. Although there have apparently been some very successful programs, these are not the panacea, either. Many content mastery classes have provided a setting that supports the practice of the regular education teacher being largely ignored by the student with LD. The student "listens" to the regular classroom teacher give instruction and directions and then goes to another teacher who "explains" what the regular classroom teacher said and did. Many students who have participated in such programs fail to listen or attend at all in the regular classroom; have no skills (skills may not be taught to mastery in the content-mastery class, and the student certainly doesn't acquire skills through osmosis in the regular classroom); and function permanently below grade placement.

In the 1990s, the new panacea for educating students with disabilities has become "inclusion." Inclusion has a number of meanings. For the child with mental retardation who has been on a separate campus, in a separate classroom, away from even the sight of nondisabled peers for 6 hours a day, inclusion may provide a means for modeling normal behavior. For the blind child, inclusion may provide exposure to normal language. For the physically challenged child, inclusion may provide access to friends and neighbors that had been denied in previous educational settings. Normal groupings of physically able youngsters and students who use wheelchairs are common in many neighborhoods and in many schools.

But what of students with learning disabilities? They are usually referred to SPECIAL educators because they are unable to read, write, spell, compute, or comprehend spoken or written language at a level commensurate with their peers or their potential. Students with LD are not visibly discernible, but they may be unable to function in classroom settings with large numbers of students. Despite modifications by the classroom teacher, the legacy of students with learning disabilities may be tears and frustration.

What has changed in education since the time my son was in elementary school that would ensure successful inclusion? The answer is, unfortunately, nothing really. Teachers are still working with students as their teachers worked with them. There is different terminology for describing what teachers do, but nothing has radically changed in most classrooms when the door is closed. There are exceptions of course—schools where teachers have high expectations for all students and provide the educational environments necessary for students to succeed. Unfortunately, these schools are so rare that they are shown on national television programs about schools that "break the molds."

What *has* changed in most schools is that today's teachers and schools are under tremendous pressure regarding achievement on paper-and-pencil assessments. In state after state, assessments are being used to measure pupil progress. Results are reported by the mass media and used as measuring sticks, not for individual students, but for teachers, principals, and schools. Research on schools with such high-stakes testing programs has found that the number of students who are retained and referred to special education is rising. The pressure of high-stakes testing plus the pressures of dealing with today's angry, violent children makes teaching an extremely stressful profession, and having to deal with students with disabilities in the classroom will not make it any easier.

There has been no massive teacher training about effective ways to teach students with disabilities. Efforts to get states to require even 6 college hours of study of the characteristics and needs of students with disabilities have been largely unsuccessful. What, then, will become of these students if inclusion becomes the rule rather than the exception? What will be different between the classrooms of the 1990s and those of when my son attended school? Again, the answer is "Nothing." Students with severe and pervasive learning disabilities will seek their own solutions. I predict that if inclusion becomes a reality, the dropout rate for students with LD will soar to a nationally disgraceful figure. I predict that the number of teenagers turning to drugs or alcohol will soar. I predict that an epidemic of teenage suicides will wrap families in despair and grief. I predict that all of us in LDA who have labored for these many years will realize we have lost not only the battle but also the war. Special education services for youth with learning disabilities will no longer be available anywhere in America's public schools.

Inclusionists counter that services for all students with handicaps will be enhanced in the regular classroom with assistive teachers, aides, and other support. Given the scarcity of funding for education today, does it make sense to assume that a school can provide a trained teacher to work with every regular classroom teacher having a child with a disability in his or her classroom? Does it really make sense, is it real to think, that an Individualized Education Program (IEP) committee would agree that a child with LD is unable to benefit from classroom instruction without the aid of a personal computer or occupational therapy? Adequate support and assistance for students with learning disabilities in the regular classroom would be prohibitive in cost because of the numbers of students involved. Does it make sense that with the growing need for earlier, more comprehensive, appropriate educational services for our poor and minority children, millions would be spent to support students with LD in regular classrooms?

Where does that leave children with learning disabilities? Unfortunately, it will leave many children waiting for that temporary transfer to their father's private school . . . a transfer that, of course, will never come.

Chapter 15

Mainstreaming, Schools for the Blind, and Full Inclusion: What Shall the Future of Education for Blind Children Be?

Michael Bina

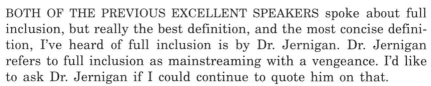

BOTH OF THE PREVIOUS EXCELLENT SPEAKERS spoke about full inclusion, but really the best definition, and the most concise definition, I've heard of full inclusion is by Dr. Jernigan. Dr. Jernigan refers to full inclusion as mainstreaming with a vengeance. I'd like to ask Dr. Jernigan if I could continue to quote him on that.

Perhaps I will shock some of you today when I say residential schools are a thing of the past. But, before you think I have lost my mind, I also want to add that residential schools are also very much a thing of the present and most definitely a very much needed provision in the future.

As a residential school superintendent nowadays, I have to be very honest; my colleagues and I sometimes feel apologetic. Others would have us think we run second-class operations, things of the past, dinosaurs on the verge of extinction. Rather I contend we are places of distinction, and therefore I make no apology. I am proud that in the past and today and clearly in the future these schools are and will continue to be valid, beneficial, and very necessary for kids. Who can deny the success of our many graduates, like so many of you in the audience today? Please do not consider any of my comments today as anti-public school. I worked in public schools, and I strongly believe that they definitely have their place also.

Residential schools today, though, unfortunately are considered placements of last resort. The presumption under the law is that public schools are considered the first and many times the only option. The playing field needs to be leveled so that residential schools can be viewed in the same positive light the public schools currently enjoy. Residential schools (please listen carefully to this because I feel very strongly about this) also need to be rightfully on the menu so that parents and others who make decisions can fully consider and ultimately choose this option if it is in the child's best interest.

In Indiana, unfortunately, we had the parent choice provision taken away by OSEP (the Office of Special Education Programs) last year at a time when President Bush was calling for parent choice in regular education as a method of reform. Taking choice away from parents of blind kids and giving it to parents of non-handicapped students is what I call adverse discrimination.[Applause] While school for the blind programs have adjusted and changed, many people's attitudes about them have not changed. Today many myths persist which negatively influence decision makers, but most disturbing to me is that many children are being excluded from attending these schools to the point that today only seven percent of blind children in our country attend schools for the blind.

I'd like to go over some of these myths that make the playing field unlevel. This first one is that residential schools segregate blind children from society. We are told by others, most of whom have never set foot on a school for the blind campus, that we are segregationists. Well this to me is a very negative and inflammatory word choice. These well-educated experts are advocates for severely handicapped individuals and are not trained in blindness. Yet they are more than very strongly pushing for elimination of residential schools and, as the other speakers have already said, even public school resource rooms. These full-inclusion initiatives are counter to federal law, which mandates a full array of services.

Think of this as an analogy: in medicine it would be gross malpractice if doctors removed any proven reliable treatment or medicine from their arsenal which would have the potential to benefit even one patient and they substituted an unproven drug. I contend we should be widening our options and not in any way reducing them. Education, as well as medicine, would be taking a step backwards by doing so.

Residential schools do not segregate or restrict in a discriminatory manner, but rather positively and purposefully bring together children as do science, math, and music magnet schools, which consolidate students with special interests and aptitudes. And, interestingly, magnet schools are being advanced as a way to improve America's schools. Yet, in spite of schools for the blind's proven track record as very productive places for boosting self-image, confidence, and solid skills for future success, they continue to be underutilized and not given the respect I feel they deserve. Doctors separate people needing medical treatment in hospitals, so is it inappropriate that we at some times, for some students when they need specialized placements, do so in special schools?

I am extremely proud of the Committee on Joint Organizational Effort and the position paper which Dr. Hatlen mentioned. This position paper challenges very strongly the requirement in the law that says, to the maximum extent possible, handicapped children must be educated with non-handicapped students. I feel that blind children shouldn't avoid contact with other blind children and that such contact is clearly beneficial. This requirement just doesn't make sense to me, but I guess the lawmakers are a whole lot smarter than I am.

One parent said it best: "How dare the lawmakers tell me who my child's friends will be! Is my child someone who should be avoided by other children?" I have seen in my experience awfully good friendships and counseling going on between blind students that our Ph.D. psychologists couldn't begin to match.[applause]

A 1991 study showed that fifty percent of residential school students were integrated in public school programs, where they could have the best of both worlds. We are vastly underutilizing our residential schools. We have some classrooms which are nearly empty at a time when blind children in public schools are not receiving all of the services specified in their IEPs. Both placements should be used to benefit the child. Many would agree that all blind children can clearly benefit from residential school some of the time and that some can benefit from residential schools all of the time.

Meaningful integration is very possible in segregated settings, and just because a child lives at home, attends a neighborhood school, and is in physical proximity to non-handicapped children, that doesn't necessarily mean that they are truly integrated.[applause] We are all aware of integrated public school students who are isolated islands in the mainstream, but our critics don't call this inappropriate isolation segregation. It is less important to me where children go to school than that, wherever they go, they get what they need when they need it in a positive climate.[applause]

Today we hear calls for full inclusion in schools, but I contend the goal needs to be full inclusion in society. For too long we have been preparing students for graduation when we should have been preparing them with skills for life.[applause] Without this solid foundation like Braille and mobility skills, positive integration into schools now or later in life becomes extremely difficult. Swimming teachers (and I used to be one when I was younger) have long since abandoned throwing their students into the deep end of the pool to teach them to swim without carefully developing prerequisite skills. But our policy makers keep overzealously pushing integration before the regular education staff are trained, attitudes are adjusted, and the blind child has the skills to survive—much less to be successful. The standard must be thriving and purposefully going in a positive forward direction as opposed to just surviving or just keeping your head above water. Integration should never become submerging.

We must admit and also address the fact that we have large numbers of underserved students in many programs throughout our country that are advertised as comprehensive when they are not. Two hours of Braille instruction per week, or worse, per month is clearly an intolerable injustice.[applause] In many cases these students are being shortchanged, and fortunately a strong outcry from parents, consumers, and professionals is increasing in intensity. An Indiana parent summed it up beautifully for me. She said, "We need to decide if we want our kids to be social or to be educated."

There is another myth, that our schools are only for students with multiple disabilities. I've had parents come to our school after many, many years of public education and say we wish we could have sent our son or daughter earlier. You have high functioning students there, and our child could have thrived in your environment, but our local district kept telling us that your school was only for multi-handicapped children. There was a study done in 1985 that predicted that by 1991 all residential schools would be primarily for multi-handicapped students. Another study done last year showed that over forty-five percent of the students in residential schools are in academic programs and that over thirty-nine percent of these students went on to college.

Another myth is that residential schools are too expensive. We spend approximately $30,000 per child on a national average, and the public schools spend about $3,000 per child per year. Our per capita costs are high, yes, but we likewise offer more than bare bones service. Using another medical analogy, we don't seem to worry about the cost for medical treatment when we roll our child, our spouse, or ourselves in for life-saving surgery. Why do we keep letting our pocketbooks rather than our consciences drive our educational decisions? I'd rather pay now than have some of our students pay for it later in life.

Quality and intensive programs come with a price tag, and I contend most strongly that not learning to read and write Braille or other skills well, when they should be learned, to me qualifies most clearly as life-threatening. Would you agree?[applause]

Also myth number four: local programs are better than center-based programs. We don't have a college or university in every city or town across the United States; yet in our field we are trying, even in light of the personnel shortage, to apply the chicken-in-every-pot, car-in-every-garage, vision-program-in-each-public-school-building philosophy. When we centralize like this, I feel we are spreading our services so thinly that we can barely tell that the services exist.

Also myth number five: residential schools are old-fashioned. To that I want to say, yes, to the extent that we model, require, and encourage old-fashioned basic skills, values, and manners. On solid skills I'd have to say we are old-fashioned.

In conclusion I want to say that we have made many changes, and I only hope that we succeed in educating the public that we are proud places for children to be educated and also that public attitudes need to be changed so that children can have the benefit of all options for them. Also, as AER President, if I could just add this little plug right here. I am very optimistic about the Committee on Joint Organizational Effort (JOE), and I'm excited about the JOE position paper on inclusion. We are developing another position on categorical services, and I pledge very strong leadership in AER to coming together as a field, consumers and professionals. That is our goal; and, as we have been cooperatively doing recently, I hope that we can continue to make the progress we have been. Thank you very much.

Chapter 16

The Education of Deaf Children: Drowning in the Mainstream and the Sidestream

Harlan Lane

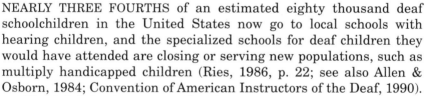

NEARLY THREE FOURTHS of an estimated eighty thousand deaf schoolchildren in the United States now go to local schools with hearing children, and the specialized schools for deaf children they would have attended are closing or serving new populations, such as multiply handicapped children (Ries, 1986, p. 22; see also Allen & Osborn, 1984; Convention of American Instructors of the Deaf, 1990).

The label "mainstreaming" embraces so wide a range of educational arrangements that, as with the label "total communication," people with divergent beliefs about deaf education can be gulled into endorsing it. In some urban schools, there are classes of deaf children, grouped by grade, without any contact with hearing children, or just the odd shared class in art or sports. Often these "self-contained" classes are only nominally within a public school—they are located in temporary trailers, separate buildings, remote corners

Excerpts from pp. 135–143, 272–278, with changes, from "The education of deaf children: Drowning in the mainstream and the sidestream." In *THE MASK OF BENEVOLENCE: Disabling the Deaf Community,* by Harlan Lane, 1992. New York: Knopf. Copyright © 1992 by Harlan Lane. Reprinted, with changes, by permission of Alfred A. Knopf Inc.

of buildings, or in basements (Goodstein, 1988). In less densely popu-
lated areas, on the other hand, the deaf child may have no one with
whom he can communicate; he is left to "make do" in the midst of a
hearing class and in the occasional coaching session with a few deaf
children of various ages and abilities. Most deaf children are in
schools where there are only one or two other deaf children (Siegel,
1991).

An ASL interpreter may be provided for the mainstreamed deaf
child in some classes; but many of these interpreters are insuffi-
ciently skilled to cover the range of academic subjects required, and
very few are board certified. Many communities can neither recruit
nor afford qualified interpreters. Few schools in America would
appoint a nurse, a counselor, or an audiologist without certification;
standards are much lower when it comes to finding an ASL interpreter. Then, too, the child who depends on an interpreter relates
very little, if at all, to the teacher. Moreover, he must keep his eyes
glued on the interpreter for long stretches while classroom events
suit his hearing classmates: maps are unfurled, slides are projected,
tables of numbers are displayed, and all the while the teacher talks,
the interpreter interprets, and the deaf child must never look away
from the interpreter (Estes, 1991).

Immersed in a hearing, English-speaking environment, the deaf
child frequently drowns in the mainstream.

"I have experienced both, mainstream and deaf school," eighth-
grader Jesse Thomas testified to the National Council on Disabilities. He first explained, "I'm not disabled, just deaf," and then gave
his reasons for opposing mainstreaming: "Learning through an interpreter is very hard; it's bad socially in the mainstream; you are
always outnumbered; you don't feel like it's your school; you never
know deaf adults; you don't belong; you don't feel comfortable as a
deaf person" (Thomas, 1989). That's the gist of surveys of deaf college
students who have attended mainstream high school or elementary school programs. Reports one study: "Almost every informant
described their social life in terms of loneliness, rejection, and social
isolation" (Foster, 1989, p. 44). In order to cope as best he can in a
mainstream class, the deaf child hides his hearing aid, pretends he
understands lessons when he does not, copies other pupils' work,
rarely asks questions in class or volunteers to answer them, speaks
as little as possible to hearing students, or even to other deaf students (Booth, 1988; see also Gaustad & Kluwin, 1991). Writes one
child trying to pass in the mainstream: "I hate it if people know I am
deaf" (Booth, 1988, 113).

Mainstreaming is a part of a wider movement in the United States that has removed large numbers of mentally and physically handicapped children and adults from custodial institutions. "Deinstitutionalization," as the movement was called, was accompanied by the promise of more normal life-styles for all and services in the community for those who needed them. There is a consensus that, overall, the promise was not fulfilled, not least perhaps because one motive for the change in policy was cost containment: It is less expensive to foist a deaf child on the local school, even with an allocation for special services, such as an itinerant special teacher or a resource room, than it is to provide education in a residential setting (Emerson & Pretty, 1987; see also Moores, 1991).

Deaf children were thus swept up in the movement to mainstream indiscriminately nearly all previously "institutionalized" children. The old custodial institutions were not only costly; they embraced many more mentally and physically handicapped children than needed to be there, and they fostered dependency and restricted freedom with no countervailing gain. This was not true of the residential schools for deaf children, however. Yes, the audist staffs of these "sidestream" schools frequently infantilized their charges, could not communicate with them, and were ineffective as teachers. Nonetheless, the residential school offered something of immense value: language—the ability to communicate with other human beings. For most deaf children, who came from hearing, languageless homes, this was a boon indeed, as was the community and the culture they found in the residential school. Although manual language was not used in class—although, indeed, it was often forbidden—still the school was a signing community, where the deaf student could get help after class with coursework, discuss local, national, and international events, obtain counseling, participate in student activities, develop friendships with other deaf students, emulate older students and deaf staff, and acquire self-respect as a deaf person (see Mertens, 1989; Stewart & Stinson, 1991).

None of these advantages is available to the deaf child in an ordinary public school, where ASL, deaf adults, and a deaf community are absent. Moreover, in this setting the deaf child is hampered in learning the "indirect messages" of education: the implied and unintentionally taught beliefs, feelings, attitudes, and social skills. Since only one schoolchild in a thousand is deaf, most school districts have too few deaf children to establish an effective program with properly trained staff, a peer group of reasonable size at each age level, and extracurricular activities. The only plausible alternative to residential schools for deaf children, then, is regional programs, but children in those programs may spend almost as much time in the bus as in class, reducing the time they can devote to extracurricular activities, to homework, and to their families. Moreover, their deaf friends are likely to live out of reach (Kluwin, 1991a, 1991b).

Granted that the conditions in the local public school for the deaf child's social and emotional growth are quite poor. Is the child receiving a better education in the "three Rs" there? Not at all. The first report cards on mainstreamed deaf children show no improvement in their blighted English or mathematics attributable to mainstreaming, even though the first to be mainstreamed were the children with the best speech and hearing, and the academic qualifications of their teachers frequently surpass those in the residential schools (Allen & Karchmer, 1990, p. 55). Indeed, there is some evidence that when achievement scores are corrected statistically for differences in the makeup of the deaf student bodies in residential and mainstream schools, the deaf child in the mainstream is at an academic disadvantage (see Note).

The deaf children who do best in school, mainstream or residential, are—note it well—the fortunate 10 percent who learned ASL as a native language from their deaf parents, the core of this linguistic minority. These native speakers of ASL outperform their deaf classmates from hearing homes in most subjects, including reading and writing English—an achievement that is all the more remarkable when we reflect that they come from poorer homes, generally a disadvantage, and that the schools they attend, whether mainstream or residential, do not capitalize on their native language skills (Mindel & Vernon, 1971; see also Brasel, 1975; Corson, 1973; Geers & Schick, 1988; Israelite, Ewoldt, & Hoffmeister, 1989; Weisel & Reichstein, 1987; Zweibel, 1987). Deaf children arriving at school with a knowledge of ASL are also better adjusted, better socialized, and have more positive attitudes than their counterparts who have been deprived of effective communication (Mindel & Vernon, 1971; see also Harris, 1978; Johnson, Liddell, & Erting, 1989). Similar findings come from other lands. In Israel, deaf children of deaf parents were found more successful than those of hearing parents in reading comprehension, emotional development, self-image, and initiative to communicate; in Greece, they were found superior in expressive and receptive communication and in lip-reading; in Denmark, they communicated more effectively with peers (Hansen & Kjaer-Sorensen, 1967; Kourbetis, 1987; Weisel & Reichstein, 1987).

The superior performance of deaf children from deaf homes highlights the changes that most need to be made in the education of deaf children: namely, a return to manual language, deaf teachers, and deaf administrators directing residential schools—successful practices in the last century, when American deaf children studied all their subjects in their most fluent language, ASL. These changes have long been advocated by the deaf community itself. "How could we ever learn to cope as deaf people, without the shared experiences of other deaf people all around us?" asks a California deaf leader, assailing mainstreaming. "It guarantees the emergence of a deaf adult with serious doubts about himself. How can a child, probably with a reading problem and almost certainly intimidated by the sometimes hostile and generally distractive atmosphere of a mainstreamed classroom, learn comfortably through an interpreter (possibly one with minimal skills) and without direct contact with the teacher? It's puzzling to me that the parent will permit this" (White, 1990, p. 2). But parents are badly advised by the experts, who, in any event, ride roughshod over their wishes.

A further obstacle to revitalizing and expanding the residential schools and other specialized programs for deaf children is placed in the way by spokesmen for people with disabilities. Now that advocates for people with disabilities have gained their hard-won integration of mentally and physically handicapped children in the public schools, they fear that segregated schooling of deaf children, who belong to a language minority, would set a precedent for backsliding on mainstreaming of disabled children. That is why such advocates mounted a major campaign in 1990 to close the American School for the Deaf in Hartford, Connecticut. Deaf leaders from around the country, outraged at this assault on America's oldest residential school, which had spawned so many others, beat back the attack. Such discord between leaders of the deaf community and of the disability rights movement arises only because neither group has control of its destiny and must persuade a third group, the nondeaf, nondisabled experts, whose incomprehension each fears.

Advocates for children with disabilities are joined in their insistence on mainstreaming for all by those in the audist establishment who believe that education without assimilation is a failure and that assimilation can be achieved by brute force (Conference of Executives of American Schools for the Deaf, 1977; see also National Association of the Deaf, 1986, 1987). This is the counsel many hearing parents want to receive, as they prefer, understandably, to have their child live at home. According to the Commission on the Education of the Deaf (1988), the intent of the law to have all handicapped children placed in the "least restrictive environment" was misinterpreted to mean mainstreaming in the local school for nearly all deaf children—precisely the most restrictive environment for those children, given the communicative and social barriers in the local school. The

U.S. Supreme Court has ruled that when Congress passed the Education for All Handicapped Children Act in 1975, it recognized that "regular classrooms simply would not be a suitable setting for the education of many handicapped children" and it provided for alternative placements (see Duncan, 1984). The Code of Federal Regulations implementing the act also requires that educational placement be "appropriate," that potential harmful effects on the child must be considered, and that a child can be removed from "regular" classes when education cannot be achieved satisfactorily (34 C.F.R. 300.550, 300.552, 300.550(b)(2), cited in Siegel, 1991). One judge ruled in 1988 that "mainstreaming that interferes with the acquisition of fundamental language skills is foolishness mistaken for wisdom" (*Visco by Visco v. School District of Pittsburg,* cited in Siegel, 1991, p. 137). But the federal and state departments of education and local school boards, frequently encouraged by the audist establishment, have largely ignored provisions of the act, of federal regulations, and of court rulings when full compliance favors placing a deaf child in a specialized program with other deaf children.

Like many mothers of bright ASL-using children, Jesse Thomas's mother appealed the local school board's insistence on mainstreaming Jesse; she agreed with her son's wish to go to the state residential school for deaf children. (Because she is hearing and could not provide a model of manual language for her son, Mrs. Thomas had made a point of placing Jesse in the company of deaf children and adults since his infancy.) The local experts claimed to know Jesse's best interests better than his mother did, however, and she lost her appeal. Teachers and administrators have their ways of keeping parents at bay, despite the law requiring that the parents participate in deciding the Individualized Educational Plan for their child (Bennett, 1988). These ways include withholding information, presenting major issues as minor ones, limiting the topics on which parents may have a say, authoritatively identifying the source of problems as the child and not the school, and choosing the time, place, manner, and language in which the discussion is conducted. Although the professional's judgment may be based on class differences, on stereotypes, on invalid test results, or on an inability to communicate with the child, many parents are intimidated, the more so if they belong to an ethnic minority. Both parties believe that the parents need the professional more than the converse.

The experts present advice, which is really a demand for confirmation of their judgment; the parent is not invited to form a plan collaboratively but asked to accede to the audist's plan. Moreover, parents are encouraged to be compliant by their fear that protest will have harmful repercussions for their child. Determined and resourceful parents can sometimes outwit the establishment, however. Mrs. Thomas had heard of a county that sent its deaf children exclusively to oral programs. Informed that those programs would not accept pupils who used ASL, the Thomases moved to that very county. As they had hoped, the program administrators would not consider Jesse for admission and saw no alternative but to send him to the state residential school for deaf children.

When Susan Dutton, who is deaf, moved with her deaf son, Mark, to Harveys Lake, Pennsylvania, the boy was placed in a local school, in a special-needs class with children ranging in age from eight to eighteen. Mark was fluent in ASL, but neither the teacher nor the other students could sign. There was an "interpreter/aide" present, who had completed one class in sign language. When the school convened a meeting to formulate Mark's Individualized Educational Plan, Mrs. Dutton was not provided with an interpreter and was told that "despite my wishes, despite my right as a parent to decide what is best for my son, Mark would have to remain in the local school and be mainstreamed into fourth grade classes with hearing students two years younger than he." Since deaf peers, culture, and role models were utterly lacking in the mainstream and there was little effective communication, Mrs. Dutton refused to sign the IEP. A hearing was convened before the school assistant superintendent: "There was no interpreter present. There was no discussion. The assistant superintendent came into this meeting having already made his decision, and he communicated it to me via note writing. It was, of course, in support of mainstreaming." Mrs. Dutton consulted a lawyer, and nine nights of hearings ensued before a hearing officer employed by the Pennsylvania State Department of Education (Dutton, 1991; Levitan, 1991). The school district's lawyer argued that the mainstream was the least restrictive environment for Mark Dutton. Susan and Mark's lawyer and several scholars contended that the local school was the most restrictive environment for Mark's education since he could not understand his teachers and peers nor they him, and since the school could not nurture his linguistic and cultural development as a deaf person. The school district prevailed, but the Duttons appealed the hearing officer's decision, and it was overturned by a panel of two lawyers and an educator who affirmed that "communication is the essence of education" and that the hearing officer had misinterpreted the law. Susan and Mark were relieved to see their year-long struggle and expense finally end in success—until they learned that the school district had filed an appeal which as of this writing is before a federal court.

Confronted with the mainstreaming tragedy in Britain, members of the British National Union of the Deaf formally charged their government with a violation of the United Nations Convention on the Prevention and Punishment of the Crime of Genocide. That treaty prohibits inflicting mental harm on the children of an ethnic group, and it prohibits forcibly transferring them to another group. According to this deaf organization, mainstreaming will gravely injure "not only deaf children but deaf children's rightful language and culture." Their published *Charter of the Rights of the Deaf* asserts that "deaf schools are being effectively forced to close and therefore children of one ethnic/linguistic minority group, that is, deaf people, are being forcibly transferred to another group, that is, hearing people," in violation of the U.N. convention (National Union of the Deaf, 1982).

For nearly a century, parents of deaf children were told to place them in specialized programs that would teach them to speak and lip-read; at home, they were to drill their child in speech and never let him make a sign. Then, fifteen years ago, most parents were told that individual signs could be used at the same time as speech. Some were told that English expressed on the hands through real and invented signs held out the greatest hope for their child's mastery of English. Ten years ago, parents were told to place their deaf child in the local hearing school. Now they are increasingly told that an ear operation combined with oral drills and no sign is his best hope. If the local school cannot provide sufficient training in speech and hearing, they may need to enroll their child in specialized programs that teach him to speak and lip-read; at home, they are to drill their child in speech and never let him make a sign. So the advice comes full circle. The audits keep changing the rules because they have the power to do so as each version of the audist regime becomes a blatant failure. Moreover, the failure of a stage of forced assimilation, far from undermining the establishment and its normalizing principles, leads to an expansion of its regime. So, too, the prison system is offered as the remedy for its own ills and the failures of applied social science justify more research. The fundamental enterprise is never placed in question; instead, bio-power establishes as the question, how best to implement the fixed, accepted goals.

The deaf community, however, has held unswervingly to a single truth: deaf identity, hence deaf language and culture. "Methods are not acquired naturally like languages," writes deaf linguist M. J. Bienvenu (1990, p. 133), "they are invented by individuals for specific purposes."

NOTE

In 1981, Allen and Karchmer examined the reading and mathematics scores on the Stanford Achievement Test of a random sample of 330 deaf students in elementary and high school who were deafened because their mothers contracted German measles during pregnancy. Those students who were partially integrated into mainstream settings had higher achievement scores to begin with (as well as lesser hearing losses), so this difference between them and deaf students in specialized programs had to be factored out statistically. When that was done, there was no reliable advantage to mainstreaming. Holt and Allen (1989), as part of a larger study, examined the reading and mathematics achievement of about sixty deaf students in special schools and in mainstream settings for whom prior achievement scores were available. When students were, in effect, matched statistically on this and several other variables, there was no difference in reading scores obtained in the two settings. However, deaf students who were fully integrated with hearing students for mathematics instruction achieve lower mathematics scores than their peers in special schools.

Four studies have been cited by some authors as supporting mainstreaming of deaf children. That conclusion, however, does not withstand close inspection. With an avowedly strong mainstreaming bias, Van der Horst (1971) published a report in the British journal *The Teacher of the Deaf* (*69*, 398–414) on matched groups of twelve "auditory defectives," enrolled in a special school (DS) or in a local school for hearing children (HS). The groups were matched on average hearing loss, age, sex, and nonverbal IQ; they were not matched with respect to the socioeconomic level of their homes, nor with respect to the training their teachers had received, although both factors are known to influence academic achievement. The two groups did not differ on one verbal IQ test, but they did differ, in favor of the HS pupils, on a second; we are told the difference was statistically significant but we are not told its size. Moreover, three of the five subtests on this second IQ test showed no difference between the groups. A comparison of the two groups on writing tests showed no difference, but the DS pupils showed less improvement from age eight to age eleven on one writing measure. Using personal records and psychological tests they fail to identify, the authors assigned emotional stability ratings to pupils. These data favor the special school children, who were labeled normal 86 percent of the time compared with only 54 percent for the deaf children in the hearing school. Because of its failure to control important variables, and the finding of no difference on the first verbal IQ test and three of the five subtests of the second IQ test, I believe it is inappropriate to cite this study as showing an advantage to mainstreaming. A 1975 study published by the Toronto Board of Education (Reich, Hambleton, & Klein) found higher raw scores on reading, language, and speech intelligibility from HS students than from DS, but "when hearing loss as well as other differences in background were taken into account, there was little remaining difference between groups to unequivocally attest to the superiority of one method over another. . . . However, the results do not support the view that integration is *harmful*." [italics theirs]. As was evident in the first study mentioned, a problem that bedevils comparisons of the achievement of HS and DS deaf students is the lack of comparability of the students who attend the two kinds of schools. In 1984, Allen and Osborne made a sophisticated attempt to render comparable by statistical methods noncomparable samples of deaf students taught in HS and DS environments. If one knew the contribution of, say, socioeconomic background to reading achievement in deaf students, and if the HS group on the average came from more upper-class homes, one could lower their average reading scores appropriately in order to render them comparable to the DS students.

A problem with this approach arises, however, when the groups differ in several important respects, for it is not obvious that the advantage arising from a wealthier background and that arising from, say, residual hearing are simply additive. This statistical issue would be less critical if a substantial difference remained after the corrections, but in fact "the actual proportion of achievement variance accounted for by integration status alone was very small for all three variables" (a reading test and two math tests). The authors go on to point out, moreover, that such differences as remain "cannot be interpreted as representing a causal relationship between integration status and achievement." They also recognize that there were many uncontrolled variables, such as prior academic ability, not imputable to the demographic variables controlled for. Moreover, there may have been differences between the groups compared in math and language aptitude and in the preparation of their teachers—to mention just two more unexamined factors. Since the slight difference in scores could be attributed to the correction procedures or to uncontrolled variables, and cannot be causally attributed to integration status, it is inappropriate to cite this study as supporting mainstreaming. Kluwin and Moores (1985) studied the effects of mainstreaming on mathematics achievement in a nonrandom sample of eighty deaf students in three high schools. The authors used a different method of post hoc corrections for some but not all of the group differences, leaving a small residual (one third of a standard deviation) advantage for the integrated students. They conclude "that the greatest amount of variance may be accounted for by the fact that regular mathematics teachers are subject matter specialists and have more teaching experience." None of the teachers in the special school, who averaged six years experience, were math specialists; all of the teachers in the hearing school had master's degrees in mathematics, except one who had a Ph.D.; they averaged eighteen years of experience. The same authors again found only trivial effects of placement on the academic achievements of deaf students in a later study: T. Kluwin and D. Moores (1989). Kluwin has concluded: "Mainstreaming per se is not a solution to improving the academic achievement of deaf students" (Kluwin, 1991a, p. 274).

To the best of my knowledge there are no studies that support the premise that a deaf child will fare substantially better in a mainstream school than in a special school for deaf children. One study that compared hearing-impaired students in the mainstream with hearing students in the same classes found that hearing-impaired seniors had "greater academic difficulties, took fewer academic courses, evidenced less school motivation, did even less homework and appeared less goal-oriented . . . than their normally hearing peers" (Gregory, Shanahan, & Walberg, 1984, p. 16).

REFERENCES

Allen, T. E., & Karchmer, M. (1981). Influences on academic achievement of hearing-impaired students born during the 1963–65 rubella epidemic. *Directions, 2,* 40–54.

Allen, T. E., & Karchmer, M. (1990). Communication in classrooms for deaf students: Student, teacher, and program characteristics. In H.

Bornstein (Ed.), *Manual communication: Implications for education* (pp. 45–66). Washington, DC: Gallaudet University Press.

Allen, T. E., & Osborn, T. I. (1984). Academic integration of hearing-impaired students: Demographic, handicapping, and achievement factors. *American Annals of the Deaf, 129,* 100–113.

Bennett, A. T. (1988). Gateway to powerless: Incorporating Hispanic deaf children and families into formal schooling. *Disability, Handicap and Society, 3,* 119–151.

Bienvenu, M. J. (1990). Letter to the editor. *Deaf American, 40,* 133.

Booth, T. (1988). Challenging conceptions of integration. In L. Barton (Ed.), *The politics of special educational needs* (pp. 99–122). Philadelphia: Falmer Press.

Brasel, K. E. (1975). *The influence of early language and communication environments on the development of language in deaf children.* Unpublished doctoral dissertation, University of Illinois, Urbana.

Commission on the Education of the Deaf. (1988). *Toward equality, education of the deaf.* Washington, DC: U.S. Government Printing Office.

Conference of Executives of American Schools for the Deaf. (1977). Statement on "least restrictive" placements for deaf students. *American Annals of the Deaf, 122,* 62–69.

Convention of American Instructors of the Deaf. (1990). Schools and classes for the deaf in the United States. *American Annals of the Deaf, 135,* 135.

Corson, H. (1973). *Comparing deaf children of oral deaf parents and deaf parents using manual communication with deaf children of hearing parents on academic, social, and communicative functioning.* Unpublished doctoral dissertation, University of Cincinnati, Cincinnati, OH.

Duncan, J. G. (1984). Recent legislation affecting hearing-impaired persons. *American Annals of the Deaf, 129,* 83–94.

Dutton, S. (1991). Deaf education: Who decides. *The Bicultural Center News, 33,* 1–2.

Emerson, E. B., & Pretty, G. M. H. (1987). Enhancing the social relevance of evaluation practice. *Disability, Handicap, and Society, 2,* 151–162.

Estes, C. (1991, April). Bestest from Estes. *The National Association of the Deaf Broadcaster, 13,* p. 3.

Foster, S. (1989). Reflections of a group of deaf adults on their experiences in mainstream and residential school programs in the United States. *Disability, Handicap and Society, 4,* 37–56.

Gaustad, M. G., & Kluwin, T. (1991). Patterns of communication among deaf and hearing adolescents in public school programs. In T. Kluwin, D. F. Moores, & M. G. Gaustad, *Defining the effective public school program for deaf students* (pp. 124–146). Unpublished manuscript, Gallaudet University, Washington, DC.

Geers, A. E., & Schick, B. (1988). Acquisition of spoken and signed English by hearing-impaired children of hearing-impaired or hearing parents. *Journal of Speech and Hearing Disorders, 53,* 136–143.

Goodstein, H. (1988). *What is mainstreaming?* Paper prepared for the Gallaudet Research Institute Roundtable on Mainstreaming. Gallaudet University, Washington, DC.

Gregory, J. F., Shanahan, T., & Walberg, H. J. (1984). Mainstreamed hearing-impaired high school seniors: A reanalysis of a national survey. *American Annals of the Deaf, 129,* 11–16.

Hansen, B., & Kjaer-Sorensen, R. (1967). *The sign language of deaf children in Denmark.* Copenhagen, Denmark: The School for the Deaf.

Harris, R. (1978). Impulse control in deaf children. In L. Liben (Ed.), *Deaf children: Developmental perspectives.* New York: Academic Press.

Holt, J., & Allen, T. (1989). The effects of schools and their curricula on the reading and mathematics achievement of hearing-impaired students. *International Journal of Educational Research, 13,* 547–562.

Israelite, N., Ewoldt, C., & Hoffmeister, R. (1989). *A review of the literature on effective use of native sign language on the acquisition of a majority language by hearing-impaired students.* Unpublished report, Boston University Center for the Study of Communication and Deafness.

Johnson, R. E., Liddell, S. K., & Erting, C. J. (1989). Unlocking the curriculum: Principles for achieving access in deaf education. *Gallaudet Research Institute Working Papers,* p. 10.

Kluwin, T. (1991a). Some reflections on defining the effective program. In T. Kluwin, D. F. Moores, & M. G. Gaustad, *Defining the effective public school program for deaf students* (pp. 272–282). Unpublished manuscript, Gallaudet University, Washington, DC.

Kluwin, T. (1991b). What does "local public school program" mean? In T. Kluwin, D. F. Moores, & M. G. Gaustad, *Defining the effective public school program for deaf students* (pp. 35–55). Unpublished manuscript, Gallaudet University, Washington, DC.

Kluwin, T., & Moores, D. (1985). The effects of integration on mathematics achievement of hearing-impaired adolescents. *Exceptional Children, 52,* 153–161.

Kluwin, T., & Moores, D. (1989). Mathematics achievements of hearing-impaired adolescents in different placements. *Exceptional Children, 55,* 327–335.

Kourbetis, V. (1987). *Deaf children of deaf parents and deaf children of hearing parents in Greece: A comparative study.* Unpublished doctoral dissertation, Boston University.

Levitan, L. (1991, December). Mark Dutton: An educational tragedy. *Deaf Life,* pp. 10–17.

Mertens, D. (1989). Social experiences of hearing-impaired high school youth. *American Annals of the Deaf, 134,* 15–19.

Mindel, E. D., & Vernon, M. (1971). *They grow in silence.* Silver Spring, MD: National Association of the Deaf.

Moores, D. (1991). An historical perspective on school placement of deaf students. In T. Kluwin, D. F. Moores, & M. G. Gaustad, *Defining the effective public school program for deaf students* (pp. 7–34). Unpublished manuscript, Gallaudet University, Washington, DC.

National Association of the Deaf. (1986). Public Law 94–142 and the least restrictive environment: A position paper of the National Association of the Deaf. *NAD Broadcaster, 8,* 1.

National Association of the Deaf. (1987). NAD recommends to the Commission on Education of the Deaf. *NAD Broadcaster, 9* [suppl.], 1–8.

National Union of the Deaf. (1982). *Charter of the rights of the deaf.* Bedfort, Middlesex, England: Author.

Reich, C., Hambleton, R., & Klein, R. (1975). *The integration of hearing-impaired children in regular classrooms.* Toronto: Board of Education.

Ries, P. (1986). Characteristics of hearing-impaired youth in the general population and of students in special education programs for the hearing-impaired. In A. N. Schildroth & M. A. Karchmer (Eds.), *Deaf children in America* (pp. 1–32). San Diego, CA: College Hill.

Siegel, L. (1991). The least restrictive environment? *Deaf American, 41,* 135–139.

Stewart, D. A., & Stinson, M. S. (1991). The role of sport and extracurricular activities in shaping the socialization patterns of deaf and hard of hearing students. In T. Kluwin, D. F. Moores, & M. G. Gaustad, *Defining the effective public school program for deaf students* (pp. 147–170). Unpublished manuscript, Gallaudet University, Washington, DC.

Thomas, J. (1989, June 8). Testimony before the National Council on Disabilities. Special Schools.

Weisel, A., & Reichstein, J. (1987). Parental hearing status, reading comprehension skills, and socio-emotional adjustment. In R. Ojala (Ed.), *Proceedings of the Tenth World Congress of the World Federation of the Deaf.* Helsinki: Finnish Association of the Deaf.

White, B. (1990, January). Deaf education: A game people play. *DCARA News,* p. 2.

Zweibel, A. (1987). More on the effects of early manual communication on the cognitive development of deaf children. *American Annals of the Deaf, 132,* 16–20.

Chapter 17

Inclusive Education: Right For _Some_

Bernard Rimland

IS THERE THE PARENT of an autistic child who wouldn't be delighted beyond words if the child would simply blend smoothly into a regular classroom? That is a dream we all share. For a few, the dream becomes a reality. Over the years, I have heard from a number of parents who have shared with us their joy, their pride, and their good fortune: "Billy has been included in a regular classroom! He is having a hard time adjusting, but he is making it!" But, for every parent whose child "makes it," there are many more who are not so fortunate.

Much as my wife and I would like to have our autistic son Mark be able to cope successfully in a normal school, it is very clear to us that he could not have done so. He has come along much farther than we ever dared hope, and we are quite confident it is because he was always in special classes, taught by experienced, skilled, caring teachers, exhibiting monumental patience, who had gone to great lengths to train themselves in methods that would help Mark and children like him achieve their full potential.

If a child can be effectively "included," he probably should be. Lovaas got excellent results by mainstreaming the most successful of his early intervention group, but only after intensive training (story on page 1). But there is a difference between inclusion and over-inclusion.

If your child functions far below the normal child intellectually, academically, and socially, does it make sense to insist that he or she be "included" in a regular classroom? Certainly not, in my view, and in the view of many, if not the vast majority, of parents of autistic children.

Today, special schools and special classes for autistic children are under heavy attack by people promoting "full inclusion." What is full inclusion? Full inclusion means abolishing the special education provisions that are vitally important to autistic children.

Unfortunately, many professionals and parents have adopted the ideology that full inclusion is the *only* option that should be made available for any child, irrespective of how inappropriate it may be for that child, and irrespective of the wishes of the parents of that child. What is worse, these people have managed to sway legislative and educational policy so that other options are prohibited. A quarter of a century ago, those of us who pioneered public education for autistic children struggled long and hard to compel the educational system to provide things that we knew were necessary to the appropriate education of our children. This included, first and foremost, teachers who were trained in the techniques of behavior modification and who understood the peculiarities of autistic children.

In the last issue of the ARRI we published a small article titled "Full Inclusion: The Right Choice?" Our article was based on a report by Simpson and Sasso in which they noted that there was no empirical evidence showing that full inclusion was beneficial to autistic children. That short article brought a surprisingly strong response from our readers. It seems that the full inclusion movement has been so quickly bought by the educational establishment that those who believe that a full range of options should be available have not had time to organize any meaningful opposition. We received many letters and calls of thanks from parents who were pleased to see that we were addressing this issue (see Letters).

Several years ago I received an urgent plea for help from a group of parents in Michigan whose children attended the Burger Center for Autistic Children. I was invited to speak there and made a tour of the facility. I was impressed. The staff were obviously very much involved with autism, the teaching of autistic children, and all the details of autism. They communicated with each other with ideas and suggestions and enthusiasm that won my admiration. They certainly had the support of the parent group. The problem was that full inclusion was being heavily promoted in Michigan, and rational and efficient programs like the Burger School program for autism were in dire threat of being closed down.

I have no quarrel with inclusionists if they are content to insist upon inclusion for their children, or for children of other parents who feel that it is optimum for their children. But when they try to force me and other unwilling parents to dance to their tune, I find it highly objectionable and quite intolerable. Parents need *options.*

If there are no objective data showing that full inclusion works better than giving people several options, why is it being promoted so avidly? Douglas Biklen attempts to answer that question solely on ideological grounds. In his book, *Achieving the Complete School,* he says of mainstreaming, "To ask, Does it work? is to ask the wrong question." He believes that full inclusion and mainstreaming should be the only choice available to us because it is the right choice, the *right thing to do.* He makes an analogy with slavery. Slavery, he says, was abolished because it was morally wrong, not because it didn't work. He also asserts that objective scientific data are irrelevant because the issue is a moral one.

I disagree strongly with Biklen on both counts. Biklen has the slavery analogy exactly backward: making full inclusion the only option does not resemble the *abolition* of slavery, but instead the *imposition* of slavery. Like slavery, full inclusion rejects the idea that people should be free to choose for themselves the options they desire, and compels them to accede to the wishes of others. And as for Biklen's rejection of scientific data, I want my children educated in ways that will assure the best outcome, as learned from scientific studies, not in ways that accord with someone's theory, or ideology, or the educational fad of the year.

Special education consultant Laurence Lieberman is one of the very few educators with the courage to speak out and tell the compulsory full inclusionists that they are wrong. Recently the National Association of State Boards of Education endorsed the principle of full inclusion of students with disabilities. Lieberman's insightful response, published as a letter to the editor in *Education Week* for December 16, 1992, is a classic, and is reprinted here in part:

> People involved in education cannot agree on school choice, on promotion policies, on achievement testing, on curricula, teaching approaches, or the distribution of condoms. But all the state boards of education can agree on full inclusion for all disabled students?
>
> This is obviously a money issue, pure and simple. The key may be found in the paragraph in your story that says a new report from

NASBE proposes that funds be provided on the basis of instructional need, not head counts. That need seems to have been already predetermined by the organization: full inclusion in regular classrooms for all disabled students.

The article—and quite possibly the report—refuses to deal with the real nature of some children, which might require that they not be in a regular classroom.

Some educators would place the issue of full inclusion solely in the realm of morality. Anything separate is evil. There may be a higher immorality than separateness: lack of progress, lack of achievement, lack of skills, and splintered learning of meaningless academic trivia.

There is the issue that special education hasn't been effective. Where, and for whom and why? Because it has been too separate? Unlikely. The regular classroom is not separate by definition. Has it worked? Sometimes, but not all the time. Placing severely disabled students in regular classrooms presupposes a level of individualization that does not exist.

Some educators believe that disabled children will be much more accepted, and society as a whole will show much greater compassion for the disabled, if all children are in regular classrooms. Knowledge does not necessarily lead to compassion.

There is a common belief that when disabled children are in physical proximity to normal children they will tend to adopt more normal behavior patterns. This is obviously not the case with many autistic children, who generally begin life surrounded by normal families.

Full inclusion is not *the* right thing to do. It is one right thing to do, sometimes.

Any organization ... that endorses full inclusion is taking an extremist position that has no place in an educational system and a society that prides itself on its choices and multiple ways to achieve a desired quality of life.

I agree with Lieberman. If special education for autism is destroyed, it will be lost for at least one generation, and perhaps several.

Chapter 18

Mainstreaming and the Philosophy of Normalization

Edward Zigler and Nancy Hall

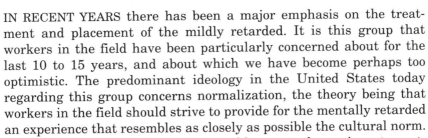

IN RECENT YEARS there has been a major emphasis on the treatment and placement of the mildly retarded. It is this group that workers in the field have been particularly concerned about for the last 10 to 15 years, and about which we have become perhaps too optimistic. The predominant ideology in the United States today regarding this group concerns normalization, the theory being that workers in the field should strive to provide for the mentally retarded an experience that resembles as closely as possible the cultural norm.

Although at first glance this would seem to be an incontrovertible point of view, it has split and polarized the intellectual community concerned with mental retardation. Care must be taken that we do not adopt an all-or-nothing attitude towards normalization. There will always be a need for the institution, and there are a number of eminent workers who have shown us that there can be habitable and humanized institutions. Unfortunately, many of the forces at work, such as that represented by the judicial system, depict the issues surrounding normalization as win–lose, either–or choices, driving out the moderate middle ground position. Those who polarize the situation by promoting either normalization or institutionalization to the complete exclusion of the other do the situation and its complexity a grave injustice.

After more than a decade of promoting normalization it remains basically ephemeral construct, backed by relatively little sound research. The characterization of normalization as "a banner in search of some data" (Zigler, 1976) is still a fair one. As yet we have no clearly articulated operational definition of normalization, with the result being that we are not able to set down clear guidelines for the formulation and implementation of social policies based on the normalization ideology (Zigler, 1985).

ORIGINS OF THE MAINSTREAMING MOVEMENT

One of the social policy manifestations of normalization that has been widely promulgated in the past decade is mainstreaming. Mainstreaming is usually viewed as an outgrowth of Public Law 94-142, the Education for All Handicapped Children Act of 1975, which provided the legislative leverage for handicapped children and their families to gain access to often-denied educational services. Under the protection of this law, these children have gained an inlet into a network of essential services, and their families have been supported in the desire for a voice in the education of their children.

Even though the term mainstreaming does not actually appear in the wording of the legislation, the administrators of institutions and school systems have typically interpreted the phrase "least restrictive alternative" to mean integrated classes. The authors concur with Gottlieb's charge (1981) that the least restrictive alternative is still unknown. What is the operation by which we define it? All too often, school systems, pressed by this legislation's failure to pay for the services it mandates, have been forced to equate "least restrictive" with least expensive (Zigler & Muenchow, 1979). Caught between a federal mandate and state and local budget cuts, school administrators may have little choice about the placement of handicapped children. In the long run, the law may even result in a failure by school systems to provide sufficient special classes. The use of high-quality but expensive private services for handicapped children may also be severely curtailed if school systems cannot pay for them. One of the top priorities, when considering the merits of various settings—home, institution or group home, special class, private school, or regular classroom—must be to respect certain basic principles of development, the most crucial of these being the principle of continuity. We cannot, with impunity, continue to move the retarded about like cattle under the banner of normalization. The positive effects of any setting must be weighed against the possible damaging effects of a move.

Public Law 94-142 may have built-in flaws. Ironically, the very law that was designed to safeguard the options of handicapped children and their parents may, in the end, act to constrict their choices and result in disservice to the very children the legislators sought to help, by forcing schools to place them in programs that are not equipped to meet their needs. The normalization principle and the practice of mainstreaming may have deleterious effects on some children by denying them their right to be different.

The variability that is so essential to our understanding of handicapped individuals is ignored by these trends. Underlying the very idea of normalization is a push toward homogeneity, which is unfair to those children whose special needs may come to be viewed as unacceptable. We must face the fact that normalization can entail nonacceptance of an individual's differences. This attitude could prove to be damaging both to individual children and adults and to the progress of the field as a whole.

It will take more than a rewriting of social policy to bring about the changes in social attitude that are required here. Training is needed for the teachers affected by this mandate. More research is necessary to determine just how P.L. 94-142 is being implemented across the nation. Specific criteria for determining who should be mainstreamed, and to what extent, are still, after almost 10 years, conspicuous by their absence.

In the face of this relative lack of research and education on the most compassionate and efficacious implementation of mainstreaming, why has it been so widely championed and so heavily promoted? Is this widespread implementation justified? Gottlieb (1981) has reviewed in some detail the reasons behind the push toward the mainstreaming of handicapped children and, in examining the evidence in support of these reasons, has found them to be sorely lacking.

The first argument Gottlieb reviews claims to demonstrate the superiority of regular over special classrooms with regard to pupil achievement. Gottlieb's thorough search fails to uncover much evidence in favor of this argument, and suggests that a truly appropriate course for stimulating higher academic achievement in educable mentally retarded (EMR) children has still not been found. The authors feel it should be noted that, with very few exceptions, the studies that gave rise to the purported superiority of regular classroom placement (Kirk, 1964) were measures of cognitive ability, and excluded social competence indices.

A second concern of investigators in the 1960s and 1970s revolved around the stigma and the social isolation that were thought to be associated with placement in a special classroom. Mainstreaming, it was felt, would increase the level of acceptance of EMR children by their nonhandicapped peers. Gottlieb points to three areas of research that are relevant to this argument. First, he reports that the devaluing of retarded children by their peers is not as global as critics of the segregated classroom seem to feel, and that indeed, many EMR children are as well accepted as nonretarded children. He then goes on to describe the results of work which shows that the social status of EMR children placed in regular classrooms can be improved. This is an area in which special programs for teachers would be useful. Where social isolation does exist, it is likely to be exacerbated by placement in a regular classroom, in which the handicapped child's behavioral differences take on an increased visibility through comparison with his classmates. In this case, mainstreaming may cause as many problems as it corrects.

A third force in the push towards mainstreaming was a direct outgrowth of the civil rights movement, on whose heels it followed. Many critics noted that classes for the handicapped contained a disproportionate percentage of minority students, so that a side effect of special class placement was often racial segregation. Gottlieb's data on this point indicate that this was indeed the case, but, regardless of the extent of mainstreaming, it continues to be true. Special classes are still racially imbalanced, and moving children to racially segregated regular classrooms does not alleviate the problem.

Finally, proponents of mainstreaming point to the value of individualized curriculum in a regular classroom. Again, the available data do not support this point, but suggest that there are few differences in teaching methods between regular and special classrooms. Gottlieb (1981) sums up this and his other arguments by saying:

> ... mainstreaming evolved from a disenchantment with self-contained classes. The changes that occurred were entirely administrative. New educational techniques or approaches were not introduced. The main expectation was that EMR children would do no worse in mainstreamed classes than in self-contained classes

(Semmel, 1979). The expectation was not that they would do better. To date, the expectation has been confirmed [p. 124].

THE EFFECTS OF MAINSTREAMING

In examining some of the effects of mainstreaming that have been documented, the best that can be said about the body of data is that they are inconclusive and often contradictory. In addition to the possibility of increasing or decreasing social stigma, mainstreaming may have an effect on a number of other behavioral variables, such as expectancy of success, responsivity to social reinforcement, outer-directedness or imitativeness, self-image and wariness of adults. Motivational factors such as these have the potential to impact on such cognitive and achievement measures as IQ score and academic performance, in addition to relating directly to social competence. There is little evidence that mainstreamed retarded children exhibit more socially competent behaviors with regard to these motivational variables than do nonmainstreamed retarded children. The one statement that can be made with certainty is that the effects of mainstreaming on the behavior of mildly retarded children are extremely complex (Caparulo & Zigler, 1983). One must consider the degree and definition of the mainstreaming in question, the social histories of the children, age, and gender, to name but a few of the variables that have been shown to account for variation in behavior. We cannot assume that mainstreaming is a simple variable that has a unidirectional effect on the children involved.

The variation in the effects of mainstreaming points out the fact that we *must* define the "appropriate education" that is guaranteed by the Education for All Handicapped Children Act. It is time to work on defining the criteria for the appropriateness of an educational program, to recognize the need for a differentiated approach to this problem and in doing so attend to the daily experiences of retarded children in a variety of settings.

EVALUATION OF MAINSTREAMING

One of the most important components of any program of services is evaluation, and mainstreaming represents no exception to this rule. Here again, objective and well-defined criteria are essential. The best evaluation of mainstreaming, which is yet to come, would look at adults who experienced a variety of mainstreamed and nonmainstreamed programs during their school years. How does classroom placement effect these individuals later in life? With either adults or children, it is clear that we cannot view cognitive measures, such as IQ, to be the most useful tool for evaluation, but should strive for a more global picture of optimal human development. Social competence must be our ultimate criterion for the evaluation of programs for the handicapped.

Consider the situation of familial retarded individuals in Sweden (Zigler, Balla, & Hodapp, 1984). Sweden purports to have no retarded individuals in this category. In reality, the percentage of familial retarded in Sweden is the same as it is in the United States, but there they are not labeled as retarded. These children pass from grade to grade till adulthood. Following their graduation and entry into society, however, these individuals often find that, because they were not labeled as retarded, they were not able to benefit from the excellent special education programs that would have prepared them for competent functioning in an adult world. Many, in fact, return to the school system and ask to be labeled retarded and educated appropriately so that they can find employment. Care must be taken that we do not duplicate this system in the United States. We should be cautious that we do not mainstream handicapped children away from training programs that will enable them to become socially competent and independent adults.

AN ECOLOGICAL APPROACH

We are beyond the point at which we can cling to the simplistic notion of some model retarded individual for whom there is a single indisputable optimal placement. The time has come instead for us to adopt a more complex systems approach in which relevant subsystems are viewed as being in interaction. An ecological model, such as that defined by Bronfenbrenner (1979), would typify such a systems approach. But any global view of the retarded would minimally have to include the retarded individual, the family (regardless of whether the individual resides at home), the workers in any nonfamily residential setting, and teachers and administrative personnel responsible for the care and education of the individual.

Both family and nonfamily residential settings exist as part of a larger community. This system includes, as integral parts, the professionals and paraprofessionals who work on the problems of the mentally retarded in medicine, psychology, and other social services. Within this system there is tremendous complexity associated with the interaction of these different disciplines. There is another relevant plane of interface: The plane between the private or for profit and governmental and nonprofit sectors. The legal system at all levels is also inextricably bound up in how we view and treat the placement of our retarded citizens, and is a strong force behind the move towards an increasing degree of normalization and mainstreaming. Another facet of this system is represented by the media, which is charged with reporting accomplishments as well as failures, and can have an enormous impact on how the field is viewed by the general public.

In addition to attending to the complexity of their world, we must be mindful of the heterogeneity of retarded individuals. There is a wide range of behaviors in those whose IQs range from 0 to 70, and an equally wide variety of factors that impinge on these behaviors. It is essential that we appreciate fully the considerable variability that exists even among the severely and profoundly retarded, and it is because of this complexity that we cannot allow ourselves to be sanguine about simplistic views of the treatment of the retarded. The retarded individual may have exacerbating physical handicaps and medical problems. There may be accompanying emotional or behavioral problems, or a concurrent psychopathology. Even in the absence of relatively major complications such as these, we must take care not to ignore the effects of less controversial variables. The age of the retarded individual, for example, is an important determinant of problems and social reactions. The needs and the adaptation of retarded individuals change as the decades go by. For some time the field has been so child-centered that we have underinvestigated the needs of the retarded adult. The lifespan approach which has had such a positive impact on developmental psychology could be put to good use by workers in the mental retardation field.

Gender is another important variable that should be taken more seriously. Mental retardation and developmental disability do not swamp sex role effects. As we make progress in the field of mental retardation we still have not produced a major study concerning the intersect of mental retardation and gender. Recognizing that such variables affect the retarded with as much force as they affect any of us may require that we humanize both ourselves and our approach to retarded persons.

What seem to be such simple and noncontroversial variables as chronological age (CA) and mental age (MA) must also be investigated thoroughly. Those of us who champion a developmental approach to retardation would argue for comparison of subject groups matched for mental age; other theorists believe that chronological age is the more important matching criterion. Until this issue is settled, researchers must continue to examine the controversy from both sides.

Another characteristic of importance is the individual's level of retardation, which has been shown to affect the way in which others interact with the individual (Zigler, Balla, & Styfco, in press). Level of retardation is largely determined by yet another highly relevant variable, namely etiology. We have long argued that researchers must distinguish between those whose retardation stems from an organic dysfunction and those whose retardation may be defined as cultural–familial. Numerous behavioral differences are associated with this etiological distinction.

The deviance in the life of a mentally retarded individual is not limited to that accounted for by the retardation itself. Leaving aside questions of cause and effect, we must simply note that the retarded are more likely to have experienced a high degree of social deprivation than are those with higher IQs.

In recognizing the variability among retarded individuals and the various factors that impinge on their development and behavior, we must acknowledge the need for an interdisciplinary effort on their behalf. Pediatricians and geneticists, psychologists and psychiatrists, policy makers and educators alike must join forces in a cooperative effort if we are to achieve any real progress toward solving the problems of retardation.

We should be wary of those who tell us that we need not examine all alternatives and to proceed on the basis of commonsense. This often turns out to be more common than sensible. It is also important to know and to bear in mind the history of this field if we are to escape Santayana's prophecy that in forgetting our history we would be forced to relive it. Many of our new ideas are actually old ideas. The treatment of the handicapped has progressed in cycles, dominated by trends that seem to have had an average lifespan of about a decade. Think back to Seguin (1866) with his emphasis on moral training, promising that normal development for the retarded would follow as a result of the right treatment. There sprang up at this time a proliferation of state schools, and the prevailing mood was one of boundless optimism. This effort did not, of course, make the retarded normal, and the pendulum swung in the opposite direction, toward a time of unwarranted pessimism. Then it was felt that nothing could be done for the retarded and they were warehoused in large institutions, often sterilized, and frequently, dehumanized. The current era of normalization represents another move toward optimism. Let us hope that our expectations for progress in this direction are tempered with realism and compassion.

THE ROLE OF PROFESSIONALS

The relatively new ideology concerning the education and placement of the handicapped makes new demands on professionals and policy makers in the field. How do we define the changing and often controversial roles of such workers? What are the tasks set before them? It was not so very long ago that professionals who worked with retarded individuals were virtually unanimous in their recommendation of institutionalization. Today the zeitgeist is such that parents who consider institutionalization are made to feel guilty and inadequate by professionals. It is troubling that we as scholars and professionals have become so intrusive in the lives of families of the retarded. Our role is not to tell families what decision to make, but to advise them on how best to make it—to give counsel, information, and support where they are needed. One humane and ethical model for such interaction has been proposed by Duff (1983), who speaks of the "moral community." In this model, the family is counseled best by those who know them and their situation best, i.e., their physician, religious counselor, or own family members. Professionals in a truly enlightened society would provide viable and available alternatives from which parents could choose in the best interest of their child.

In the best of all possible worlds, choices regarding placement and education of a handicapped person would be made according to such a model. Teachers and school administrators would also play a role in such decision making. But before this can become truly feasible we must educate our educators. We must also provide specially trained support personnel for these teachers. And we must recognize that such training, and the effective and human integration of handicapped children into mainstream settings, is going to be expensive.

Public Law 94-142 provides for less than 10% of the money needed to implement the changes it mandates. Compare this to, for example, Head Start, for which federal legislation provides 80% of the program's costs. It is clear that our nation's financial priorities have not kept pace with the needs of our handicapped citizens. It is still true, for instance, that economic incentives are provided to families choosing to institutionalize a severely handicapped child.

OUTLOOK FOR THE FUTURE

What lies in the future for normalization and its two most apparent manifestations, deinstitutionalization and mainstreaming? New directions will be affected by, among other things, the course taken by institutions. We have finally seen that the size of a treatment facility per se does not determine its social–psychological characteristics, and tells little about the daily experiences of its residents. The normalization adherents have not yet appreciated the variability of even large institutions. There is some value left in such places: In a comprehensive system of care for the retarded a large institution could serve as the hub of a network of services. For an example of such a system, examine the model developed at the Ellwyn Conference (Crissey, in press).

The future of the field of mental retardation is also being influenced in a constructive way by a strengthened commitment to interdisciplinary work. Only a cooperative effort involving physicians, psychologists, educators, social workers, sociologists, and public policy makers, to name but a few, can lead to real progress in formulating a comprehensive model to help the retarded. The significant improvements in the treatment of the retarded which we have witnessed over the past two decades have been a result of just such interdisciplinary work. Further improvements depend on our recognition of the importance of continued sound research, and of ongoing and longitudinal evaluations of treatment programs.

The only safeguards we have against fads in treatment trends lie in the results of our research. Solid scientific underpinnings are essential to the development of policies and treatments that are both effective and humane. Quality programs and comprehensive research studies are often expensive and we must take care to make them as cost-effective as possible, tempering our rhetoric with financial realism. Advocacy for rational and compassionate budgetary priorities is essential, but at the same time we should be willing to listen and to compromise in our interactions with decision-makers. We must, as workers concerned with the retarded, support and guide our advocates and policy-makers by sharing with them our knowledge.

There is a new note of optimism among those concerned with the retarded. The heat of the once virulent debate over normalization has cooled in recent years, and a new sanity and synthesis has emerged. Although the principle of normalization is not without merit, we cannot allow ourselves to lose sight of long-term goals in our anxiousness to produce quick and visible results. The positive effects of normalization and its social policy manifestations with be many if we do not allow these policies to become empty slogans by ignoring sound developmental principles. Responsibility for protecting these principles and safeguarding choices for the treatment of the retarded rests with us all.

REFERENCES

Bronfenbrenner, U. (1979). *The ecology of human development: Experiments by nature and design.* Cambridge, MA: Harvard University Press.

Caparulo, B., & Zigler, E. (1983). The effects of mainstreaming on success expectancy and imitation in mildly retarded children. *Peabody Journal of Education, 60*(3), 85–98.

Crissey, M. A. (in press). *The residential institution: A community resource.* Baltimore: University Park Press.

Duff, R. (1983, February). Decision-making in extreme situations: Infant Doe and related matters. Paper presented at the Bush Luncheon in Child Development and Social Policy, Yale University, New Haven, CT.

Gottlieb, J. (1981). Mainstreaming: Fulfilling the promise? *American Journal of Mental Deficiency 86*(2), 115–126.

Kirk, S. A. (1964). Research in education. In H. A. Stevens & R. Heber (Eds.), *Mental retardation: A review of research.* Chicago: University of Chicago Press.

Public Law 94-142, Education for All Handicapped Children Act, November 29, 1975.

Seguin, E. (1866) *Idiocy: And its treatment by the physiological method.* New York: Wood.

Zigler, E. (1985). Handicapped children and their families. In E. Schopler & G. B. Mesibov (Eds.), *The effects of autism on the family.* New York: Plenum.

Zigler, E. Testimony presented to the Senate and House Appropriations Committee, March 1976.

Zigler, E., Balla, D., & Hodapp, R. (1984). On the definition and classification of mental retardation. *American Journal of Mental Deficiency, 89,* 215–230.

Zigler, E., Balla, D., & Styfco, S. (in press). New directions for the study of the effects of institutionalization on retarded persons. In *Proceedings of the NICHD Conference on Learning and Cognition in the Mentally Retarded,* Nashville, TN, September 16–18, 1980.

Zigler, E., & Muenchow, S. (1979). Mainstreaming: The proof is in the implementation. *American Psychologist, 34*(10), 993–996.

Appendix

FULL INCLUSION OF STUDENTS WHO ARE BLIND AND VISUALLY IMPAIRED: A POSITION STATEMENT

prepared by the American Council of the Blind, the American Foundation for the Blind, the Association for Education and Rehabilitation for the Blind and Visually Impaired, the Blinded Veterans Association, the Canadian Council of the Blind, the Canadian National Institute for the Blind, the National Federation of the Blind, and the National Library Service for the Blind and Physically Handicapped

"Full Inclusion," a philosophical concept currently advanced by a number of educators, is not a federal legal requirement in special education law. Proponents of "full inclusion" nevertheless take the position that all students with disabilities must receive their total instruction in the regular public school classroom regardless of individual needs. Unfortunately, "full inclusion" would eliminate all special placements, including "pull out" services, resource rooms and specialized schools. Such an arrangement would be seriously detrimental to the educational development of many students with disabilities.

We, the national organizations of and for the blind listed here are firmly committed to appropriate educational opportunities designed to provide students with the competencies necessary to ensure full participation in society. It is significant to recognize that our field was the first to develop a broad range of special education options beginning with specialized schools as early as 1829, and extending to public school programs since 1900. These options have provided critically important educational preparation for several generations of highly successful and independent blind people. Based on this long and impressive record of success in making optimal use of both special and public school programs to meet the diverse needs of blind students, we strongly agree upon the following:

- If provided with timely and adequate specialized services by appropriately certified teachers, students who are blind or visually impaired can develop skills that will enable them to achieve success and independence as responsible

From Joint Organizational Effort Committee. (1993). Full inclusion of students who are blind and visually impaired: A position paper. *The Braille Forum,* July 1993, *32*(1), 44–47. Copyright © 1993 by the American Council of the Blind. Reprinted by permission.

citizens in a fully integrated society. If these students do not receive appropriate instruction designed to develop competencies that meet the sensory deficits of blindness and low vision, critical learning opportunities will be lost, thus diminishing the potential for future accomplishments. In this context, ample opportunities for instruction in such areas as braille, abacus, orientation and mobility, and use of prescribed optical devices must be made available to students, as needed.

- Educational decisions must be made on a case by case basis consistent with the Individuals with Disabilities Education Act (IDEA), which guarantees a Free Appropriate Public Education in the Least Restrictive Environment (LRE) from among a Full Continuum of Alternative Placements based on the Individual Education Plan for each student. Educational decisions should not be made simply on the basis of philosophy, limited school budgets, administrative convenience, or concerns about socialization.

- Full inclusion in regular education classrooms for all students with disabilities irrespective of individual needs is in sharp conflict with procedural guarantees of IDEA.

- Least Restrictive Environment and Full Continuum of Alternative Placements are critically important IDEA provisions. LRE is not one sole physical location. It is, rather, a principle, which if properly applied, matches the need of the student with an appropriate school setting which provides meaningful challenges, realistic expectations, and maximum opportunities for achievement and development of a healthy self-esteem.

- The regular education classroom may be considered the LRE if the student possesses sufficient readiness and survival skills and can be provided adequate supports, specialized services (from personnel trained in education of the visually impaired), and opportunities to develop skills commensurate with his or her potential. Extreme caution must be exercised so that full inclusion does not result in "full submersion," social isolation, "lowered" self-esteem, poor performance, or a setting in which services are unavailable.

- In cases where the needs of the student cannot be met in the regular classrooms, an alternative education placement must be provided and be recognized as the LRE for that particular student. Such alternative placements should not be negatively viewed as discriminatory or as "segregated" settings when legitimately warranted to develop the needed skills for future integration in school and society.

- Since it has been clearly demonstrated that blind children benefit from interacting with disabled and nondisabled children, both interaction opportunities should be fully encouraged in whatever setting that is considered appropriate. We believe that the mandate in IDEA which states that, "to the maximum extent appropriate, children with disabilities [should be] educated with children who are nondisabled," does not intend that blind children avoid interaction with each other.

We strongly urge that decision makers carefully consider and be sensitive to the impact of reform initiatives on the education of students with visual disabilities. Caution must be exercised to insure that educational philosophy and trends such as full inclusion do not seriously endanger appropriate and specialized services for students who are blind and visually impaired. If properly implemented, IDEA can provide legal safeguards to insure that all individual children can realize their full potential for independence and success.

AMERICAN FEDERATION OF TEACHERS RESOLUTION: INCLUSION OF STUDENTS WITH DISABILITIES

Adopted by the AFT Executive Council on October 27, 1993

AFT Resolution on the policy known variously as inclusion, full integration of students with disabilities, the regular education initiative, unified system, or inclusive education.

WHEREAS there is no legal mandate or consistent definition for "inclusion," let it be known that for AFT policy we define inclusion as the placement of all students with disabilities in general education classrooms without regard to the nature or severity of the students' disabilities, their ability to behave and function appropriately in the classroom, or the educational benefits they can derive.

WHEREAS the mission of the public schools and of the AFT is to provide high standards, rich and challenging classroom experiences, and maximum achievement for ALL students, including students with disabilities as well as nondisabled students in general education classes;

WHEREAS public schools, particularly in urban areas, already are facing severe burdens because of the inequities in funding that plague them, overcrowding, the persistent social problems that surround them, and demands that they resolve the immense problems that students bring to school, severely reducing the schools' ability to provide a high quality educational program for any student;

WHEREAS two years before the twentieth anniversary of the passage of the Education for All Handicapped Children Act (P.L. 94-142), Congress' continuing cynicism in funding the mandates of the law at under 10 percent of costs instead of the 40 percent promised has compromised schools' ability to provide appropriate services to students with disabilities, and has placed even greater strains on education generally by requiring that higher and higher percentages of funding go to special education:

WHEREAS inclusion is being championed as the only placement for all students with disabilities by a movement of some advocacy groups—in the face of opposition from the parents of many students with disabilities and many respected advocates for the disabled— when there is no clear evidence that inclusion is appropriate or pro-

---

Reprinted by permission of the American Federation of Teachers.

vides an educational benefit for all students with disabilities, and no clear evidence of its benefit for the other students;

WHEREAS there are deep concerns about the high percentage of minority children in some classes for students with disabilities, and inclusion is viewed by some advocates and parents as the only means of getting minority children out of those classes;

WHEREAS inclusion is being adopted by a large number of local school boards, state departments of education, legislators, and other policymakers all over the country as a means to save money by placing all students with disabilities in general education classrooms and curtailing special education supports and services;

WHEREAS inclusion is being adopted in contradiction to the mandates of P.L. 94-142 and the Individuals with Disabilities Education Act (IDEA, the revision of P.L. 94-142) that require students to be evaluated and, based on individual needs, assigned to the "least restrictive environment" (LRE) that exists within a continuum, or range, of placements;

WHEREAS even when students with disabilities are appropriately placed, general and special education staff who work with them are not receiving the training they need that they are entitled to by law;

WHEREAS the federal law and court decisions forbid school districts from removing disruptive students with disabilities from programs for more than 10 days a year, and require that, in the absence of school district and parental consent to an interim placement or a court order, such students "stay put" in the class while their placement is being evaluated and adjudicated;

WHEREAS the existing federal legislation limits the ability of teachers to challenge legally inappropriate placements of students with disabilities in general education classrooms;

WHEREAS insufficient medical personnel are employed by school districts to care for medically fragile children under existing circumstances, and inclusion would place these students in medical danger and increase the responsibilities of teachers and paraprofessionals;

WHEREAS inclusion threatens to overwhelm schools and systems that are already extremely vulnerable—particularly in areas with great poverty and social needs—by placing additional responsibilities on teachers, paraprofessionals, and support professionals, thus threatening the ability of schools to meet the educational needs of all students;

WHEREAS students with disabilities have frequently been placed in programs that failed to serve their needs to meet high educational standards, fueling the desire of their parents to have their children in general education classrooms even when such placements are not appropriate;

RESOLVED that the AFT continue to seek high, national achievement standards for education, applicable to ALL students, disabled and nondisabled alike;

RESOLVED that the AFT oppose inclusion—that is, any movement or program that has the goal of placing all students with disabilities in general education classrooms regardless of the nature or severity of their disabilities, their ability to behave or function appropriately in the classroom, or the educational benefits they and their general education peers can derive;

RESOLVED that the AFT denounce the appalling administrative practices that have accompanied the inclusion movement. These include, but are not limited to, placing too many students with disabilities in individual general classrooms; placing students with disabilities in general education classrooms without services, professional development, or paraprofessional assistance; refusing to assist teachers who are having problems meeting the unique needs of students with disabilities; and changing IEPs en masse so that students with disabilities may be placed in general education classrooms without supports and services and irrespective of the appropriateness of the placement;

RESOLVED that the AFT seek alliances with organizations that support the continuum of alternative placements and the educational placement of students with disabilities within the least restrictive environment appropriate to the individual needs of the students;

RESOLVED that the AFT seek with its allies to reopen P.L. 94-142 and IDEA, convincing Congress both to recognize in the law the high costs and complex problems of special education, and to respond by providing:

1. full funding for all of its mandates;

2. a 5-year reauthorization of the laws for educating students with disabilities—just as every other education act requires—to realize the benefits of new hearings and discussions of problems that arise;

3. the legal right for teachers to attend the IEP meetings of children they teach; the right to appeal inappropriate placements; and the right to be fully represented during due process hearings without reprisal, i.e., intimidation, coercion, or retaliation, for being a child

advocate; and the right to be involved in the assessment of delivery of services, staff training, and availability of resources to ensure the effectiveness of the program as intended by Congress;

4. the reauthorization and enforcement of the continuum of placements, which includes mainstreaming as an existing alternative strategy within the range of services for students with disabilities;

5. that criteria for placement in general education require the proximate ability of students to function appropriately both academically and behaviorally when supplementary aids and services are provided by the district;

6. support for districts in maintaining consistent discipline policies for ALL students who disrupt classrooms or engage in dangerous behavior;

7. removal of the "stay put" provision, thus allowing districts to make responsible alternative arrangements for disruptive and/or dangerous students during the appeals process;

8. reauthorization of and insistence on comprehensive professional development;

9. negation of court decisions concerning students with disabilities which are detrimental to educational programs—such as the "stay put" provision, limitations on the discipline of students with disabilities, and decisions that favor inclusion;

10. for limitations on the number of students with disabilities in self-contained and general classrooms;

RESOLVED that the AFT seek with its allies to address the problem of the high percentages of minority students in special education; and

RESOLVED that the AFT renew our longstanding commitment to meeting the needs of ALL students for high standards, rich and challenging classroom experiences, and maximum achievement, whatever their educational placements might be.

RESOLUTION ON INCLUSIVE EDUCATION

Prepared by The Association for Persons with Severe Handicaps (TASH)

Preamble

The United States Congress, in passing the Americans with Disabilities Act (ADA) in 1990, found that there were approximately 43 million Americans with disabilities and found that these individuals had been isolated and segregated, faced restrictions and limitations, occupied an inferior status and had been seriously disadvantaged. The implications of this situation have been evident in the field of education.

Resolution

WHEREAS the democratic ideals of American society can be best served and protected when diversity is highly valued and seen as the norm in all schools; when *all* students are viewed as active, fully participating members of the school community; and when the reciprocal benefits of full inclusion for all students is understood and celebrated;

BE IT RESOLVED that TASH reaffirms a definition of inclusion that begins with the educational and moral imperatives that students with disabilities belong in general education classrooms and that they receive the supports and services necessary to benefit from their education in the general education setting. Inclusion proceeds to and is fully defined by a new way of thinking based upon current understandings about how *all* children and young people are educated—a new way of thinking that embraces a sociology of acceptance of *all* children into the school community as active, fully participating members; that views diversity as the norm and maintains a high quality education for each student by assuring effective teaching, powerful pedagogies and necessary supports to each child in the general education setting.

BE IT FURTHER RESOLVED that TASH calls upon local, state, provincial, regional and federal governments, as well as all related organizations, to stand accountable for the development and maintenance of educational opportunities for *all* students that are fully inclusive and ultimately effective; and that the United States Government be urged to vigorously enforce, at all levels, legislation *already enacted* that assures such accountability, development and maintenance.

BE IT FURTHER RESOLVED that TASH recognizes the many highly successful inclusionary practices already in place in classrooms, schools, and school districts across the nation and beyond, and calls upon all those who can make a difference to combine their efforts in a cooperative manner to support and celebrate these efforts and at the same time continue to work as agents of change to bring inclusion to all those who have not yet experienced this new way of thinking.

Research findings and documented experience offer overwhelming support for the following components as essential to the creation of fully inclusive schools:

General

- Teaching which uses heterogeneous groupings and a variety of age-appropriate instructional strategies based upon students' learning needs and which emphasize active learning strategies;

- High expectations for all students and teachers who treat each student as a uniquely important individual;

- Program philosophy which emphasizes the value of diversity, multiculturalism, social inclusion and belonging for everyone;

- Access for all students to campuses and classrooms, including co-curricular and extracurricular activities, that are free from prejudice and other physical and psychological barriers;

- Comprehensive, sensible and culturally competent curricula which are effective for the full range of learners;

- Opportunities for all secondary school students to participate in work study or other community and/or job skill development programs which will not negatively impact participation and full membership in the high school community;

Assessment

- Thorough analysis of the learning needs of *all* students;

- Broad use of unbiased and culturally sensitive assessment procedures that enhance students' strengths and assist in the identification of their needs;

- Accountability for achievement which is based on each student's personal potential and educational experience;

Communication

- Emphasis on the importance of family involvement and home–school communication structures that are culturally responsive and which empower families;
- Conscious creation of a strong sense of community and fostering of mutual respect and support among education staff, parents, and students;
- Collaboration among teachers, other personnel, family members, students, and peers to plan and deliver educational services;
- Well-delineated processes for problem-solving as defined by the family, student, and classmates;

Staff Development

- Teacher training programs that are inclusive and collaborative of general and special education teachers so that all teachers will be prepared to teach all students effectively;
- Necessary and appropriate staff development programs for teachers and related services staff which will develop the necessary new understanding, beliefs, skills, and behaviors;

Supports

- The necessary and appropriate supports and services to provide *all* students with opportunity for success;
- A broad range of support services (e.g., speech, reading, occupational therapy, assistive technology) which are closely coordinated with the general education classroom's goals and activities and which are provided in general education settings; and
- Creative ways to allocate special and general education resources, with funding obstacles removed.

Resolved on this day, December 17, 1993.

Note. Originally adopted: December 1988; Revised: December 17, 1993.

RESOLUTION ON THE REDEFINITION OF THE CONTINUUM OF SERVICES

prepared by The Association for Persons with Severe Handicaps (TASH)

Children and adults with severe disabilities require specialized and individualized services that traditionally have not been made available in typical school and other community environments. Instead, access to such services has been tied to categorical placements which increasingly isolate persons with disabilities from relationships with their family, peers, and other citizens. In the past, the concept of a continuum of services has been used to foster the notion that persons with severe disabilities must earn the right to lead integrated lives in the community. TASH believes therefore that a redefinition of the continuum is vitally needed.

The Association for Persons with Severe Handicaps believes that specialized and individualized services can be readily and effectively provided in integrated settings, and need not preclude opportunities to develop peer and other social relationships which are so critical to the achievement of full participation in society.

TASH further believes that effective methodologies and models which can be applied in integrated settings now exist, and that the focus of new significant and systematic research and development efforts should now be upon the development, implementation, validation, and dissemination of such alternatives to outdated practices which segregate persons with disabilities from their families, peers, and the community by requiring placement in handicapped-only and categorically grouped services and settings.

THEREFORE, TASH calls for a redefinition of the continuum of services which emphasizes the attainment of the following characteristics and components:

1. The provision of specialized staff, resources, and services to meet individual needs in the regular classroom, neighborhood school, home and family, and community program and setting;

2. The substantive training and retraining of personnel, both special and generic service professionals—to

prepare them for providing instruction to a variety of heterogeneous groups of learners;

3. The systematic shifting of service delivery design and services away from a categorical, homogeneously grouped, and separate model to one which requires integration and thrives on a variety of grouping arrangements;

4. The philosophical and administrative merger of special and regular education and specialized and generic services into one service delivery system, evidenced by the integration of both professional staff and students; and

5. An unambiguous model of the Least Restrictive Environment which is marked without exception by integration into normalized community environments and proximity to family and peers and other citizens who do not have disabilities.

FURTHERMORE, The Association for Persons with Severe Handicaps commits its resources and energies to support and to promote such components of an integrated continuum of services, through advocacy, dissemination, research, training, and program development in collaboration with consumers, colleagues, families, professional training programs, research centers, and community services.

Note. ORIGINAL RESOLUTION "I.Q. TESTS" ADOPTED OCTOBER 1979; REVISED NOVEMBER 1986.

CH.A.D.D. POSITION ON INCLUSION

Adopted by CH.A.D.D. (Children and Adults with Attention Deficit Disorders) National Board of Directors on May 4, 1993

CH.A.D.D. believes that every child in America is entitled to a free and appropriate public education. The needs of many children are adequately met through regular education and placement in the regular classroom. There are times, however, when regular education is not sufficient to ensure that all children succeed in school. Access to a continuum of special education placements and services is especially important for many children with disabilities. This ensures their right to receive a free and appropriate public education designed to meet their unique needs and which facilitates their achievement in school.

There was a time in America when a free and appropriate public education was not guaranteed by law. Indeed, it was not all that long ago that children with undetected disabilities languished unnoticed in classrooms, and parents of children with identified disabilities were frequently told that their children could not be educated in the public schools because no special education services were available. That all changed with the passage in 1975 of Public Law 94-142 which CH.A.D.D. considers to be a benchmark in meeting the educational needs of all children.

Since renamed the Individuals with Disabilities Education Act (IDEA), this landmark legislation, among other things, mandates:

- a free and appropriate public education in the least restrictive environment designed to meet the unique needs of children with disabilities;

- the right to a comprehensive, multidisciplinary assessment;

- a team approved Individualized Education Program (IEP) that includes current functioning levels, instructional goals and objectives, placement and services decisions, and procedures for evaluation of program effectiveness;

- the availability of a continuum of special education services and placements appropriate to the child's specific learning needs; and

---

Reprinted by permission of CH.A.D.D.

- procedural safeguards to ensure the rights of children with disabilities and their parents are protected.

The principles embodied in the IDEA are as valid today as they were when P.L. 94-142 was passed eighteen years ago. The problems facing the education of children with disabilities in public schools are not the result of the Act, but rather its incomplete implementation. While it may be true that there are some children who are being excluded from the regular education classroom without sufficient reason, it is equally true that many children with attention deficit disorders (ADD) and other disabilities continue to be denied access to an appropriate range of special education and related services and settings.

We believe that the concept of inclusion should reflect society's commitment that every child be educated in the environment that is most appropriate to that child's identified needs. CH.A.D.D. supports inclusion defined as education which provides access to appropriate support and remediation at every level to facilitate each child's ability to participate and achieve. The environment in which these services can best be delivered depends on the needs of the individual student.

Many children with disabilities are educated successfully in regular classrooms with appropriate accommodations and supports. However, others require alternative environments to optimize their achievement. CH.A.D.D. supports this continuum of services and placements. As state and federal governments proceed with the reform of public education, they must ensure that schools continue to be required to accommodate to the individual needs of children with disabilities by providing a variety of options in support of the right of each child to a free and appropriate education.

Children with attention deficit disorders, like children with other disabilities, can exhibit a range of impairment, thus requiring a continuum of educational services. For some children with attention deficit disorders, screening and prereferral adaptation in the classroom may be all that is needed. For others, it will be necessary to refer for a more comprehensive assessment which could lead to a formalized IEP process. Children with attention deficit disorders have diverse needs and will require enhanced teacher preparation in identification, as well as the planning and implementation of a variety of intervention and instructional strategies.

As Congress debates education reform, let it not lose sight of the integrity of the principles embodied in IDEA. Specifically, we recommend:

- a continued recognition of the importance of the availability of a continuum of special education services and placement settings designed to meet the individual needs of each child with a disability;

- increased monitoring of the mandated practices and procedural protections contained within the IDEA to ensure better compliance with the law;

- maintenance of the integrity of funding streams for special education to ensure that we do not return to the days when a public school could tell a parent of a child with a disability that the school cannot "afford" to provide special education and related services;

- a renewed commitment to preservice and inservice teacher training and staff development so that all educators can competently recognize the educational needs of all students and, when necessary, make appropriate accommodations and referrals for comprehensive assessments; and

- stronger collaboration between regular and special education teachers.

Adherence to the principles embodied in IDEA will ensure that all children are included in the federal mandate for a free and appropriate public education. We welcome the opportunity to continue to be a part of the education reform movement.

POSITION STATEMENT ON FULL INCLUSION

prepared by the Consumer Action Network of, by, and for Deaf and Hard of Hearing Americans

I. The Consumer Action Network (CAN)

The Consumer Action Network (CAN) is a coalition of national organizations of, by and for deaf and hard of hearing people. Founded in March 1993, CAN addresses advocacy and legislative issues of importance to deaf and hard of hearing persons. Such issues include shaping public policy, ensuring the rights of deaf and hard-of-hearing persons and improving their quality of life; empowerment of consumer leadership and self-representation; and equal educational, employment, health and technology access.

II. The Problem: The Full Inclusion Educational Model Does Not Meet the Educational Needs of Deaf Children

A. Implications of Deafness

A hearing loss can have a devastating effect on an individual's ability to participate in a regular educational environment and in society. Being deaf creates a communication difference. Deaf people, as a result of their hearing loss, are visually oriented individuals, and may have considerable difficulty participating in an environment that relies primarily on sounds to communicate and learn. Deaf people use many different approaches to communicate. No two deaf people are alike. It is incorrect to assume that all deaf people can be taught to lipread or all deaf people can be taught to speak or use hearing aids. It is also incorrect to assume that becoming fluent in sign language is easy and can be accomplished in a few months. Some people who are deaf use American Sign Language (ASL). Others use a combination of sign language and speech. While some deaf

---

Reprinted by permission of the Consumer Action Network.

people are able to lipread to some degree, many cannot do so. CAN believes that every deaf person has the right to use whatever communication style bests suits him or her in a given situation.

The difficulties associated with educating deaf students in a regular educational environment were recently discussed in a federal policy guidance for deaf students (Federal Register, October 30, 1992).

> The disability of deafness often results in significant and unique educational needs for the individual child. The major barriers to learning associated with deafness relate to language and communication, which in turn profoundly affect most aspects of the educational process.
>
> Because deafness is a low incidence disability, there is a not widespread understanding of its educational implications, even among special educators. This lack of knowledge contributes to the already substantial barriers to deaf students in receiving appropriate educational services.

CAN believes that regardless of which educational placement option is chosen, it is vital to meet the communication needs of each individual child, youth or young adult.

CAN believes that, in addition to addressing the communication needs of all deaf children, the educational placement decision must consider the cultural background of the deaf student. One of these cultural features is the use of ASL for language and communication. ASL is a visual language with its own rules of syntax and grammar.

Deaf culture is also expressed through theater, sports, and poetry. Works of art by deaf people often express pride in being deaf as they struggle to gain equal footing with their hearing peers.

When deaf people are among their peers there is no feeling of being left out or missing critical aspects of communication. Communication is much more easily accomplished and the cultural aspects are both understood and accepted. If a person could hear and was not fluent in sign language was placed with a group of deaf people, that person would immediately experience isolation. The situation, not the hearing loss, creates the barrier to effective and fluent communication.

CAN believes that a large majority of regular classroom teachers are not able to fully understand and therefore, cannot adequately address these cultural aspects of being deaf. In sum, a Full Inclusion Model will impede development of some deaf children's cultural needs.

B. The Full Inclusion Model and the Educational Requirements of Deaf Children

In schools that use the Full Inclusion Model, all students, regardless of their hearing loss, are placed with their hearing peers in the "home" school or regular educational class. The emphasis is on the physical placement of the student in the community school with an informal support system rather than on providing a full spectrum of services. Specifically, it is assumed that the regular classroom teacher will be able to educate and communicate with these deaf children. It is also assumed that hearing peers will be able to communicate with the deaf students in a positive manner. People in support of full inclusion believe that the emphasis in placement decisions for students should be on choice-based approaches rather than on an individualized assessment and planning process. Further, those who are supportive of full inclusion believe that placement of students in a separate school, such as schools for the deaf, or separate classrooms within regular educational programs, segregates and is therefore unacceptable.

CAN believes that the philosophy of Full Inclusion puts undue emphasis on the physical placement of deaf children with hearing peers at the expense of the needs of deaf students. Placement of deaf students without consideration for their communication, cultural, academic, social, and emotional needs would result in turning a potential ability situation into a disability situation.

C. The Full Inclusion Model and Its Legality

Under the Individuals with Disabilities Education Act (IDEA), a free appropriate education must be provided in accordance with individualized education plan requirements.

Section 300.551 requires that each public agency ensure that a continuum of alternative placements is available to meet the needs of handicapped children for special education and related services. The continuum required must include instruction in regular classes, special classes, special schools, home instruction, and instruction in hospitals and institutions, and make provisions for supplementary services (such as resource room or itinerant instruction to be provided in conjunction with regular class placements).

Section 300.552(d) requires that each public agency ensure that in selecting the least restrictive environment, consideration is given to any potential harmful effect on the child or on the quality of services he or she needs.

CAN believes that the philosophy of full inclusion for all deaf students is clearly in violation of IDEA since it does not ensure the availability of a continuum of alternative placements. Many deaf and hard of hearing students cannot progress satisfactorily in a regular education environment even with the use of supplementary aids and services. The emphasis for deaf children, youth and young adults should be on providing a "satisfactory" education, not simply placing them with their hearing peers. Educational placement of deaf students in regular classrooms without consideration of communication needs may cause undue academic, social, emotional and cultural damage.

CAN believes that if the federal government really wanted to require education for all deaf children in the regular educational environment, then the regulations under 34 CFR 300.551–.552(d) related to ensuring a continuum of alternative placements and considering harmful effects in placing students in the least restrictive environment would not have been needed. These two sections are used to balance the preference of regular classroom placement with the realization that certain individuals should not be educated in that setting.

CAN believes that for some deaf children, whose communication and cultural needs cannot be met in the regular educational setting, the school for the deaf may be considered the appropriate placement as determined on the basis of the IEP. Local school systems should be encouraged to develop their programs around the needs of children and not force students into inflexible programs. Each placement recommendation should emphasize opportunity for exemplary development. Accordingly, placement decisions are based on the Individualized Education Plan (IEP) which should include:

1. Academic, social, cultural and emotional needs;

2. Severity of hearing loss and potential for using residual hearing;

3. Curriculum content and method of curriculum delivery;

4. Need for special services; and

5. Current, preferred, and most appropriate mode of communication.

Once the IEP has been developed by professionals, parents, and when appropriate, students knowledgeable about deaf related issues and needs of the particular child, the placement decision can be made. This placement decision must consider whether the appropriate trained personnel are available to implement it.

D. The Full Inclusion Model and the Lack of Appropriate Educational Resources

CAN believes that the majority of regular educational teachers are both unprepared and unequipped to deal with the multitude of needs for deaf children. Special education teachers often do not receive adequate training necessary to meet the full range of communication needs of deaf children. A person with a master's degree in special education, for example, may have never interacted with deaf people or be aware of the different communication options that deaf people may use.

CAN recognizes that there are not enough interpreters in the United States and that interpreting services do not guarantee education for all deaf children. The cost of interpreting services can be quite high and even greater than the salary of a teacher. This makes it financially demanding on school systems. Education departments in some states have not even established personnel standards for educational interpreters in the same manner that standards have been established for speech pathologists, occupational therapists, physical therapists, etc. As a result, many interpreters employed in public educational settings do not meet the minimum standards for educational interpreters established and endorsed by the American Society for Deaf Children (ASDC), Alexander Graham Bell Association for the Deaf (AGBAD), Association of College Educators-Deaf and Hard of Hearing (ACE-DHH), Conference of Educational Administrators Serving the Deaf (CEASD), Conference of Interpreter Trainers (CIT), Convention of American Instructors of the Deaf (CAID), National Association of the Deaf (NAD), and the Registry of Interpreters for the Deaf (RID). Thus, even students who have the ability to use interpreters effectively are often missing information critical to their academic, social and emotional performance in the regular educational environment. In addition, not every deaf student knows how to use interpreters effectively. To a large degree, the education acquired by a deaf child in full inclusion settings may depend not so much on the deaf student's ability, but rather on the ability of teachers, interpreters and other service providers to communicate clearly and effectively.

CAN believes that without the ability to provide adequate funding, necessary professional training, and staff to meet the individual needs of all deaf children, youth and young adults within a regular educational environment, it is impossible to provide an appropriate education for all deaf children in the regular class even if all the deaf students were academically, socially, and emotionally capable of this placement.

III. Position Statement

It is the position of the Consumer Action Network (CAN) that all deaf children, youth and young adults are entitled to a continuum of educational placements. This includes residential and day programs for deaf students, center schools in public education environments, self contained classes within a public school setting, and other educational placements that are deemed appropriate, based on a thorough assessment of each child's unique abilities. The educational placement decision for deaf children, youth and young adults should take into consideration each individual's communication, academic, social, emotional and cultural needs. CAN urges that students, parents, families, and professionals recommending the educational placement option take into consideration all of the necessary factors and the desired outcomes to be pursued. Further, CAN believes that, deaf adults, while having the same desired outcomes and careers as those of their hearing peers, cannot attain these goals unless their education places appropriate emphasis on the unique communication and cultural needs that deafness presents.

It is the position of CAN that education in a local public school setting will not meet the individual needs of ALL deaf children, youth and young adults. CAN believes that programming of this type will not meet the unique communication, culture, academic, social and emotional needs of all deaf children. In addition, CAN also recognizes that there is a severe shortage of trained personnel, including teachers familiar with the implications that deafness presents and qualified interpreters to facilitate communication.

IV. Conclusion

The position paper addresses the needs of deaf children, youth and young adults in an educational environment—needs that can only be addressed by consumers, parents, students (when appropriate) and professionals involved in the education of the deaf. CAN does not support the philosophy of full inclusion for all deaf children, youth and young adults. CAN believes that educational placements based on a Full Inclusion Model are unable to meet the unique communication, cultural, academic, social and emotional needs of all deaf children, youth and young adults because of the latitude of services needed, and the lack of trained personnel available to provide services. Thus, for many deaf children, youth and young adults, full inclusion placements present inordinate barriers in terms of providing appropriate education and allowing individual pursuit of careers of their choice.

Note. Founding members of CAN: American Association of the Deaf-Blind, American Athletic Association of the Deaf, American Society for Deaf Children, Association of Late Deafened Adults, Deaf and Hard of Hearing Entrepreneurs Council, Deaf Women United, Inc., National Association of the Deaf, National Black Deaf Advocates, National Congress of the Jewish Deaf, National Fraternal Society of the Deaf, National Hispanic Council of Deaf and Hard of Hearing People, Telecommunications for the Deaf, Inc.

POSITION PAPER ON DELIVERY OF SERVICES TO STUDENTS WITH DISABILITIES

prepared by the Council of Administrators of Special Education, Inc.

Introduction

During the past year, numerous requests have been received from the members for the Council of Administrators of Special Education, Inc. (CASE) to issue an update to the position paper on the subject of Least Restrictive Environment (LRE) as it relates to the topic of full inclusion of students with disabilities. The CASE Strategic Plan indicates CASE "will establish position statements that are reflective of the issues generated by the membership." This paper is therefore being written in response to the CASE Strategic Plan and membership requests.

All students, both disabled and nondisabled, have educational needs which must be met. CASE believes public schools should be held accountable for meeting the educational needs of all students.

The development and establishment of special education programs in the United States has been an evolutionary process over several decades. Each incremental stage in the process has led to increased knowledge and implementation of the best practices known and available for the times and to corresponding adjustments in the belief systems and attitude held by the educational community. The LRE requirement in the special education regulations has led the education system to establish a continuum of educational placements (environments) over the past two decades. A "special" education system was implemented that came to operate parallel to the general education system within public education.

Currently, rather than a focus upon the environment, a focus upon levels of scope and intensity of educational services (least restrictive alternatives) is considered appropriate. Special education (specially designed instruction) is not a site or setting, but a service delivery system that is responsive to the unique needs of each child. The educational community is increasingly advocating for a more "inclusive" public education system for ALL children. The result is

---

Reprinted by permission of the Council of Administrators of Special Education, Inc.

an evolving philosophy and practice of inclusionary programming for
our nation's students with disabilities

Inclusion Rationale

Inclusion is the result of a major shift in the historic beliefs and
practices of educational communities regarding the provision of services to children and youth with disabilities. Inclusion means that
students with disabilities are educated in supported, heterogeneous,
age-appropriate, and natural and student-centered classroom, school
and community environments for the purpose of preparing them for
full participation in a diverse and integrated society. The practice of
inclusion transcends the idea of physical locations and incorporates
basic values that promote participation, friendships and interactions
in all aspects of education and community life.

The CASE position in the Least Restrictive Environment position paper was: "CASE does *not* support inclusion as a policy/practice
in which ALL students with disabilities, *regardless* of the severity of
their disabilities and needs for related services, receive their total
education within the regular classroom setting in the school they
would attend if not disabled." CASE does support, however, the evolving practice of inclusion as an appropriate goal of a unified education
system for ALL students.

The implementation of inclusion requires:

- development of a local board policy supporting inclusion;

- a goal of participatory membership for all students;

- sufficient supports to students and staff;

- effective leadership, commitments, and a shared responsibility for all students;

- active partnerships with parents;

- appropriate pre-service and ongoing inservice training for
  all staff;

- curriculum and methods which are adapted for individual
  needs;

- a strong sense of "community" in the classroom, throughout
  the school and with parents/caregivers;

- the study and celebration of diversity; and

- the ultimate establishment of a unified education system responsible for serving ALL students.

An inclusive education provides benefits for all students. Inclusive schools will assist in the development of future citizens who value all people, regardless of their learning, physical or emotional characteristics. The best preparation for adult life in a diverse society is education in a diverse classroom. Of particular benefit to students with special needs will be:

- opportunities for friendship and a true sense of belonging;

- the natural availability of role models;

- facilitation of language and communication skills development;

- the development of appropriate social skills.

Position

CASE believes in and supports the evolving practice of inclusion for all students as an appropriate goal of our educational community. CASE believes that the decisions about an appropriate education for students must be made on an individual student basis. While there are those exceptions where full inclusion is not appropriate, we believe strongly in the goal of including ALL children with disabilities into their own school and community. This necessitates a shift in the focus of the IEP teams *from* the place for a student *to* the intensity and scope of services that a student needs to be appropriately educated.

CASE encourages all professionals involved in developing and/or providing educational services to endorse the position stated in this paper.

(subject to revision)

CEC POLICY ON INCLUSIVE SCHOOLS AND COMMUNITY SETTINGS

prepared by The Council for Exceptional Children

The Council for Exceptional Children (CEC) believes all children, youth, and youth adults with disabilities are entitled to a free and appropriate education and/or services that lead to an adult life characterized by satisfying relations with others, independent living, productive engagement in the community, and participation in society at large. To achieve such outcomes, there must exist for all children, youth, and young adults a rich variety of early intervention, educational, and vocational program options and experiences. Access to these programs and experiences should be based on individual educational need and desired outcomes. Further, students and their families or guardians, as members of the planning team, may recommend the placement, curriculum option, and the exit document to be pursued.

CEC believes that a continuum of services must be available for all children, youth, and young adults. CEC also believes that the concept of inclusion is a meaningful goal to be pursued in our schools and communities. In addition, CEC believes children, youth, and young adults with disabilities should be served whenever possible in general education classrooms in inclusive neighborhood schools and community settings. Such settings should be strengthened and supported by an infusion of specially trained personnel and other appropriate supportive practices according to the individual needs of the child.

Policy Implications

Schools

In inclusive schools, the building administrator and staff with assistance from the special education administration should be primarily responsible for the education of children, youth, and young adults with disabilities. The administrator(s) and other school per-

---

sonnel must have available to them appropriate support and technical assistance to enable them to fulfill their responsibilities. Leaders
in state/provincial and local governments must redefine rules and
regulations as necessary, and grant school personnel greater authority to make decisions regarding curriculum, materials, instructional
practice, and staffing patterns. In return for greater autonomy, the
school administrator and staff should establish high standards for
each child and youth and should be held accountable for his or her
progress toward outcomes.

Communities

Inclusive schools must be located in inclusive communities; therefore, CEC invites all educators, other professionals, and family members to work together to create early intervention, educational, and
vocational programs and experiences that are collegial, inclusive,
and responsive to the diversity of children, youth, and young adults.
Policy makers at the highest levels of state/provincial and local government, as well as school administration, also must support inclusion in the educational reforms they espouse. Further, the policy
makers should fund programs in nutrition, early intervention, health
care, parent education, and other social support programs that prepare all children, youth, and young adults to do well in school. There
can be no meaningful school reform, nor inclusive schools, without
funding of these key prerequisites. As important, there must be interagency agreements and collaboration with local governments and
business to help prepare students to assume a constructive role in an
inclusive community.

Professional Development

And finally, state/provincial departments of education, local
educational districts, and colleges and universities must provide high-
quality preservice and continuing professional development experiences that prepare all general educators to work effectively with
children, youth, and young adults representing a wide range of abilities and disabilities, experiences, cultural and linguistic backgrounds,
attitudes, and expectations. Moreover, special educators should be
trained with an emphasis on their roles in inclusive schools and
community settings. They also must learn the importance of establishing ambitious goals for their students and of using appropriate

means of monitoring the progress of children, youth, and young adults.

Note. Adopted by the CEC Delegate Assembly, 1993, San Antonio, Texas.

CONCERNS ABOUT THE FULL INCLUSION OF STUDENTS WITH LEARNING DISABILITIES IN REGULAR EDUCATION CLASSROOMS

prepared by the Council for Learning Disabilities

The Board of Trustees of the Council for Learning Disabilities (CLD) SUPPORTS school reform efforts that enhance the education of all students, including those with learning disabilities (LD). The Council SUPPORTS the education of students with LD in general education classrooms *when deemed appropriate* by the Individual Education Program (IEP) team. Such inclusion efforts require the provision of needed support services in order to be successful.

One policy that the Council CANNOT SUPPORT is the indiscriminate full-time placement of ALL students with LD in the regular education classroom, a policy often referred to as "full inclusion." CLD has grave concerns about any placement policy that ignores a critical component of special education service delivery: Program placement of each student should be based on an evaluation of that student's individual needs. The Council CANNOT SUPPORT any policy that minimizes or eliminates service options designed to enhance the education of students with LD and that are guaranteed by the Individuals with Disabilities Education Act.

From Council for Learning Disabilities. (1993). Concerns about the full inclusion of students with learning disabilities in regular education classrooms. *Learning Disability Quarterly, 16*(2), 126. Copyright © 1993 by the Council for Learning Disabilities. Reprinted by permission.

Note. Approved by the Board of Trustees, April 19, 1993.

INCLUSION: WHAT DOES IT MEAN FOR STUDENTS WITH LEARNING DISABILITIES?

prepared by the Division for Learning Disabilities (DLD) of
The Council for Exceptional Children

What Is the Law?

Free appropriate public education is required by law for students with specific learning disabilities:

... IDEA, The Individuals with Disabilities Education Act

... 504, Section 504 of the Vocational Rehabilitation Act.

Availability of a continuum of placement options is required by law:

• Special classes provide intensive, highly individualized instruction;

• Resource help provides specific skill instruction daily or several times each week focused on individual needs;

• Consultation provides support to general education teachers who have students with learning disabilities;

• Accommodations and modifications in the general classroom provide the minor support needed for individuals to meet group expectations.

Mainstreaming and Inclusion Are Not in Federal Statutes or Regulations

Placement in a least restrictive environment (LRE) is required by law.

Intensive educational services are appropriate and necessary to meet the needs of some students with learning disabilities.

Any given learning environment may be restrictive for an individual student if a continuum of options is not available:

• Without intensive daily help Maria's severe reading disability will continue to interfere with and restrict her academic success;

Reprinted by permission of the Division for Learning Disabilities of The Council for Exceptional Children.

- Without using a word processor in his fourth grade class, Leon's ability to express his good ideas would be restricted by his inefficient and poorly formed handwriting.

Pivotal Policies

An Individualized Education Plan (IEP) ensures parent and/or student participation in establishing placement, related services and student program goals.

Options across the continuum must be available to meet the needs of individuals with disabilities:

- Mark's specific needs and IEP require that an LD specialist guide his sixth grade teacher in determining accommodations;

- Anna's specific needs and IEP require that an LD specialist guide her in an intensive, small group setting for three hours per week.

Related or supportive services must be available based on individual student need.

If a Continuum of Service Options Is Not Available to Individual Students with Specific Learning Disabilities, the Intent of IDEA Is Not Being Met

Many state and local budget allocations and reimbursements are categorical, based on the recognition that students with learning disabilities often require specialized programs, personnel, and resources.

Teacher competencies, certification standards, and licensure criteria identify specific professional skills that are critical to effective teaching of students with learning disabilities.

Implications for Practice

A regular classroom setting cannot provide the specific and/or intensive instructional services appropriate for some students with learning disabilities.

Students with learning disabilities who are placed in general education classrooms will need consultation, support services, and/or direct services from an LD specialist at varying points in their school careers to be successful.

The IEP must be formulated *prior* to determination of the appropriate placement option.

General education teachers can assist students with learning disabilities by using appropriate accommodations and auxiliary aids in the classroom.

Personnel who possess specialized skills in learning disabilities must be available to assess learning and guide general education teachers in determining appropriate accommodations, adaptations, and aids.

Special education and general education must actively work with each family and student to maximize integration with peers and independence at home, in school, and in the workplace.

A Range of Program, Personnel, and Service Options Must Be Available to Permit Selection Based on Individual Student Needs

The different professional competencies possessed by LD specialists and general education personnel are both needed to achieve positive educational outcomes for all students with learning disabilities.

The Annual IEP Review must ensure a free, appropriate public education for each individual student with learning disabilities.

Some Current Philosophies

Mainstreaming and the regular education initiative (REI) encourage the participation of students with learning disabilities in general education classes to the extent it is appropriate to their needs and provides the least restrictive environment.

General education refers to the educational experiences provided in regular classrooms, rather than in special education settings.

Inclusion and inclusive schools refer to the placement of students with disabilities in general education buildings or classrooms.

Full inclusion is used by some people to refer to the full-time placement in general education classrooms of *all* students, including those with disabilities.

A "Full-Inclusion" Program as Defined by Its Advocates, Provides Placements ONLY in General Education Classes for Students with Learning Disabilities

In practice, mainstreaming, inclusion, and full inclusion are often used interchangeably.

Research Ramifications

Although statistics indicate that more than 80% of students with learning disabilities are *in regular classrooms,* the data included all students with learning disabilities who spend *any* time in regular classrooms.

There Is No Validated Body of Research to Support Large Scale Adoption of Inclusion as the Service Delivery Model for ALL Students with Learning Disabilities

Reports of studies focused on students with learning disabilities in special, resource, and general education settings are often based on preliminary findings or only partially reported.

Studies reporting the progress of students with learning disabilities in various settings are inconclusive concerning *academic growth.*

A number of large-scale federally funded studies targeting the issue of inclusion are in the final stages of data analysis.

Action Plan

DLD is initiating an effort to examine and analyze research and practice related to inclusion for students with learning disabilities.

Resources

Position Papers on Full Inclusion of All Students with Learning Disabilities in the Regular Education Classroom. Learning Disabilities Association of America, 1993

A Reaction to "Full Inclusion": A Reaffirmation of the Right of Students with Learning Disabilities to a Continuum of Services. National Joint Committee on Learning Disabilities, 1993

POSITION PAPER ON FULL INCLUSION OF ALL STUDENTS WITH LEARNING DISABILITIES IN THE REGULAR EDUCATION CLASSROOM

prepared by the Learning Disabilities Association of America

The Learning Disabilities Association of America, LDA, is a national not-for-profit organization of parents, professionals, and persons with learning disabilities, concerned about the welfare of individuals with learning disabilities. During the 1990–91 school year, 2,117,087 children in public schools in the United States were identified as having learning disabilities. This is more than fifty percent of the total number of students identified in all disability categories.

"Full inclusion," "full integration," "unified system," "inclusive education" are terms used to describe a popular policy/practice in which all students with disabilities, regardless of the nature or the severity of the disability and need for related services, receive their total education within the regular education classroom in their home school.

The Learning Disabilities Association of America does not support "full inclusion" or any policies that mandate the same placement, instruction, or treatment for *ALL* students with learning disabilities. Many students with learning disabilities benefit from being served in the regular education classroom. However, the regular education classroom is not the appropriate placement for a number of students with learning disabilities who may need alternative instructional environments, teaching strategies, and/or materials that cannot or will not be provided within the context of a regular classroom placement.

LDA believes that decisions regarding education placement of students with disabilities must be based on the needs of each individual student rather than administrative convenience or budgetary considerations and must be the results of a cooperative effort involving the educators, parents, and the student when appropriate.

LDA Strongly Supports the Individuals with Disabilities Education Act (IDEA) Which Mandates:

- a free and appropriate public education in the least restrictive environment appropriate for the student's specific learning needs.

- a team approved Individualized Education Program (IEP) that includes current functioning levels, instructional goals and objectives, placement and services decisions, and procedures for evaluation of program effectiveness.

- a placement decision must be made on an individual basis and considered only after the development of the IEP.

- a continuum of alternative placements to meet the needs of students with disabilities for special education and related services.

- a system for the continuing education of regular and special education and related services personnel to enable these personnel to meet the needs of children with disabilities.

LDA believes that the placement of *ALL* children with disabilities in the regular classroom is as great a violation of IDEA as is the placement of *ALL* children in separate classrooms on the basis of their type of disability.

LDA URGES THE U.S. DEPARTMENT OF EDUCATION AND EACH STATE TO MOVE DELIBERATELY AND REFLECTIVELY IN SCHOOL RESTRUCTURING, USING THE INDIVIDUALS WITH DISABILITIES EDUCATION ACT AS A FOUNDATION— MINDFUL OF THE BEST INTERESTS OF ALL CHILDREN WITH DISABILITIES.

APPROPRIATE INCLUSION

prepared by the National Education Association

The National Education Association is committed to equal educational opportunity, the highest quality education, and a safe learning environment for all students. The Association supports and encourages **appropriate inclusion. Appropriate inclusion** is characterized by practices and programs that provide for the following on a sustained basis:

- A full continuum of placement options and services within each option. Placement and services must be determined for each student by a team that includes all stakeholders and must be specified in the Individualized Education Program.

- Appropriate professional development, as part of normal work activity, of all educators and support staff associated with such programs. Appropriate training must also be provided for administrators, parents, and other stakeholders.

- Adequate time, as part of the normal school day, to engage in coordinated and collaborative planning on behalf of all students.

- Class sizes that are responsive to student needs.

- Staff and technical assistance that is specifically appropriate to student and teacher needs. Inclusion practices and programs that lack these fundamental characteristics are inappropriate and must end.

Reprinted by permission of the National Education Association.

NEA-CEC-AASA Statement on the Relationship Between Special Education and General Education

**prepared by The National Education Association, The Council
for Exceptional Children, and the American Association
of School Administrators**

The National Education Association (NEA), *The Council for Exceptional Children* (CEC), and the *American Association of School Administrators* (AASA) recognize and commend the significant growth and improvement that has occurred over the past decade in the provision of special education and related services to exceptional children as a result of the efforts of educators and other advocates. Past school practices of excluding some exceptional students from educational opportunity have been all but eliminated. Most exceptional students now have available, protected by law, a free appropriate public education guaranteeing them the special education and related services they need. The age ranges of exceptional children served have expanded with increasing focus on interventions in the very earliest years to education programs extending through age 21. Further, we are pleased with the growing collaborative efforts on the part of general educators and special educators which have led to increasing integration, where appropriate, of exceptional children with other children.

We are, however, concerned about trends and events which we believe to be regressive to the continued improvement of efforts to meet the special educational needs of exceptional children. Recent education reform movements have focused on increased performance standards for students and changes in the ways professional educators are trained and evaluated. While many of these reforms are having a positive impact on education as a whole, they are often insensitive to the needs of students for whom the standard curriculum and approaches to learning may not be appropriate. Similarly, some recent efforts to reform the professional preparation of educators have not taken into consideration the need for highly qualified special educators. We are also concerned that limited educational resources are constraining educational alternatives and quality of

---

education for all students, and we are particularly concerned that limited special education resources are resulting in increased class sizes and case loads, reduced related services, referral backlogs, and strained relationships between educators and educators and parents. Finally, we are concerned about a growing insensitivity on the part of some public officials and advocates to the unique learning needs of exceptional children, the fundamental right for placement decision to be based on the individual needs of each exceptional child, and the capability of all schools and educators to meet the educational needs of exceptional children.

Because of our longstanding commitment to ensuring all exceptional children quality, free appropriate public education and our concern over recent movements that may be counterproductive to this goal, we urge the members of our organizations and other advocates to increase their advocacy on behalf of exceptional children in accordance with the following principles.

The *National Education Association,* the *Council for Exceptional Children,* and the *American Association of School Administrators* believe that:

1. The strength of our education system is in its diversity—diversity of students, professionals, and learning environments. Exceptional students, be they handicapped or gifted and talented, are one group of diverse learners both in terms of what they need to learn and how they can best learn. Special educators are the educational professionals qualified to provide specially designed instruction to exceptional children who require such instruction, and special education programs are an integral part of the necessary diverse education provided to children.

2. Some children with exceptionalities can benefit from the instruction provided by general education, but many exceptional children are not able to benefit from some or all of such instruction because of their unique learning styles or because they require a differentiated curriculum.

3. Decisions about the appropriate education for an exceptional child must be individually determined; conducted in a manner that protects the rights of the child and the persons who work with the child; considerate of the child's educational needs, of home, school and com-

munity relationships, and of personal preferences; and made with the active involvement of the varied professionals, including teachers, who have knowledge about the needs of the child and the educational environment in which the child might be placed.

4. The professional and legal principle of least restrictive environment, within the context of individual decision making, assures each exceptional child access to a full continuum of quality special education alternatives. Each child must have the alternatives which are most educationally appropriate to his or her needs.

5. Efforts on the part of professionals, parents, consumers, and other advocates over the past several decades have led to greater integration of exceptional children on school campuses. We call for continued efforts in this regard to the degree that they are consistent with the individual educational needs of the exceptional child, the educational needs of the other children with whom the child will be educated, and the ability of the professionals involved to provide the education all of the children require.

6. The critical components of ensuring exceptional children the quality education they require are an adequate supply of qualified special education and related services personnel; the appropriate conditions under which to practice; sufficient instructional resources; and adequate federal, state, and local funding. Recognizing the unique role the federal government plays in this regard, we call upon the federal government to focus its resources on supporting the training of special education and related services personnel who meet state and professionally recognized standards; conducting research and development activities leading to the availability of improved technology, media, and materials that can be used effectively by special education and related services personnel; and increasing its financial obligations to the support of special education services.

7. Since many exceptional children will receive some of their education from non-special education professionals, we urge professional preparation programs, states, and school districts to provide such personnel with increased

learning opportunities to improve their knowledge and understanding of exceptionality so they can facilitate the participation of exceptional children in their classrooms and work as a team with special educators.

8. Collaborative efforts among special educators, other members of the educational system, and various public and private agencies can help improve and expand the services available to exceptional children and, we hope, improve and expand the services available to all children. We encourage the further development of collaborative efforts that appropriately and effectively utilize professional and other resources at the local level.

Note. May 13, 1987.

A REACTION TO FULL INCLUSION: A REAFFIRMATION OF THE RIGHT OF STUDENTS WITH LEARNING DISABILITIES TO A CONTINUUM OF SERVICES

prepared by the National Joint Committee on Learning Disabilities

The National Joint Committee on Learning Disabilities (NJCLD) supports many aspects of school reform. However, one aspect of school reform that the NJCLD cannot support is the idea that *all* students with learning disabilities must be served only in regular education classrooms, frequently referred to as *full inclusion.* **The Committee believes that *full inclusion,* when defined this way, violates the rights of parents and students with disabilities as mandated by the Individuals with Disabilities Education Act (IDEA).**

Because each student with learning disabilities has unique needs, an individualized program must be tailored to meet those needs. For one student, the program may be provided in the regular classroom; yet for another student, the regular classroom may be an inappropriate placement. Therefore, the NJCLD supports the use of a continuum of services and rejects the arbitrary placement of all students in any one setting.

In *Issues in the Delivery of Educational Services to Individuals with Learning Disabilities* (1982) . . . the NJCLD stated its support and commitment to "a continuum of education placements, including the regular education classroom that must be available to all students with learning disabilities and must be flexible enough to meet their changing needs." This was reaffirmed in 1991 . . . in *Providing Appropriate Education for Students with Learning Disabilities in Regular Education Classrooms,* which recommended that public and private education agencies should "establish system-wide and state-based plans for educating students with learning disabilities in the regular education classroom when such placement is appropriate. The responsibility for developing plans must be shared by regular and special educators, parents, and student consumers of the services. Once developed, a plan must be supported at all levels of the educational system."

In summary, the NJCLD supports educational reform and efforts to restructure schools. As stated in "School Reform: Opportunities for Excellence and Equity for Individuals with Learning Disabilities" (1992, see *Newsbriefs* Jan/Feb 1992, p. 3), "NJCLD demonstrates a deep concern and desire that parents, professionals, and policy makers work cooperatively in planning and implementing reforms. We strongly urge that strategies be developed within the reform movement to improve education for students with learning disabilities." As these strategies are developed, it is necessary to ensure that each student with a learning disability is provided a continuum of service options that will guarantee a free, appropriate public education based on the student's individual needs.

Note. This position paper was developed by the National Joint Committee on Learning Disabilities and approved by the member organizations, January 1993.

Contributors

Barbara D. Bateman, Department of Special Education, University of Oregon, Eugene, OR 97403

Michael Bina, Indiana School for the Blind, 7725 N. College Avenue, Indianapolis, IN 46240

Margaret N. Carr, Woodway Elementary School, 6701 Woodway Drive, Fort Worth, TX 76133

Stanley C. Diamond, 403 East Allens Lane, Philadelphia, PA 19119

Douglas Fuchs, Department of Special Education, George Peabody College for Teachers, Vanderbilt University, Nashville, TN 37203

Lynn S. Fuchs, Department of Special Education, George Peabody College for Teachers, Vanderbilt University, Nashville, TN 37203

James J. Gallagher, Frank Porter Graham Child Development Center, Nations Bank, B Plaza, Suite 300, 137 E. Franklin Street, Chapel Hill, NC 27514

Michael M. Gerber, Graduate School of Education, University of California, Santa Barbara, CA 93106

Nancy Hall, Yale University, P.O. Box 208205, New Haven, CT 06520-8205

Daniel P. Hallahan, Curry School of Education, University of Virginia, 405 Emmet Street, Charlottesville, VA 22903

Peter Idstein, Wilmington College, 320 Dupont Highway, Newcastle, DE 19720

James M. Kauffman, Curry School of Education, University of Virginia, 405 Emmet Street, Charlottesville, VA 22903

Harlan Lane, Northeastern University, Psychology Department, 125 NI, 360 Huntington Avenue, Boston, MA 02115

Donald L. MacMillan, School of Education, University of California, Riverside, CA 92521

William C. Morse, Department of Special Education, College of Education, University of South Florida, 4202 E. Fowler Avenue, Tampa, FL 33620

Bernard Rimland, Autism Research Institute, 4182 Adams Avenue, San Diego, CA 92116

Melvyn I. Semmel, Graduate School of Education, University of California, Santa Barbara, CA 93106

Edward F. Zigler, Yale University, P.O. Box 208205, New Haven, CT 06520-8205

Author Index

Subject Index